STEWART COWLEY

THE GARDENER'S DIARY IN COLOUR

Marshall Cavendish · London & New York

Edited by Vivien Bowler

Published by Marshall Cavendish Books Limited,
58 Old Compton Street,
London, W1V 5PA

This material was first published by Marshall Cavendish Limited
in the publication *The Encyclopedia of Gardening*

Printed in Great Britain

ISBN 0 85685 148 5

About this book . . .

Over three hundred colour-packed pages of gardening expertise make this diary a valuable addition to any gardener's book-shelf.
Month by month it shows you exactly what needs to be done in the garden and how best to set about it. The thorough but simple instructions are backed up with lavish colour photographs and for each month there is a beautiful selection of the plants you can expect to be adorning your garden.
The Jobs of the Month charts are a special feature of the book; with these you can tell at a glance which aspect of your garden needs most attention this month—and you can be sure that all the advice has been compiled by experts.
The active gardener really cannot do without this diary, but the 'armchair' gardener too can get an immense amount of pleasure from a book which combines down-to-earth advice with a glorious record of the changing seasons.

Contents

Pictures supplied by:
Bernard Alfieri 226
Heather Angel 143, 171, 199, 227, 254
Amateur Gardening 34, 36
D. C. Arminson 28, 53, 58, 59, 82, 91, 119, 121,122, 153, 157, 170, 183, 185, 197, 220, 223, 224, 325, 332
P. Ayres 72, 245, 246, 256
P. Becker 304
Pamela Booth 257, 286
James Browne 136
J. K. Burras 10, 32, 33, 36, 87
R. A. Chand 294
R. J. Corbin 10, 13, 17, 21, 22, 23, 24, 26, 29, 31, 40, 45, 49, 52, 53, 57, 58, 66, 72, 73, 78, 80, 81, 85, 86, 87, 97, 100, 101, 105, 106, 109, 110, 112, 114, 115, 125, 127, 129, 132, 138, 139, 142, 153, 154, 155, 156, 157, 160, 161, 162, 163, 164, 165, 167, 169, 181, 182, 184, 190, 192, 195, 209, 210, 211, 216, 222, 223, 225, 226, 239, 241, 246, 249, 254, 269, 272, 275, 277, 279, 283, 290, 302, 305, 307, 308, 309, 311, 321, 322
J. K. Cowley 59, 78, 82, 86, 87, 93, 97, 101, 104, 108, 118, 123, 127, 155, 156, 163, 167, 176, 177, 189, 191, 197, 203, 213, 218, 219, 258, 314, 325
J. E. Downward 25, 33, 34, 35, 36, 65, 66, 83, 258, 261, 290, 317, 332
Valerie Finnis 9, 10, 35, 39, 45, 51, 62, 65, 71, 82, 125, 138, 140, 142, 147, 166, 253, 261, 262, 291, 307, 318, 319, 339
B. Furner 170, 171, 197, 283, 310, 334, 336
I. Hardwick 68, 72, 94, 122, 160, 204, 283
Ron Hatfield 6, 133, 142, 253
R. E. Heath 83
J. C. W. Howden 141
A. J. Huxley 7, 66, 178, 290
G. Hyde 10, 36, 49, 51, 60, 62, 80, 90, 94, 111, 116, 118, 132, 177, 231, 232, 260, 284, 288, 304, 315
courtesy I.C.I. Ltd. 302
Leslie Johns 5, 6, 9, 10, 17, 20, 23, 24, 25, 27, 30, 31, 33, 37, 38, 50, 55, 56, 62, 64, 65, 69, 79, 82, 91, 92, 98, 113, 118, 119, 121, 122, 123, 179, 238, 300, 306, 314, 323
F. Lane 116, 144
Anton Last 68, 337
Alfred Leutrscher 27
J. Maddams 123
John Markham 6, 35, 60, 76, 77, 78, 88, 92, 116, 145, 172, 200, 202, 207, 228, 231, 233, 255, 259, 285, 312
E. M. Megson 71, 147, 150, 168, 179, 230, 232, 234, 235, 259, 286, 288, 289, 291, 315
P. Morby 324
Natural History Photographic Agency 284
National Trust 294, 295 (Moseley Hall, Staffordshire)
Morris Nimmo 7, 8, 37, 95, 235, 259, 260, 287, 289, 316, 317
S. J. Orme 9, 150, 151, 230, 231, 232, 263, 286, 315
Photo Researchers/Jane Burton 256, 284
Ray Proctor 123, 164, 166, 196, 220, 255, 301, 303, 311
I. Ruthven 272
Ruth Rutter 221, 330, 338
Kay N. Sanecki 219, 254, 293
Joy Simpson 297
Donald Smith 12, 27, 309, 336
Harry Smith 7, 8, 17, 32, 34, 35, 36, 37, 38, 40, 41, 42, 43, 44, 45, 56, 61, 62, 63, 65, 66, 73, 89, 90, 91, 93, 94, 95, 105, 106, 113, 117, 118, 119, 120, 121, 122, 123, 125, 126, 138, 141, 146, 149, 154, 165, 176, 178, 198, 199, 201, 203, 206, 207, 213, 227, 229, 234, 241, 247, 248, 251, 252, 262, 263, 269, 273, 276, 278, 281, 287, 289, 290, 292, 313, 314, 319, 324, 328, 330, 331, 333, 334, 339, 340
Spectrum 305
Violet Stevenson 50, 69, 71
Suttons Seeds 135
Tourist Photo Library 42
D. Wildridge 71, 90, 93, 95, 117, 120, 148, 172, 174, 175, 178, 204, 205, 207, 230, 258, 268, 288, 333
Dennis Woodland 261

The Month of January

January is usually considered to be the month for plants in the greenhouse. Yet, outside, the snowdrops are beginning to show and such shrubs as Jasminum nudiflorum and Viburnum tinus are in mid-winter flower. In mild conditions there can be unexpected joys; polyanthus, primroses, wallflowers, honesty and Brompton stocks may flower until curtailed by frost.

Begonia semperflorens, the fibrous-rooted winter-flowering Begonia with many varieties, usually pink, red or white, and called 'everflowering' because some plants can, in fact, be kept in flower the whole year through.

1 The double form of the common snowdrop. As soon as the flowers begin to fade, or while they are in flower, the clumps can be lifted, separated and replanted immediately at the original depth. They are good plants for naturalising in grass as the leaves will have died down when the grass is ready to be cut.

2 The bright little flowers of Crocus tomasinianus are among the earliest of the genus to open. The orange-yellow anthers are prominent when the flowers open.

3 Anthurium scherzerianum (Flamingo Flower) is a house plant flowering constantly, given humidity.

4 Birds like these Robins are January visitors to a well-stocked bird table in the garden. Suet, dough, table scraps are suitable food.

1

2

3

1 Salix alba chermesina, a red-barked form of the golden willow. To keep the shoots vividly coloured prune them hard in February or March. This promotes fresh new growth for the following winter.
2 Thuja plicata, the Western Red Cedar, grows best in moist lime-free soil. Although it is a good tree for screens it must have shelter from strong winds. Its distinctive varieties include those with golden and 'zebra' variegated foliage.
3 Garrya elliptica needs the protection of a south-facing wall or other sheltered place. Catkins decorate the tree from November to February.

1 Hamamelis mollis makes a 10-foot shrub with fragrant flowers. It is the best of the Witch Hazels. A paler form turns an attractive yellow in the autumn.
2 One of the best of all mid-winter flowering shrubs, Jasminum nudiflorum is usually grown as a climber against a wall but may be trained as a pillar or left to sprawl as ground cover.

1

2

3

3 Hazel catkins are the male flowers of the Corylus. Females, which develop into cob nuts, are inconspicuous. Several varieties include the decorative golden and purple leaved forms and the form contorta with corkscrew stems.
4 Chimonanthus praecox is often known by its synonym C. fragrans. Its flowers are sweetly scented and appear from November to March before the leaves. It is quite hardy but given the protection of a south-facing wall the flowers will be earlier and more abundant.
5 Viburnum tinus, formerly known as Laurustinus, a lovely evergreen shrub flowering through the winter. Its clusters of deep pink buds become more noticeable at the end of November. Varieties include purple and variegated leaf forms.

4

5

1

2

3

1 Closely related to the Hawthorn, the Pyracantha provides much vivid winter colour. The shrubs can be grown as specimens, in mixed borders or as a covering for a wall, even on the north.

2 Cotoneaster frigida is one of several Cotoneasters that carry berries throughout winter. There is a yellow form and a pendulous one. In ideal conditions the shrub will grow to about 30 feet. Although birds take the berries, enough are usually spared to provide good winter colour.

3 Pernettya mucronata is among the loveliest of all hardy berry-producing plants. It belongs to the heather family and like most of them it prefers a lime-free soil.

1 The vivid, nodding, yellow-green flowers of Helleborus argutifolius are some two inches across and contrast handsomely with the great glabrous evergreen foliage. Most hellebores like rich, moist, well-drained soil, partial shade.
2 Although at their best and flowering most freely in April, Primroses produce a few flowers even during the shortest days of a mild winter. They like a semi-shady position and are easily propagated by division.
3 Helleborus niger, the Christmas Rose. To get unsullied long-stemmed blooms, cover the plant with a cloche or a small frame topped with a pane of glass or clear plastic.
4 In early January the young shoots of Helleborus foetidus that protect the blooms are vivid green. One of the sub-shrubby Hellebores, the plant stays handsome for several weeks.

1

2

3

4

Lachenalia aloides is parent of many hybrids like this L. a. nelsonii. After flowering, the bulbs should be dried off, then ripened outdoors.

The Saintpaulia or African Violet is unrelated to the common Violet. There are hundreds of varieties. The leaves can be smooth or furry.

Narcissus 'Soleil d'Or', one of the earliest of all varieties. It can be grown in soil, bulb fibre or in a bowl of pebbles and water.

The good earth

Soil is the foundation of successful gardening. First find out what kind of soil you have inherited. Then plan to improve it and adapt your planting schemes to it

Any soil will grow something and because of this gardeners are apt to take their soil for granted. But good soil, rich, sweet and healthy, can enable a gardener to double his crop with half the labour he would have to expend on bad soil.

All soil was once rock. Rain, frost, sun, subterranean disturbance, bacteria, animals and plants have over the centuries gradually broken down the surface to form soil. These rock particles, with additions, are the basic part of garden soil today.

Soil is not pulverised rock alone, however. A good garden soil is made up of:

Rock particles	40 per cent
Air	25 per cent
Water	25 per cent
Humus	10 per cent

Rock particles can vary in size from stones anything over ¼ inch or so in size, useless because they cannot hold or absorb water, to a very fine substance almost like powder, so fine that it binds together like glue and forms clay.

Where limestone is the basic rock, a limy or calcareous soil is the result. Sandstone can produce a coarse and porous sand or, if the grains are more finely ground and an intensely gluey substance known as alumina is present, it produces clay.

Sandy soil will not hold water. Moisture escapes through it quickly and easily, leaching away soil foods. So although sandy soils are warm and well aerated, they will not produce a good crop unless they are conditioned.

Unlike sand, clay does hold water well. So well, in fact, that it will admit little air. Because it is filled with water it is both heavy and cold. It will produce only a late crop and a poor one.

Half-way between sand and clay is silt, and nearer still to the sand base is the ideal loam, defined as having 6–15 per cent clay, 40–60 per cent silt and 20–50 per cent sand. If the soil originated in limestone or chalk it will contain much calcium and will be known as marl.

For the ordinary gardener, loams or marls are the most productive soils. Although clay or heavy soil is likely to be alkaline, and sandy or light soils acid, loam can be either.

In a relatively small area such as a garden it is possible to have several different kinds of soil. This is generally due less to physical differences in soil chemistry than to the period during which it has been under cultivation, for soil tends to become more acid the more it is used.

It is readily apparent whether a soil is light or heavy. But to discover whether it is acid or alkaline requires chemical investigation. Several soil test kits are on the market which will indicate not only alkalinity and acidity, but deficiencies in nitrogen, phosphorus and potash, three major essentials.

Soil acidity or alkalinity is measured in units known as the pH; complex logarithmic and unnecessary to explain. Neutral soil, neither acid nor alkaline, has a pH of 7.0. If the pH is above 7.0 then the soil is alkaline, and if below this figure it is acid. The best round figure to aim at is between 6.5 and 7.0.

Once acidity or alkalinity has been determined, it is easy to discover in general terms the physical composition of a soil, remembering always that it can differ in separate sections of a plot.

Two thirds fill a clear glass with clean water. Into this drop a good tablespoonful of earth from the garden and stir vigorously. Stones and sand will fall immediately to the bottom. Loam, having a proportion of sand, will form the next layer. Clay, light and powdery, will dissolve and do little more than colour the water, remaining suspended. The humus will float on top of the water. This test must be carried out with comparatively dry soil, or the clay, already waterlogged, will tend to fall immediately to the base and dissolve too slowly to permit accurate interpretation.

More people grumble about clay soil than any other type. It is difficult to work, wet, sticky, heavy and cold. In summer it bakes to a brick-like consistency. But it is rich in plant foods and minerals which cannot get washed out of the sticky mass.

A long-term cure for clay soils is a thorough drainage system, not, alas, always possible in a small suburban garden. Land drains should be laid herring-bone fashion according to the slope of the land or the position of the main drain. If there is neither drain nor slope, lead the land drain system into an adequate pit or soakaway. This should be up to 4 feet square and deep, filled with broken bricks, clinker and similar materials. The upper foot or so can have its top soil replaced and so conceal the pit below. If a land drain system is unfeasible, the provision of just one or two soakaway pits will help to drain the land of excess moisture.

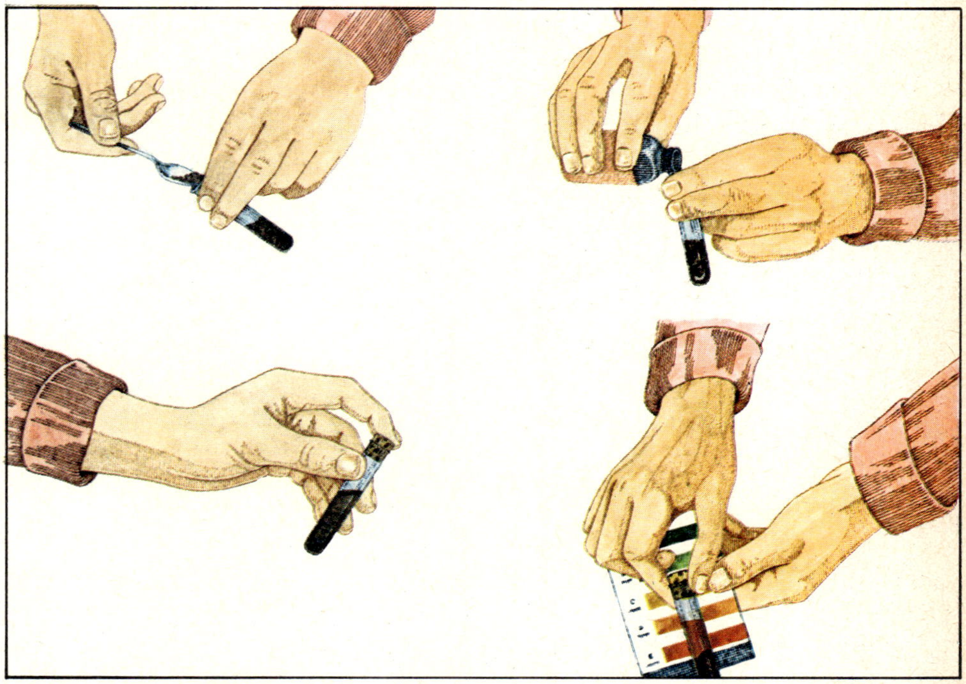

Testing soil for acidity. *Top left* **dry soil is put into a test tube with a dry spoon.** *Top right* **the acidity-testing solution is poured carefully on the soil sample.** *Below left* **put a cork in the neck of the test tube before shaking.** *Below right* **the resultant solution is matched for colour with the test card and read. Reading is** ***p*****H 7.0.**

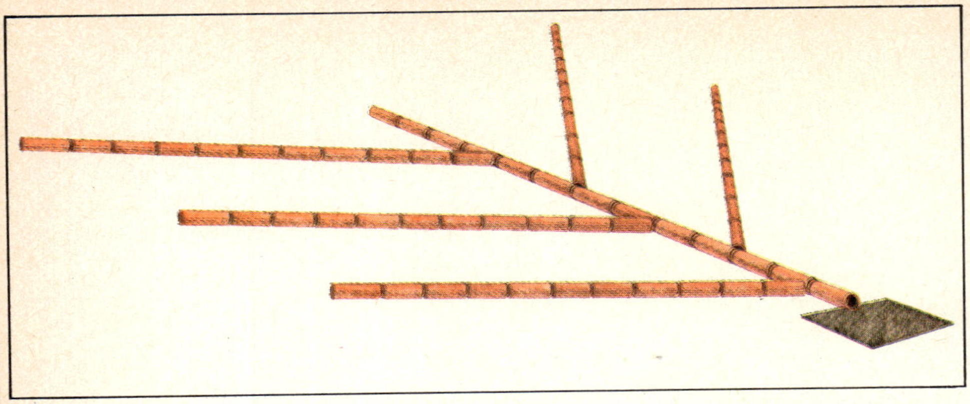

1

2

1 **Drainage tiles laid in a herring-bone pattern lead to a soakaway. They are laid following the direction of the slope and the soakaway is at the lowest point.**
2 The drain runs into the soakaway.
3 The junction of the drain is not sealed to form a joint but is left open. Tiles are placed over the joint to prevent silt from washing into the pipes and blocking them.
4 A section through a tile drain. It is laid in a bed of rough material to assist sharp drainage, very necessary in clay soils. In sandy soils sharp drainage can be harmful.

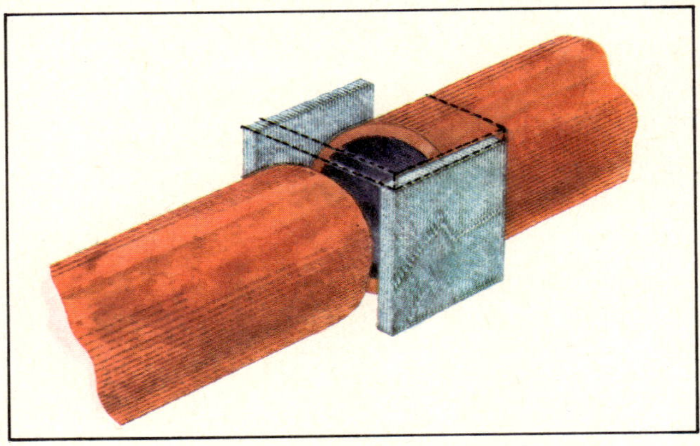

3

4

Once a clay soil is drained it will tend to bake hard in summer unless its texture is improved. Weather can help here. The clay should be dug and left in great lumps during the winter for wind, rain, frost and snow to break it up. In spring, dress the surface at least 2 inches deep with peat, spent hops, leafmould, rotted compost or farmyard manure, all of which will give body to the clay and help to break it up into finer particles.

Hydrated lime, about ½ lb per square yard, merely sprinkled into the clods of clay in late autumn or winter will be washed down to the deeper soil and will also help to break up the soil mass.

Where clay soils need draining to clear some of the surplus moisture, sandy soils suffer because they are too sharply drained. Water runs through too quickly, carrying with it plant foods and minerals. Sandy soil is often poor and hungry.

So give sandy soil as much bulk and

great aid here is the same material that should be used for conditioning clay; peat and similar humus-making material. In autumn dig this in. Apply lime (to neutralise excess acidity) in spring. Never apply farmyard manures and lime at the same time or chemical reactions will waste the goodness of both. For the average garden an acid soil with a pH of slightly less than 7.0 is best. It will grow almost anything so long as the slight acidity is due to the constitution of the soil and not to bad drainage and poor aeration. If the soil is found to be both acid and frequently flooded, see to drainage at once.

Over-acidity can be conveniently corrected by the application of lime. Spread this on the surface in winter and allow rains and frosts to dig it in for you.

It is much easier to change a pH figure upwards than downwards. Chalky soils can be improved and made more acid by liberal applications of peat. Research has shown that calcifuges or lime haters such as rhododendrons, fail to grow in an alkaline soil not so much because of the lime in the soil but because this lime locks up essential iron.

Calcifuges can be grown in naturally limy soils by digging a substantial hole, lining this with impervious plastic material and planting in a special acid peat mixture. However, this is not very satisfactory for long periods. For, although lime from the soil is prevented from being washed into the roots, the soil mixture tends to dry out quickly. A better method is to build a peat or acid hill on top of the calcareous soil and plant in this. Water contaminated by the soil-held lime moves upwards far less rapidly than downwards and the plants will live for many years.

For a guide to whether a local soil is acid or alkaline, look around you at the wild vegetation. Acid soils will be indicated by wild rhododendrons, heathers, bilberries, pines. Alkaline soils can sometimes be recognised by their

Digging out a drainage trench. The top soil can be replaced to conceal the system after the drain is laid.

The drain is bedded down in clinker. Drainage will not itself help with clay. The soil texture needs improving.

grey or white colour and by wild clematis, wild cherries, scabious, stonecrops and beech trees.

Whether acid or alkaline, all soils must contain both air and moisture in the spaces between the soil particles. Air in these spaces contains more carbon dioxide and less oxygen than in the air above soil level, and the moisture is not pure water but a solution of salts. Plant roots breathe out carbon dioxide at a rate proportionate to that at which leaves absorb it. So if the soil particles are so small (as in clay) that pore spaces hardly exist at all, a high concentration of carbon dioxide is built up in a short time. It can double in less than two hours and increase tenfold during a single hot day. This is why some plants can actually be seen to wilt and die in the hot sun. Watering, the usual cure, succeeds not so much by feeding the plant roots with moisture as by opening up the pore spaces and allowing excess carbon dioxide to escape through the soil.

Watering a soil is important for two reasons: it provides the necessary moisture to the roots and, as it courses down through the soil, it drags air down after it. This explains why it is vital when watering a plant to do it thoroughly.

A soil containing a high proportion of humus is open in texture and spongy in character, so it holds plenty of both air and moisture. Humus is the dark coloured granular substance that is retained when organic matter (leaves, other forms of decayed or decaying vegetation or animal manures) rots and returns to the soil. Humus is essential to good soil. It improves soil texture and it provides the necessary conditions for bacterial activity. This bacterial activity breaks down the constituents of the soil into chemicals that are absorbed in liquid form by the roots of plants.

Uncultivated soil, whether woodland or meadow, is normally sufficiently supplied with humus for its needs because of the dropping of leaves, the rotting of vegetable matter such as tree trunks and grass, and the droppings of animals.

But few natural deposits are allowed to lie in the cultivated garden. Leaves are cleared after they fall. Grass is cut and removed. All the emphasis is on taking away from the soil and none is on replacement. If the garden deposits are stored neatly in one place, aided in their natural decaying processes and then returned to the soil, both soil condition and soil productivity are improved. The way to do this is to make compost, in a heap or a bin.

The compost heap should be built up with leaves, grass, dead flowers, outer leaves of lettuce and cabbage, potato peelings, organic waste from the vacuum cleaner and any similar material that is not so hard or woody that decomposition will take too long.

As the heap becomes too large or the bin is filled, fork the contents into the second, turning the outsides to the centre and vice versa. After a few months, depending on weather and contents, the vegetation will have decomposed into a rich, brown, friable material ready for use in the garden.

Loam can be made by much the same method but using turf instead of vegetable matter. When making a new flower bed in the grass, skim off the turf in manageable rectangles and lay these, grass downwards, in a pile. The grass will rot and you will be left with rich, friable, fibrous loam.

1

3
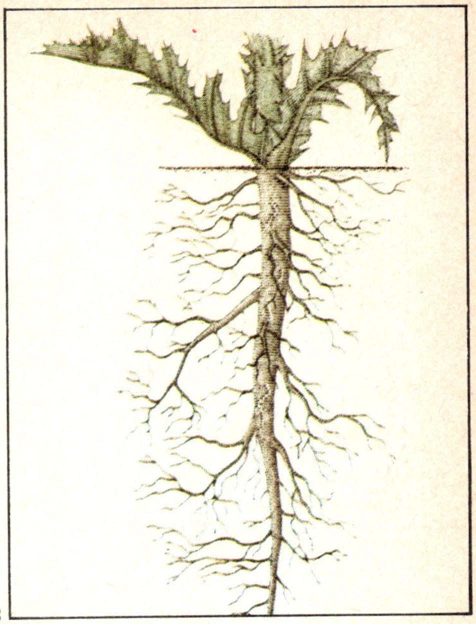

2

4
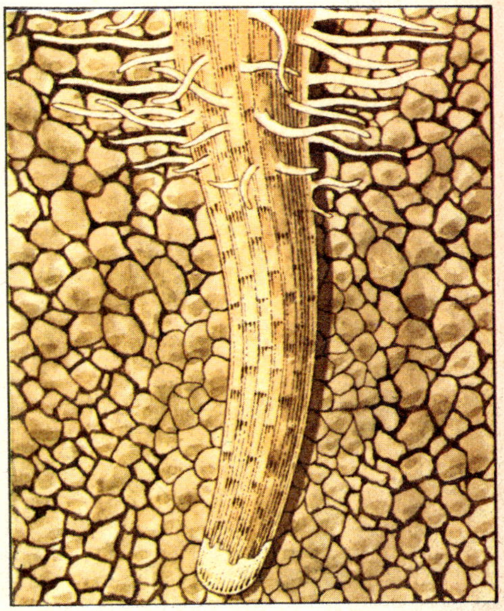

1 An example of a tuber forming or tuberous root like a Dahlia's.
2 A fibrous root can insinuate itself among the soil particles and spread as far underground as the plant does above the ground.

3 A tap root delves deep into the ground and often has thin subsidiary roots emanating from it.
4 The root tip protected by a root cap forces its way through the soil, compressing the soil particles.

When lime is required to reduce the acidity of the soil it is spread by hand over the surface in winter.

Greenprint

To design a garden is to harness the nature of the site to your particular family needs. That is the objective; fulfilling it is a many-faceted task

Garden design had its origin in the landscape around us, which was created by climate, geology, land form, aspect—and man. The house and its environment have developed from the factor of mere shelter to the factor of shelter within an aesthetically pleasing setting. Flowering plants of all sizes, forms and textures are placed near the house, while trees and shrubs form the background to the garden. The former create an effect of interest and excitement. The latter are more functional.

Your first task in planning your garden is to study and interpret those signs of nature that enable you to create a successful plan. Local nurserymen and the Parks Department will be able to provide you with invaluable information on local conditions: climate, rainfall and geology that govern the basic plant ecology of the area. These are the fingerprints of nature and within them lie the secrets of a garden's success.

While technical information can be supplied by specialists, what cannot be explained are the particular characteristics of your garden. You should be prepared to spend a little time studying your property: the way the house is orientated within the site, the area it covers and the effect it has on the garden.

The orientation of the house and garden will affect design appreciably. Where the garden faces north and east, shelter from the cold winds will be necessary, just as screening from prevailing winds will be essential in open areas. A wall facing south will assist establishment of tender plants, while facing north or east prohibits all but the hardiest.

Remember, too, that gardens are to be appreciated from both inside and outside the house. Nor are views seen beyond the garden to be ignored. An attractive building, a group of trees or an opening into the countryside can be emphasised; an ugly wall or rubbish dump blotted out, or at least its impact on your environment reduced.

In large gardens one major space should be emphasised, with spaces of varying sizes linked to it visibly or invisibly, for equal distribution of equal-sized spaces reduces the impact of any and every space. In small gardens, restricted to one space only, carefully designed details will help develop greater potential.

Changes of level, trees or large shrubs control views and define spaces. Ground sloping towards the windows can be exploited by creating a small flat area, enclosed by retaining walls. Ground sloping away may call for terrace development overlooking the garden. Near the house a large tree may create a shady area under its canopy. Positioned farther away it can become the climax to a garden. Another consideration is a garden must be designed with its function in mind. A large hard-surfaced area should be provided for children in a large family, unless the garden is big enough to take the wear and tear.

Some people can create a garden intuitively. But, obviously, those who can spare the time to put all the site information, dimensions and levels on paper will leave less to chance.

A design on paper should develop from the garden's existing conditions and the functions it is to fulfil—for example: a sitting area, sheltered and with controlled views from it; an open area of grass; paths which lead logically through the garden to subsidiary spaces such as the kitchen garden, tool shed, compost area or greenhouse. Each area must be clearly defined but boundaries should not be over-emphasised lest the garden loses its overall unity.

Every space should appear in logical progression from the one preceding it. Thus a terrace physically linked to the house will have paths and steps leading naturally off it in the direction of the garden's next attraction. Paths along the lawn should move round objects easily. A curved line can increase the sense of space but it must be gentle—for curves on the ground appear stronger than they do on paper. Straight paths, however. are the easiest to construct and

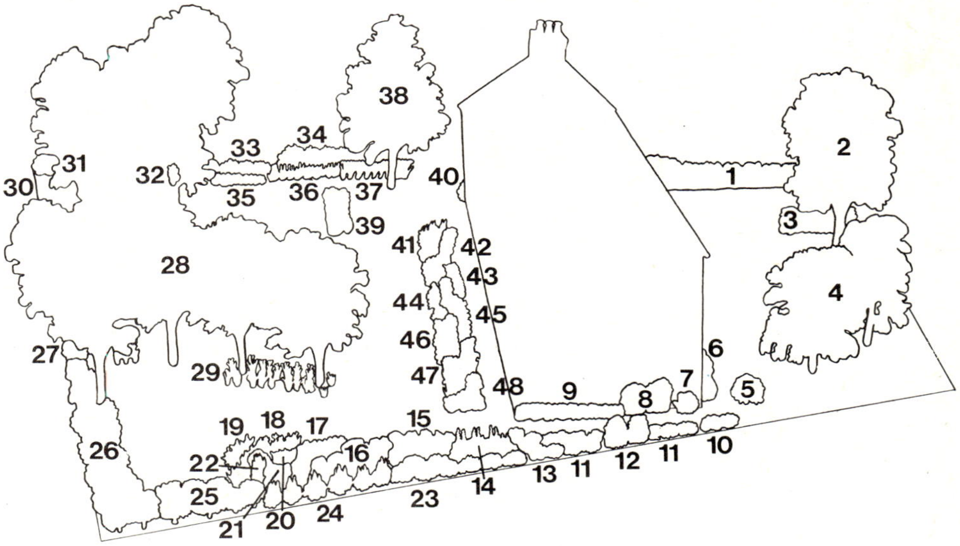

Fulfilment of a garden design and planting plan for a fairly typical wedge-shaped plot *left, below* **is expressed in the drawing** *left, top*. **For identification and comparison the whole garden is shown in flower** *far left*. **In actuality, of course, the plants would flower seasonally.**

KEY

(1) 12 Hypericum patulum 'Hidcote' at 2 feet spaces centre to centre. (2) 1 Fraxinus excelsior. (3) 9 Skimmia japonica at 3 feet. (4) 2 Betula pendula (5) 1 Phillyrea decora. (6) 12 Rosa 'Iceberg' at 2½ feet underplanted with Myosotis alpestris and Iberis umbellata (7) Viburnum davidii. (8) 2 Hydrangea petiolaris (climber). (9) 9 Viburnum davidii at 2½ feet. (10) 2 Hypericum patulum 'Hidcote'. (11) 12 Berberis candidula at 2½ feet. (12) 2 Rosa Paul's Scarlet Climber. (13) 5 Potentilla fruticosa at 2½ feet. (14) 7 Salvia officinalis at 2½ feet. (15) 9 Hypericum patulum 'Hidcote' at 2 feet. (16) 5 Senecio laxifolius at 3 feet. (17) 4 Viburnum davidii at 2½ feet. (18) 6 Hemerocallis fulva maculata at 2½ feet. (19) 3 Hosta crispula at 2 feet. (20) 3 Lilium hansonii at 2 feet. (21) 5 Helleborus argutifolius at 2 feet. (22) 1 Macleaya cordata. (23) 8 Viburnum opulus compactum at 3 feet. (24) 6 Syringa 'Maud Notcutt' at 4 feet. (25) 7 Viburnum opulus at 3 feet. (26) 14 Viburnum tinus at 3 feet. (27) 9 Mahonia japonica at 3 feet. (28) Oak trees. (29) Spring Bulbs. (30) Compost. (31) 15 Viburnum tinus at 3 feet. (32) 6 Pieris forrestii at 3 feet. (33) 5 Viburnum opulus compactum at 3 feet. (34) 6 Philadelphus lemoinei at 4 feet. (35) 6 Potentilla fruticosa at 2½ feet. (36) 11 Salvia superba at 2 feet. (37) 11 Iris kaempferi 'Dresden China' at 2 feet. (38) 1 Robinia pseudacacia. (39) 7 Rubus cockburnianus at 3 feet. (40) 8 Hypericum calycinum at 2 feet. (41) 6 Rosmarinus officinalis at 2½ feet. (42) 8 Rosa 'Frensham' at 2½ feet. (43) 6 Gypsophila paniculata at 2½ feet. (45) 10 Erigeron 'Elstead Pink' at 2 feet. (46) 6 Rosa 'Super Star' at 2½ feet. (47) 12 Iris pseudacorus at 2 feet. (48) 9 Chrysanthemum maximum at 2 feet.

maintain, a point to be remembered. When you have met all these necessary space requirements, the individual character of each area can be developed. Visual excitement and interest can be created by using, in close proximity, plants of contrasting form, by exploiting the silhouette of graceful shrubs against a dark wall surface or—if using building materials—by harmonising the paving materials with the house. Surface colours act by illusion to increase or decrease the apparent size of any space. Bright colours, such as scarlet and yellow, appear to reduce its size. Cool colours, such as blue and white, increase it. When used within a restricted space, small-scale materials—brick, slate, small-leaved plants like cotoneaster (dwarf types), hebe, hypericum and vinca—will increase its apparent size, while large, coarse materials—large paving slabs, large-leaved plants such as hosta, mahonia, viburnum and acanthus—will reduce it.

Hard surfaces in the garden, such as paved sitting areas, can be softened, by leaving small areas open for flowering plants and herbs. Beware, however, of too many interruptions as they will tend to confuse the general effect. Pierced concrete blocks, wood and plants can be used to screen and shelter a sitting area. Pierced concrete block screen units are available in various colours and designs. Wooden screens, with vertical or horizontal slats, are effective natural material that acts as a foil to climbing plants, jasmine, ivy, roses or wisteria.

Water is an element that adds character to a garden. Natural pools should follow the contours of the land closely. Artificial pools in terraces are best kept simple, their shape regular and their edging clearly defined.

Planting schemes should exploit seasonal effects. In winter, for example, evergreen shrubs planted on the boundaries will produce a prominent background. Summer should bring a blaze of flowers, and the autumn garden make the most of the changing colours of foliage. Plants are best grouped. A collection of individual plant specimens will only destroy the unity of the garden because no single plant can create the effect of a group.

The backbone planting of your garden is all-important. It will probably comprise trees and shrubs. A large garden can absorb a range of various plant sizes, from ground carpeting plants to large trees. A medium garden is best suited to medium and small trees such as *Cornus kousa* and *Quercus ilex*. A small garden will accommodate only small trees, such as *Rhus typhina*, *Aesculus parviflora* and *Arbutus unedo*, and perhaps medium to small-sized shrubs.

What about the sequence of operations?

All drawings and details should be completed before the physical work starts. Next, all areas to be developed should be cleared of weeds, dug over, and manure and fertilisers applied. Existing plants you wish to retain should be pruned, lifted carefully and heeled in.

The aim of any garden is to provide a place to relax, contemplate and play; somewhere you can feel close to nature. The thought of the pleasure your garden will give you will be a constant encouragement as you work to create and maintain it.

Jobs of the month

January gardening can be more rewardingly active than you might suppose. And the month's "armchair" gardening — selecting from catalogue, ordering seeds and plants — may make or mar your garden later. In the following pages the Jobs of the Month are described under 16 main subject headings — from Bulbs to Wildlife. Which of the suggestions you follow, which tasks you carry out will depend, of course, on the locality, the nature of your garden, the kind of weather and personal inclination. Below, to start with, is a summary of Jobs of the Month.

Bulbs

Start to bring plunged or covered hyacinths and narcissi indoors for gradual warming up

Flowers for cutting

You can cut and use ornamental kale or cabbage as though they were great roses

Fruit

Weather allowing, plant newly arrived fruit trees and bushes. Prune existing stock

Greenhouse

List future needs. Remove dead flowers, fading leaves. Take cuttings of chrysanthemums. Sow seeds of lilies, *Begonia semperflorens* and sweet peas

Hedges

Before planting a new hedge prepare the site and let it settle for a few weeks

Herbaceous Plants

Start sowing for Summer and take root cuttings to fill gaps in perennial borders

House Plants

Don't over-water Christmas comers. But avoid a too dry atmosphere (with humidifiers) and give them light

Lawns

An early first mowing may be feasible. Trim edges

Patios

Remove leaves, debris from the area and from drainage vents

Paths

Survey faults for later action. Clear leaves, algae, moss from paving

Rock Gardens

Clear around emerging bulb flowers and give them a chance to shine

Roses

You can start first-stage pruning. Obtain manure now for early Spring application

Trees & Shrubs

Plant new arrivals with an eye to their maturity

Vegetables

Study seed catalogues and note latest introductions. You can sow round-seeded peas, early broad beans, shallots

Water Gardens

If the surface is frozen ensure there's a hole open in the ice

Wildlife

Food you put out for birds should be rich in carbohydrates

The climate In general the climatic pattern in the British Isles is such that the cycle of growth in the south is between two and four weeks ahead of that in the north.

Bulbs

If you have plunged or covered pots of hyacinths and narcissi outdoors you should begin bringing them into the warmth of the house or greenhouse. (*Plunging* means submerging a potted plant just under the surface of the soil, peat, ashes, sand or clinker. *Covering* means storing a plant in a sack, polythene bag or similar container in a dark, dry, cold place, outdoors or indoors.)

Inspect the bowls or pots before you bring them in. The buds of hyacinths should not only be showing but be well out of the neck of the bulbs. If they are brought in too soon the result will be a short-stemmed flower hidden inside long leaves. Hyacinths do much better and become richer in both colour and scent if they are given liquid fertiliser. But apply the fertiliser only in the dilutions and at the intervals recommended by the makers.

Shoots of narcissi should be about 4 inches long. Again, the flower buds should be well out of the neck of the bulbs before they are brought indoors. If the bulbs are 'double nosed' some of the shoots will not have flowers within them. Nip these off so that the plant's energies are concentrated on those shoots that do contain flowers. Once indoors the flower stem will elongate and the bud which is vertical at first will gradually become 'goosenecked'. Just before this stage, at a time when you can see that the flower is almost ready, spray the buds lightly with water twice a day. Once the petals open, do not spray.

Tulips take longer to mature and should not be brought in yet. Neither should small bulbs such as crocuses and snowdrops be brought indoors until the flower bud is showing colour and is about to break from its sheath; otherwise the blooms will not open.

Having been brought into the greenhouse or indoors, hyacinths and narcissi should not be hurried. Bring them first to a temperature of about 50°F (10°C), no more. Gradually, day by day, increase this to 60°F (16°C). That should be the maximum, for only a spring day's temperature is needed for good results. During this 'warming up' period do not forget to keep the bulbs watered.

Hippeastrums, often called amaryllis in bulb catalogues, should be potted in John Innes compost No 2. Place the bulbs in individual pots. They should fit fairly tightly, with no more than ¾-inch between bulb and pot. Allow an inch between soil surface and pot rim for watering. Hippeastrums are not given a preliminary period outdoors but are started straight away in a temperature of about 60°F (16°C). No water should be given then for two weeks. Then give them small amounts sufficient only to stimulate growth. Depending on

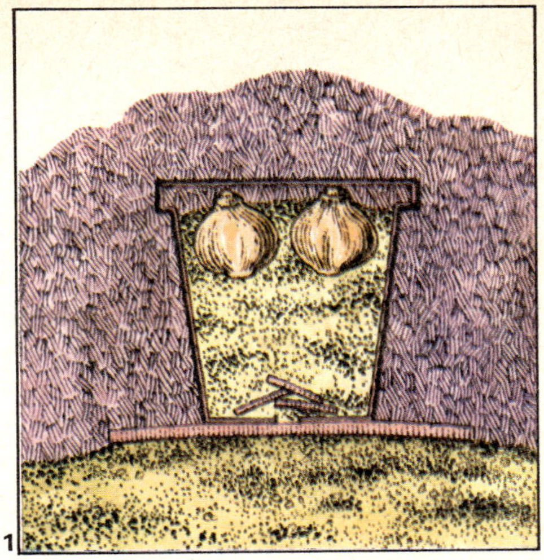
1

2

3

4

1 When Hyacinths in pots are immersed in the plunge bed the whole pot is covered with a few inches of soil to ensure that the bulbs are kept cool and in the darkness. This encourages the bulb to make a good strong root system. The bulbs can be removed from the plunge bed when the buds have emerged well out of the necks of the bulbs.
2 Hyacinth bulbs with buds well out and plump shoots.
3 Hyacinths in full flower indoors. Never place them over a radiator.
4 Snowdrops braving the snow. They are the toughest of the January bulbs and the first to flower out of doors.

RECOGNITION CHART

Tree Portraits

This guide presents 10 principal tree forms and shapes. They include the bush form and the "artificial" fan and cordon

FASTIGIATE
The Lombardy Poplar, Populus nigra italica. Widely grown because of its form and quick growth. Other examples: Prunus 'Amanogawa', Carpinus pyramidalis, Taxus baccata fastigiata

BUSH **Berberis vulgaris. Berberis species in general and many flowering shrubs are of true bush form – i.e. growth springs from the base. Other examples: Hydrangea macrophylla, Syringa vulgaris, Spiraea thunbergii**

FAN-SHAPED
The Fig, Ficus carica. Often grown against a wall and fan-trained to utilise reflected heat from the wall. This helps to ripen the fruit and give protection against Spring frosts. Other examples: apricots, peaches, nectarines

CONE-SHAPED
(sometimes called bush-shaped) Picea omorika. An evergreen conifer, quick-growing in early stages. Other examples: Taxodium distichum, Abies nordmanniana

CORDON
Like the fan, an artificial form. Apples (shown here in oblique cordon form) and pears are commonly grown this way, a method of intensive cultivation to produce maximum fruit from minimum space

ANDARD
ıe, Tilia platyphyllos. A tree with eetly scented flowers. Characteristic the form – with a clear bole before the ad of the tree breaks. Other examples: axinus excelsior (the common ash), er campestre (field maple or sycamore)

COLUMNAR
Thuya occidentalis columnaris. A conifer of stylised form with the head of the tree breaking some feet above ground. Other example: Thuja occidentalis 'Rosenthalii'

PROSTRATE
A prostrate plant lies down on the ground (as opposed to creeping over it) and growth is usually rigid. Good for covering a bank if put at the top. Excellent for camouflaging manholes, inspection covers etc. Example: Juniper

EEPING
eping Willow, Salix babylonica, uick-growing tree, often lden very early in the year, amples: Fraxinus excelsior ndula (weeping ash), Betula ndula (common birch), nus 'Cheal's Weeping', eeping cherry)

HORIZONTAL-GROWING
Cedar of Lebanon, Cedrus libani. Branches are held horizontally and appear to be in layers. An evergreen. Usually grown as a specimen tree on lawns. Other example: Pinus laricio (Corsican or black pine)

temperature and watering, the flowers should begin to appear before the leaves after a further three weeks or so have elapsed. Now begin watering the plants liberally, feed with liquid manure and syringe twice daily. Humidity is important. A day temperature rising to 65–70°F (18–21°C) is allowable. Night temperature should never fall below 60°F (16°C).

In the house, bulbs should be placed near a window but never over a radiator. If radiators underline virtually all your window sills, the best thing to do is to place the bulbs on a table as near as possible to a window.

Flowers for cutting

At this season the value of every bit of fresh green, every speck of blossom, the tiniest flower and the brightest leaf is at its greatest. It is surprising what colour one can find.

Should you have been wise enough to grow ornamental kale or cabbage, you will have real treasures to draw upon. If they have been grown quite closely they will not be too large and can now be cut and used as though they were great roses.

If you wish to use them in tall arrangements, say against a framework of forced blossom and newly opened buds, then pull up the entire plant. Wash the roots but do not remove them. Arrange the cabbages as though they were long-stemmed flowers. When the arrangement has passed its best you can even re-plant them. They may take a little time to revive, but you will then have more coloured leaves for later in the season and will not have wasted an entire plant.

Cut a few quite short, as though you were cutting cabbage for cooking, and use these to serve two purposes: to make a lovely rosette of colour at the foot of long-stemmed flowers, say an arc of narcissi, and to hide the pinholder on which the flowers are impaled.

Helleborus niger, the Christmas rose, should be throwing up a succession of flowers. These are often very short-stemmed and really can be admired only if they are arranged in a low bowl, perhaps among moss or ivy. To make the stems grow longer and at the same time to protect the petals from being splashed with mud, it is as well to cover the plants. A cloche can be used. But so can a wooden box without top or base. Even a bottomless bucket or tin will serve.

Sometimes when cut these flowers will not take water and tend to wilt very quickly. To prevent this, place all newly cut stems in water that has been heated to baby-bath temperature—70°F (21°C). As a general rule, always split stem ends upwards a little way for all but bulb flowers and very slim stems. All flowers should have a long, deep drink before arrangement, up to just below the bloom but not over the petals except in rare cases. Once the stems and leaves are turgid you can arrange them in shallow water without fear of their wilting.

While you are at it, winter-prune the bushes. Take the weak, spindly and twisted stems rather than the strongly growing ones which will look so handsome in the garden later in the season. Choose first those shrubs you know open early, like the flowering currant, *Ribes sanguineum*, *Cornus mas*, the common plum, and of course *Prunus subhirtella* and the early viburnums. Cut also the coloured stems of willow and dogwood. They are attractive even when bare, but their buds will slowly open in the warmth of the house to bring a touch of early spring.

Ornamental Kale is invaluable for winter flower arrangement. It adds colour and form and the leaves are rigid. Use the entire plant, roots and all.

If shoots of the Flowering Currant, Ribes sanguineum, are cut early in the year and taken indoors the flowers will open.

Tulips you buy can be arranged excitingly by the addition of some Hazel catkins. The small Red Cabbage makes a rosette.

Fruit

Continue planting fruit trees and bushes as they arrive from the nursery unless the soil is too wet or frosted, in which case open the packages except around the root ball and keep the plants in a frost-free shed until the weather improves.

During periods of bad weather inspect all stakes, supports and particularly wires for cordon or fan-trained trees and repair or strengthen these as necessary.

Newly planted trees and bushes should be pruned during their dormant period. Prunings, whether of young or established trees and bushes, should be burnt and the ash scattered over their roots after it has cooled but before the potash has been leached out by rains.

All fruit trees and bushes except strawberries should be sprayed with a five per cent tar-oil solution while they are dormant. This will kill the eggs of pests such as aphids, scale insects, red spider mite and caterpillars, and will clear the bark of algae growths. Wear protective clothing for the job.

No spray or splashes must come into contact with the skin. So choose a still day without wind. If contamination does occur, wash off immediately with cold water.

When the ground is frosted hard, take advantage of the situation and avoid probable damage to lawns by cutting down any old, overgrown or diseased trees. With large specimens do this in stages, starting at the top and working downwards, but leaving much of the main trunk for leverage to remove the stump entirely. If the stump cannot conveniently be removed, cut the main trunk at or below ground level and hasten its rotting away by boring holes in it and filling these either with a weedkiller such as sodium chlorate or a fertiliser mixture such as three parts Nitro-chalk mixed with one part superphosphate.

Pruning

Apples and pears All shoots on newly planted trees and bushes that are required to make new growth should be cut back by about two thirds. On trained trees merely trim the leaders to avoid excessive growth.
Blackberries, loganberries, raspberries Cut back all bushes or canes of newly planted varieties to 1 foot or so of the ground to encourage root formation and the establishment of new, strong growth from the base. *Black currant, red currant, white currant, gooseberries* Cut all leading shoots of newly planted bushes by at least half, and black currants down to ground level. *Cherries* On new plantings choose future leaders and cut these back to about 1 foot. *Peaches, nectarines, plums and damsons* Do not winter prune these trees. They are apt to bleed, and any pruning they may require should be carried out in summer when the sap will coagulate quickly. *Established fruit trees and bushes* Pruning of established trees should aim to remove diseased, crossing, broken, weak or spindly growth and to encourage the formation of fruiting spurs. This is done by shortening lateral growth to two or three strong buds.

If any fruit trees require major surgery —say the removal of a large branch— this should be carried out by degrees. First remove the lighter twiggy parts.

Then cut the branch back until only one section joining the main trunk is left. Cut upwards underneath this, flush with the main trunk, to about a third or half its thickness. Then cut downwards to meet the first cut, supporting the stump of branch during the process. This will avoid any tearing of the main trunk or tissue. Paint all large wounds with a specific dressing such as Arbrex or with a bitumen paint to prevent the entry of disease spores and to encourage the growth of new tissues over the wound.

When removing an old or damaged limb from a tree, saw close to the remaining branch. A stump should not remain.

The remaining snags are removed with a sharp knife, making sure that the bark is pared evenly and not left in a torn condition.

Paint the wound over with pitch tar or some material such as Arbrex. This is to seal the cut and prevent the entry of disease.

When pruning established Apple trees, cut back the leaders by a third or half, and prune the laterals to form fruiting spurs.

Greenhouse

Because space is limited, valuable and expensive to heat in the greenhouse, the propagating case or even cold frames, it is important to plan ahead so that it is usefully occupied. So make a list in January of all the plants you wish to grow and the seeds you wish to germinate, together with their quantities; otherwise you may find yourself heating expensive air or, worse still, without space or facilities for plants or seedlings requiring the protection or aid given by a greenhouse, propagator or frame.

If you have no greenhouse but are thinking of buying one, choose with great care. Type, constructional materials, size, heating and siting should all be taken into consideration before making a final choice.

The cheapest type of house to buy and to heat is the lean-to, for this uses as one of its walls the wall of the dwelling or boundary. Although in consequence there will be light losses, less heating will be needed. The span-type house allows good light penetration all round but loses heat more rapidly and so is more expensive to run.

Softwoods as constructional material have the drawback that they must be painted regularly to maintain the timber in good condition. Western red cedar, oak and teak are longer-lasting timbers. Steel-framed greenhouses last only as long as their rust proofing, so obtain adequate assurance on this vital question before making your purchase. The most useful modern material is probably aluminium, today produced in extruded shapes allowing channels, ridges, boxbars and non-hardening glazing compounds for durability, safety, long life, convenience and the entry of maximum light.

The size of your greenhouse will depend on the uses you have for it. Remember that the larger it is the more expensive it will be to buy and to heat, but that too small a house can lead to overcrowding of plants, frustration and to breakage of glass. Make sure you can move about easily in it and that you use it only for its functional purpose and not as a storage shed. Every pack of fertiliser, every empty flower pot it contains means a waste of space and money.

Even an unheated greenhouse can be a useful addition to garden productivity but is of little value during winter. So some facilities for keeping temperatures

The span-type greenhouse shows good light penetration all round.

slightly above freezing will help to make the most of your original investment.

Electricity, clean, versatile, demanding no stoking or regular attention and capable of providing light during the darker days, is undoubtedly the best means of heating a greenhouse.

Aim to maintain winter temperatures of at least 45°F (7°C) and bear in mind that to raise the temperature only slightly more can double or even treble your heating costs. In very cold weather

Cuttings of large exhibition Chrysanthemums are taken from the stools and trimmed. The lower leaves are removed.

Seeds of Lily are sown singly into sandy compost in pots or pans or boxes, and left in the greenhouse to germinate in due course.

The lean-to type of greenhouse is the cheapest to maintain.

a paraffin heater used in addition can significantly lower costs, though fumes and excessive condensation can be a problem. You can get the additional warmth needed from some purposes by means of a propagating case and soil warming cables, neither of which is as expensive to run as heating the entire greenhouse. But thermostatic control of all these items is essential, though inexpensive. In fact most heaters available today come complete with their thermostat.

The cuttings of the Chrysanthemums are then dibbled in round the edge of a 3-inch pot into a fine and rich sandy compost.

Sweet Pea seeds, previously chitted, are pushed singly into small pots or the labour-saving peat pots, which can be set in the soil.

Electricity is easily the best method of greenhouse heating.

Even in winter some ventilation is necessary, particularly if a paraffin heater is to be employed, so make sure your greenhouse is adequately provided with ventilators. For summer care it is helpful to have ventilators operated to some degree automatically in case the sun raises temperatures to dangerous levels while you are away. Electrical or mechanical systems are available.

Sensible siting of the greenhouse can materially cut costs. The site chosen should if possible be in full sun, yet protected from cold north and east winds. A north to south ridge will mean that throughout the year the house gets most sun, but an east to west siting allows more winter light to penetrate. Obviously correct foundations must be installed, and initial costs will be kept down if water and electricity supplies are nearby rather than having to be brought considerable distances. For future safety all electrical installations should be carried out by qualified engineers.

Greenhouses today can be filled with useful automatic equipment which can make them almost independent of human care. Shading, watering, heating, lighting and ventilating can all be automatic and the installation of mist-propagating equipment together with soil warming can simplify and make almost foolproof the propagation by means of cuttings, particularly hardwood. A separate propagating case simplifies at lower costs the production of quick and early seedlings.

Frames should be sited somewhere near the greenhouse to save time and trouble in transferring plants. They can usefully have soil-heating elements buried to increase their versatility, though these should not be switched on at all times.

In January, while temperatures are low and light poor, special attention should be given to all plants in the greenhouse. Remove dead flowers and fading leaves and take care never to overwater. Any mildewed or diseased plants or cuttings should also be removed before they infect healthy plants.

Hedges

The primary purpose of most hedges is to define a boundary, but other possible purposes include acting as a windbreak, a barrier, a screen or as a separation of one part of a garden from another. Of course many hedges serve more than one purpose.

If you intend planting a new hedge, first decide its primary purpose, for this governs the selection of the material from which it is to be made. A windbreak hedge for a bleak part of the country will not be the same as a privacy screen for the cosy suburbs. An impenetrable barrier against sheep, cattle, dogs and children will be completely different from a neat, clipped, formal boundary.

Whatever the purpose of a hedge, there are sufficient types and varieties of plants available to make it interesting or even colourful as well as purely utilitarian. And there is no reason why a single variety should be used alone. Sometimes a mixture of evergreen and deciduous, green, brown gold and purple, tall and short, flowering and berrying can be used to make a truly decorative feature.

As a hedge is almost invariably a permanent structure, it is important to give it every advantage in the initial planting. Prepare the site before the plants arrive from the nursery. This can be done at any time during the winter if the ground is neither too wet nor deeply frosted. Mark the site with a garden line and dig out a trench one spit or spade's depth deep and up to 4 feet wide. Remove the soil to the side and fork over the subsoil deeply, incorporating in this lower layer a good proportion of humus-making material such as compost, peat or farmyard manure. Replace the top soil, breaking it up well and incorporating a double handful of bonemeal to every yard of length. Leave the soil to settle for a couple of weeks or so.

1

2

3

4

1 When preparing to plant a hedge take out a trench a foot deep and about as wide and put in some good rich compost.
2 Spread the compost along the trench and fork it into the soil.

3 Put in the plants along the garden line. Mark the distance between each plant with a measuring stick or rod. Plant slowly and carefully.
4 Fill in the soil around the roots and firm with the foot.

When the plants arrive from the nursery heel them in at one end of the trench you have dug and, beginning at the other end, dig your planting trench about 1 foot deep and rather wider. Plant slowly, thoroughly and firmly. Plant at intervals, usually about 18 inches apart. This will enable each plant to touch its neighbour in about two years.

A thicker, more durable hedge is made by planting two layers, the plants in the front row alternating with those in the back and about 1 foot or 18 inches apart.

Water in the plants well and during the first season never allow the plants to become dry. Their first spring is a critical period and they will benefit

A young hedge of Berberis darwinii. This is a good hedging plant, dense-growing and ever-green, with orange flowers in May.

Escallonia macrantha is recommended as a flowering evergreen plant that forms an impenetrable barrier as a garden boundary.

Chamaecyparis lawsoniana pottenii, a coniferous plant, is reasonably quick growing and makes a good wind break. It is mature in about five years.

very much from a daily spray over their foliage.

The most commonly used and readily available hedging materials are probably beech (both green and copper), box, *Chamaecyparis lawsoniana*, *Cupresso-cyparis leylandii*. *Cupressus macrocarpa*, holly, hornbeam, laurel, *Lonicera nitida*, privet, thorn, *Thuja plicata* and *T. occidentalis* and yew. Less frequently seen but flowering and berrying and so more attractive for certain purposes are *Berberis darwinii* and *B. stenophylla*, *Cotoneaster simonsii*, escallonia, *Mahonia aquifolium*, *Rhododendron lyteum*, *R. ponticum* and roses. Most of these plants are comparatively quick growing (i.e., reasonably mature within five years or so). The slow-growing exceptions are box, holly and yew. These can take ten years or more to mature.

Herbaceous Plants

Except for the present enjoyment of the sweet white blooms of the Christmas rose, the ever-developing sharp green shoots of that other early hellebore, *foetidus*, which will be in flower next month, and the burgeoning buds of bulbs, January is mainly a month of looking ahead so far as herbaceous plants are concerned.

If attractive summer bedding schemes are to materialise there are some seeds which will have to be sown now, antirrhinums, cannas, salvias and verbenas among them. For pots, sow begonias of all kinds, gloxinias, streptocarpus and, for tubs too, some of the American hybrid pelargoniums or pot geraniums will look well.

Prepare to fill gaps in perennial borders by taking root cuttings. Just as some weeds go on growing if a little of their root is left in the ground (dandelions for example), so can some perennial garden plants be increased by portions of roots. The range is limited but it includes such showy plants as anchusas, gaillardias, oriental poppies, all varieties of the showy summer *Phlox paniculata*, romneyas, statice and verbascums.

Roots, of course, vary in thickness. Thick ones such as anchusa and poppies should be cut into pieces 1–1½ inches long. Make a square cut at the end from which the piece was taken from the parent root and a slanting one the other end. Using a dibber, plant in pots of sandy soil or John Innes cutting compost, square end upwards and just below the soil surface. The thinner roots, such as those of phlox, gaillardia and others, should be cut in roughly 2-inch lengths and strewn on the surface of boxes or pans of the soil or compost and then lightly covered with about ½ inch more.

Keep the pots, pans or boxes in an unheated frame or cold greenhouse, or in some sheltered place out of doors but protected from slugs. They should shoot by the spring and be ready by early summer for transplanting a few inches apart in a nursery bed. Once grown into good plants, they can be moved to their final positions.

Do not be in too great a hurry to tidy the herbaceous borders by removing any faded stems or by raking off windblown leaves. Although it may be possible to see some of the current year's growth on some plants, they are best not exposed. There may be more bad weather ahead.

Where the garden is on heavy clay it is best to let the stems stay on the plants until early March even though this may not always look tidy in the more prominent parts of the garden. A point to be borne in mind is that slug damage is never so bad when this concession is made.

1

2

3

1 Summer-flowering Phlox can be propagated from root cuttings, made 2 inches long.
2 Root cuttings of Oriental Poppies are usually dibbled into John Innes cutting compost.
3Papaverorientalis, the Oriental Poppy, can be grown from root cuttings.

House Plants

Largely because of the popularity of house plants as Christmas gifts, a number of the most beautiful varieties are to be seen in flower in our homes in January. Although bloom is usually fairly short lived, some flowers continue attractive for weeks on end.

Perhaps the longest-lasting 'flower' belongs to the *Aechmea rhodocyanea*, popularly known as the Greek vase plant, one of the easiest and longest-lasting of all house plants. The 2 inch-wide grey-green leaves of aechmea radiate from the centre to form a 'vase' or 'cup'. In the winter a long pink stem arises from the centre of this 'vase', opening at the top to form the flower. The flower is actually a prickly, spiky scape bearing a series of smaller flowers, pink, blue, white and purple. These smaller flowers last for several weeks and when faded they leave the attractive pink scape still projected above the leaves.

As it produces its flower, however, the plant begins to die and over the next few months gradually begins to wither, leaving one or more small young plants coming through the soil at its base. These can be split up together with a good portion of root, and re-potted where they will quickly grow away to give a further supply.

Since the appearance of new and tougher varieties, the poinsettia, *Euphorbia pulcherrima*, has achieved deserved popularity.

It is normally seen at Christmas with brilliant scarlet bracts. The bracts can also be pink or white. The actual flowers of the poinsettia are the small, berry-like, yellow protruberances on top of the scarlet bracts. Poinsettias prefer cool to warm atmospheres and generally do better in a hall or bedroom than sometimes stuffy living rooms. They like plenty of light and should be watered carefully, being kept slightly on the dry side and given water only when the leaves begin to droop and show signs of dryness. After the flowers have finished and fallen, allow the soil to dry out almost completely and then cut down the main stem to about three buds. In spring re-pot and begin to water again. Begin feeding in the warmth of a greenhouse in about September in order to bring the plants into flower again.

An interesting and attractive house

1

2

3

1 Flowering pot plants make a colourful contribution to winter.
2 House plants displaying contrasts of form and of colour.
3 Aechmea rhodocyanea, known as the Greek Vase Plant.

plant in flower in January is the zebra plant, *Aphelandra squarrosa Louisae*, which gained its popular name because of the white stripes on the green leaves. The aphelandra carries a cockscomb of yellow flowers that persist for long periods. These flowers appear in a series of yellow-green bracts, the whole inflorescence being in the shape of a small elongated pyramid.

Zygocactus truncatus, Christmas cactus or crab cactus, is another plant that will flower at this time of year, as the first of its common names indicates. The other common name refers to the flat, leaf-like stems, which are jointed like a crab's claws. The zygocactus—a true cactus—will give freely of a profusion of brilliant flowers; white, pink, scarlet or red, depending on variety.

The charming little *Saintpaulia ionantha*, or African violet, can be induced to flower at almost any time of year and a collector can have specimens in bloom for the whole 12 months. The little violet-like flowers can be pink, blue, white or red as well as violet in colour, and can be either double or single, for there are many cultivated varieties available.

Rhododendron Simsii, an ericaceous plant demanding plenty of moisture at all times and an acid soil mixture, can be a mass of bloom in January. Flowers can be white, red, pink, brick-coloured or sometimes striped. As the rootball has usually been trimmed to allow the plant to fit into a small pot, the remaining roots must always be kept damp.

The most useful indication of moisture requirements is to be seen in the tiny trunk of the plant itself. This should show a dark dampness for at least an inch from soil level.

Some general advice: house plants like as much light as possible, dislike over-warm, over-stuffy conditions. Humidifiers will correct a too-dry atmosphere, the great danger. A bowl of water near the plant will serve. Keep it topped up. Do not over-water house plants. They don't need much water at this time of year since root growth is minimal.

Lawns

There is no reason why a lawn should not be mown on a fine day in January as long as it is not too wet or frosted. Certainly this is preferable to leaving grass to grow too long and matted.

If the grass is wet, swish it over early in the morning with a long, supple and whippy cane to send water droplets down off the blades of grass into the soil so as to hasten drying. Mow quickly, lightly and with blades set high, first having swept from the surface of the lawn any dead leaves or other debris.

You can prepare now for new sowings of grass seed in the early spring and late summer by ordering seed. The best lawn seed tends to vanish from the seedsmen's stores early in the season and it is advisable to order early.

Allow for about 1½ ounces of seed per

1

2

3

4

1 The site for a new lawn must be cleared of rubbish and debris.
2 Fork over the area and break up the soil to a depth of 4 inches.

3 The perennial weeds on the site need to be lifted, not dug in.
4 Rake the surface level, making a fine tilth for seed sowing.

square yard. On this basis you will want about 1 lb for every 10 square yards. Prices vary from 50 to 95 pence per lb. Unless there are young children in the family who are likely to subject your lawn to hard wear, buy a lawn seed mixture that does not contain rye grass, even though hard-wearing mixtures containing this grass are cheaper and perennial rye grass is quick to germinate.

The best mixtures will probably contain these ingredients in varying proportions by weight: some four parts Chewing's fescue, four parts of creeping red fescue, two parts browntop.

Actual sowing of grass seed must wait. But provided weather conditions are favourable and a supply of good clean turf is available, there is no reason why a lawn should not be turfed any time between October and February. A new lawn turfed now should be ready for light use by the summer.

Turfing is rather like laying floor tiles. Once the turves are laid you have —hey presto!—a matured lawn, to the eye anyway. There is no germination period as with seed. But the cost of turfing is about three times that of sowing. Make sure drainage is satisfactory and dig the site thoroughly, clearing away all stones and perennial weeds. If, after digging, the ground is left fallow for a few weeks, weed seeds in the soil will germinate and can be cleared. The next step is to break up the soil thoroughly and rake the surface to a fine tilth while observing the necessary levels. A week before laying the turf rake into the soil a handful of bonemeal per square yard.

Lay the turves with alternate joints like bricks in a wall. Stand on a board while laying them and move this over the laid turf rather than over the soil.

A damaged lawn can be renovated by removing and replacing the turves during any dry spell in the winter.

Beat down and consolidate the turf so that it establishes firm contact with the soil below.

A light dressing of sieved compost spread over the newly turfed area and brushed into the cracks should be followed by a light rolling. If the coming spring weather is dry, ensure adequate watering of the turf.

Patios

Keep all areas swept clean of fallen leaves and other debris, for insect pests and disease spores can settle and breed there. Make sure that all pots, troughs, window boxes and other containers have their drainage holes clear of rubbish; otherwise rain and frost will kill plants and may crack containers. Examine all containers and put aside for repair any that may need it, ready for spring plantings.

Continue to give some protection to the more tender plants, particularly those in an exposed place on the patio or on a roof or balcony. Winter winds and frosts can whip around corners in these places to do considerable damage.

If trees and shrubs ordered earlier have arrived from the nursery do not hesitate to plant them in your containers. The containers should be fairly small for reasons both of space and the windy conditions usually prevailing on roof, balcony or patio.

Suitable subjects for winter interest include dwarf conifers, winter flowering heathers (mainly *Erica carnea*), several forms of ivy, camellias, *Senecio laxifolius* and *Mahonia aquifolium*.

If the depth of the containers used is sufficient, at least 1 foot, all more or less permanent plantings can be underplanted with spring flowering bulbs, which will be making growth by now and in sheltered places may even be showing their green shoots.

Although peat and peat-based composts are useful for balcony, roof and patio gardening in the summer because of their moisture retentive properties, their very lightness is a drawback where wind is a problem, for they tend to blow away when dry. So either use soil mixtures incorporating heavier soils with the peat or top-dress containers with ½ inch or so of shingle, pea gravel or lime-stone chippings. Alternatively, use peat in the lower half, or two thirds, of the container and soil for the top section.

Climbers growing in containers will frequently be used in this highly artificial form of gardening. So make sure during the winter that straining wires or climber panels fixed to walls are secure and cleaned from last year's dead growth. A panel heavily covered with dead trails can be caught in a high wind and torn from the wall, taking with

A patio near the house furnished with coniferous plants provides winter colour and shelter.

it precious plants and growing bulbs and possibly breaking the container.

Check drainage from the patio and all entrances to down pipes on balconies and roof tops to ensure that debris or fallen leaves have not choked the outlets.

Paths

This is the time of year when a good, solid path down the garden proves to be worth all the time and effort spent on making it. It will enable you to walk along to pick a handful of herbs or inspect a winter-rocked tree tie without getting your feet wet or muddy. It also enables you to wheel a barrow load of fallen leaves or shrubs for planting without tearing the soft lawn.

This is also the time of year that reveals faults in path making. Frosts may break up a badly laid pathway, crumble stone or bricks. Pools of water or ice may show in slight hollows. Soil or grass beside the pathway may be waterlogged because rain shed from the surface cannot drain away. Algae growing on the paving surface or fallen leaves may create a slippery hazard.

There is little that can be done in January weather to alleviate major faults in paths, but at least note them lest they be forgotten.

Flooded or soggy ground beside paths can be drained to some extent by spiking the surface deeply and thoroughly, preferably using a spiker that removes little plugs of soil. If the holes thus made are filled with coarse sand or grit this will ease the drainage problem.

Fallen leaves on paving should be cleared away regularly. Algae or moss can be removed with a stiff brush, using either a proprietary moss or algae killer or a solution of ordinary household bleach in hot water.

If you plan to pave or repave, order a non-slip surface type of paving. A deep foundation of broken bricks, stones and rubble will help to drain surface water away quickly and allow the path surface to dry. A slight camber to a path with a good foundation will lead excess water down below the surface.

Algae, which make paths slippery in winter, can be removed by applying tar-oil winter wash from a can.

All walls should be examined from time to time during winter to ensure that frost has not entered to break bricks or stones.

Rock Gardens

On the rock garden some of the little bulb flowers will already be pushing through the soil, making little splashes of colour. Give them a chance to shine out more brightly by clearing away the debris of winter. Leaves are almost certain to have drifted against them. These may have given valuable protection but they need not be left to hide the flowers now.

If slugs are troublesome, put down a pellet or two a few inches from the plant.

So long as the soil is not frosted, one can plant alpines throughout the winter. Survey your rock garden as it is now and ask yourself: Is it as 'fully furnished' in winter as it could be?

Many plants are handsome at all seasons. The massed rosettes of cobwebby sempervivums are both attractively

Above **Abies concolor watereri prostrata, a plant for winter effect.**
Below **Conifers provide winter colour.**

Many plants, particularly alpines which dislike dampness, need protecting from the worst of winter rain. Cover them with glass.

coloured and shaped. There are more than 40 species and some 200 hybrids of these. So the choice is wide. Sedums also offer superb contrast in colour and texture. *Sedum spathulifolium* has a lovely grey-blue bloom. Its variety, *purpureum*, has deep purple-stained leaves.

Dianthus foliage adds more contrast and liveliness, for there is even the odd winter flower on some plants. There are many evergreen shrubs and conifers. Of the latter *Picea abies* 'Reflexa', *Juniperus chinensis sargentii* and many other of its dwarf forms are invaluable, while the little creeping willow, *Salix repens*, and the lower growing *S. reticulata* bring novelty to the scene.

Roses

There are many passionately held theories about rose pruning and its timing. Of course much depends on soils and aspects, but most experts advocate gradual pruning from about the turn of the year through to March or April rather than a single, final pruning at any time of the year.

You can start to prune your roses on any January day when weather conditions are not too adverse.

First cut away all dead stems, all twiggy growth incapable of bringing forth a strong shoot and all side shoots growing into the centre of the bush. It is essential to allow light and air into the centre if strong, healthy growth is to be maintained. If there is time during the month continue the pruning process by cutting to about half their present length the remainder of the shoots, always to an eye pointing in the required direction.

You will probably have opportunities later on to hard prune. Even if you don't have, you will have done sufficient pruning to produce a fine show of blooms in the coming season and will, at the same time, have reduced the top weight of the bushes to insure against rocking in high winds and the waterlogging of roots.

You can plant roses—like all other shrubs—in January, provided the ground is not hard into frost or waterlogged.

Newly planted bushes in medium to heavy soil should be cut down to within 6 inches or so of the soil, again to an outward-pointing eye. If they are planted in light or sandy soil it is best merely to tip them in their first year and to wait until they have made a good strong root system before being more drastic.

Roses like a slightly acid soil with a pH of about 6.0 or 6.5. If your soil is alkaline it can be improved with heavy dressings of compost, farmyard manure and peat. All these should be applied in the

When Rose pruning, wear gloves and avoid windy weather; otherwise the whippy growths can be a hindrance.
1 The bush before it is pruned.
2 Dead and unwanted wood has been removed.
3 Cut back the leaders to an outward-facing bud a few inches above the ground level.
4 The finished job should look neat and leave a well-shaped skeleton to the bush. Light and air are important.

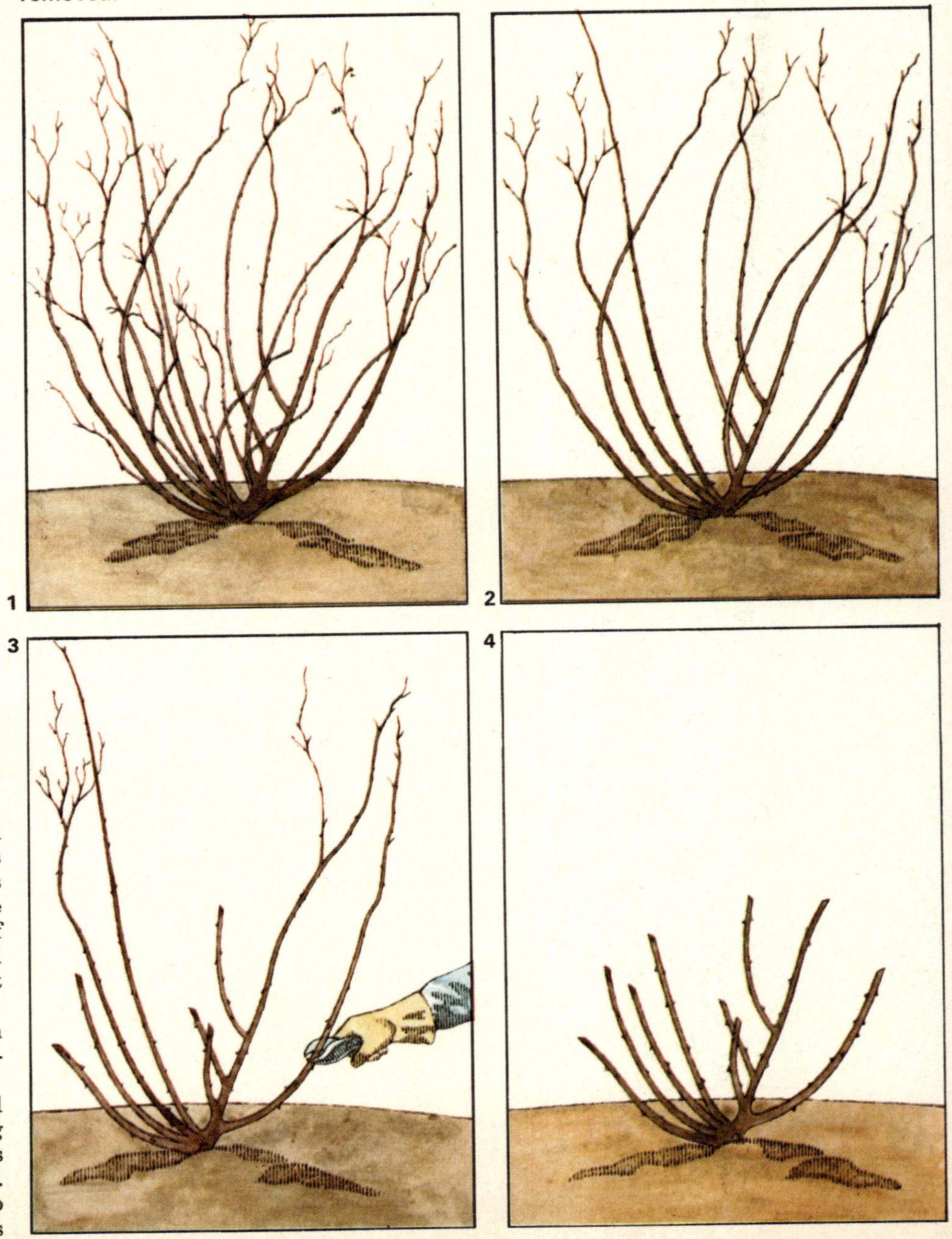

early spring, but as many farmers in January are overcrowded with manure this is a good time to obtain a supply.

Trees & Shrubs

Apart from trees and shrubs grown in canisters, which can be planted at any time of the year because their roots receive little disturbance, the winter is the normal season for all plantings. If the soil is not waterlogged or frosted, you can plant now. Should plants arrive during bad weather they can be heeled in (temporarily planted at a slant so that the sap doesn't rise too quickly) until it improves.

As new trees and shrubs will probably become permanent residents of your garden, plant them well and give them every chance to fulfil themselves. They may be planted either as specimens, alone in their grandeur, or in groups, with smaller subjects co-existent in a shrub border.

Most catalogues indicate the final size of a tree or shrub in its maturity. If you ignore this advice, you may risk planting a tiny new tree just arrived from the nursery in a location where in a year or two it will block a path, hide a cherished view or effectively bar entrance to the garage. Or, if, at the other extreme, your planting distances are excessive you may have to wait up to 20 years before you enjoy a well-stocked and proportioned garden. It is suggested that for early colour, shape and form it is preferable to plant more closely than is generally recommended with the intention of removing certain trees and shrubs after a few years.

When planting, dig the hole rather wider than necessary but not too deep; most roots spread laterally.

Break up the base of the hole with a fork and incorporate in this base seeds, farmyard manure, compost, peat or similar humus-making material as is available. After the addition of a thin layer of soil, the tree or shrub can be placed in position to see whether the planting depth is correct. It is important that soil should come no higher than the quite obvious mark on the stem indicating its previous level. If the height is correct, insert the stake up to 2 feet in the ground and as tall as the first branching stem. Holding the plant upright in the hole, sift in a few inches of soil, shaking the roots occasionally to make sure that they are in close contact with the soil. Firm thoroughly with your heel. A further layer of humus-making material can be added to the planting material before the final layer is laid, bringing the soil to ground level.

Although labour saving, trees and shrubs need some attention, particularly in their first few months. So examine newly planted specimens to make sure

1

2

3

4

1 When planting a young tree take out a hole large enough.
2 Lift the ball of soil straight into the planting hole.

3 Mark the soil level with a stick. Set the shrub to the right depth.
4 Pack fine soil firmly around the roots and level it off.

that frosts have not loosened the soil around them and that they are not dry. Harsh east winds in winter and frequently experienced spring droughts can be fatal to young trees. Give them any necessary protection and plenty of water at the roots. A fine spray over the entire plant on spring evenings will lessen damage from over-transpiration. Never allow grass and weeds to grow immediately around a newly planted tree or shrub for the first few years.

In the border, plant with an eye to overall effect rather than to the striking appearance of any one particular shrub. It is usually most effective to group two or three shrubs of one kind or family together, with a contrasting group—in colour, shape, form or texture—as neighbour. Plan heights to give an irregular, rather than an even saw-tooth, pattern.

Climbers are among the most useful shrubs in the garden, for they add to its size as well as softening a wall or fence and providing the benefit of their flowers and foliage.

All climbers need some support, whether it be the wall or fence alone for sucker or aerial rooted plants such as ivies and Virginian creeper, or wires or trellis for roses, clematis, wisteria and others. These supports should be firmly fixed to the wall or fence but are best placed just a few inches away in order to keep the wall dry and to allow air to get behind the plant's foliage.

When fixing trellis or wires it is a good tip to use long screws or nails and to use a large cotton reel between wall and trellis.

It is sometimes suggested that climbers such as ivies and Virginian creeper which cling to a wall or fence by themselves can do serious damage. They cannot, in fact, damage the fabric of a sound wall or fence within any period that is likely to worry you, but they can sometimes get into eaves or gullies and this tendency should be prevented by pruning.

Vegetables

Most of January's vegetable gardening is done at the fireside! Take time to browse through the seed catalogues and note how modern introductions can help to make your garden more productive.

You can have, for example, lettuce that does not run to seed or bolt quickly, cabbage that is called long-standing (because once it makes a good compact heart it stays like that instead of

moving on to make flower stems) radish, beet and other root crops that grow fast and are therefore tender as well as early.

In a small garden and with certain crops—most salads, for instance—it is better to sow a little and often than to fill a row at once. This way one produces a continuous crop and avoids gluts. On the other hand, a continuation of other crops, such as peas, can waste time and space.

If you have a deep freeze, you should adapt your plans to it. There will be no need to plan a continuation of first and second early, maincrop and late peas. Decide which of the varieties is best for you and sow several rows together. Once this crop is ready for picking you will be able to clear the ground and plant it with something else.

A deep freeze makes even the smallest plot productive.

Several rows of beetroot can be sown at the same time. The rows can be a little closer than if the beet were to be spaced between other crops. The roots can be lifted young and in perfect condition. An entire row of broccoli and cauliflower can be harvested at one time and the vacant space re-sown immediately. Most seedsmen now list varieties which are best for freezing, and it is worth growing these rather than an old favourite which might not have the same sugar content or which might become mushy when frozen.

If at the fireside in January you study seed catalogues and make your selections, your summer reward can be vegetables in abundant variety. New introductions, including some specially suitable for the deep-freeze, can make your garden more productive.
Right **Parsley, Petroselinum crispum, can be picked in winter.**

Order or buy your seeds early, especially if you want some of the newer introductions. Unpack them and keep them in a cool place away from damp and mice.

Much January work depends on where a garden is situated. In the mild south or in sheltered gardens some work can go ahead outdoors now. But seed should be sown only when the soil condition is favourable. If the soil sticks to the shoes, it is far too cold and wet for seeds.

The hardiest peas are round-seeded; wrinkled marrowfats are for later crops. The first can be sown from November to early March according to soil and situation. One pint is sufficient for 50 feet. The best way is to sow the peas in wide rows, say three rows 2 inches apart. Following a garden line, make flat drills 6–9 inches wide. Often a lightweight spade will do this more quickly and easily than a hoe. Drills can be made warmer by putting a light covering of peat over the base. Space out the peas on this and cover them first with a little peat and then 2–3 inches of soil. Tread this down and rake the surface lightly.

Early broad beans may also be sown now, one pint for a 50-foot single row. These can be dibbled in 2 inches deep, either in single rows 5 feet apart or 12-inch wide double rows 6 feet apart. If dwarf broad beans are sown (and these are ideal for small gardens) plant only 3 feet apart for single rows and 4 feet for double. Later, quicker-maturing lettuce, radish or corn salad can be sown between the rows.

Where soil is well drained, shallots can be planted 6 inches apart in rows 1 foot apart. Take out a small hole with a trowel to hold the depth of the bulbs and press them into this.

Order seeds or plants now for the herb garden. Seeds should be sown in the spring and plants will be delivered then. The site should be south-facing and receive some shelter from north and east. Smaller plants such as chives, marjoram, parsley and thyme should go in the front of the plot, backed by taller-growing herbs. All will then get their share of the sun.

Water Gardens

Many people are put off water gardens because they suspect they are a particularly costly feature, both in time and money. The very opposite is true. In terms of labour, water gardens are economical throughout the year—and to the point of parsimony in the winter.

In January there is nothing much to be done other than to continue to keep leaves and debris from falling into the water and, in very hard weather, making sure that if the surface has frozen there is an open hole in the ice.

Where the frost is so heavy that a small pool is likely to freeze solid for more than a day or two, any fish it contains should be netted and removed to a slightly warmer place (a pail of water, for example). But a mere surface inch or two of ice can do no harm—as long as a small hole is kept open for noxious gases to escape.

It is these gases and not the cold that harm fish. They are produced mainly by rotting vegetation, dead and dying water plants and fallen leaves. Hence the importance of keeping water clear during autumn leaf fall.

In icy conditions it is helpful to float on the water surface a rubber ball, preferably a heavy one, of 6 inches or more diameter. A heavy ball will absorb the ice pressure and can easily be removed to leave a clear gap. If the ball is too light it will merely ride up on the ice as this forms, and lie on the surface.

Alternatively, place an empty tin can on the ice and fill this periodically with boiling water. This will make and preserve a neat hole in the ice. The hole needs to be there during the whole time the pool is covered in ice. And perhaps the best means of doing this is to use one of the handy miniature floating electric heaters. By no means all pools, however, are accessible to the electricity supply. So the rubber ball or the hot water treatment may still be necessary.

Warning: use merely enough heat to make the hole. The water itself should not be warmed or plants may be started into premature growth. Remember, too, not to break the ice by breaking it forcibly. This creates shock waves in the water that can seriously harm any fish, particularly in their semi-dormant state.

Wildlife

In the garden, wildlife is frequently more varied in January than in other months. Lack of natural food compels animals and birds to go farther afield. Once they have discovered a regular supply of food they will return to it day after day.

Because of the long nights and short days it is unlikely that nocturnal animals such as foxes and badgers, at other periods surprisingly active even in many urban areas, will be seen.

Birds, on the other hand, can be observed throughout the day if food and water are provided as an inducement. The main types of bird to be seen, both in urban and country areas, are blue tits (light blue cap with a white border), great tits (black head and stripe running down breast), thrushes, blackbirds, wood pigeons, tree and house sparrows (the hedge sparrow is rarer and belongs to a different family), robins and starlings.

Any food that is put out for birds should be rich in carbohydrates to give them energy and warmth. Suet, dough and table scraps are suitable and should be put either on a bird table, best suspended from a branch, or on a path or paved area rather than among grass. Monkey nuts or a half coconut can be strung and suspended from a branch for tits. Mealworms, available from most good pet stores, are a great favourite with blackbirds. Little salty food should be made available to birds as it can harm some types, particularly birds of prey such as the kestrel or owl.

Water provides something of a problem because of frosts but is all the more essential to birds when normal supplies are frozen. If you place a supply of water in the lee of a tree or a bank there will be less risk of its freezing.

Although you may not see any foxes and badgers, close examination of snow or mud surfaces will often reveal their tracks and they can be counted on to visit rubbish or compost heaps. The tracks of a rabbit or crow may be seen around the edge of a pond or pool. Fox prints are similar to those of a dog but are longer and narrower.

Once animals and birds have been attracted into the garden, they will stay if not frightened. And if the food supply is maintained and as winter wears on they will lose much of their shyness.

A rubber ball floated on the water of a garden pool will stop ice forming solidly over the surface.

Tits and other birds welcome the bird table and will become daily visitors if food is put out.

Rabbit tracks in the snow. Scrutiny of snow or mud surfaces may yield prints of other January visitors too.

Evergreens

Their foliage, form and colour clothe winter bleakness in the garden. And there are varieties that flower throughout the year

The term evergreen is, in a sense, a misnomer. Some evergreens are, it is true, evergreen. But others can be evergold, evergrey, eversilver.

Evergreens can be flowering or berried. They can make hedges, ground covers or pot plants. They can grow to 100 feet or no more than a few inches. They can be climbers or topiary. They cover a range of the gardening alphabet from andromeda to yucca. And they are decorative in winter as well as summer.

Deciduous trees and shrubs lose their foliage in the autumn. It might appear, by contrast, that evergreens hold their leaves for ever. But this is not actually the case. Their leaves are shed, not dramatically with the coming of the frosts, but gradually throughout the entire year—and they are as constantly replaced.

The main value of evergreen is during the winter, when the green, grey, gold or glaucous blue foliage, the shining berries and the attractive flowers indicate that the garden is still very much alive. Evergreens help to extend the season and by making the right choice of varieties it is possible to have some types, such as the invaluable ericas, in flower throughout the whole year.

The facility that evergreens offer to soften the winter landscape can be extended to soften the lines of buildings and walls.

Evergreen climbers and coverers include the tough and resilient ivies and some of the honeysuckles, pyracanthas and cotoneasters, which give good service throughout the summer and then save surfaces from starkness during the winter.

A particularly pleasant twining evergreen climber is *Akebia quinata*, tough enough to grow even on a north wall, yet producing scented dark purple flowers in April high enough for the perfume to drift into bedrooms.

There are even a few evergreen clematis species, including *C. armandii*, with clusters of glistening white flowers in April and *C. balearica*, a smaller climber with yellowish white flowers produced as early as February.

Consider, too, the conifers, nearly all of them evergreen. They can be green, gold, grey, silver or blue. They can be tall and towering or wide, spreading and ground hugging. They can be erect or drooping. The quick growers among them can be kept under some sort of control by careful pinching out of leading shoots during the early years and many conifers can be bent, twisted and trained to picturesque shapes. Pot grown, they can be dwarfed and shaped bonsai fashion or left statuesque for the terrace or patio.

1

2

1 The term evergreen means that the plant holds its leaves throughout the winter. The foliage may be green, gold or grey.
2 Many Ericas flower in the winter.

When planted closely together conifers tend to lose their lower branches. To keep a conifer clothing the ground, plant it as a specimen in grass, with plenty of space, light and air around it.

Flowering evergreens include some of the most splendid garden plants: azaleas and rhododendrons, camellias, the barberries, ericas, hollies, mahonias, pyracanthas, viburnums and the magnificent *Magnolia grandiflora*, with its big leathery leaves and its huge scented flowers.

Many evergreens like an acid soil. The azaleas, rhododendrons, camellias and ericas are examples. They can be grown in containers, in special beds filled with acid soil or on peat hills. Occasional treatment with sequestrene will give them the iron they need, normally locked into alkaline soils.

Evergreens are obvious choices for hedging plants and there is a wide range. *Berberis stenophylla* is perhaps too vigorous for a hedge unless plenty of space can be devoted to it. Neater and as colourful are *B. darwinii* and *B. juliana*. Some of the escallonias make pretty hedges with their shining foliage and pink or red flowers. They are surprisingly tough and hardy and particularly useful for seaside planting. Pyracanthas, viburnums, holly and box are other alternatives, all with much to commend them.

The Month of February

The garden begins to lose its bleak appearance. Buds everywhere are swelling. The leaves of herbaceous plants appear above the soil. Early shrubs send out their flowers before their leaves; forsythias, flowering quinces and currants, plum blossom and daphnes are examples. Crocuses, scillas, hyacinths, early daffodils signal spring

1

2

3

4

1 Cymbidium 'Goblin Lydart' is an orchid of attractive form and colour. The green petals are striped with maroon and the labellum is also maroon and of a velvety texture. It is a native of Burma.
2 Paphiopedilum 'Chipmunk Vermont' is another Orchid which can be relied upon to flower at this time of the year. The labellum is rounded and shining, and is a distinguishing feature of the flower.
3 Euphorbia fulgens has numerous bright red flowers in winter and early spring. The plant is a native of Mexico. It needs greenhouse cultivation in Britain. It reaches some 3–4 feet in height. The leaves are particularly attractive and are a deep bluish green, and lanceolate.
4 Clivia miniata, known as the Kafir Lily, is a greenhouse flowering plant with a fleshy root. It produces scarlet and yellow flowers in the early spring.

1 Perpetual Carnation 'Arthur Sim', like all Carnations, does best in a house to itself where it can be given airy and rather dry conditions.
2 Fragrant Freesias can be raised from either seed or corms. They are best grown as naturally as possible because both the quality and the life of the flower are affected by forcing.
3 Primula malacoides, an ever-popular flowering plant which can be raised in the greenhouse, then enjoyed indoors.
4 Primula obconica can be had in a wide range of colour and white.
5 Frost enhances and emphasises the form of Helleborus corsicus.

1

2

3

4

5

5

3

6

4

1 Erythronium dens-canis, the Dog's Tooth Violet, belongs to the Lily family.
2 Galanthus nivalis, the Common Snowdrop, is also called Fair Maids of February. The bulbs will thrive almost anywhere and should be left undisturbed.
3 Eranthis hyemalis, the Winter Aconite, is a native plant which likes shady beds and borders under trees.
4 Iris histrioides is a bulbous Iris, flowering during February. It is a native of Asia Minor.
5 Cotoneaster horizontalis is a hardy and vigorous shrub and is often called the Fishbone Plant because of its form.
6 Ilex aquifolium, the Holly, remains beautiful throughout the winter months, and the bright red berries persist.

1

2

3

1 Salix daphnoides, one of the popular Pussy Willows. The grey furry catkins begin to burst from their buds at any time after the turn of the year, and are grey at this time of the year. Later they will be golden when the stamens ripen.
2 Daphne blagayana flowers at the end of the month. It has fragrant cream flowers close to the stem.
3 Cornus mas, also known as the Cornelian Cherry on account of its showy fruits, makes a neat tree some 15 feet in height. It is a mass of colour at blossom time and is noticeable because it flowers so early in the year.
4 Iris reticulata grows well in a pot and can be kept in a cold frame through the winter. The pots can either be allowed to remain there until the flowers appear or removed to the greenhouse or a warm room.
5 The Spanish Iris 'Canary Bird' can also be raised in a frame. The plants should never be removed to warmer conditions for forcing but allowed to flower in their own time. They make admirable cut flowers and last well in water.
6 Single early Tulip 'Brilliant Star' is one of the best recommended varieties for forcing at this time of the year. It is among the few that may be transplanted successfully to more decorative pots and bowls once the flower buds appear in the neck of the plant.
7 Crocus chrysanthus 'Blue Peter' is one of the many chrysanthus varieties which can be grown well in bowls.

4

5

6

7

1

2

3

4

1 Cedrus atlantica, the Mount Atlas Cedar, has several varieties the foliage of which comes into its own during the winter months. This one with blue-grey foliage is C. atlantica glauca; there are also argentea and aurea.
2 The evergreen Elaeagnus pungens, a colourful shrub from China and Japan. The fragrant flowers are rather insignificant later in the year but the shrub is grown for its foliage.
3 Prunus serrulata plays a dual role in the garden where the attractive dark bark shines warmly during the winter. Blossom follows in spring.
4 Rubus cockburnianus, the 'Whitewashed Bramble', is grown for the effect of its white stems in winter. It is one of the handsomest of all Brambles.

1 House plants are dependent not only on the colour of their blooms for decorative effect. Foliage adds colour in the tall Dracaena sanderiana, Cordyline terminalis and Tradescantia.
2 Impatiens petersiana has a deeper coloured foliage than the more common I. sultani, the Busy Lizzie, and because of this is sometimes called Dusky Lizzie.
3 Many plants grown in pans and pots in an alpine house provide a riot of bloom during the coldest months of the year.

1

2

3

Ruling the aspect

Light is as important to growth as moisture. While you cannot re-orientate a garden in the 'about turn' sense, you can shape and plant it to make the most of the aspect

One of the most important features of a garden is its aspect or orientation. The verb to orient properly means to place so as to face east, as for example the siting of a church with the chancel at the east. But we cannot, of course, face our gardens in any particular direction; we have to take them as they come. Nevertheless, it is important when planning or designing a garden, or even certain garden features, to take account of the aspect or orientation. Every gardener should be so aware of the points of the compass in relation to his garden that he knows almost by instinct at any time of the day just where the sun is shining, even though it may be obscured by clouds.

All plant growth demands light, as necessary to it as moisture. Light is essential to the delicate but inexorable processes of photosynthesis that create vital plant foods through the green leaves.

Light can vary in quality and intensity far more than is discernible by the human eye. Plants grow better in country districts than in towns largely because of the improved quality of the light. Many plants that grow only in southern areas even down to the equator owe their success as much to the quality of the light as to the warmth.

To find just how light can vary in different parts of a normal domestic garden depending on orientation and shadows cast by trees and buildings, it is worth measuring its power by means of a light meter or photo-electric cell. Variations in readings in the full sun or full shadow, in east or west aspects, can be dramatic. Fortunately most plants are less critical of light than the photo-electric cell but to give them the best chance of good growth it is as well to give them the type of light conditions they prefer. These vary; not all plants enjoy powerful light.

Small gardens are usually dominated by the house. Normally the house is roughly rectangular, with each of its four sides facing roughly one point of the compass.

The small house and garden underline the importance of orientation. They also present good opportunities for 'extended' planting, for the walls of a house should always be brought into a garden as far as possible. The walls give extra warmth and protection and at the same time add appreciably to the total area of the plot.

The use of vertical space extends boundaries without taking in adjoining land. A 10-foot climber, for example, adds 10 feet to the available greenery.

A south wall means that it *faces* south. So a free-standing boundary wall running between two houses is a north wall for one neighbour and a south wall for the other if it runs from east to west.

A south wall is the most valuable horticulturally, for it receives most sun and is warmest. Grow against it only those plants that require its warmth and protection or will flourish best there. Never waste a south wall on climbers such as ivy or Virginian creeper, both of which can manage with (indeed, sometimes even prefer) a north or east wall.

The sun begins to reach the face of a south-facing wall comparatively early in the morning, hits it squarely at noon (if artificial time adjustments are ignored) and stays on it at an ever-widening angle until comparatively late in the afternoon. The wall absorbs warmth all this time even though the day may be overcast.

Almost as valuable is a west wall, for the sun begins to touch its fringes at about midday, when its rays are strongest, and maintains its beneficent warmth until sunset.

Although it gets almost no direct sun, a north wall can still be useful to a gardener. Several climbers such as ampelopsis, ivies, *Hydrangea petiolaris, Polygonum baldschuanicum,* jasmine, honeysuckle and even *Clematis montana* will grow well on it. Many other plants will grow at its foot, preferring constant shade to sunshine and revelling in a cool position that usually is moist as well.

Finally—the east wall. This catches the early morning light, comparatively cold at dawn but surprisingly warm as the sun rises higher in the sky. Many climbers, including those mentioned above, will do well against an east wall.

The trees in this garden and the placing of shrubs not only produce charming vistas but filter the sunlight to the benefit of the smaller plants in the wide curved beds.

But choose them with care, for much of the worst frost damage to plants is caused not by the cold itself but by the sudden sun-induced warmth on frost-crisp petals; this can have the effect of rupturing their tissues.

To get the best light throughout the year, a greenhouse should, where possible, be orientated with the ridge running from north to south. If the shade cast by trees, house, walls, hedges or fences is disregarded, the same principle applies to a single flower bed. If it runs from north to south it will receive the greatest all-day benefit from the sun on all the plants. If, on the other hand, you wish it to be well baked by the sun you will face it to the south—that is, run it from east to west. If it can be sloped or banked up on the north side, then the south side will be as warm as is physically possible and the north side may even be in shade. This will enable you to grow sun-lovers on the south side and shade-lovers on the north.

Banks, gullies, mounds and slopes assist with orientation as well as adding interest to the appearance of the garden. Constructed with an eye to orientation, they can help the plants that are grown to live a longer and more floriferous life. They can give sun or shade, protection or exposure, sharp drainage or boggy conditions.

Shade gives many plants the conditions they require. It is sensible, for example, to site a large specimen tree in the lawn where its shadow gradually moves over a herbaceous bed or border containing moisture-loving plants such as trollius, ranunculus, mimulus, hostas and hemerocallis. Yet if the border contains, say, verbascum, echinops, nepeta, lupins, dianthus, acanthus and the like it would be better to place the tree on the north of this bed so that it does not cast its shade over these sun-lovers.

This indicates the importance of the southern boundary which, though technically a north wall, fence or hedge, is the line over which the sun will enter the garden and shine most brightly. As much sun as possible must be attracted over this boundary and the barrier kept as low as is compatible with shelter and privacy. A row of tall conifers along the south side of a garden will so reduce the amount of light received by the plants in it as to add considerably to the gardener's problems.

Where shelter from prevailing wind is concerned, a dense screen is frequently less effective than one that is lighter, which means that if the prevailing wind comes from the south both greater protection from the wind and better quality light are obtained if a light shelter of open trees is formed rather than a denser screen. Wind can be compared with water. If a flow of water meets an impenetrable barrier it builds up, flows over it and down the other side with considerable turbulence. But if it is obstructed by a more open screen it will flow through gently, its strength absorbed by the barrier.

A position in the lee of a windbreak is always comparatively warm and sheltered, even though it may face due north. As this position also tends to dry out less quickly than one in full sun or directly exposed to drying winds, it can be useful for moisture-loving plants. Ferns and similar plants are perfect for such a situation and can often be seen growing wild where these conditions prevail.

Fortunately most people do not have to garden where wind, possibly salt-laden, is a major problem. Yet even in such conditions orientation can ease the problem. The garden can be so designed as to place in the forefront of the blast those trees and shrubs that will accept it, soften it, filter it and release it tamed to the remainder of the growing garden.

One of the best trees for this purpose is the sea buckthorn, *Hippophae rhamnoides*, which will give fine grey-green foliage and, if both sexes are planted, a multiplicity of orange berries. The attractive and deceptively delicate-

Tree-enveloping cluster of Clematis montana with Hebe armstrongii in foreground. Contrivance can give Clematis the positions they need—head in sun, roots in shade.

In a shaded garden a wall can be built to provide a position where the light might be stronger and at the same time provide colour. Frequently, the more tender plants can be grown on walls.

Pelargoniums give pinnacle colour to a boundary wall. Walls can extend the planting possibilities of a garden provided the choice of subjects is made according to aspect.

looking plumes of tamarisk are also tough enough to give protection in these conditions.

The average lawn size in gardens is 1,000 square feet, half the size of the average total garden. This makes grass the most important single plant. (There is a tendency to overlook the fact that grass is a plant in its own right, demanding care equal to that bestowed on the finest rhododendron or liquidambar.) Some grasses do not grow well in continuously shaded positions and this should be considered when planting trees or shrubs that are likely to cast deep shade, although the patterned and dappled moving shade of single specimen trees planted in the lawn is little impediment.

An ideal position for many plants, particularly climbers, is one where their roots are in the shade and their heads in the sun. This ideal can be fulfilled through selective planting and in many instances is brought about by the growth habit of the plant itself. Grass, for example, shades its own roots if it is not shaved too close. At the other extreme a clematis planted against a wall can have its base completely open to the baking sun unless provision has been made to avoid this.

You may wish to grow a clematis or wisteria on a south wall but for some reason may be unable to shade the roots. It may be possible to plant the roots against an east wall and train the shoots upwards to grow around the corner to face south. Or you can plant a climbing *Hydrangea petiolaris* on the north side of an old apple tree and allow its shoots to grow upwards into the tree and wind around until the splendid flowers benefit most from the sun on the south.

Water gardens should always be placed so that they are in full sun. Paradoxically, the water itself should be shaded to a considerable extent. But

The curvature, different levels and planting scheme of this garden are designed with orientation the key factor in mind. The aim is to give sun and shade as and where they are needed.

the plants such as water lilies that carry out this task demand bright sun on their large leaf surfaces if they are to fulfil their function.

A new water garden is commonly made by digging out a hole and placing the soil on one side for the creation of an affiliated rock garden, perhaps with a pump-fed stream running down to the pool. If this raised area is situated to the north and east, then every benefit is gained. The pool is sheltered, the raised mound that faces down to the pool basks in the southern sun, and the northern edges are ideal for some of the alpine plants that shine at their happiest when they are situated out of the direct rays of the sun.

1

2

3

1 Well-placed and low-growing conifers prove labour saving in the long run. They require no clipping or pruning and give an established effect all the year round.
2 Initial outlay on clean paving and perennial plants is well justified.
3 Where much of the garden is given up to lawn, choose a slow-growing grass.

Labour-saving

The permanent features and planting schemes in a garden are the real keys to reducing time and toil and increasing the enjoyment of gardening

These days the general pattern of gardening is governed to a great extent by the motor car and television. Both of these are time consumers and both have a relationship to family life that tends to pull the gardener out of his garden and into family excursions or family viewing.

They are two of the main reasons why trees and shrubs have increased in popularity and beds of annuals have declined in popularity, why rose trees sell in millions every year, why sales of peat have risen astronomically and why some mechanised garden aids are less expensive and more widely used than might seem reasonable in an era of small gardens.

The modern gardener, however enthusiastic, has so many other calls on his leisure that he needs to achieve the best possible results with minimum labour.

A labour-saving garden is a planned garden. There is a common impression that a time-consuming plot can be changed overnight into one that can be managed in an hour or two a week by the purchase of powered tools. This is fallacious. Provided it is effectively planned, the average garden of 2,000 square feet can be maintained easily in one afternoon a week without a single powered tool.

But larger gardens, or those where considerable space is given up to vegetables, can gain from the use of powered machines. Several lightweight machines are available which will take attachments to run cultivators, ploughs, ridgers, lawn mowers, hedge cutters, circular saws, pruners, weeders, pumps and the like. Wheeled spreaders of seeds and fertilisers can be helpful and time saving in the larger garden. Knapsack pressure sprayers can save time by cutting out the necessity for constant replenishment of liquid sprays when, for example, many roses must be treated against aphids or black spot.

The most important element of labour saving, however, is the correct choice of plants and materials. To take a simple example, if a garden contains 50 feet of privet hedge this will need clipping at least twice a year. Because privet is a greedy plant the soil at its base will grow nothing else unless it is enriched regularly. But if the soil is enriched it will grow weeds and these will have to be removed. So several time-consuming operations are involved.

Yet, once constructed, a well-made wall will need little attention in a lifetime. Or if a hedge is preferred, berberis, for instance, will also require little attention and provide lavish colour throughout the year.

A labour-saving garden is frequently a necessity not so much because of shortage of time as because of the sheer physical inability of the gardener to cope with the sometimes heavy work involved. Here garden design and the construction of special features can enable the gardener to enjoy and care for his plot with the minimum of heavy digging and lifting. Even so, an intelligent selection of plants will prove his greatest asset.

There are plants that variously like acid soils or alkaline, that enjoy situations that are hot and dry or moist and boggy, bleak and windswept or warm and protected, shaded or open to the sun. There are tall trees and low growing, columnar, weeping, conical or spreading; trees and shrubs for town gardens and for the countryside; climbers and prostrate plants. There are, indeed, plants for all situations, and by choosing the right plants for the right spot the gardener enlists the aid of nature to help him grow his plants well and easily.

A gardener starting from scratch with an empty plot should look around him before he begins to plan his garden. The ecology of the neighbourhood will tell him much. In local gardens he will be able to see which plants appear to grow best, and nearby open spaces, woodland and commons will reveal what will grow on his soil and in his weather. Wild heather, pines and rhododendrons in the locality prove that the soil is acid and possibly sandy. Wild clematis in hedgerows and native beech trees suggest that the soil is alkaline. The weather-pruned sweep of tall, bowed trees will indicate the strength and source of the prevailing wind.

The gardener who insists on saving labour must accept his natural soil and grow plants that it will tolerate unless he is prepared to involve himself in considerable continuous work to change the nature of the soil.

Every virgin garden should have its soil carefully tested in several different places because significant differences can exist in a single small garden. An area that has been heavily worked is more likely to be acid than one that has lain fallow for years. Plot the differences in acidity and alkalinity as a planting reference and make careful note of any important mineral deficiencies that may be found. Soil testing kits are inexpensive to buy and simple to operate.

Then decide the primary purposes of the garden. Is it to be merely a pleasure garden? Is it to be a playground for the children? Is it to be productive, yielding fruit and vegetables?

A beautiful and labour-saving garden can be created quite cheaply. But by spending initially what can, admittedly,

Properly constructed steps and walling will require no attention and make a permanent background. The changing effect is achieved by containers.

If soil type is considered when initial planning is carried out and only plants that thrive are introduced, much work can be eliminated by choosing shrubs, both evergreen and deciduous.

amount to a considerable sum, various aids and comforts can be incorporated that, if added piecemeal at later stages, will cost even more in money and time.

These expensive extras are largely structural, in the form of paving, walling and the construction of a water garden. They may involve much heavy work that a skilled workman can undertake more quickly and easily than an amateur. But if you commission work of this kind make sure that the workmen *are* skilled. For a wrong slope in paved areas can cause a constantly boggy patch of ground, or a wall constructed without proper foundations can sink, crumble and waste the money that was spent on it.

A considerable portion of the garden will probably be put down to a lawn. Make sure that this area is well drained before it is sown or turfed. Use a slow-growing lawn seed mixture as this can save as much as one mowing a week. Avoid all tiny patches of grass, all awkward corners and sharp angles.

Modern mowers are light and easy to handle and if the area to be cut is straightforward the once or twice weekly mowing can provide a pleasant half an hour's exercise. But if the machine must be manoeuvred around difficult spots, pushed with difficulty under overhanging trees or shrubs, or even lifted by hand over steps or around obstructions, mowing the lawn becomes a time-wasting chore.

Normally a hand mower is sufficient for lawns of up to 2,000 square feet but the elderly or partially disabled gardener may require a powered machine even for this area. An electric machine, light in weight, easy to start, quiet to run, is excellent for a small lawn. It is no more difficult or dangerous to operate than a domestic vacuum cleaner. Battery mowers, too, are quiet and easy starting but considerably heavier and usually requiring an overnight charge after use. Petrol-engined machines should not be necessary except in the larger garden and here there is a choice between the cylinder type, where the blades cut with a scissors action, and the rotary type, where the grass is slashed by blades circulating parallel with the ground. Both types can be obtained with grass collecting boxes. In general the second type deals best with long grass but does not give so fine a finish.

All machines should be serviced regularly, at least twice a year, either by the maker or by a local service agent. The year's first servicing should take place well before the grass has begun to grow; otherwise delays in the workshop may mean that the grass has grown high before the machine returns.

In some country or larger suburban gardens it is possible to make an informal or 'wild' garden. The grass is allowed to grow long, rides or pathways traversing it, with occasional trees, shrubs and patches of naturalised bulbs but no formal beds whatever. The dream is usually more attractive than the reality, however. Considerable artifice must lie behind the effective wild garden, and more work and attention are required than might be expected. The long grass must be cut, if only three or four times a year, and this is a major heavy task. Rank weeds are apt to invade the area. Pest and disease attacks are more prevalent because of the protection afforded to insects and fungi in the long grass. So, by and large, a wild garden is seldom in fact a labour-saving one.

Weeds, a time-wasting nuisance for the busy gardener and a physical problem for the elderly or disabled, can be discouraged by both chemical and natural means. Weeds in lawns can be killed by applications of the hormone or selective weedkillers. When correctly applied, these kill broad-leaved weeds but do no harm to grasses. Weeds in flower, shrub or rose beds can be killed by applications of a chemical that acts only on green foliage. For example, weeds at the base of a tree can be sprayed and killed, and any drops that may fall on the brown bark of the tree will do no damage.

There is another type of weedkiller that could more properly be called a weed preventer. It kills slowly, but has an extremely long-lasting effect. It is excellent for areas such as drives, gravel paths and paving. A single application in the late winter or early spring can keep the area clear of all weeds for the whole year. So drastic a preventative cannot be used where any plants are growing but a derivation of the type has been developed for use in rose beds and similar places. It acts by

A pool surrounded by paving for easy care is one of the best features to plan in a garden when there is a minimum amount of time to spare on garden maintenance.

making a crust or barrier in the top inch or two of the soil, not deep enough to harm the roots of established plants but sufficient to kill or prevent germination of any weeds or weed seeds in this layer. The crust must not be broken by hoeing or similar action; otherwise a 'vacuum' will be created in which weeds can again grow.

Mulches and ground covers are natural means of keeping down weeds. Grass mowings make an excellent mulch that improves soil texture as well as keeping down weeds. Spread the mowings over bare soil in about inch-thick layers, keeping them away from the bases of established plants. Peat, again in about inch-thick layers, fulfils the same purpose, but always apply the peat moist, not dry. Dry peat absorbs soil moisture and forms a cover which rain takes a long time to permeate.

Ground-cover perennials that are low growing and so require no staking, have attractive flowers or foliage and help to smother weeds, include the colourful hardy perennial geraniums, or crane's bills, not to be confused with pot geraniums or pelargoniums. The hypericums, particularly *H. calycinum,* the St. John's wort, will cover a bank with their foliage and pretty yellow flowers and prevent weeds growing through. Epimedium and vinca or periwinkle are good spreading ground covers. Ivy grows well on the ground and can be obtained in many colours, shapes and forms. Heathers are obtainable in many colours and varieties, some of which will grow happily in an alkaline soil, and by careful choice it is possible to have flower colour from heathers the year through.

Disabled gardeners will find many special tools available to them; these are lightweight and usually with long handles to avoid stooping and bending. They may also find it worth while having constructed for them a few raised beds on which they can grow flowers at waist level and thus tend them easily. The added advantage here is that the flowers can be seen, touched and smelt at this height, a pleasure usually not possible for the partially crippled.

It is also feasible to construct a small water garden at waist level. It can house both fish and water plants to be enjoyed close to without bending or stooping.

The essence of labour-saving as of all aspects of gardening is clear assessment of your individual requirements and inclinations and a practical plan to meet them. Thus the expression 'week-end gardener' need not be a contradiction in terms.

If hanging baskets are put in a spot where the dripping water can do no harm, there is no need to lift the baskets down more than once a week.

The use of a mechanical fertiliser spreader is justified in all but the smallest garden. It ensures that the fertiliser is spread evenly.

RECOGNITION CHART

Bud formations

Buds help to identify trees still barren of foliage. More important, buds are a key to correct pruning and propagation.

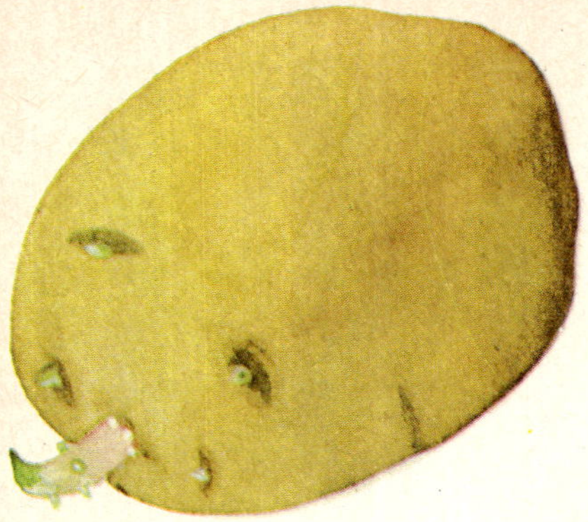

The eyes of the potato are in fact buds. When seed potatoes are put in the dark to sprout before planting the shoots grow from these eyes or buds

Brussels sprout provides an example of an axilliary bud that remains a bud instead of forming another shoot. The buds expand to cluster around the main stem. The section shows how Brussels sprout leaves fold over one another

An axilliary bud is one that arises in the axil of the leaf or in the angle between the leaf stalk and main stem. Example: the catalpa

Budding a rose on to other stock: the bud is removed from the stem, a T-shaped cut made in the stock and the bud slipped in and bound with raffia

On apple, pear and other fruit trees, the fat rounded buds are fruit buds, giving blossom, then fruit. The smaller, thinner buds are growth buds producing shoots

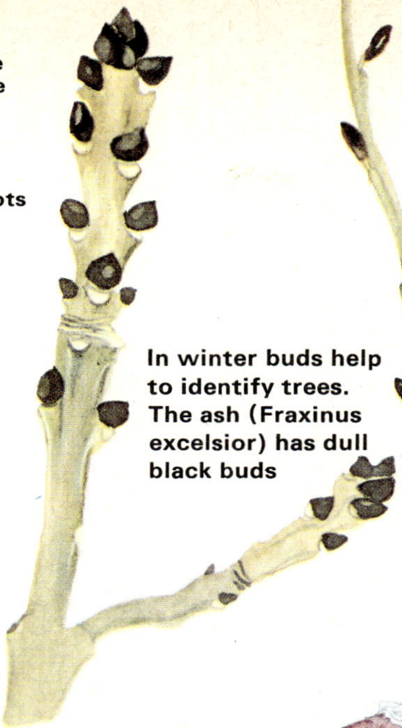

In winter buds help to identify trees. The ash (Fraxinus excelsior) has dull black buds

The alder (Alnus glutinosa) has stalked buds

The beech (Fagus sylvatica) has thin, pointed buds

The strawberry has bud-bearing stolons or runners. The buds produce roots and leaves and can make new plants severed from the parent

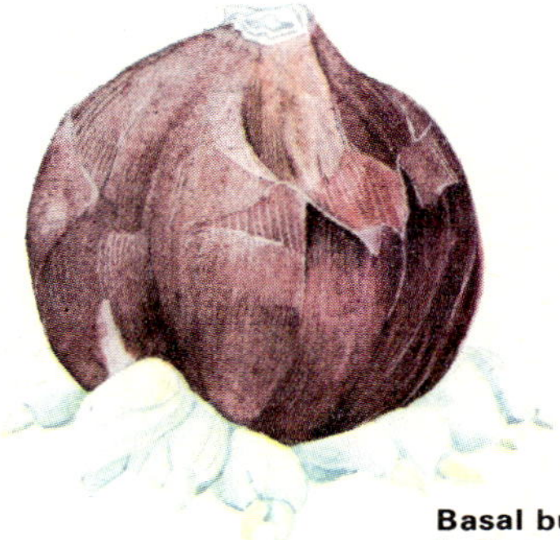

Basal bulbils on a hyacinth bulb are in effect buds and can serve as propagators

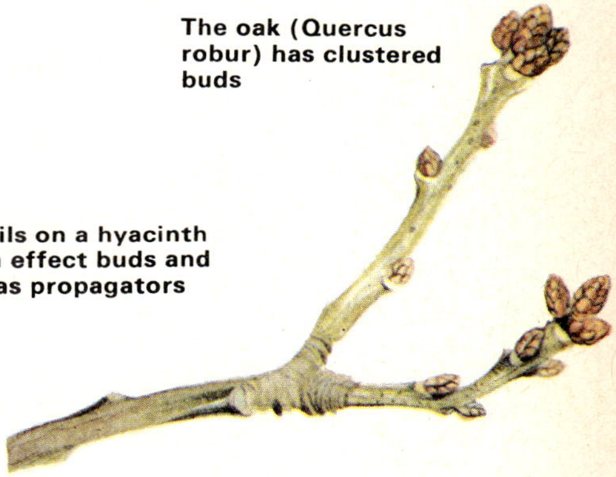

The oak (Quercus robur) has clustered buds

Shoot-budding asparagus. The edible sticks are cut as the bud tips break the soil surface

The horse chestnut provides an example of terminal buds. These grow at the tip of a shoot and protect the growing area. The horse chestnut's buds ('sticky buds') have a leaf scar below them in the form of a horse shoe

The magnolia, too, bears terminal buds. They swell in February and March to become features of the as yet bare tree

Some lilies produce black or brownish bulbils in the axils of of the leaves. Sown in sandy compost, these will yield new plants

Stem cutting of a vine is called the eye. Taken with a bud, the cutting is pinned down into sandy compost, bud uppermost. A new plant will result

Jobs of the month

February for the gardener is a betwixt-and-between month, in some years winter's long and bitter tail-end, in others a harbinger of spring. You can complete your armchair planning of new garden features and your selection of new varieties. Outdoors, there is the robust challenge of preparing the ground for new plantings next month. Below is a summary of Jobs of the Month for February, described fully in the following pages under 16 main subject headings.

Bulbs

Move overcrowded snowdrops. Plant corms of *Anemone coronaria,* ranunculus tubers, *Camassia quamash.* Indoors, keep hyacinths and narcissi moist

Flowers for cutting

Harden protected flowers before arranging them. Plan the sowing of everlastings

Fruit

Before growth starts, prune young plums and peaches that are to be fan-trained. Prepare to protect blossom from frost. Apply artificial fertilisers

Greenhouse

Sow summer bedding plants and tomatoes. Start off winter-stored dormant plants including pelargoniums, fuchsias, tuberous begonias

Hedges

Clear pest-harbouring rubbish, fork over the soil and apply a light dressing. Prepare the ground for a new hedge

Herbaceous Plants

Take cuttings of delphiniums and dahlias. Clear established borders and fork in a dressing between the plants

House Plants

Ensure against plants on window sills being frosted through the glass. And provide adequate humidity

Lawns

If the lawn is soggy, pierce the surface with a fork at 6-inch intervals. Then sprinkle a dressing over it

Paths, Walls & Fencing

Complete repairs and kill weeds before they grow on paths and driveways. Examine climbers' supports

Patios, Window Boxes & Roof Gardens

Order stores of soils and composts. Clean out window boxes, tubs, troughs. On sunny days, move plants to give them a sunbath

Rock Gardens

After clearing debris, loosen the surface of the rock garden and apply a top dressing with appropriate chippings over it

Roses

Double-dig a bed for new roses and incorporate humus before planting. Remove exhausted or twiggy wood from established plants

Trees & Shrubs

In favourable conditions, plant ornamental trees and deciduous shrubs. Prune early summer and later-flowering clematis hybrids. Also prune wisterias and ornamental grape vines

Vegetables

In the greenhouse or under frames or cloches sow vegetables including Brussels sprouts, cabbage, cauliflower, lettuce, leeks. If the weather is right, sow broad beans in the open

Water Gardens

Plan to construct a marsh garden as an extension of the main pool. If frogs prove a nuisance in the pool, net and remove them

Wildlife

Put out pans of water for birds and animals. Replace the water if it has frozen

Bulbs

Early flowering crocus species like *ancyrensis, biflorus, chrysanthus, imperati,* and *susianus* all open their short cup-shaped flowers when the sun comes out in February, revealing far brighter colours within the petals. All these species will establish themselves in the garden.

Move *Galanthus* species, snowdrops, that are overcrowded or have spread beyond their allotted limit now while they are still in full flower—or certainly before the leaves turn yellow next month. The tiny bulbs can be separated and planted singly at the same time.

Mix them among the cyclamen so that the snowdrops may benefit in effectiveness from the foliage of the cyclamen. The leaves of *Cyclamen coum* will have appeared in autumn but by now the flowers will have pushed through.

In the rock garden and in drier patches under trees and bushes *Anemone blanda* and its cultivars will withstand the wind after mid-February and live up to their name of windflower.

Where the soil is not too wet and soggy it is a good time to start planting corms of *Anemone coronaria* of the du Caen and St. Brigid strains, the flowers single in the former and mostly double in the latter. Choose a spot where the soil has been well prepared, is rich in humus and will not dry out too much. Put in the corms 3 inches deep and 6 inches apart.

At the very end of the month plant a few ranunculus tubers, strange claw-like objects, at the base of a sunny wall or somewhere where sharp drainage has been provided, mixing plenty of decayed leafmould in with the top soil to provide moisture. The growing bud is at the junction of the claw, so put the tuber in with the claw pointing downwards. Label the bed so that the spot does not get filled up with other things in the early spring before the shoots appear.

Also plant *Camassia quamash* (syn. *C. esculenta*) fairly closely for a good display, detaching the offsets and planting them separately to increase the stock.

Sturdy shoots of bulbous irises, scillas, muscari and tulips, the last-named seemingly of stagnant growth at this time, will be showing well by now. Resist the temptation to fork around them in an effort to spring clean but scratch out some of the winter debris by the light use of a springbok rake.

Indoors, some hyacinths and narcissi will be scenting the living room. Keep pots and bowls nicely moist and never allow them to dry out. Keep them in a well-lighted spot and turn the bowl round each day to prevent the plants from developing a permanent inclination towards the window.

1

2

1 Gladiolus corms are put into boxes or pans of moist peat to encourage them to start into growth before they are planted out of doors.
2 The pale mauve flowers of Crocus tomasinianus can be relied upon to flower in February.

Do not attempt to hurry bulbs indoors, especially daffodils, if they appear to be slow; you will get a good crop of leaves but the flower stem will become 'strangled' in the neck of the bulb. If daffodil pots had thin stakes inserted when they were brought into the light, by February the roots will have grown around them without damage and the stakes will be firm enough to support the mass of leaves the plant produces.

Bring in more tulips from the plunge bed when the growth has reached nearly 3 inches and put them in a dark place where the temperature never exceeds 60°F (16°C) to allow the stems to lengthen. After two or three weeks put the pots in a light place but not in direct sunlight. Never encourage tulips to hurry. Grown at their own pace in a maximum temperature of 68°F (20°C) they will produce flowers which will be as sturdy as when the plants are grown in outdoor conditions.

Many imported lily bulbs are on sale now and make good pot plants. Choose plump bulbs if possible. Otherwise tone them up by putting them in trays of moistened peat and leafmould in a frost-proof place for a week or two. When potting lilies provide plenty of crocks at the base of the pot and bury the bulb completely. Plant stem rooting lilies with the base of the bulb about 2 inches above the crocks and just cover it with compost, leaving space for more soil to be added as it grows.

Flowers for cutting

If frames or cloches are placed over violets, anemones, polyanthus and even wallflowers and calendula the plants will be protected and warm and so induced to produce some early flowers. Just as important as their earliness is the fact that flowers protected in this way from mud splashes are so much cleaner.

An important reservation: protected flowers usually need hardening well before they are arranged. This means that they must have a long deep drink up to but not over their petals. Even after arrangement, wallflowers, polyanthus and calendula should have at least two thirds of their stem length under water or the flower may wilt badly, but first strip the portion of stem ends that are to go under water, because leaves will quickly decompose, foul the water and kill the flowers.

Because they like such deep water these flowers are really best posied in mugs or beakers rather than arranged loosely in taller containers. For this reason they are good flowers to place on low tables where one can look down on them.

Like the hellebores to which they are closely related, anemones tend to wilt inexplicably. They should receive the same preliminary treatment as the hellebores; the newly cut stems should be placed in water heated to a temperature of 70°F (21°C).

If, after arrangement, a flower of whatever kind (other than a bulb flower) wilts, remove it and stand its stem in an inch of boiling water. Keep the flower in the water until it has cooled. It will now be turgid again and it can be put back into the arrangement. Bulb flowers are an exception.

Violets, which bloom so valiantly out of doors, often cannot take a stuffy atmosphere indoors and wither very rapidly. The best way of keeping them fresh and sweet for days is to use a large brandy balloon type of container.

First bunch them into a loose posy collared with leaves and tie them, not too tightly, just under the leaves. Pour a little gravel into the base of the glass deep enough to take the trimmed stems of the violet bunch so that the flowers and leaves are resting on the gravel. Pour in water to come just level with the top of the gravel. The violets will last for days.

Now is the time to look forward to next winter's flower arrangements and perhaps Christmas gifts, too. An early start with sowing everlastings, immortelles and other perpetuelles is essential if the flowers are to be gathered under the best conditions in summer, long bebefore autumn rains and frosts.

All are easy to grow. Helipterums, usually listed as acrocliniums, and

1

2

1 The first few flowers to brave the cold can make compact arrangements, eked out with coloured leaves.

2 Branches of long-lasting Camellia foliage make a framework for early double Tulips with Bilbergia.

1 Fruit trees trained as cordons form an archway over the path in a kitchen garden. Flowers for cutting provide an early spring crop.
2 Preventive spraying with lime sulphur is necessary against Peach Leaf Curl.
3 Pollinate Peach blossom under glass.

rhodanthe are dainty white and rose daisies. Helichrysums are the everlastings or straw daisies and these are usually sold as mixed but they can be bought in separate colours. Statice or limonium are also available mixed or in separate colours. Ammobium, a white daisy, lonas, like a tiny yellow tansy, and xeranthemum, mainly white, are others.

Ornamental grasses are invaluable. It is usually recommended that these should be sown where they are to be grown.

Fruit

Young plums and peaches that are to be trained as fans should be pruned immediately before growth starts. At this season wounds heal quickly and risk of silver leaf disease infection is therefore limited. If a maiden was planted, cut if possible to a sideshoot 2 feet above soil level. Where there is no convenient sideshoot, cut to a growth bud beneath which there are two more growth buds. Cut off any other laterals flush with the stem.

If the 'fan' already has two ribs, cut these back to a bud about 12–18 inches from the vertical stem. The following February cut back all branches to leave from 24–30 inches of ripened wood. This process can be repeated for one more year if there is still an area of wall to be 'furnished'.

Prune nut bushes, taking care not to remove too many of the male catkins as these are necessary for pollinating the flowers. Remove basal suckers and cut laterals back to a flower bud to keep the bush open and uncrowded.

Where a starting temperature of 70–80°F (21–27°C) is available, melon seeds may be sown singly in 3-inch pots of John Innes or no-soil potting compost for a hothouse crop. Lower the temperature to 60°F (16°C) by night after germination. Suitable varieties are 'Best of All', 'Blenheim Orange', 'King George' or 'Watermelon Florida Favourite'.

Leaf curl is often a serious trouble with outdoor peaches, nectarines and almonds. Preventive spraying is necessary before the leaves appear, just before the buds begin to swell. Use lime-sulphur, Bordeaux mixture or any proprietary copper preparation. This will also check red spider mite.

At a slightly later stage of growth—when the buds are just breaking—apples and plums should be treated with an approved spray if red spider mite was in evidence the previous year.

Watch wall-trained trees and be ready to provide some kind of protection should frost threaten when the blossom is out. Apricots, peaches, nectarines and plums will flower in that order. A fine-mesh net hung over a tree may prevent radiation frost damage but old curtains, sheets or tablecloths may all be pressed into service.

When fruit blossom is out at this time, it may be too cold for pollinating insects to be flying and so it helps to transfer pollen by hand from the blossom of one tree to that of another of the same kind, using a dab of cotton wool or, better, a dry camel-hair brush. This hand pollination should always be practised with fruits flowering under glass.

The end of this month is the time for applying artificial fertilisers to fruit. Do not go by rule-of-thumb but vary doses according to performance, giving more if growth has been poor and crops heavy but reducing nitrogen or omitting it entirely if growth has been vigorous but cropping disappointing.

Average dressings per square yard are 1 ounce sulphate of ammonia, ⅓ ounce sulphate of potash annually and, every two years, 1 ounce superphosphate. Black currants and plums may need twice as much sulphate of ammonia and the potash dressing should be increased to 1 ounce per square yard where symptoms of deficiency were noted last summer.

Scatter the fertilisers over the soil and, with a rake, scuffle them gently into the surface.

To obtain extra-early strawberries, cover some first-year plants with cloches or a polythene 'tunnel', about mid-month.

Greenhouse

If a temperature of about 50°F (10°C) can be maintained in the greenhouse or propagating frame, some of the summer bedding plants, invaluable for a colourful display, can be sown now.

In addition to *Begonia semperflorens*, the sowing of antirrhinums, lobelia, ageratum and *Salvia splendens* can now take place. But note that *Salvia splendens* needs a higher temperature, of at least 60°F (16°C), and it should not be sown until this can be maintained.

Sow the seeds in John Innes seed compost made firm and level in well-drained pots or boxes, with the seed covered to about twice its depth except in the case of very tiny seeds, which should be merely pressed into the surface. After sowing, soak the boxes or pots from underneath until the moisture seeps through to the surface. Then cover them with glass and paper. Turn the glass daily to remove condensation and never let the compost become dry.

For a more unusual display, cannas may be used in mild, sunny areas. They will make very showy pot-plants. To avoid root disturbance later on, the large black seeds are best sown singly an inch deep in 3-inch pots of John Innes potting compost No 1 after the hard outer covering has first been filed through or the seeds soaked in warm water for 24 hours. A temperature of at least 70°F (21°C) is needed for good germination but a slightly lower temperature will do for dormant canna roots, which may be bought now and boxed up in moist peat or leafmould.

For a colourful greenhouse display sow *Primula obconica*, celosias ('cockscombs'), tuberous begonias, gloxinias and the 'Christmas Cherry' (*Solanum capsicastrum*). A temperature of 60°F (16°C) will do for most of these seeds. But gloxinias need a temperature of at least 65–70°F (18–21°C). So if this temperature cannot be maintained yet, leave the gloxinias until next month.

For 'home-grown' tomatoes, seed should also be sown now, ¼-inch deep and 1 inch apart in the J.I.P.1, in at least a temperature of 60°F (16°C). But much cooler conditions will do for such vegetables as Brussels sprouts, cauliflowers, cabbages, leeks, lettuce and onions, all of which may be sown in boxes or pots for planting out later.

Dormant plants stored through the winter should also be started off now. If zonal pelargoniums ('geraniums') have been stored close together in boxes, pot them up singly in the J.I.P.1. When they start to grow, cut them back to about 6 inches high.

To start fuchsias into growth cut them well back before increasing the water supply and keeping them well syringed. But on no account must hydrangeas be cut back now or there will be no blooms. Stand these in full light and give them more water gradually.

Other dormant plants that may also be started now are gloxinias, tuberous begonias and hippeastrums. Bed the tubers of the first two close together in boxes of moist peat or leafmould so that their tops (the concave side) are just visible. Then keep them just moist at a temperature of 55°F (13°C) for begonias and 65°F (18°C) for gloxinias. Hippeastrums need repotting only every three or four years and until then all they need is the renewal of the top inch of compost. When this has been done, cut off any remaining leaves from the plants before keeping them almost dry in plenty of warmth.

When cuttings of the large exhibition chrysanthemums taken last month are making obvious growth, pot them up singly into 3-inch pots of the J.I.P.1, burying as little of the actual stem as possible. Cuttings of the reflexed and incurved decorative varieties may also be taken now, together with those of the early-flowering outdoor varieties. Use basal shoots about 2 inches long, insert them firmly in boxes of the J.I.P.1, and after a thorough soaking allow them to become practically dry before soaking them again.

Perpetual carnation cuttings may still be taken up to mid-February, using young shoots about 4 inches long from about half way up the plant. After trimming these off beneath a joint remove the leaves from the bottom inch of stem, then dibble the cuttings ¾-inch deep in clean sand or vermiculite in a propagating frame at a temperature of about 50°F (10°C).

Cuttings rooted earlier should be potted into 3-inch pots of the J.I.P.1, with only their roots firmly covered. To get them quickly on the move again a temperature of about 55°F (13°C) is needed.

For a spring display in the cold greenhouse, pot up a few wallflowers, forget-me-nots, polyanthuses and primroses in ordinary soil with some sharp sand for drainage. Ample ventilation is needed for these.

Cuttings of perpetual-flowering Carnations can be taken up to mid-February.

Trim the cutting below a joint and remove the leaves from the bottom inch of the stem.

The prepared cuttings are dibbled in round the edge of small pots of clean sand.

1

2

1 The evergreen Cotoneaster x cornubia bears a heavy crop of berries in winter.
2 An established hedge of Escallonia 'Apple Blossom' provides attractive flowers in summer and is also evergreen, so furnishes the garden very well in winter.

Hedges

February is a good month for tidying-up operations in the garden, and hedges should not be neglected in this annual spring cleaning.

A lot of pest-harbouring rubbish tends to collect in and around the bottom of hedges, and winds blow the leaves into drifts at their base. Such collections of decaying vegetable material make ideal breeding grounds for slugs, snails and other garden pests.

Leaves and rotting vegetation can be raked out and added to the compost heap but it is better to burn dead twigs and branches. These can be a potential source of fungus diseases, such as coral spot, rusts and mildew.

After tidying up is completed, the soil should be lightly forked over. A light dressing of bonemeal or a good general fertiliser can be pricked in at the same time.

As noted in The Month of January, preparation of the site for a new hedge should, weather and soil conditions permitting, be carried out about a month in advance of actual planting. This will give the soil time to settle.

March to early April is a good time for planting both deciduous and evergreen hedges, so that February is a particularly appropriate time to carry out the preparatory work a month or so in advance of actual planting, given a spell of reasonably fine weather.

Thorough digging over of the bed is essential to the subsequent health and vigour of the hedge. Neglect at this initial stage often leads to weak, uneven growth when the plants come to maturity.

The subsoil should be well broken up with a fork as digging progresses and plenty of humus-rich material should be incorporated in the lower spit of soil. This can consist of well-rotted animal manure—where it is obtainable—matured garden compost, leafmould or peat.

A generous dressing of a slow-acting organic fertiliser such as bonemeal or hoof and horn can be given at the rate of 3 to 4 ounces to the square yard. This will look after the hedging plants' requirements during their first season, supplemented, where necessary, by mulches during the summer months.

Herbaceous Plants

New herbaceous borders or alterations to existing flower beds can be planned from an armchair when conditions are unsuitable for outdoor gardening.

Ideas seem to snowball if you put them down on paper. Don't think only in terms of straight flower beds, one each side of a lawn. Often a curved border fits in better with the general layout; or an island bed, oblong, oval, round or heart-shaped, can look very attractive.

Having decided on the outline of the border, tackle the ground soon in readiness for spring planting.

Work plenty of hop manure, rotted compost, farm manure, seaweed or horticultural peat into the lower spit when digging, adding a complete fertiliser to the top spit, having in mind that most perennials will remain in the same spot for at least three or four years.

Established borders should be cleared of decaying vegetation now. After clearing, sprinkle bonemeal (4 ounces per square yard) and hoof and horn (2 ounces per square yard) over the surface, lightly forking it in between the plants.

Christmas roses *(Helleborus niger)* move best immediately after flowering, but do not transplant them until absolutely necessary. These beauties enjoy moist, well-drained loamy soil and partial shade, together with an annual mulch of rotted manure or compost in February.

The hardy montbretias tend to run to leaf unless lifted and replanted every two years. The corms should be planted 3 to 4 inches apart, 3 inches deep, in groups of a dozen or more in sandy loam manured for a previous crop. Freshly manured ground is not suitable for this plant but bonemeal or fish manure may be added a few weeks before planting.

Delphiniums and dahlias are easily increased by cuttings taken this month. Delphinium roots should be covered at once with cloche or bell glass to encourage suitable growth. When shoots are 3 to 4 inches high, about a pencil thickness, remove with a sharp knife from below soil level, preferably with a heel of old wood attached, and trim off the lower leaves before planting firmly, 1 inch deep, round the edge of an earthenware pot filled with equal parts of damp peat and silver sand. Cover with a

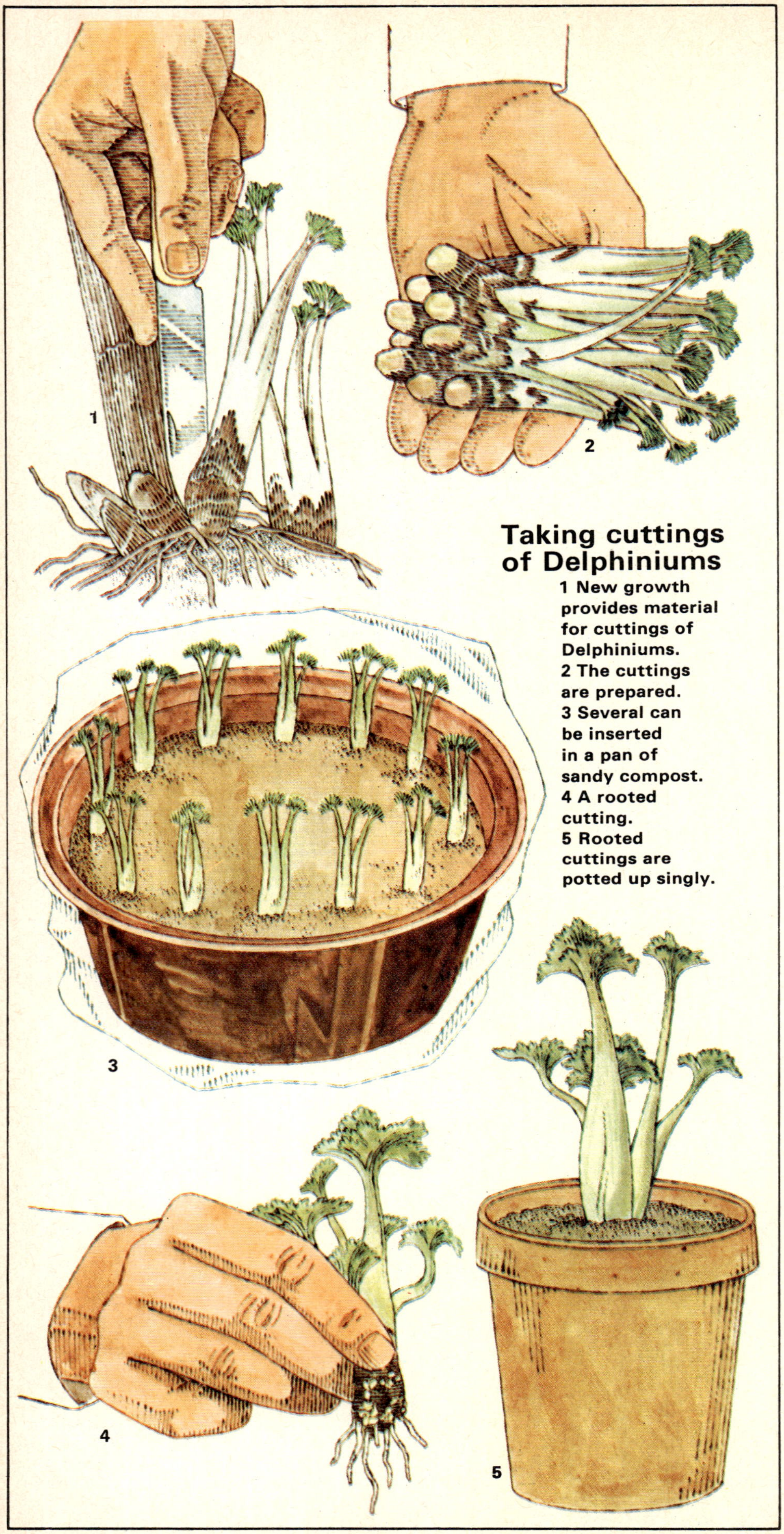

Taking cuttings of Delphiniums

1 New growth provides material for cuttings of Delphiniums.
2 The cuttings are prepared.
3 Several can be inserted in a pan of sandy compost.
4 A rooted cutting.
5 Rooted cuttings are potted up singly.

tent of polythene and stand in a frame or on a sunny window-sill. As soon as rooted—usually four to five weeks—transplant the cuttings singly into peat pots filled with John Innes potting compost No 1 leaving them to grow on until moved into the open border in early summer.

Place dahlia tubers in boxes of damp soil where there is gentle warmth to induce growth. Cuttings should be 2 to 3 inches high, removed just below a node and planted in small pots of sifted loam and sand. To offset undue transpiration, stand them on a layer of damp peat in a propagating frame or glass-covered box until rooted.

The half-hardy and tuberous-rooted begonias with their big showy blooms are wonderful for gap filling during summer and autumn. Tubers intended for transplanting into the open after the frosts should be started into growth in a warm room or greenhouse towards the end of the month or beginning of March. They should be planted 3–4 inches apart, hollow side uppermost, just covered with soil, in shallow boxes of John Innes potting compost or good loam mixed with rotted manure.

Lily-of-the-valley *(Convallaria)* beds need a mulch of decayed manure or leafmould now.

House Plants

The combination of indoor warmth with lengthening daylight begins to awaken house plants into new growth in February.

It can be a dangerous month for some plants. Outside, nights can be bitterly cold. If house plants are placed too close to a window, although they benefit from the light they can sometimes be frosted through the glass. Never allow any plants to stand on a window-sill between the glass and drawn curtains, lest cold air enters and is trapped around the plants. Bring the plants into the room before drawing the curtains.

Another problem is that any new growth that plants may begin to make is young, tender and succulent. It needs a moister, more humid atmosphere than generally prevails indoors. Some extra humidity is easy to provide and is beneficial not only to plants. The human skin enjoys the softer atmosphere. So does furniture.

The simplest means of providing greater humidity is to place a pan or dish of clean water in one or two places. The water evaporates speedily and requires topping up every day or two. Purpose-made humidifiers carry out the same function more efficiently. They range from china or earthenware water containers that can be suspended from radiators to more complex and expensive electrical machines.

1

2

3

4

1 Philodendron scandens.
2 Peperomia hederafolia.
3 Philodendron imbe 'Burgundy'.
4 Construct a humidity bath to provide the necessary humidity for Saintpaulias by putting the pot into a waterproof container and then plunging this into a basin filled with boiling water.

An uncostly humidity meter will indicate needs and register improvement. In most comfortably warm homes the relative humidity will register a reading of about 50°F. This is too dry for plants (and human beings). The aim should be to raise the reading to between 60–65°F (16–18°C).

Some plants need more humidity than others and may require a 'local' source. One good solution is to plunge the pot inside a larger container with the space between the two filled with moist peat or some other absorbent material. This packing material should be kept constantly moist. From it will arise minute quantities of moist air to surround and bathe the plant's leaves.

A more drastic method, that of making a 'humidity bath', is sometimes recommended for plants such as the popular saintpaulia or African violet. Here the plant pot is placed inside a waterproof container and this in turn is placed in the centre of a large basin. Boiling water is poured into the basin and steam creates a moist atmosphere around the plant. This is obviously not a continuous process but one to use occasionally when a particular plant seems to need a special dose of humidity.

Probably the best way of providing local humidity is simply to spray the foliage of the plants with a fine spray or atomiser.

Lawns

It is useful to inspect grass areas two or three times during this month. As it is a period when ground can be at its wettest, February offers a good opportunity to find out what sort of soil conditions exist below grass level.

If you find that the lawn has water lying on the surface for several days, after rain or snow, or that your foot prints indent $\frac{1}{2}$-inch to one inch in a muddy lawn surface, you can be fairly certain that soil conditions and drainage are not as good as they should be. On the other hand, if there are no puddles and the surface is springy to walk upon, the soil is probably in good condition and free-draining.

In the latter case no action is required now. But if the lawn is soggy it is advisable to do something about it if you want a good lawn for the summer.

If conditions do not appear to be too bad, dig in an ordinary garden fork 4 inches deep at 6-inch intervals over the lawn area. Push the fork to and fro a couple of times before making the next set of holes. Follow this operation by sprinkling over the surface a $\frac{1}{2}$-inch layer of a 50/50 mixture of a good coarse grade of peat and coarse gritty sand or a proprietary organic lawn dressing. Brush this in. The addition of an organic soil conditioning material (one based on seaweed, for example) is advantageous.

If the lawn gets badly water-logged, use a hollow-tined fork instead of an ordinary garden fork. This will bring up cores of soil which will be replaced by brushing in the peat/sand mixture.

Using a hollow-tined fork can be hard work, so do not try to cover too large an area at one time.

Paths, Walls & Fencing

February is the month to prepare all paths, all paving, walling and fencing for the spring season. Any repair or renewal tasks should be completed as quickly as possible to allow for more creative decorative work later on.

Weeds have not yet begun to grow so the thing to do now is to prevent them coming and thus save hours of work later in the year.

All gravel paths or driveways which have no plants growing in them should be treated in February with a proprietary long term weed-killer. There are types now available that will keep the surface clear of all weeds for the whole of the year without further attention. These consist of a powder that is mixed with water and sprinkled on the pathway. The powder does not dissolve in the water but remains in suspension, so when it is sprinkled on the ground it remains as a fine film or crust in the top inch or two. Thus it does not travel through the soil and can be sprayed next to growing plants without affecting them.

Make sure that every inch of the path is sprayed, for if portions are missed weeds will grow through.

Clear any existing weed growth from the bases of walls and fences and at the same time examine any climbing shrubs growing there to make sure that supports are firm and ready to accept the new growth that will come. Prune away weak and spindly growth and any that is dead or diseased. Move any shoots that have grown on top of others so as to allow light and air to enter.

If new paving has been laid on sand or directly on to the soil, fill all cracks with cement to prevent weed growth.

The best way to do this without leaving unsightly marks on the paving slabs is to use a dry mix of four parts sand to one of cement. Mix this thoroughly and tamp it down well into the cracks between the paving slabs so that it travels just under the slabs. Then water lightly, allowing the water to get into the cracks and moisten the dry mix. It will set hard, help to anchor the slabs and prevent any weeds from growing through.

Patios, Window Boxes & Roof Gardens

You should continue to keep containers of plants that are slightly tender in a sheltered position or protected with straw or sacking. If you move a container to a sheltered position, make sure it does not become too dry, for sometimes a protective wall that keeps off the coldest winds also keeps off the rain.

There will be little growth as yet but if spring bulbs are planted in terrace pots, in window-boxes or on the roof, have a look at them occasionally to ensure that nothing is resting on the shoots that may be coming through.

Continue to clear away any windblown leaves or other debris that collect in corners and around the bases of containers. Stone troughs or similar containers that contain winter hardy plants will also collect debris at the bases of the plants. Clear this away.

On the patio and on the roof garden complete the pruning and clearing of vines and climbers. Examine all supports, trellis or straining wires to make sure they are undamaged and secure. A loose or damaged section will quickly come away from the wall and do considerable damage in the spring gales.

Any window-boxes, tubs or troughs that were put away before the winter should be brought out, cleaned and repaired ready for the coming season and stores of soils and composts should be ordered or mixed ready for planting next month.

As the winter is coming to its end, you should know by now what extra winter features or colour you will require for next year. Dwarf or prostrate conifers, ivies, heathers and the like can be collected from nurseryman or garden centre and planted up now in the terrace pots or on the roof garden. Give newly planted subjects an occasional gentle spray over all their foliage on days when the weather is not actually frosty.

1

2

1 A niche in the wall of a patio can be filled in winter by a hardy plant in a container. Bonsai culture provides examples of plants suitable for use in this way.
2 February is the time to complete the plans for a good summer effect on the patio and roof garden. Choose labour-saving plants for foliage effect as well as for flower quality.

Take advantage of the occasional sunny days and move plants to a spot where they can take a sun bath. If they are too heavy to move except to their permanent quarters, either lift them on to a wheeled platform or strap them to a two-handled stretcher so that they can safely and easily be moved by two people.

Really large containers may be found almost impossible to move once they have been filled with soil, so take them to their permanent positions before filling them. This applies specially to window-boxes.

When filling window-boxes, tubs and troughs with soil, remember that this is one of the rare cases in gardening where it is possible to vary conditions according to the requirements of particular plants. For example, a trough filled with heathers and perhaps a dwarf conifer or two can be made to flourish to a greater extent than normally possible by using certain quantities of acid peat instead of neutral.

As each container is separate, each can be filled with a tailor-made soil, perhaps including a handful of lime or a bucket of acid peat or allowing for more than normal drainage.

Rock Gardens

All dead leaves and other winter debris should be moved from the rock garden, taking special care that none is allowed to remain on the plants themselves. Not only do dead leaves and debris provide a good hiding place for slugs and other pests but they are a repository for fungus diseases.

However, herbaceous rock plants that retain their dead leaves over the winter should not be disturbed, as these form a protection for new shoots emerging from the soil and are best left until the shoots are well above the surface.

Dead rosettes of evergreen herbs like saxifrages, silenes and other cushion plants are best removed. Do not fill the resulting gaps, as is often suggested, with sand or other materials. Instead, work a top dressing of chippings, either of limestone or granite, depending on whether the plants are lime-tolerant or lime-hating, around the circumference of the cushion. This will effectively close gaps.

When the rock garden has been cleared of debris the surface should be slightly loosened with a small hand fork, taking care not to go too deep for fear of causing root disturbance. Then a top dressing should be applied. The contents of the dressing will differ according to type and position of the plants. For the normal species of easily grown trailing or mat-forming plants, such as aubrieta, arabis, alyssum, phlox and most sun-lovers, it should consist of two parts loam and equal parts of coarse sand and peat, all by bulk not weight.

After mixing thoroughly, work the compost, used fairly dry, well down among the trailing laterals but without covering them completely.

This has a twofold action. It provides a fresh supply of food and also a rooting medium for the trailing laterals.

When planting Roses, the hole should not be made any deeper than is necessary and should be wide enough to allow the roots to be spread.

The cushion plants and those growing in a scree mixture require a top dressing of two parts coarse sand and equal parts of leafmould or peat. The compost should be applied round the plants, not directly to the plants themselves. Rain will wash it into the soil.

After the top dressings have been applied, the surface of the rock garden can be given a final dressing of the appropriate chippings.

Roses

Most of February work among roses will be concerned with planting and pruning. If the autumn and winter have been very wet, many autumn-purchased plants may still be heeled-in, awaiting sufficiently dry soil conditions. A friable soil is essential to successful planting. If the soil is a little too wet but not soggy, its condition can be made suitable by thoroughly incorporating some granulated peat.

Ideally, the rose bed should have been prepared several weeks earlier to allow the soil to consolidate. If this was not possible, it should be dug now.

Double digging in strips is best, the top soil from the second strip being thrown forward on top of the loosened subsoil of the first strip. The top soil from the first strip will be transferred to the opposite end of the bed to provide top soil for the final strip. By this method the fertile top soil is kept on the surface.

As much humus as can be spared should be incorporated as the digging proceeds. Mix it well in. Do not leave it as a separate layer. Well-rotted animal manure is ideal. But granulated peat, spent hops, garden compost, old hay and

The rock garden in winter. Ericas, or heathers, provide colour. Old growth is left until the very early spring to give protection to the crowns.

straw, leafmould, old chopped turf, sacking and waste of vegetable origin generally will all rot down to form valuable humus.

Before planting is started, a planting mixture should be prepared, consisting of a large bucketful of moist granulated peat into which two handfuls of either meat and bonemeal or sterilised bonemeal have been mixed. A shallow hole is taken out in the prepared bed, not more than 6 inches deep and wide enough to accommodate the roots without bending them. Several handfuls of the planting mixture should be added and the plant stood in the hole to check correct planting depth (so that the budding point is just covered). More planting mixture is thrown over the roots, together with some fine soil. The plant should then be gently raised and lowered to eliminate any air pockets. Further soil is added and then firmed moderately with the feet, starting on the outside edge of the hole and working towards the centre to avoid upsetting the level of the plant. The hole should be filled, finishing off with an inch or so of loose soil or peat.

Any dead or obviously exhausted or twiggy wood should be removed from established plants to simplify pruning later in the month or early in March.

Trees & Shrubs

Ornamental trees and deciduous shrubs can be safely planted this month, provided that weather and soil conditions are favourable. If the soil is frozen or too wet and sticky for planting, orders that arrive from nurserymen should either be opened up and heeled into a trench or, if the soil is too frozen to dig, should be stored in a frostproof shed or garage. Thanks to the efficiency of modern packing methods, it will be quite all right if the storage period lasts as long as two or three weeks.

Clematis figure very prominently in this month's work programme. It should now be safe to get new plants in.

Pruning of the early summer and later-flowering hybrids can now go ahead. Where the very early-flowering species such as *Clematis montana, C. alpina* or *C. armandii* are concerned, it is better to wait until they have finished blooming, when all the old flowering shoots can be cut back.

There are two different pruning procedures to be adopted now with the remainder. With the large-flowered hybrids that come into bloom before midsummer, pruning should not be drastic but more of a tidying-up operation. All dead growths should be cut right out for a start. After this, those which remain should be disentangled (this can be something of a headache!) and cut down to the lowest pair of strong-growing buds before being tied back to their supports.

Clematis that flower from July onwards, including the popular *C. jackmanii* and its varieties, will need more drastic treatment. All shoots must be cut back to a strong pair of buds about 3 feet above soil level.

It can be noted that other clematis requiring this treatment include the intensely fragrant *C. flammula,* which blooms so profusely from August to October, *C. tangutica,* with silken spidery seedheads and yellow Chinese lantern flowers, 'Comtesse de Bouchaud' and 'Gipsy Queen'.

Clematis are long-lived plants and it is, therefore, worth spending time and trouble on the preparation of the planting holes.

Contrary to what is often thought, these plants do not require large quantities of lime. They will grow quite happily in acid soil conditions and planting in holes with plenty of compost, peat or well-rotted manure will be sufficient for their cultural needs. It helps, too, if the lower spit of soil in the planting hole is replaced by neat compost or rotted manure.

1

2

1 Dwarf Bean 'The Sutton' sown under cloches in November is now getting away well.
2 Lettuce seedlings of the variety 'Cobham Green' have been pricked out 60 to a box.

Among the other climbing shrubs that can be pruned in February are the ornamental grape vines (varieties of *Vitis vinifera*) and wisterias, both of which should now have their lateral growths shortened down to one or two buds. This will keep them tidy and encourage new growth.

Pruning Vitis vinifera. The weak and unwanted growth is cut out, then the lateral growth is cut back.

The retained growth is tied in to the supports for training and to prevent it from getting broken by the wind.

Vegetables

February can exasperate the vegetable gardener. If the winter has been long and hard the soil will be undug and unmanured. Even if the sun shines to warm the soil, the hasty gardener may find that late snows and frosts take their toll.

1

2

1 Rows of Garden Peas 'Feltham First' which were sown last November have come through the winter well and will provide an early crop.
2 The leaves of Chives can be pulled through the winter months.

A quickly maturing crop like Radishes can be sown as a catch-crop between rows of a slower-growing crop. For example, if Lettuce, Peas or Parsnips are sown in rows A and C, Radish can be sown along row B and will soon be harvested.

Consequently, it is well to try to use greenhouse, frame and cloche for those types of vegetables that can be raised in warmth and transplanted later.

Both French and broad beans may be sown individually in pots or in deep seed boxes. But guard against mice which will literally have a beanfeast unless traps are set.

Brussels sprouts, cabbage, cauliflower, lettuce and leeks may be sown in frames or under cloches and transplanted later. Short-horn carrots, globe beetroot, white Lisbon onions and radishes can all be sown in rows in frames in rich soil, grown fast and pulled young. If you have enough frames, spinach, turnips, cauliflowers and potatoes can also be left to mature. Even one frame of potatoes can provide a welcome early crop but only varieties suitable for forcing should be grown.

Mustard and cress can be grown continuously in boxes in the greenhouse. Cress, which germinates more quickly, should be sown four days before mustard. The temperature should be maintained at 60–65°F (16–18°C) or the seedlings will damp off.

Celery and celeriac are both more successful when the seed is sown early. The important thing is to prick out the seedlings as soon as they are large enough to handle, two inches each way. They must not be planted out until June or July.

If no frame is available, lettuce may be sown in boxes in the greenhouse, pricked out and transplanted later. If they can be covered by cloches after planting they will be hastened. Make sure that the seed leaves are not buried in pricking out or transplanting.

Wherever crops are sown in rows under cloches, you can often use the space at the edge of the rows for catch-crops of quick maturing radish. Fill the shallow drills with peat, and water this well before sowing the seed thinly. Grown without check, radishes will soon mature and can be out of the way the main crop needs more room.

Onions can also be sown in boxes or, alternatively, in rows under cloches. Gardeners in a hurry can plant onion sets that will provide young onions while the seed-sown crop matures. Autumn-sown onions (spring onions) can be transplanted now. Shallots should be planted two-thirds their depth and cloves or garlic (these are the portions of the old bulb) should be just covered. Both should be about 6 inches apart.

In the right weather conditions broad beans can be sown in the open from about the second week of the month. It is not necessary to draw a drill. Seeds may be dibbled, 2 inches deep, 6 inches apart in rows 2 feet apart. Soil that is too rich produces lush plants and many pods but too few beans. Apply manure or compost at roughly 1 cwt to 15 square yards. Alternatively, grow beans on soil previously enriched for cauliflowers or potatoes. Where no manure is available use a good quality fertiliser.

Take a look at standing crops. Perpetual spinach and parsnips will both be running to seed soon. Keep cutting spinach hard to get the full value. Lift parsnips and store them.

Keep broccoli curds unblemished and protected by snapping the midribs of one or more of the outer leaves so that these bend over and cover, but do not rest on, the heart of the plant.

Jerusalem artichokes provide delicious tubers in winter and the sunflower-like plants make a fine windbreak. Seven lb of tubers planted 1 foot apart will make a 50-foot row.

Water Gardens

During February's customary alternation between birdsong and blizzards the water garden makes only one demand—that a hole be kept open in any surface ice that forms (see The Month of January). A floating pool heater shoulders this day-and-night responsibility at the touch of a switch, leaving the gardener to the fireside study of catalogues and the planning of new features.

One of the new features might be the creation of an area suitable for marsh plants. This should be sited, as one would expect to find it in nature, adjacent to the pool proper and an area that is shaded will not be found a

A spell of mild weather in February will bring frogs to the pool to spawn. The resulting tadpoles will eat algae.

disadvantage. A badly drained hollow that is waterlogged in winter and dries out in summer will not do, since it is in the summer growing season that an abundance of moisture is essential.

The most effective way to create a marsh garden is to construct it as an extension of the main pool, as an integral part of the water garden layout.

If the main pool has already been completed, whether in concrete or plastic, it is not possible to tack on an extension. Nevertheless, a marsh can be made close enough to the pool to appear part of it, although in fact there is no connection.

This is achieved by excavating the area to a depth of 12 inches and laying a sheet of polythene before returning the soil, liberally mixed with damp peat. The polythene can have a few holes and need not be turned up at the edges, since the aim is to impede drainage but not prevent water movement entirely. Soaking in dry spells will be necessary and is best provided by means of a length of ¾-inch polythene tubing, pierced with holes at 12-inch intervals and buried 6 inches above the polythene. One end is stopped; the other left above the surface to be connected, via a length of garden hose, to the water supply in periods of drought.

The assurance of ample moisture in the growing season will provide ideal conditions for such attractive plants as calthas (marsh marigolds), lythrum, primulas, *Iris kaempferi* and *Iris sibirica*, mimulus, rodgersia, trollius, menyanthes, peltiphyllum and the splendid ferns, osmunda and onoclea.

If the weather see-saw brings in a mild spell at the month's end, frogs may appear in the pool. They are seldom harmful, though rare cases occur of a male frog short-sightedly clasping a fish instead of a female frog. The adult frogs will leave the pool after spawning and the tadpoles will eat algae, plant remains and other detritus. All the same, they can be a nuisance in the courting stage when their activities stir up the mud and even overturn containers.

They can be netted out and removed in a large plastic bag with only a little water. But they will have to be moved some distance—preferably to a country pond—or their heads will be bobbing about in the pool again next day.

Wildlife

From December until February, wild life in the garden has been dominated by resident birds such as the thrushes and tits and those animals that did not hibernate all through the winter. Now some other birds begin to appear, among them chiff-chaffs, wheatears and blackcaps. And as if to make way for these immigrants, the winter visitors, the fieldfares and redwings and those blackbirds, starlings and greenfinches that wish to summer in cooler climes, leave for the north via eastern Europe.

February frosts can cut off all water supplies to birds and animals. So put out pans of water for them, replacing it promptly if it has frozen.

Animals that have been asleep through the winter begin to make their first hunting trips of the year. For example, the hedgehog, a more common animal than is generally realised, comes out of hiding and begins to make up for its two or three months of fasting. The hedgehog is a real friend to the gardener and is to be valued as a four-legged pest-destroyer. It generally forages among hedges and less cultivated parts of the garden. As it wanders about, snouting out slugs and beetles, it leaves behind in the mud its tiny, five-toed prints, rather like human hands in miniature.

A pest the hedgehog cannot control is the rabbit, which returns again after being ravaged by disease and is one of the most damaging of mammals, to be found in town and country alike. By the end of the month the first litters will be adding to the rabbit problem and when the warmer weather comes this litter will be producing still another generation.

The grey squirrel, during its brief and cautious hibernation period, has been making short visits to the outer world to fill its pouches with the nuts it buried in the autumn and is now beginning to come out for the year.

Reptiles, especially the slow-worm, come out occasionally to bask in the weak February sun. The slow-worm is not a snake but a limbless lizard, completely harmless to humans. It has value in the garden in keeping down slugs and similar pests.

In the highest trees, rooks may begin to build their nests, and in almost any receptacle from a drainpipe to a cast-out kettle, from a conifer to a creeper, other prospective parents will build. Those thrushes that did not travel north will start making their nests of grass, roots, moss and mud in the fork of a tree, a bush or a creeper. A relative of the thrush, the robin, will build anywhere, in a wall, an old tin can, a piece of drainpipe or even a shed. The house sparrow will build near any human habitation, for man is its main food source.

The birds become more active during February and nest building starts. A Chiffchaff at the entrance to its nest.

The Rooks will be building their nests this month in high trees. They build in colonies, making large untidy nests.

The Month of March

Lengthening days now induce some plants to bloom even when the weather is severe. Early showpieces include shrubs like hazels, whose catkins are wind-pollinated and so do not depend on insects. The winter-flowering heather seems impervious to bad weather and flowers even under the snow. In sheltered spots, violets, primrose and hellebores will begin to open.

Early-flowering Rhododendron arboreum is a 'tree' type growing as high as 40 feet

1 Where it has been grown in a sheltered position, *Camellia japonica tricolor* has white flowers striped with pink and a group of golden stamens in March.
2 *Camellia japonica* has many cultivars, all of which can be grown out of doors in favourable spots. *Camellia* 'Governor Mouton' has clear deep pink flowers.
3 *Magnolia soulangeana* is one of the easiest Magnolias to grow. It flowers while the tree is still young, and on bare wood, in March. The large flowers are held upright on the branches.
4 *Prunus spinosa*, the Blackthorn or Sloe, one of the showiest of British early-flowering plants. In the autumn it has hard blue-black fruits which can be used for Sloe gin.

1

2

3

4

1

2

3

1 Viburnum burkwoodii is one of the evergreen kinds of Viburnum. The flowers are fragrant and appear in 'balls' of white early in the year.
2 Pieris japonica is one of a group of evergreen shrubs outstanding for their beauty and of great value in the garden. They prefer an acid soil.
3 Corylopsis spicata, with sweetly scented blossoms due in early March, is a Japanese shrub. It flowers on bare wood with hanging bunches of yellow bell-shaped flowers.

1

2

3

4

5

1 Cyclamen persicum 'Silver Strain', so called for the beauty of its foliage. Most types of pot cyclamen have handsome leaves, but unlike 'Silver Strain' they are mainly green.
2 Cinerarias are extremely diverse. The showy florists' flowers are progeny of Senecio cruentus and vary considerably in both size and colour. But the range of gay colours makes the plants popular.
3 Euphorbia pulcherrima, the Poinsettia, has several forms, in red, pinks and even white. The large 'petals' are really bracts and the plants are comparatively hardy compared with the older types.
4 Many double Narcissi force well and are splendid for pots and bowls. Not only do the double flowers give extra colour but they grow shabby less quickly than the single forms.
5 Like other alpine plants, the miniature Narcissi grow well in pans in the greenhouse They should not be forced but like to be allowed to grow naturally.

1

2

3

4

5

1 Spathiphyllum wallisii are ideal plants to grow in the darker corners of the house. They will, for example, like being in a dark hall. When they are grown in the greenhouse they need to be shaded.
2 Primula kewensis, a candelabra-type hybrid, brings a different colour from other Primulas flowering at this time of the year. The yellow flowers are welcome among the pinks and mauves of such species as malacoides and obconica.
3 Strelitzia reginae, the Bird of Paradise Flower, so called because of its striking form and colour, can be raised from seed under glass as well as from offsets or division of old plants.
4 The double-flowered Doronicum, D. caucasicum 'Spring Beauty' is a modern form of Leopard's Bane. It is lower growing than the type.
5 Helleborus orientalis, the Lenten Rose, is a member of the buttercup family and the name 'rose' was applied presumably because of the likeness to single roses.

1

2

3

4

5

1 Tulipa kaufmanniana, known as the Water-lily Tulip from the way they open their flowers wide to the sun. Many fine and beautiful hybrids are available.
2 The large flowered crocuses which are at their best this month are Dutch hybrids. These grow well in borders with other plants, often forming a carpet around shrubs and also in grass.
3 Chionodoxa lucillae, or Glory of the Snow, so named because it is so hardy that it will follow the snow line. It is very free flowering and will soon establish itself in any garden.
4 Narcissus bulbocodium, the Hooped Petticoat Daffodil, will soon become naturalised in sandy loam. Dwarf Narcissi of all kinds are ideal for the rock garden now.
5 Scilla sibirica 'Spring Beauty' is one of the many deep blue Scillas which never fail to provide patches of bright blue as the days begin to lengthen. It is a bulbous plant from Asia Minor.

Jobs of the month

March marks the start of the gardener's eight-month active season. In general, now is the final chance before the autumn to plant shrubs and fruit trees. There is pruning to be done and vigorous new growth to be protected and shaped. For summer promise to be fulfilled the herbaceous border may need a new quota of perennials and edging plants. And the lawn begins to make its regular demands. Summarised below are the Jobs of the Month for March. They are set out fully on the following pages in 16 main sections.

Bulbs

Survey the flowering bulbs in the garden. Decide which need moving and which need supplementing. Plant gladioli corms and hardy oxalis species

Flowers for cutting

Use still – gay winter-flowering heathers as the fabric for an embroidery arrangement of smaller spring flowers. Sow exotic foliage plants – e.g. *Atriplex hortensis cupreata,* ricinus, perilla

Fruit

In most areas the first fortnight of March gives a final chance of fruit planting, Refirm the soil around earlier plantings, secure ties and apply a mulch

Greenhouse

Sow alyssum, nemesia, stocks, asters, marigolds, petunias, Pick out earlier-sown tomatoes and other plants. Water cacti thoroughly to start them and where necessary transfer them to larger pots

Hedges

Plant evergreen or deciduous hedges, ideally a two-man operation. On exposed sites protect the young hedge with wattle hurdling

Herbaceous Plants

In a new border, plant hardy perennials to a colour scheme. In an established border, lift and divide plants that require this. Put in edging plants including primulas, pansies, violas

House Plants

Increase watering and feed plants more frequently. Remove apparently backward plants from their pots, inspect them and replace if need be in a pot one size larger

Lawns

Sweep, lightly roll and rake the lawn before mowing. Prepare the ground for a new lawn, either seed-sown or turfed

Paths, Walls, & Fencing

Plant offsets into a dry-stone wall as you build it or insert them in crevices of an existing wall

Patios, Window Boxes and Roof Gardens

If you have no green-house and wish to raise patio plants from seed, make a 'miniature green-house' by putting a seed tray in a plastic bag; then inflate and seal the bag

Rock Gardens

Replace winter casualties and plant out newly acquired specimens. Construct a scree of any size upwards of 2 square feet

Roses

Complete planting and prune the bushes in the hand before doing so. Prune established roses according to type: Floribundas, Ramblers, Hybrid Teas, Shrub Roses, Climbers

Trees & Shrubs

Lightly hoe shrub borders or begin a mulching cycle. Prune certain shrubs. Syringe camellias with water against frost damage and protect chaenomeles (japonica) from bud-ravaging birds

Vegetables

In easily workable soil sow successional crops. Develop seedlings in a raised or mounded nursery bed. Use fill-in space in flower borders for vegetables

Water Gardens

To complement a watercourse, plant 'trailers' (aubretia, alyssum, helianthemum). In the pool itself, plant *Hottonia palustris,* the water violet

Wildlife

In readiness for spring broods, clean out and repair any nesting boxes around the garden. Fix new nesting boxes on the north side of trees

Bulbs

March is the month in which the autumn planning and planting of spring-flowering bulbs really bear results. In shrub borders, in grass, in beds, window-boxes and tubs, daffodils and narcissi of all types are coming into flower.

Popular species of miniature narcissi such as *bulbocodium*, the hoop petticoat daffodil, and *cyclamineus*, the cyclamen flowered daffodil (better suited to peaty soil), will be adorning grassy banks with less well-known species like *nanus*, *juncifolius* and the clear white-flowered *watieri*. A good bulb for stony ground, *Eranthis hyemalis*, the winter aconite, will be nestling among its leafy growth.

The full array of crocuses is flowering, whatever the March weather, and the various cultivars of *C. sieberi* are specially colourful. The short-stemmed tulips, many with mottled or striped leaves, hybrids and cultivars of *Tulipa kaufmanniana*, the water-lily tulip, are the first tulips to flower at the end of the month.

With bulbs flowering in the garden, now is the time to assess their total effect and to decide which need moving and which need supplementing for better results next spring. Do not under-estimate newly planted bulbs. They frequently take a year or two to settle down.

The most fascinating bulb flowers of the month are the bulbous irises, some of them delicately scented. *Iris histrioides* produces its purple flowers whatever the weather. *Iris reticulata* and its varieties look particularly well in pans and troughs and mix well with crocuses for effect. *Leucojum vernum*, the spring snowflake, and muscari can also be relied upon to make a show now.

If window-boxes have been empty through the winter, plunge pots of daffodils raised out of doors or in a cold greenhouse into the soil in the window-boxes and top dress with peat. Avoid the temptation of turning the plants out of their pots. The mass of root will not appreciate such sudden freedom.

Prepare areas in the perennial border or in raised beds in which to plant lilies at the end of the month. Choose spots where they will get some shade during the middle of the day or where there is a living mulch provided by other plants.

In all but freezing springs the end of the month is not too early in favourable districts to plant gladioli corms for some early flowers. Put the corms in pockets of sand in previously prepared open ground. The pockets of sand are a protection against soil-borne disease and encourage root action. Put the corms 5 or 6 inches down with sand beneath. In stony soils pack fine soil above the corms to avoid a permanently curved spike when growth begins. For the best effect, plant the corms in clumps, say 5 or 7 together in a flat-bottomed hole, placing them about 5 inches apart. Cover them with fine soil.

Other plants to put in now are the hardy summer and autumn flowering species of oxalis, attractive for edging. Try potting up five or six bulbs in a 5-inch pot for summer pot work or get *Oxalis floribunda* going for summer adornment of hanging baskets.

Indoors, as hyacinths and daffodils growing in pots and bowls fade, cut off the flower stems at the base. Reduce the watering but keep the fibre or soil just moist until the foliage has faded completely.

The pots are rather unsightly at this period, so remove them from living rooms to a spare bedroom or an airy light shed. Or if the weather is mild, plant them directly from their containers in a corner out of doors.

Flowers for cutting

While buds are burgeoning everywhere in March and many flowers are bravely trying to bloom, there are few which are yet showing in the great masses that will give delight later. But even two or three from a plant here and there can be combined to make a large bowl of colour.

Make use of the winter flowering heathers, still gay and bright, to form a fabric on which the embroidery of smaller, softer flowers can be set. It will do the heathers more good than harm to take a good handful of short stemmed snippets from them. These, massed in a low container, will prove to be as good as any other stem holder and more colourful, too.

Clusters or little posies of two or more primroses, daisies, scillas, saxifrages, pulmonaria, tiny narcissi, irises, crocuses and other modest flowers all lend themselves to the 'embroidery' type of arrangement. Depending on how many flowers are available, containers can vary from a shallow oven dish to a giant old-fashioned wash basin.

Branches of blossom can still be brought indoors and forced. Use small side stems and snippets to give height

1

2

1 Anemone blanda, a useful little bulbous plant for many places in the garden—not only under trees, but also in the rock garden.
2 A window-box planted with Daffodils, Hyacinths and early Tulips—for effect in March. The small conifers can be either permanent or in containers.

1

2

3

to arrangements featuring little flowers.

Many evergreens look well with spring flowers. The lovely grey-green catkin-hung *Garrya elliptica* blends well with the clear pastel hues of hyacinths and tulips. Yellow spotted glossy aucuba leaves and scarlet berries match poppy anemones. Use box, myrtle, eleagnus, camellia and any other glossy leaves for contrast. Try the pretty bosses of *Viburnum tinus,* leaf and flower, to eke out a few blooms.

As the flowering greenhouse and house plants, such as cyclamen and azaleas, come to an end, gather the last flowers from the plants to use in arrangements. This way the fading plants can be dispatched to their summer quarters and their few flowers placed in a more attractive setting.

Meanwhile look ahead for summer arrangements. Hardy annuals sown in rows as though vegetables are easy to gather and easily supported to keep stems straight and flowers well off the ground.

In a large area, rows of each kind can be sown according to taste and requirements. But in a small garden the flower

1 Mahonia leaves look well with many spring flowers and bring a double value to the arrangement if they have changed colour.
2 Small-leaved Rhododendrons or other dainty evergreens are useful with the leafless stems of Narcissi.
3 The dried arrangements that have been used throughout the winter are still in prominence in March.

arranger might consider sowing a packet of tall annuals mixed, which seedsmen offer at a cheap rate. Sow all seed very thinly to avoid wastage by thinning later.

Many exotic-looking foliage plants are easily grown from seed. Among those that should be sown now are ornamental cabbage and kale, purple-black *Atriplex hortensis cupreata,* silvery, downy *Cineraria maritima* varieties, ricinus, the castor oil plant with wine-bronze leaves, and perilla, also bronze with finer laciniated leaves.

Cobaea scandens, the cup and saucer flower, a handsome climber, should be sown in a temperature of 60–65°F (15–18°C). Its handsome violet-green flowers bring beauty and distinction to arrangements, and even when the corolla has fallen the star-like calyx left behind is pretty enough to be used, especially in green arrangements.

For those who like all-green ensembles there are green zinnias and nicotiana, while the long tassels of green love-lies-bleeding, *Amaranthus caudatus viridus,* can be used fresh or, alternatively, carefully dried for arrangement.

Fruit

Except in very cold and climatically backward regions and in markedly late seasons, the first fortnight of March provides the final opportunity for fruit planting, as this should be carried out while the trees are still dormant. Exceptions are the container-grown soft fruits sometimes available at garden centres. These may be planted out at any time provided great care is taken not to break up the root ball.

With March fruit planting, the condition of the soil is still a vital con-

1 Small branches are prepared as scions and labelled.

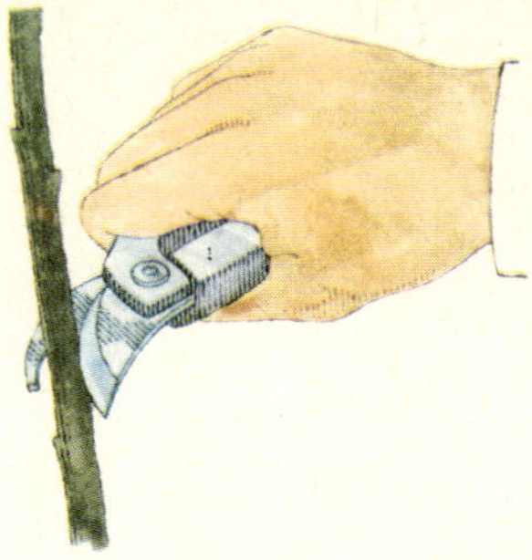

2 A clean cut is made with secateurs across the stock.

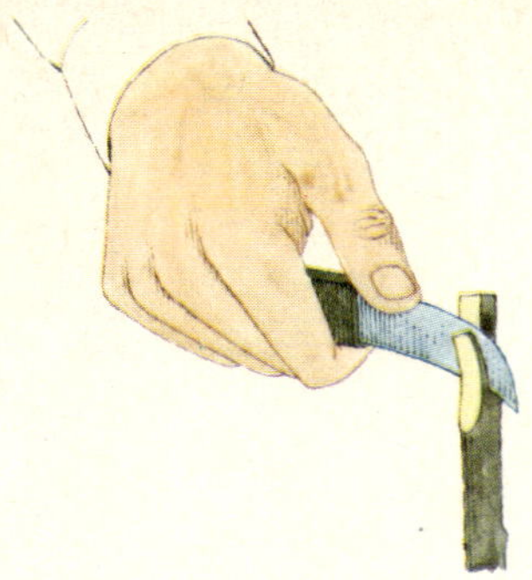

3 A knife is used to make an oblique cut, then a tongue.

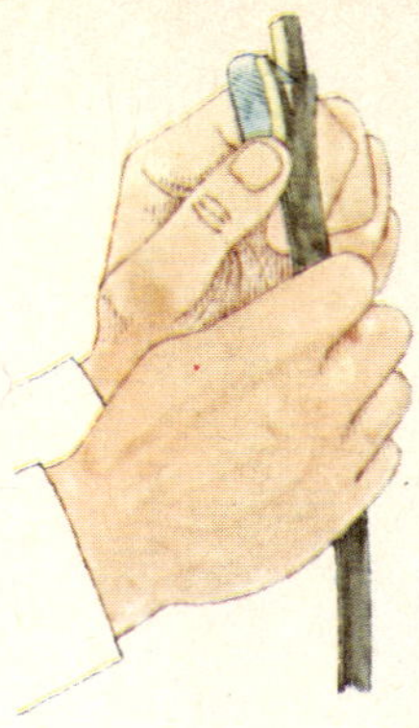

4 The tongue must be of even thickness yet not too thick.

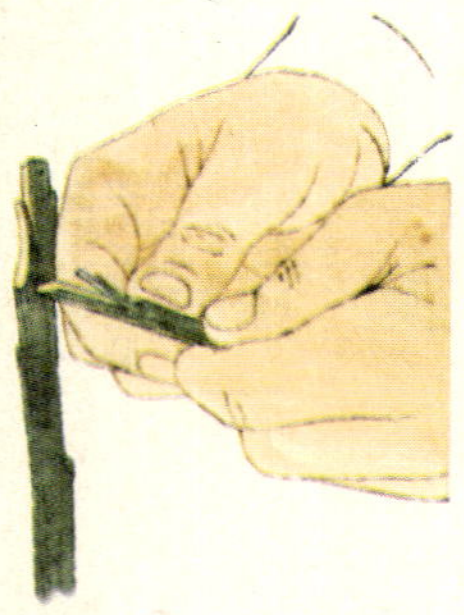

5 The scion is cut, to match the stock, the tongue thinner.

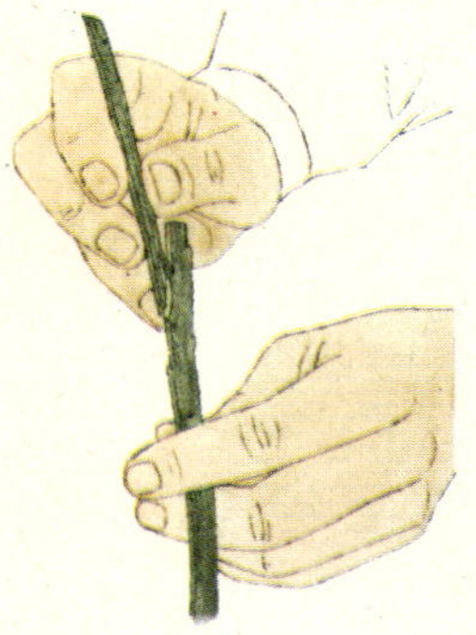

6 The cut surfaces are brought together and should match.

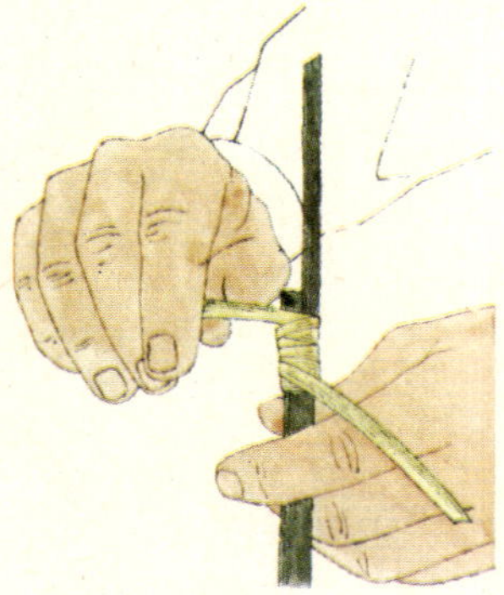

7 The union is held firmly in position with raffia.

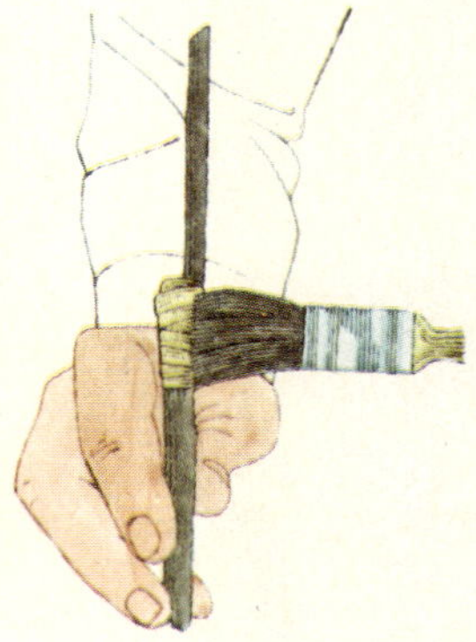

8 Grease or tar is painted over the raffia to exclude air.

sideration. The soil that is worked among and around the roots of the new plants must be crumbly and friable—not frozen and not too wet. Good soil condition is more important than a slavish following of the calendar.

It is particularly important to see that spring-planted trees and bushes do not want for moisture. They do not need feeding during their first season but a 2-inch mulch of moist peat spread over the soil surface will prevent loss by evaporation. Late-planted trees, too, may open more leaves than the roots can keep supplied, especially in windy weather when evaporation from the leaf surfaces is greater. Some sort of windshield of sacking or polythene arranged on the windy side of March-planted trees is therefore a help. So is overhead syringeing with clear water on warm days.

Inspect all trees which were planted earlier to see that hard frosts during the winter have not lifted them. Refirm the soil around them by treading and, at the same time, see that ties are still doing their job. Wall-trained trees need critical inspection because sometimes the soil settles but, of course, the wall to which they are fastened does not. A tree may be literally hanging from its fastenings and, if so, the close contact between soil and new roots necessary for quick re-establishment is lost.

If these earlier planted trees have not been mulched, attend to this now. Peat will serve for this as feeding is not required the first season.

Where fertilisers have not yet been given to older trees they should be applied now along the lines described in **The Month of February**.

Soft fruit should have first call on available supplies of well-rotted dung, garden compost or spent hops. Old mushroom bed material is also excellent provided the soil is not already neutral or alkaline, this form of manure usually having a proportion of chalk mixed in it.

Keep a close eye on the weather. If there is a spring drought, as often happens, all fruits planted this season should be watered generously. Trees against walls are particularly liable to suffer.

Although late summer or early autumn is the best time for planting the summer-fruiting varieties of strawberries, they may also be planted in March. In this case, however, they should never be allowed to fruit their first summer and all blossom trusses should be nipped off as soon as seen. Water thoroughly immediately after planting.

Perpetual fruiting strawberries (also known as remontants or ever-bearers) may be planted now, too. In cold districts and on heavy soil, this is a better time than October. A crop the first year is permissible but the plants must be given a reasonable chance to get established first. So remove all blossom until the end of May or early June. Early blossom removal may also be carried out with established perpetual strawberries so as to obtain a maximum autumn crop.

Sow alpine strawberry seed $\frac{1}{8}$-inch deep either outdoors where the plants are to fruit or in a seed pan in greenhouse or frame for transference outdoors later. These little berries have a flavour like that of the wild strawberry, make good jam and can be safely eaten by sufferers from rheumatism. The green-

1

2

1 Raspberries pruned last autumn and the new canes tied in may need to be looked over at this time of the year and any canes that have been blown about retied.
2 Clearing between the rows of Raspberries (and other soft fruit) is a job to do once the land is dry.

Raspberry canes planted this season should now be cut back to about 8 inches from the soil. Make the cut to a visibly live bud.

Once the sap is rising freely, old trees which were cut back in December can be regrafted with more modern and more desirable varieties. Whatever method of grafting is adopted, remember that all cut surfaces should be protected as soon as possible by painting with grafting wax or sealing compound to keep out disease.

Where trees were regrafted last year, one or two branches may have been left full length as sap drawers. Saw these off now, flush with the main trunk or branch, pare the wound smooth with a knife and paint over with white-lead paint or proprietary sealing compound to keep out disease.

Where gooseberry pruning has been deferred because the birds take so many buds in winter, do this now. Cut back leaders by a third and spur-prune side-shoots to two live buds for largest berries and to 1½ inches for smaller berries but heavier crops.

Towards the end of the month a grape vine in an unheated greenhouse can be started into growth by syringeing each morning with slightly warm water. Close the ventilators entirely at night and allow only a little top ventilation by day.

Old grease bands may need to be renewed, especially if the winter has been hard. Burn the old bands. Alternatively more grease can be smeared directly on to the trunks of the trees. If the weather is mild and there is the promise of an early spring hay bands can be prepared.

Greenhouse

There is still time to sow the summer bedding plants mentioned in the notes in The Month of February. If desired, to them may now be added alyssum, nemesia, stocks, asters, *Mesembryanthemum criniflorum*, French and African marigolds, petunias, kochias, *Phlox drummondii* and cosmeas. All should be sown in the same way as the earlier ones. In cold greenhouses sowing should take place preferably towards the end of the month.

Tuberous begonias, gloxinias, celosias, *Primula obconica* and *Solanum capsicastrum* may also still be sown as in February, with in addition the beautiful schizanthus or poor man's orchid, as it is sometimes called, easily raised from seed to flower in summer in cool airy conditions.

As the winter-flowering pot plants come to an end, *Azalea indica*, cyclamens and *Solanum capsicastrum* can be kept for next year but cinerarias and calceolarias are best discarded. Trim the faded flowers off the azaleas, then keep the plants well watered and syringed in the greenhouse to induce new growth.

Cyclamens need gradually less water until they die down, while the solanums

house sowing can be made quite early in the month but the outdoor sowing must wait until the sun has warmed and dried the soil.

In the event of really warm weather later in the month, strawberries that are being forwarded under cloches or polythene tunnels will need ventilation during the middle part of the day.

Should there be cold nights, be ready to give anti-frost protection to wall fruit trees already in flower. Pollinate the blossom by hand in the manner already described.

Where for some reason winter-washing with tar-oil has not been carried out during the dormant period or where red spider mite has been troublesome (tar-oil, unfortunately, does not kill red spider mite but does kill some of the mite's natural foes), spray apples with any good insecticide just as the green tips appear out of the buds. This wash kills many pests besides red spider eggs but not apple blossom weevil. The maggots inside the blossom make it turn brown and it never opens. To counteract this, malathion may be added to the spray.

The Butterfly-flowered Schizanthus or Poor Man's Orchid, decorates the greenhouse, from autumn-sown seed.

The fragrant blooms of Stephanotis floribunda can be a generous addition to the greenhouse in early spring.

1 Where cacti are grown in a greenhouse, be it on a large scale, as shown here, or as a modest collection, March is the time to repot, move and reorganise.
2 Calceolarias and Cinerarias make an excellent show under glass now.
3 The earlier sown Tomatoes are ready for pricking off into small pots.

should be cut back to about 6 inches high and repotted into pots one size larger, using John Innes potting compost No 1 plus a pinch of Epsom salts (magnesium sulphate).

Tomatoes may still be sown as in February but where earlier-sown ones have already made their seed leaves (the first pair formed) these will be ready for pricking out.

Bedding plants and pot plants sown earlier will also need pricking out as soon as they are large enough to handle, in most cases at about $\frac{1}{4}$-inch high.

This pricking out needs care, particularly with tomatoes. Use clean, well-drained seed boxes almost filled to the rim with the J.I.P.1 made firm and level. Use a small fork or trowel to lift the seedlings out of the seed compost, making sure that they are moist beforehand. Then dibble them firmly into the new compost at about $1\frac{1}{2}$ inches apart.

Handle the seedlings by the leaves, not the stem, and bury those with an obvious stem right up to the seed leaves; the others should only 'sit' on the surface, with their roots well anchored.

The dormant plants mentioned in the February notes may still be started into growth but where this has already been done cuttings should be taken as they become available. For zonal pelargoniums ('geraniums') use young shoots about 4 inches long, trimmed off beneath a joint, These should be inserted about an inch deep in the J.I.P.1 or in clean sand or vermiculite, in warm, airy conditions in full light.

For fuchsia cuttings use young shoots about 2 inches long. Remove the leaves from the lower inch of stem before inserting the cuttings in the same way as the zonal pelargoniums but preferably in a propagating frame—although they can be rooted more slowly on the open greenhouse bench in gentle heat.

If any fuchsia cuttings were rooted last summer, a few of these can be grown on as 'standards' by removing all the side shoots (but not the leaves) from the main stem until this reaches the height that is required.

Gloxinias and tuberous begonias may also still be started into growth. But where those started earlier have already made an inch or two of growth, pot them up singly in well-drained 3-inch pots of the J.I.P.1.

Water them sparingly until growth starts again, which should soon be seen to take place if the begonias are kept at a temperature of about 50°F (10°C) and the gloxinias at 60°F (15°C).

With the coming of March, cacti need more water. So give them a thorough soaking to start them off. If their growth, including the spines, has reached the sides of the pot they should then be transferred to pots a size larger, using the J.I.P.1 mixed with a sixth part of sharp sand, grit and crushed brick, over a deep layer of broken brick to provide drainage.

If a little heat is available, dahlias can be started early in the month by standing them upright in boxes and working some light, peaty soil in among them until only the tops of the actual tubers are visible. Do not bury the base of the stem. If the soil is kept just moist there should soon be plenty of shoots to use as cuttings.

Continue to take cuttings of decorative and early-flowering chrysanthemums and to pot up those that are already rooted. After potting make sure that they get ample light and ventilation; this is essential to ensure strong, sturdy plants.

Cuttings of perpetual carnations should be potted up as they become rooted, while those that have already nearly filled the 3-inch pots with roots should be moved on into 6-inch ones, using the J.I.P.2 over perfect drainage. Maximum light and air must be given to these plants now, with only enough heat to keep them safe from frost.

Climbing plants are not advisable incumbents in greenhouses devoted to tomatoes, chrysanthemums or carnations but otherwise they make most attractive features. *Hoya carnosa,* wax flower; *Plumbago capensis,* cape leadwort; *Passiflora caerulea,* passion flower; and *Stephanotis floribunda* are all fine ones to grow in pots. Use a rough, peaty compost for the *Hoya carnosa* and the J.I.P.2 for the others. For the *Stephanotis floribunda* try to keep the temperature above 50°F (10°C) but the others need only to be safe from frost. Established plants of the passion flower should be thinned out and cut well back now.

Make sure that violas, pansies, bedding calceolarias and penstemons rooted in cold frames now get plenty of air by removing the frame lights whenever there is no risk of frost.

1

2

3

4

5

1 March is a good month for planting both evergreen and deciduous hedges, and there is a wide choice of plants for this purpose. Few are better than Berberis x stenophylla, which makes a decorative but impenetrable hedge.
2 The evergreen Privet, Ligustrum ovalifolium, makes a good hedge to provide privacy all year round.
3 Young hedge plants frequently need protection from prevailing wind until the plants are established.
4 The Beech hedge holds its leaves in winter.
5 The Quickthorn, or Hawthorn, before it breaks into bud in March.

Hedges

Both evergreen and deciduous hedging subjects can be safely planted during March. It is well to remember that, although you may be planting in dozens or even hundreds, each shrub is still an individual plant and should be treated accordingly. Although the quickest planting method, with the help of a garden line, is to take out a trench the length of the site, shrubs normally get away better in separate planting holes.

In any case, the roots must not be bunched or over-crowded and the plants should be firm in the ground. They should be laid out along the length of the row at the appropriate planting distances before they actually go in. This will ensure that they are evenly spaced.

Ideally, planting should be a two-man operation, with one partner to hold the shrub in position while the other fills in around the roots and makes the soil firm. Smaller shrubs, however, such as lavender, rosemary or box, which are used for interior dividing hedges, can be planted with a trowel in a similar manner to bedding plants.

Deciduous hedging plants should be pruned back to about 6 inches from ground level before or immediately after planting. This will result in vigorous basal shoots and the hedge will be well-furnished at the bottom.

Evergreens should have less drastic treatment but all plants should be trimmed back to a uniform height before they go in.

Conifers and evergreens, such as rhododendrons and azaleas, come from the nursery with their roots 'balled' in sacking or polythene. This material should be removed but the tight ball of fibrous roots should never be disturbed. Conifers should not be trimmed for the first few seasons, by which time they should be well established.

If the soil is dry when the plants go in, they should have a thorough soaking, two gallons at least to each. This watering should continue throughout the rest of the first spring and summer season whenever dry conditions are prevalent. With conifers and evergreens, overhead spraying or syringeing in dry weather will help to counteract loss of moisture through excessive leaf transpiration.

Among deciduous hedges, *Crataegus monogyna,* or quickthorn, is one of the cheapest hedging plants of all. It will rapidly make a hedge that is practically impenetrable by man or beast. But it affords little privacy during winter. Beech and hornbeam, which both retain their russet dead foliage in winter when trimmed as hedges, are much better all-rounders.

An excellent and colourful ornamental flowering hedge can be made from *Ribes atrosanguineum,* the flowering currant, whose pink or carmine flowers are so attractive in spring. Such a hedge will remain compact up to 8 feet tall, while the snowberry, *Symphoricarpus laevigatus alba,* with its fascinating white 'mothball' berries, will perform an equally decorative function in winter.

There is a wide choice of evergreen hedging material, especially among the cotoneasters and barberries, which declare an autumn and winter bonus in

RECOGNITION CHART

Leaf portraits

The guide identifies 18 leaf forms ranging from ovate and lanceolate to digitate and fleshy, showing examples of each form

OVATE
Oval-shaped. Examples: Parrot tree, Parrotia persica, with coloured foliage; holly, Ilex aquifolium; poplar, Populus serotina (triangular ovate)

LANCEOLATE
Lance-shaped. The willow (Salix species)

LINEAR
Long, thin, grass-like. Schizostylis. Daffodils (Narcissus species). Carnations (Dianthus species). Iris species

RENIFORM
Kidney-shaped. Pelargonium species. Often with attractive zones of colour

CORDATE
Heart-shaped. Cyclamen persicum. Other examples: violets

ELLIPTICAL
Spindle tree Euonymus europaeus

SPATULATE
Spoon- or spatula-shaped.
Top: London Pride, Saxifraga umbrosa. Haberlea species.
At right:
Primula species

TRIFOLIATE
Three leaves together as in clover. Oxalis species

FILIFORM
Thread-like. Coreopsis verticillata.
Nigella damascena

ACICULAR
Needle-like. Spruce.
Pine (Pinus species)

SQUAMOUS
Sheathed, stem-clinging.
Chamaecyparis species

SAGITTATE
Arrow-like. Caladium bicolor

OBOVATE
Generally oval but blunted slightly at end away from leaf stalk.
Magnolia obovata

PELTATE
Shield- or target-shaped.
Canary creeper, Tropaeolum speciosum

DIGITATE
Finger-like. Lupin. Horse chestnut, Aesculus hippocastanum

ORBICULAR
Flattened form of obovate.
Alder, Alnus glutinosa

PALMATE
Palm-like. Fig, Ficus carica. Ivy (Hedera species). Vine (Vitis species)

FLESHY
The form of many cacti and succulents. Houseleeks (Sempervivum species)

the shape of attractive berries. Holly, yew and box are a longer term planting proposition, since all of them are comparatively slow-growing.

Even the much-maligned privet makes an effective and compact evergreen hedge if it is properly maintained—that is, clipped regularly and often during its growing season. *Ligustrum ovalifolium*, the oval-leaved privet, is the species most widely used. It is a greedy feeder and an inveterate soil robber. This makes it unsuitable for planting in the neighbourhood of choice shrubs or border plants or for a hedge in the fruit or vegetable garden.

For acid soils, rhododendrons and azaleas make first-rate evergreen flowering hedges, although the initial outlay for plants is heavier than for most other hedging subjects. As a long-term investment, however, few other plants could be more effective or trouble-saving.

Conifers, such as the various forms of *Chamaecyparis lawsoniana, Cupressus leylandii* and *Thuja plicata*, make some of the finest evergreen hedges of all. They will need little attention and will remain well-clothed and dense right down to ground level.

Newly planted hedges of conifers and evergreens, which will have to stand up to the full force of spring and summer gales, should be staked, if possible, especially in open or exposed situations. Staking acts as a safeguard against wind-rock, which can do serious damage to the young fibrous roots. Stakes provide a firm support until the plants develop their own anchoring roots. They need not be large. Fairly stout canes will be sufficient for the purpose.

Where hedges are exposed to the north and east, some kind of temporary screen may be advisable, not only to protect the young hedge from the weather but also to fulfil the functions of shelter and privacy that the hedge will take over as it matures.

One of the best and cheapest materials for the purpose is wattle hurdling. With a useful garden life of from 7 to 10 years, this makes an ideal screen and shelter.

Herbaceous Plants

March is a busy month in the herbaceous border as elsewhere. Although, strictly speaking, herbaceous borders should consist of perennials that die down in winter and appear again in spring, most borders usually include one or two evergreens together with a few bulbs, bedding plants and annuals.

If you are stocking a new border, the hardy perennials should be planted at once. Arrange them in groups of three or more of a kind rather than dotted about singly, keeping the tall plants towards the back in a single-sided border and in the middle section of a

double-sided border.

Popular perennials for a mixed border:

Blue, purple and mauve: delphiniums, anchusa, phlox, campanula, *Tradescantia kreisler, Iris germanica*, lupins, Michaelmas daisies (asters) and *Nepeta mussinii*.

Yellow and orange: coreopsis, *Achillea* 'Coronation Gold', heliopsis, *Geum* 'Princess Juliana', helenium, *Rudbeckia deamii* and solidago.

Pink: pyrethrum, sidalcea, *Anemone japonica, Delphinium* 'Pink Sensation', phlox, heuchera, Michaelmas daisy, pinks, border carnations.

Red: scarlet bergamot (*Monarda didyma*), oriental poppies *(Papaver orientalis), Lychnis chalcedonica*, carnations, and *Geum* 'Mrs Bradshaw'.

White: Achillea 'The Pearl', Michaelmas daisy, delphinium, *Chrysanthemum maximum*, gypsophila, *Pyrethrum* 'Avalanche', *Tradescantia* 'Osprey' and carnations.

Suitable plants for a shady border include astrantia, foxgloves (digitalis), polyanthus, *Anemone japonica*, phlox, lily-of-the-valley *(convallaria)*, doronicum, columbine *(aquilegia), Campanula persicifolia*, solidago, astilbe, Michael-

The semi-double flowers of Heliopsis patula, a strong-growing herbaceous perennial, somewhat resistant to drought.

By considering the selection of both plants and cultivars a good colourful effect can be maintained on the herbaceous border for many weeks. Most herbaceous perennials have only one flowering period, but several cultivars flower just a week or two apart. By including such plants in the border continuous effect can be aimed at. Variation in colour as well as height should be the object when planning a border of this kind. The best results will be achieved if the border is carefully planned on paper before any planting is started. By colouring in the various areas that will be in flower, say in June and then again in July, changing effects can be forecast. Use an overlay of thin or transparent paper on top of the basic plan to arrange the juxtaposition of the plants. This way it will be seen clearly where gaps are likely to appear after flowering, and thus where some other plant needs to be introduced to cover the fading foliage.
1 Aster; 2 Heliopsis; 3 Delphinium; 4 Aster; 5 Helenium; 6 Delphinium; 7 Aster; 8 Geranium; 9 Erigeron; 10 Kniphofia; 11 Campanula; 12 Phlox; 13 Sidalcea; 14 Gypsophila; 15 Eremurus; 16 Pyrethrum; 17 Lupin; 18 Iris; 19 Hemerocalis; 20 Delphinium; 21 Salvia; 22 Lupin; 23 Iris; 24 Lavendula; 25 Dianthus; 26 Physostegia; 27 Erigeron; 28 Scabious; 29 Aster; 30 Artemisia; 31 Nepeta; 32 Lychnis.

Border Phlox are available in a wide range of colour and by selecting cultivars a succession of bloom is assured.

Lychnis chalcedonica is a useful herbaceous perennial. Without it, colour tends to be lacking in the border during July.

mas daisy and violas.

Plants that need dividing in established borders can be lifted. Replant only the fresh growth round the outer edge rather than the hard woody centre of the clump.

Border carnations are quite hardy but well-drained, recently limed ground is essential if the plants are to thrive. They are happiest in friable loam but can be grown in clay soil if grit, rotted manure and peat are added when preparing the ground. Plant them 15 inches apart, firmly but not too deeply; deep planting tends to rot the stems.

Coming from the same family (dianthus), pinks enjoy similar conditions. Planted 9 inches apart as an edging to an herbaceous border, they can look quite lovely when interplanted with mauve catmint *(Nepeta* x *faassenii)*.

Other edging plants that can be put in this month include polyanthus (primula), spaced 6 inches apart, pansies and violas, 10 inches apart, or a miniature lavender *Lavandula spica* 'Baby Blue' (10 to 12 inches high).

Plant gladioli corms from now until the middle of May, at fortnightly intervals to provide a succession of bloom. The colours of these stately flowers with their sword-like foliage are brightest when grown in full sun, planted 4 inches deep, 9 inches apart, in clumps of 6 or more in deep, rich, well-drained soil.

The giant-flowered double and semi-

1 Pinks make a good edging in midsummer and are very fragrant.
2 Border Phlox, P. decussata 'Nora Leigh', is popular because of its variegated foliage, which gives a touch of lightness to the border.
3 The Prairie Mallow or Sidalcea has good upright spikes of flower from June to August or September.
4 Monarda didyma 'Cambridge Scarlet', the Oswego Tea Plant, likes plenty of moisture in the soil to thrive.
5 The Obedient Plant, so called because the flowers can be moved from one position to another, is Physostegia.

double ranunculus, with blooms as much as 3 inches across in brilliant shades of crimson, scarlet, pink and yellow, on stems 15 to 18 inches high, can be planted during March and April also. So, too, can the large-flowered hybrid montbretias which are hardy only in mild districts.

Choose a well-drained sunny part of the border for both these delightful flowers, planting the tuberous roots of ranunculus with the claws pointing downwards, 2 inches deep, 6 inches apart, and montbretia 3 inches deep, 3 inches apart, lifting the bulbs in November and storing in a frostproof place.

Make sure of sweet scent in summer by planting stem-rooting lilies. The golden-rayed hill lily of Japan *(Lilium auratum), Lilium regale, Lilium brownii, Lilium sargentiae*, the shell-pink, pink spotted *Lilium speciosum* 'Cinderella' and the deep crimson red *Lilium speciosum rubrum* 'Uchida Kanoka', for instance, are all delightfully fragrant.

The bulbs of these should be planted 3 to 4 inches deep in open porous soil enriched with plenty of peat and leaf-mould (lime-free soil for *Lilium auratum* and *Lilium regale).* A mulch of rotted compost, leafmould or moss peat should be applied as the stem roots appear.

The modern day lilies *(hemerocallis),* in colours ranging from primrose to orange, light cherry-red, deep crimson, orchid shades, pink and bi-colours, should not be overlooked when planting a border. These gorgeous flowers are perfectly hardy and while preferring good friable loam they can be grown in almost any type of well-drained soil if rotted compost or peat is worked in before planting. Plant them 2 feet apart with the crown about ½-inch below the surface, spreading the roots carefully and scattering slug pellets over the ground to prevent the young shoots being eaten.

Autumn sown antirrhinum and Brompton stock wintered under glass should be hardened off now in readiness for transplanting into open borders towards the end of the month.

Finish preparing the ground for hardy annual sowings, working damp horticultural peat into the top 3 or 4 inches and raking the surface to a very fine tilth.

House Plants

By now many house plants will be making appreciable growth and the amount of water they are given can gradually be increased. Still keep them slightly on the dry side but give them more than in the short and cold days.

If a plant appears to be making little growth or if water appears to rush through the soil and collect in the saucer, it is likely that the plant will require repotting. If the plant is small enough, take it up in the hand with the fingers spread over the soil surface and, turning it upside down, knock the pot rim sharply against a hard surface. The plant and root ball will slip out from the pot into the hand.

Examine the root ball carefully. If the roots appear to take up all the space and coil around the outer edges, then the plant certainly needs repotting. Choose a pot only one size larger and crock or disc the drainage hole at the base.

Using John Innes compost No 2 or a suitable proprietary potting compost, sift sufficient into the base of the pot to allow the root ball to come just under the level of the rim and then very gently tease some of the old soil away from the roots.

Having done this, place the roots in the new pot and gently sift soil or compost around them, firming the soil as you go and making sure that every root hair is in intimate contact with the soil and that the plant stands upright in its new pot. Water thoroughly and then put aside to drain.

Allow the newly repotted plant to become almost dry at the roots before watering again and thereafter maintain a regular watering programme

Sometimes, particularly with larger plants, it is not necessary to repot completely. Yet the provision of fresh soil will give new life to the plant. In these circumstances gently scrape away some of the soil at the top of the pot, taking care not to damage the roots. Replace this exhausted soil with fresh.

As the plants are examined to discover whether they require repotting, it is also possible to trim and groom them after their winter of comparative inactivity. Some shoots may be weak and spindly. Some leaves may either be dead or dying. Go over the entire plant carefully and clean it up ready for the coming season's growth.

The beginning of spring is also the time to begin a new feeding programme for house plants. Where they have been fed only once a month or so during their semi-dormant period in the winter, they can now be introduced gradually to more frequent doses of fertiliser, perhaps once a fortnight for the first 6 to 8 weeks and weekly thereafter. Always read carefully the instructions provided by the fertiliser manufacturer and never exceed the recommended dose.

The aim of every house plant enthusiast should be to maintain his plants in good health but to allow them to make growth only slowly. House plants that by excessive feeding are made to grow too quickly will both exhaust themselves and grow too large for their positions in the home. Sometimes, on the other hand, certain plants are required to grow quickly, perhaps to form a screen or cover a wall, and flowering plants require a constant succession of bloom to look at their best.

During the winter any cacti or succulents grown as house plants should have been kept almost bone dry, being given

1

2

3

4

1 To turn out a pot plant to examine the ball of soil and the roots, take it in the hand with the fingers spread over the soil surface and upturn the pot. Strike the rim sharply on a firm surface, like the edge of a table, and the pot can then be lifted clear of the ball of soil.
2 When indoor Azaleas, A. indica, have finished flowering they can be plunged out of doors for the summer. Do not do this until the danger of frost is past, and then choose a sheltered spot. The pot should be sunk so that the rim is level with the soil surface.
3 ***Behind*** **Peperomia glabella;** ***in front*** **Peperomia magnoliaefolia.**
4 Pandanus veitchii.

just sufficient water to keep them plump and healthy. Now is the time to begin encouraging them into new growth to induce them to produce their flowers, so often surprisingly gay and attractive, yet usually so short lived.

Never begin to feed cacti or succulents until their roots have become accustomed once again to regular moisture. Begin to increase their watering now so that their swollen stems are fat and turgid and then begin feeding next month. Give them as much light as possible, keeping them always close to the glass in a south facing window unless the weather is too cold outside, in which case bring them back a little way into the room while ensuring that they still get the benefit of good light.

Those flowering plants such as *Azalea indica* that have produced their rich blooms indoors during the cold winter months and that are now past their best should gradually be allowed to dry out. Give longer intervals between watering. They can be plunged in a sheltered spot in the garden for the summer where they will benefit from the more natural conditions than obtained indoors. But do not do this until all danger of frost has passed.

Flowering bulbs that have passed their best should also be allowed to dry out gradually before they are lifted from their soil and planted out in the garden. As with bulbs in garden soil their foliage should be allowed to remain.

Lawns

March is the beginning of a new year for lawns.

With a birch broom, sweep the lawn clear of any winter rubbish. Follow this by a light rolling (when the soil is not too wet) to consolidate any frost pockets created. Then rake the lawn, with a wire spring-back lawn rake, to remove matted growth and lift weeds for cutting. One or two lawn mowings will probably be required but, to prevent 'scalping', the cutter blades should be set 1 to 1½ inches high.

Where a new lawn is to be made, March is a good month to prepare the ground for either seed sowing or turfing in April. (The best months for lawn ground preparation are July for August seed sowing, and September for October turfing; there is less likelihood of drought and the grass has time to become established before being used the following summer.)

If yours is a new garden, a general plan of its future design needs to be put in hand first.

It is not necessary to have a square or rectangular shaped lawn. Even if the garden area appears to hold little scope for imaginative design, it is possible to introduce gentle curves to give a softer, more pleasing effect. Equally, it is not necessary for the lawn to be absolutely flat. Where space allows, many of the most pleasing lawns have a gradual, natural-looking slope, or their levels are broken by terraces or grassed or shrub-planted banks.

For ease of maintenance, however, it is advisable not to introduce flower beds within the lawn area itself. Concentrate these around its perimeter.

All too often, a new lawn has to be made on what is virtually a rubbish heap left by the builders. It is no good hoping that a quick levelling operation and a scattering of grass seed will produce a healthy lawn—because it will not. There is nothing for it but to put in several hours' hard labour.

First remove all obvious rubbish, scrub, tree roots and deep-rooted weeds. Rough grass and shallow-rooted weeds can be forked in deeply during digging.

Then examine the site to discover whether there are 6 inches of top soil overall (a minimum of 4 inches will serve). If you want to make a sloping lawn, say 1 in 80, and have *in situ* top soil to a depth greater than 6 inches, some of the top soil can be transferred

1

2

3

1 A good easy-care lawn is free from central beds. March is the month to sweep it and start with a light rolling. The date of the first mowing will vary with the season.

Deep-rooted weeds to be grubbed out:
2 The long tap-rooted Dandelion, Taraxacum officinale.
3 Bulbous Buttercup, Ranunculus bulbosus.

to form the incline. Alternatively, buy in top soil to give the required levels.

If steeper slopes are to be created, the top soil will have to be dug off, placed on one side and the sub-soil gradients altered prior to returning the top soil.

If the soil has not been over-compacted, if water does not lie on it and if there is not overmuch poor sub-soil mixed into the top soil, then a thorough digging over of the top 6 to 8 inches will be sufficient.

However good the soil, it is a sound practice to fork in organic matter at this stage, for example, a good grade of granulated peat at 5 to 7 lb per square yard. If the soil tends to be heavy, incorporate 1 cwt of gritty, lime-free sand per square yard to improve drainage. Leave the area rough dug until the end of the month.

If too much sub-soil is near the surface, it should be removed and replaced, if necessary, with bought in top soil to rasie the ground level.

Badly compacted or naturally very heavy and poor draining soil will require more thorough treatment. For small lawn areas, double digging is advised. Incorporate the previously recommended rates of peat and sand into both the sub-soil and top-soil layers. Where large areas are involved, it is recommended that a mechanical tractor-drawn sub-soiler be used.

It is rare that a garden lawn site requires soakaway, tile or drain-pipe drainage. Should a large area of very heavy, wet ground be involved, however, it would be advisable to go to the trouble and expense of laying a suitable drainage system. Again, care should be taken to keep top-soil and sub-soil layers separate, and the organic materials recommended previously should be incorporated into each layer.

Towards the end of March, having left the roughly prepared area to settle for 2 to 3 weeks, any weeds that have appeared should be dealt with.

Shallow-rooted weeds can be hoed and raked up or a quick-acting weed-killer may be sprayed on. The former method is preferable. Deep-rooted and bulbous weeds, for example *Taraxacum officinale* (dandelion), *Rumex* species (docks) and *Ranunculus bulbosus* (bulbous buttercup), are best forked out, with roots and bulbs intact, and destroyed.

After weeding, and when the soil is fairly dry, fork over the top soil and mix in a general fertiliser (at the recommended rate). Then tread the ground, with your feet moving close together and your body weight over your heels. Follow this by roughly raking the site with a wide-toothed rake. Repeat the treading and raking but this time at right angles to the first operation.

Paths, Walls & Fencing

A dry stone wall, whether free-standing or retaining a bank of soil, is an ideal place to grow some kinds of plants. This is proved by the fact that a new wall will, after a period, show evidence of natural growth. Windblown or bird-borne seeds lodging in the wall will germinate and grow. Only small quantities of soil are necessary.

If the wall is still being built, it is a simple matter to plant or sow seed as you go. Bed each course of stone in a layer of good loamy soil, just thick enough to prevent the stones grating on one another. One or two seeds can be sown at the outer edges. But dot them about at different levels to obtain an engaging irregularity rather than straight lines of plants. Offsets of certain plants can be inserted in crevices.

If the wall is already built, offsets can usually be inserted in crevices, their roots surrounded by a little ball of mud and some good compost rammed in after them with a stick. Seeds can be inserted in the same way, in a ball of mud.

In general, mat-forming plants with a fine root system should be used. Some ferns grow well, particularly on the north side of walls where they do not get too baked by the sun. But as the roots of these wall plants are generally protected by the walling stones and seldom dry out completely, it is also possible to grow many other plants such as campanulas, dianthus, some antirrhinums, iberis, scabious and the lovely sedums and sempervivums.

Offsets of sempervivums can be detached in March and planted up to make good tufts of starry plants quickly. There are more than 40 species and a couple of hundred hybrids of sempervivum, so the choice is wide.

As retaining walls usually separate two different levels in the garden it is sometimes necessary to have steps leading up or down. Never skimp on steps. Make them well with a good wide tread of at least 8 inches and shallow but even risers. Where possible and where necessary incorporate a slope so that a mower or wheelbarrow can be taken up or down with little difficulty

Undoubtedly the best time to introduce small plants into the crevices between stones of a wall is when the wall is being built. But existing walls can be softened in appearance by tucking in suitable plants, in spring.
1 Plants from small pots are used.
2 The whole ball of soil is tucked in.
3 Then rammed in with a trowel handle.
4 Roots and plant should be horizontal.

1

2

3

4

1 Campanula poscharskyana provides a mass of starry mauve-blue flowers.
2 Ramondas are useful for tucking between the stones of a north-facing wall.

3 The golden leaved Ericas are colourful even when not in flower.
4 Another plant useful for tucking into the wall is Helichrysum selago.

and no risk of damage to the step edges.

Never place any paving plants on steps. They can too easily lead to a bad fall. If a flight of steps appears stark and forbidding, plant at the edges to soften the hard lines. A *Cotoneaster horizontalis* spread along the side, its fishbone patterned stems sweeping along the edges, will hug the surface and not get in the way of feet.

Even a slight balustrade can be given extra dignity and importance by placing a well planted stone urn at the top. Where required, the balustrade can be in a different colour, texture or material from that of the steps themselves. But always keep each tread the same in every way, as differences can confuse the eyes, particularly of the elderly. Make sure, too, that each tread has a very slight forward slope to carry water away and prevent the formation of ice in frosty weather.

Patios, Window Boxes and Roof Gardens

Plants grown in containers are usually a little warmer and therefore a little more ahead than plants grown in the open soil. So tub, trough and window-box plants will be showing definite movement by now.

All danger of frost has not yet passed, however, and although there is the temptation in the warmer and longer days to use some of the more tender and colourful plants, this should be resisted unless you are prepared to gamble on the possibility that they may be killed and have to be replaced.

Preparations can be made now for raising annuals and other bright decorative features for the window-boxes and troughs.

If a greenhouse is available, the plants can be raised in it and grown on until the frosts have finished. But even without this aid, much can be done by the urban gardener wishing to beautify his window-boxes or roof garden.

Many seeds will germinate quite happily in the normal warmth of the home. Sow them in the usual way in pots or seed trays and then slip these, one by one, into a transparent plastic bag, blowing the bag full of air and then sealing the opening tightly with a rubber band. This in effect makes a miniature greenhouse, warm and humid, where the seeds will quickly start to shoot.

Examine the bags each day and, if the condensation inside is too great, gently remove the pot or tray, turn the bag inside out and put the pot or tray back inside it.

Keep the sealed bags in a warm spot at first. An airing cupboard is ideal. When the seeds have germinated, remove them to a window-sill where they get good light and not quite so much warmth.

If the plants get too large before they can be planted out they can be transferred into a larger bag or placed out of doors on a warm day in a sunny and sheltered position.

Because space is at a premium in patio, window-box or roof top gardening, it is not practicable to wait for the early bulbs that have finished flowering to die down, as in the case of a larger garden. And at this stage they look unsightly in situations where they are the focus of attention. So lift the spent flowers from the soil complete with the bulb. If you have the space for the purpose, they can be stored like this, the bulbs lying in a box buried in peat or soil. If you have inadequate space, the best thing to do is give them away to a friend with space enough in his garden, where they can be heeled in ready for

A miniature 'greenhouse'

planting again later in the year.

Many hardy annuals can be sown now directly into the containers in which they are to grow and they will flower from about June onwards. But this will mean that the tubs or troughs are comparatively dull and uninteresting for much of the spring period when they should be at their brightest.

So to fill empty containers with plants that will give instant results it may be desirable to use dwarf trees and shrubs and some of the lovely alpines and rock plants that are always sold pot-grown and are capable of being planted in containers at any time of year.

Any seed sown or cuttings taken directly into outdoor containers can be both hastened into growth and protected from inclement weather by placing a pane of glass over the top of the pot. This, in effect, makes a miniature cold frame. But because winds can lift and break the glass it is wise to place a stone or some other comparatively heavy object on top.

Containers that hold newly sown seed or newly inserted plants should never be allowed to dry out completely. Because there is no subterranean reservoir for containers, as there is for plants grown in the open soil, the compost is apt to dry out quickly and from March onwards a constant watch must be kept on all containers to make sure that they are not dry.

A good watering may well result in the water rushing through the pot and out of the drainage hole with much of the root ball still remaining comparatively dry. So the practice to be followed is to water the plants thoroughly and gently and then to repeat the process so there can be no doubt that all the soil in the container is uniformly moist.

Where established plants are beginning to show signs of new growth, start feeding them now. Use a liquid or granular fertiliser, preferably at a little less than the recommended rate this early in the season. The plants should be growing away strongly before you give them the full dose.

Rock Gardens

The rock garden takes on a new lease of life during March and, although the plants are slow to start, by the time April approaches the scene will have rapidly changed.

There are many jobs that require attention in the rock garden during March, such as the replacement of winter casualties and the planting out of newly acquired specimens.

The snowdrops are beginning to go over and this is the time that they can be transplanted if so desired, for they re-establish themselves much more easily if moved before the foliage has died away.

There are a number of snowdrop species on the market if you want to experiment or grow a collection. The following are best purchased while in flower, not as dried bulbs, and will add lustre to the rock garden: *Galanthus elwesii*, a large species from the Aegean Islands; *G. nivalis* 'Lutescens', the common snowdrop with yellow markings instead of green on the inner petals; and *G. plicatus* from the Crimea, large solid flowers with green markings on the scalloped tips of the inner petals.

The spring flowering crocus species are also at their best during this month. Here again there is wide scope for selection among crocuses that are just as easy to grow as the Dutch forms more commonly seen and they are certainly daintier, with an elfin charm all their own.

1

2

1 A slightly raised bed can be made into a scree garden, and provides a labour-saving feature along the path. It is colourful in March and, by careful selection, can be interesting all year.
2 A colourful selection of early bulbs.

Notable species and varieties include *C. chrysanthus*, orange with brownish purple veinings on the petals, and its many forms ranging from ivory-white to dark orange; *C. balansae* (Asia Minor), bright orange with deep mahogany feathering; *C. biflorus* (s.w. Europe), large flowers with creamy-buff exterior and feathered purple and silvery-lavender interior; *C. etruscus* (Italy), lilac-blue with the outer three petals pale yellow-feathered purple; *C. fleischeri* (Asia Minor), pure white with slender petals and deep orange-red anthers; *C. sieberi* (Greece), goblets of purple-blue, shaded orange at throat.

These are just a few of the many available and this is the best period to buy them as they are in flower and a range to suit your taste can be obtained at nurseries.

The latter part of March is an ideal time to plant out rock plants, either newly purchased or from well-grown seedlings or rooted cuttings that have been grown on from the previous year.

Never buy plants that have outgrown their pots. These will often fail when transplanted to a permanent position. Small well-rooted specimens will establish better.

Cushion plants should be compact and free from dead or dying rosettes. The foliage of the plants should look healthy.

Any planting that has to be carried out should be done during open dryish periods. On no account must it be attempted if frost is present. Gently take the plant from its pot and remove the drainage crocks. Loosen the ball of soil. Remove a small amount of compost from the neck of the plant, at the same time disposing of any weed seedlings or grass.

Make a hole large enough in the rock garden to accommodate the plant easily. After working in the soil round the roots, make the planting firm and top dress with the appropriate chippings. Where space allows, the smaller species and varieties are best planted in threes.

Most nurserymen's catalogues of rock plants have the words 'Suitable for the scree' added to the names of many of the plants, which include a number of the best and most floriferous of rock plants.

March is a perfect time for the construction and planting of a scree. It can be of any size from a couple of square feet upwards, depending on the overall size of the rock garden. Any aspect from sunny to half shade is suitable for the cultivation of plants requiring varying degrees of sunlight.

The soil should be removed to a depth of approximately 15 inches, and the scree bed partially filled with 9 inches of drainage material topped by 1 inch of peat or leaf roughage. The top 5 inches should then be filled with a mixture of equal parts of good loam, leafmould or peat and three parts of really sharp sand and stone chippings. Allow the bed to settle. Subsequently rocks for decoration or to provide root and partial shade for the plants can be placed in position. Finally give the scree bed a top dressing of stone or gravel chippings.

Roses

Rose planting should be completed if at all possible during March. When planting during this month it is normal practice to prune in the hand before doing so. Take care to cut away all weak, damaged and dead wood and cut back the remaining sound wood to 3 or 4 eyes from the base.

The pruning of established roses should be undertaken early in the month before the new shoots become too long, as these will be on the upper half of the stems that will have to be cut away. Roses are best pruned when they are dormant and the dormant period varies from year to year according to severity of the winter. After a period of frosts or heavy snow it may be that the roses will still be dormant early in March but normally they should have started into new growth.

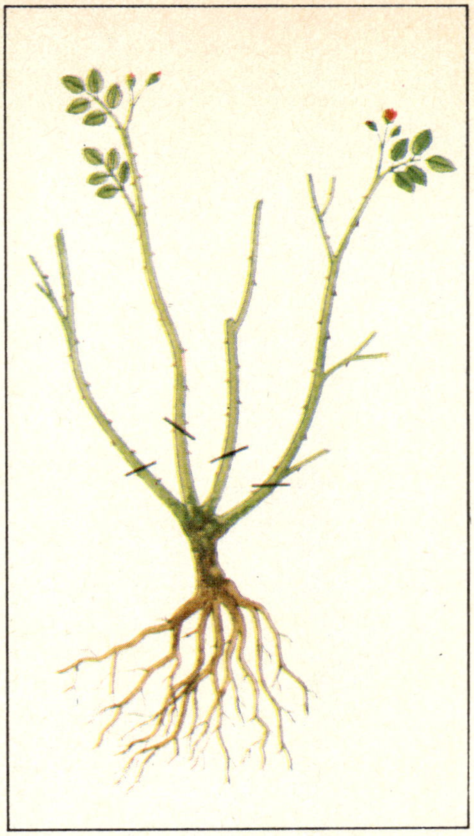

When a Rose is received from the nursery ready for planting it sometimes looks a straggly plant. When planting, allow plenty of room for the roots to be spread out and make them very firm. The growth should be cut right back to within a few inches of the ground. The position of the cuts is indicated.

There is considerable variation in pruning methods depending partly on the requirements of the grower. Is he, for example, interested mainly in exhibition roses or in general garden display? The various main groups of roses call for various pruning methods and the type of soil on which roses are growing is also a differential factor.

Really hard pruning, which used to be widely practised for exhibition and formal bedding, is no longer considered essential with modern varieties. Many of them, particularly in shades of yellow, resent hard pruning that may result in sparse flowering and split blooms. Most hybrid teas in shades of yellow, apricot, orange and flame give better results from moderate pruning.

There are certain preliminary operations common to all groups and to all methods of pruning. All dead, dying, badly diseased, damaged, thin, twiggy and unripe wood must first of all be cut away. So should any badly placed shoots, that is, those crossing other shoots or growing inwards to the centre of the plant, which should be kept open. When pruning, a sharp pair of secateurs should be used and all cuts should be made on the slant just above an outward facing eye, which is a dormant shoot bud.

Having removed the superfluous wood, you will get a better idea of the healthy wood that remains and needs to be shortened. This is explained below.

Hybrid Teas

This type may be pruned by one of three methods: *Light pruning* This involves cutting back any basal shoots of the previous season to just above the first or second outward-pointing eye below the footstalks of the old flowers. Laterals from older wood should be cut back by about a third of their length. The system is recommended for use on very hungry soils. Mulching the surface of the beds with organic matter is also advisable. *Moderate pruning* For garden display and the provision of cut flowers for the house, this method gives good results on most soils. It involves shortening growths made during the previous season by about half—rather more than this if they are slender and rather less if they are strong and sturdy. *Hard pruning* This method is more suited to the needs of the exhibitor of specimen blooms but it may also be preferred where formal beds on lawns require the plants to be kept compact and not to overhang the turf. Only the strongest of the healthy growths are retained. These are cut back to about 4 or 5 eyes from the base and any laterals or side shoots are restricted to 2 or 3 eyes. A rich soil and liberal feeding are recommended under this system to give good results over a lengthy period.

Floribundas

New basal shoots of the previous season should be left almost full length. Merely cut back to the first outward-pointing eye below the old footstalks. Laterals from 2-year-old wood should be cut back halfway and older wood which has not produced flowering laterals should be cut back hard to 3 eyes from the base.

Ramblers

The category covers the wichuraianas and the multiflora ramblers. Those that renew themselves with new canes from the base every season should have all the old canes cut out after flowering and the new ones tied in to fill the space. Others that do not renew themselves completely from the base should have as much of the old wood cut away as can be spared and all the new canes retained.

Climbers

The category includes modern recurrent climbers. Apart from removing old and twiggy wood and cutting back laterals to 3 eyes, little formal pruning is necessary. But horizontal training, to force the dormant eyes into growth along the length of the canes, is most important.

Shrub roses

These include Old Garden roses. Apart from the removal of twiggy wood and thinning out to avoid overcrowding, pruning is aimed at maintaining a symmetrical outline and avoiding bareness at the base. The aim is achieved by cutting back 1 or 2 main stems to within a foot or 15 inches of the soil as necessary. All prunings should be removed and burnt without delay.

Trees & Shrubs

March is one of the busiest months of any in the shrub border. The planting of deciduous shrubs can still continue. It is also a good month for getting in evergreens and conifers as well as evergreys and silver-leaved shrubs like lavender, rosemary, santolina and artemisia, all of which it is risky to plant in autumn or winter.

The shrub borders will look all the better for a light going-over with the hoe or border fork this month. This loosens the surface soil that will have been compacted by winter rain and/or snow. Such cultivation, however, must be only very shallow.

Mulching can begin now and continue throughout the summer months. Peat, partly rotted leaves, garden compost and lawn clippings all make good mulching material. It is not advisable, however, to use lawn clippings if the turf is very weedy or has recently been treated with selective weedkiller.

Quite a number of shrubs will need pruning in March. Newly-planted trees, too, should have their side branches cut back by about a third and their leaders lightly tipped. It is better, if possible, to cut back to that oft-quoted but elusive 'outward-pointing bud' to ensure that the tree or shrub under treatment develops a good shape with an open centre.

The shrubs that need pruning at this time of year are mainly those that flower on their current season's growth. In general, such pruning should be drastic for shrubs like *Buddleia davidii* (the butterfly bush), *Hydrangea paniculata, Caryopteris* x *clandonensis* (the blue spiraea) and for smaller aromatic shrubs such as *Perovskia atriplicifolia* (the Russian sage) and cotton lavender, *Santolina chamaecyparissus nana*. Many shrubs, however, will survive quite happily without energetic pruning.

The camellia buds will be starting to show colour, and this marks the beginning of the dangerous period where frost damage is concerned. The damage,

1

2

3

4

5

1 A firm support for a climbing plant can be provided by a stout trellis attached to the wall. A cane sometimes needs to be put in by the young plant until the growth is tall enough to be tied to the trellis.
2 When a trellis has to take the weight of much growth, as it does with Roses trained on it to form a screen, it is wise to erect the uprights in a base of concrete.
3 Fine netting can be hung over wall shrubs to protect them from frost or from the attentions of the birds.
4 Buddleia variabilis needs to be pruned back very hard early in the year.
5 The finished work looks clean.

1 Santolina chamaecyparissus nana is one of the shrubs that need pretty drastic pruning at this time of the year.
2 When Camellia buds start to colour, the danger of frost damage is likely.

which takes the form of petal-browning or bud-dropping, is most severe when a clear frosty night is followed by a bright sunny morning.

Much can be done to avert it if plants are sited on a north or westerly aspect, where the sun does not get to them until after mid-day. Syringeing the plants with cold water early in the morning is also a help.

Chaenomeles, the so-called 'japonica' or Japanese quince, will be opening its flowers early this month. These lovely wall shrubs flower on the bare wood, and bullfinches are very partial to the flower buds. They will strip the branches completely unless the plants are adequately protected. With a wall-trained specimen this is a simple matter. Netting can be draped over the branches to provide almost complete protection.

Supporting wires and trellises have an irritating habit of coming adrift just as the plants reach the peak of their flowering display. It pays, therefore, to anticipate trouble by checking all wall supports and putting any faults right now.

Poles, posts and pergolas, too, should be examined for symptoms of decay and any timber that is suspect should be renewed or reinforced. Supports for new climbers and wall shrubs should be put up at the same time as these are planted. Any such work is much more easily done when the wall plants are dormant.

For most clinging, twisting and twining shrubs, a simple wall support of wire netting, secured to vine eyes or wall nails, will suffice.

Heavier wall shrubs may need a wooden trellis. Ideally, this should be constructed of fairly stout oak battens. But compromise is often necessary and the expanding, ready-to-erect type of trellis sold in garden shops and hardware stores can be very effective.

These and any other similar maintenance tasks relating to shrubs and climbers should be completed, if possible, before the end of the month.

Vegetables

Most families find it more convenient to have a steady succession of vegetables than to have to cope with glut-filled periods.

The only exception is where a deep freeze unit is installed. Then one can clear the entire crop at once and this does away with the necessity of sowing, say, early, main crop and late peas. Most seedsmen offer varieties of many vegetables that are particularly suitable for deep freezing. But even with a deep freeze, you still need to maintain a steady supply of salad crops.

March gives the green light to go ahead with the succession programme. A reminder: seedsmen have more and more quickly maturing varieties, so study your catalogues carefully. For example, peas can be sown from now until the end of June.

Lettuce can be sown in their permanent positions at about three-weekly intervals; a good guide here is to sow when the previous sowing appears above the soil. By varying the type—cabbage, cos or the cos-cabbage cross such as 'Webb's Wonderful'—one can ensure a steady supply. Carrots, chervil and turnips are also successional crops.

In many cases it is more practical to raise seedlings in a specially prepared nursery bed and to transplant them later to their permanent quarters. By doing this one can use small areas: the border of a path, for instance, at the foot of fan-trained bushes or perhaps a raised bed near or between frames.

3 On sandy soils Broad Bean seeds can be dibbled in at stations, put in about two inches deep, during March.
4 The earlier sown Onions will be ready for transplanting now, and should be put in with a dibber, along a line.

A nursery bed is better drained and warmer if it is raised or mounded. The soil should be fine so that the shallow drills, only $\frac{1}{2}$-inch to $\frac{3}{4}$-inch, can be easily made.

It is important that the seed is sown thinly. Otherwise the seedlings will become crowded and drawn. Because of the competition, drawn plants produce strong tap roots that become broken when the plants are moved. This causes a check on the growth of the plants. To be really succulent it is essential for vegetables to grow quickly and smoothly without any such retardation. The plants should develop a mass of fibrous roots that can be lifted in a good root ball when the time comes for them to be

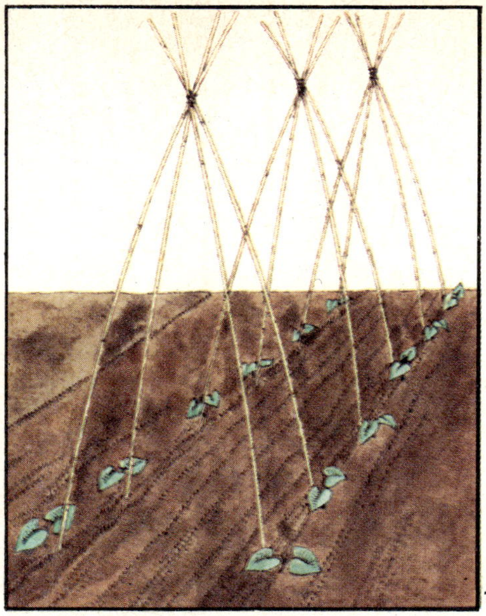

1

2

1 Once runner Beans have germinated and been thinned to the stoutest plant, canes for support later in the summer can be erected along the rows.
2 Lettuce seedlings can be thinned now as they become large enough to handle.

moved.

All the brassicas, cabbages, savoys, Brussels sprouts, broccoli, cauliflowers and kales are best raised this way, leeks also. The rows need to be only 6 inches apart and it is best to move the plants as soon as they have developed two real leaves.

It is important to make an early start with vegetables. It is even more important that seed should be sown only when the soil is in perfect condition.

As soon as the soil can be easily raked and drills drawn, and provided there is no strong wind, the following can be sown: early maturing varieties of stump-rooted carrots (there are good new introductions) to pull as soon as they are ready; cabbage lettuce, endive, spinach and onions to store, broad beans, early peas and, finally, parsnips and turnips if these have not already been sown.

Potatoes can be planted in the warmest part of the vegetable garden. Peas and broad beans that were sown earlier in frames and greenhouse should be gradually hardened by giving them ventilation as the days and nights become warmer. By the end of the month they should be ready to plant out.

During the last week of March annual herb seeds may be sown. These include bush basil, sweet basil, borage, chervil (this is best sown in succession from the beginning of the month), coriander, florence fennel (sow this in rows and treat as for parsnip), sweet marjoram, purslane (sow in rows and treat as for spinach) and summer savory.

Not all gardens, it is true, have a large amount of space which can conveniently be set aside and regarded solely as a place in which vegetables may be grown. At the same time, there are many people who would like to be able to grow enough of those vegetables which come in so usefully for salads, especially in the summer months, or perhaps produce some of the kinds that cannot easily be bought in the shops. So a little ingenuity must be exercised in creating such a space or spaces.

There are many places in the garden where vegetables can be grown near or even among other plants. Lettuce or spinach can be planted in a row behind a row of rose bushes. Beetroot is attractive enough to be planted in groups among annuals.

Runner beans, more especially the purple podded kinds, can be grown on tripods at the back of a border. Alternatively, they and marrows can be grown over a child's teepee made of lashed poles.

Lettuce, parsley, chervil, chives, carrots and beetroot can be sown in ribbons down the side of a path with flowers or perennial herbs behind them. Cut-and-come-again vegetables, such as the handsome Swiss chard and its coloured variety, 'Ruby Chard', and the oak-leaved salad bowl lettuce, can be grown in groups among flowers where they can stay until the summer's end.

Prepare the soil now to have it ready for those vegetables that should be sown later.

Water Gardens

Whatever signs of spring may be evidenced elsewhere in the garden, there are few so far in the pool, except for leaf growth on calthas (marsh marigolds) and the pinkish new shoots of the striped grass, *Glyceria spectabilis variegata*. Entwined among these might be found long strings of black-beads-set-in-jelly,

3

4

3 Lysichitum americanum is a striking and unusual plant for the waterside.
4 Hosta fortunei albo picta is one of the plants that enjoy being at the margin of a pool.

the spawn of toads. They usually appear about two weeks later than frogs.

If there is little else that demands attention in the established pool, opportunities will certainly exist for beautifying or improving the area around it. During open weather this month and next, rock plants and dwarf conifers and waterside perennials can be planted, as well as the marsh plants mentioned in The Month of February.

When an informal pool is constructed, the excavated soil is frequently built up at the side to form the foundation for a rockery. This resolves the problem of what to do with the soil and at the same time creates an opportunity to introduce the charm of a waterfall splashing down the rocks into the pool. The simple mechanics of such an arrangement are detailed in the notes for November.

It is appropriate to refer briefly now to those rockery or alpine plants that seem particularly suitable for association with a watercourse because their trailing growth flowing down the rocks repeats and complements the movement of the water.

Such plants as aubretia, alyssum, *Campanula poscharskyana* and *C.* 'Birch Hybrid', helianthemums, *Phlox temiscaming, Saponaria ocymoides* and *Thymus serpyllum albus,* if planted now, will clothe the rocks rapidly with growth and cascades of vivid colour. They are admirably complemented by the dark green of *Dryas octopetala* and sprawling conifers like *Juniperus sabina repandens. Cotoneaster dammeri,* a vigorous shrub with prostrate contour-hugging stems, rounds off the season with bright red berries.

Even where there is no rockery, many of these plants can be grown to advantage in gaps in the paving around the pool, to trail in the water and soften and disguise the edges.

'Waterside plants' is a term used to embrace those that do not grow within the pool proper but need an ample supply of water during the summer months and thus find conditions ideal on the banks of natural lakes and streams.

The soil around an artificial pool, having no contact with the water in it, does not provide the degree of moisture needed (unless an area is specially created). So the following plants are useful mainly for lake and streamside planting.

Few gardens nowadays can spare the room for that most impressive of waterside plants, *Gunnera manicata,* with 8-foot wide leaves on 7-foot stems, but a scaled-down effect can be achieved with such ornamental rhubarbs as *Rheum palmatum* and *Rheum emodi.* Both hostas and rodgersias are admirable for foliage effect, giving the lush, oasis-like character the water garden needs without demanding too much space. Pre-eminent among flowering waterside plants are the varieties of *Iris sibirica* and *Iris kaempferi,* particularly the Higo strain of the latter, which has massive, mostly double blooms.

Primulas are another invaluable moist-soil family, particularly in shady areas, where drifts of the candelabra varieties can be used to glorious effect. *Primula bulleyana* (buff-orange), *Primula japonica* (carmine), *Primula pulverulenta* (pink shades) and *Primula sikkimensis* (yellow) are very fine.

The double marsh marigold *(Caltha palustris plena)* grows as well in moist soil as in water, flowering profusely from March to May. A striking plant for the very edge of the water is lysichitum. Its 2 to 3-foot high flower spathe, hooded like a giant cuckoo-pint, and either yellow or white according to species, appears in April.

Other good waterside subjects, worth investigating in specialists' catalogues, are astilbe, aruncus, hemerocallis, lythrum, mimulus, miscanthus, peltiphyllum and trollius as well as such ferns as osmunda and matteuccia.

Weeping willows, showering leaves and twigs from a height of 50 feet, should be left to public parks and stately homes. *Salix wehrhahnii,* making bushy growth to barely 5 feet and spangled with April catkins, is not a weeper but a far better choice for modern gardens.

One plant only qualifies for planting in the pool this month, *Hottonia palustris,* the water violet. It has soft green submerged foliage and spikes of pale lilac flowers held above the water. It is temperamental, sometimes disappearing for 12 months after planting, and a nuisance to suppliers because it is seldom fit to plant at the same time as other oxygenators. But it is worth having and should be planted now if obtainable. If it is not available, order it now for planting when it is fit to move again, in October.

Wildlife

The exodus of winter birds emigrating to the north reaches its peak in March, and by the end of the month most of the summer residents will have arrived. The migrants that reached southern Britain in February have by now moved to the north of the country to give place to the swallows, martins, warblers and wagtails that come flying in from Africa.

The Wood Mouse or Long-tailed Field Mouse (Apodemus sylvaticus) starts to move about in the open garden again.

In the garden this tends to produce a fairly healthy balance between the insectivores and the insects—nature's way of keeping down the insect population to the benefit of plant life, and the gardener's.

The birds that remain—tits, robins, some of the thrushes, blackbirds and starlings—flutter around finding nesting materials. The thrushes and robins will have a brood of hungry mouths to feed before the end of the month.

In readiness for spring broods, clean out and repair any nesting boxes that you may have around the garden. If you are thinking of putting out new nesting boxes, fix them on the north side of trees so that the sun will not shine into them.

The many mice, voles and shrews begin to leave their runs, burrows, nests and holes in walls, tree roots, banks and barns to travel abroad again. And consequently the owls need to travel shorter distances and spend less time searching for their food.

The mice, shrews and voles on which the owls feed do not actually hibernate but merely hide in more sheltered spots during the winter. In the spring they come out of their burrows and travel about their runs.

Principal types of owl that use the garden for a hunting ground are the little owls and tawny owls.

The little owl was introduced to Britain from Holland as recently as 80 years ago and is now the most common owl but is seen less frequently than the barn and tawny owls because of its shyer disposition.

The tawny owl is the real hooter of the family. But this is not the only sound it makes, for both it and its smaller brother have a considerable vocabulary of shrieks, screams, whistles and plaintive 'pheets' which they employ according to circumstances.

Owls, hawks, weasels, stoats, foxes and other creatures generally manage to keep down the rodent population of the garden. Over a period of a few years they increase in numbers until a balancing increase of predators arrives to reduce them.

Underground, among the garden pests at work, is the European mole. The runs and mounds that scar the garden and uproot plants are not the mole's living quarters but the passages that it is for ever making to find enough food for its insatiable appetite. The real home of the mole is a large semi-spherical mound about 18 inches high and 2 feet across. In this is a network of tunnels and passages in which the boar and sow mate in March.

In wilder parts of the countryside—but surprisingly near houses on occasion—the sow badger has dragged into its enormous city of holes and passages new bracken fronds for the young that were born about the beginning of the month.

The Month of April

April may be a showery month but it has its share of warm sunshine heralding the approach of summer. The plants, too, feel that summer is on the way and there are many lovely blooms in the garden now.

Euphorbia robbiae, sometimes called E. amygdaloides, grows up to 2½ feet high.

1

3

2

4

1 Primula auricula, like all its kind, prefers a rich soil in a shady border. The flowers are usually in heads of about seven, like those of the Polyanthus. They come in many different and fascinating colours—greens, greys, reds, blues and yellows.
2 This showy little plant is Primula allionii. Like most of the true alpines, it grows close to the ground.
3 A dwarf variety of Doronicum, or Leopard's Bane, is 'Spring Beauty', an ideal plant for a tree-shaded border. The early-flowering Doronicums last well when cut for an arrangement.
4 The double Marsh Marigold, Caltha palustris, gives a most glorious display of the brightest golden yellow. This plant enjoys a moist soil and will do well planted around the edge of a garden pool.

1

2

3

4

1 There are a great many neat cushion-forming plants in the rock garden. This is Saxifraga jenkinsae and is one of the earliest to flower.
2 Viola calcarata is a delightful alpine Pansy, but when this plant is grown in gardens it is often very variable. The colour and form can change from garden to garden.
3 What glorious colour Aubrieta deltoides, the Rock Cress, gives to the rock garden. Its blossoms appear at their best when they cascade over the edge of rocks, as can be seen in this picture. The Rock Cress has many lovely forms and varieties.
4 Tulipa tarda, sometimes called T. dasystemon, came originally from Turkestan, and is a most attractive little plant.

1

2

3

1 The beautiful showy Tulipa greigii has produced many splendid hybrids, like this 'Oriental Splendour'. The blooms really seem to glow with rich colour.
2 This tulip is 'Sparkling Fire', another of the greigii hybrids. The attractive glaucous foliage, usually with purple-brown stripes, is a characteristic of these Tulips, which also have downy stems.
3 The Crown Imperial, or Fritillaria imperialis, prefers to be planted in a shady spot in the border. With its nodding, bell-shaped acid-yellow flowers this is a most beautiful bulbous plant.

1

2

3

1 Narcissus 'Sweetness' is a Jonquil hybrid. It is worth cultivating, not only for the bright, cheerful display it gives, but also for its delicious perfume.
2 Many of the new varieties of the Snake's Head Lilies, Fritillaria meleagris, have large handsome blooms and are strong growers.
3 Scilla campanulata has been cultivated in our gardens for centuries. It is very like the Bluebell, which is often seen growing wild in woods. The Bluebell, Endymion non-scriptus, is usually included in Scilla, but it is botanically a small separate genus.

1

1 The Ornamental Flowering Cherries are among the first to blossom, and what a really magnificent sight they present with their branches laden with blossom.
2 Magnolia kobus, a deciduous tree from Japan, is a joy for the gardener with chalky soil. This is one of the few Magnolias that will grow in these conditions.
3 The Malus, or Flowering Crab, produces very pretty blossom in spring and has the added attraction of often bearing richly coloured autumn fruits. Malus is a genus of about 25 species and almost every gardener will find one to suit any type of situation.

2

3

1

2

3

1 Cattleya 'Virtue' is one of the beautiful hybrids of this race. The Cattleya is a genus of about 70 species of epiphytic Orchids, natives of tropical America. In summer Cattleyas need a warm, moist shaded condition.
2 Freesias are South African cormous plants with heavily fragrant flowers. The fragrance is especially distinctive in the orange varieties.
3 'Globe', a handsome Cymbidium variety, with firm, thick-petalled flowers. Cymbidiums, a genus of orchids originally from north India, are much appreciated by amateur growers and the cut-flower producers mainly because they are of easy cultivation and require minimum heating.

Jobs of the month

April is a month when you will be busy with sowing, potting up and pruning. But it is also a time of year when insect pests become active. So make quite sure that you are as active with your spraying and fumigating. Many jobs in the garden, like pruning roses, depend very much on locality. But wherever you live, April *is* a busy month.

Bulbs

Narcissi should have dead flower stems cut off. Hand weed tulip beds. Sow lily seeds and complete the planting of lily bulbs. Lightly top dress gladioli at the end of the month

Flowers for cutting

Sow seeds for ornamental gourds. Young shoots are just right for flower arrangements – but need special treatment

Fruit

Spray to ensure pest and disease-free fruits. Cut back leaders of maiden plums. Start dis-budding established fan-trained peaches and nectarines. Pinch out any blossoms on new trees

Greenhouse

Increase the amount of water given to plants, including cacti. Stop fuchsias and pot on begonias and gloxinias. Pot up cyclamen seedlings. Sow seeds for tomatoes and cucumbers

Hedges

Prune flowering hedging shrubs. Hoe around newly planted shrubs. Keep a sharp look-out for caterpillars

Herbaceous plants

Plant out dahlia tubers. Sow hardy annuals where they are to flower. Feed plants with liquid fertiliser. Weed, dig and mulch established borders

House plants

Increase your stock of house plants by propagation

Lawns

Prepare the ground. Sow seed or lay turf for a new lawn. Give established lawns their first feed of the year. Deal with moss

Paths, fences and walls

Lay new paths that will be decorative as well as functional

Patios, balconies, roof gardens and window boxes

All planting should be completed. Supports for climbing plants must be ready

Rock gardens

Some of the easier grown plants can be divided. If you haven't done so, catalogue and label your plants. Seed of several rock plants can be sown

Roses

When pruning is completed, apply an organic fertiliser. Mulching with animal manure is best done this month to avoid breaking off young shoots that will have grown by May.

Shrubs, trees and climbers

Trees and shrubs will appreciate mulching. Clematis plants ex pots can be planted. Treat shrubs with systemic sprays to prevent aphids and red spider

Vegetables

Plant out broad beans and peas. Transplant brassicas. Seed sowing is among the month's main jobs

Water gardens

Complete new pools. Spring clean established pools. Build up fish to breeding condition. Place orders for new aquatic plants

Wildlife

Parent birds are busy feeding their young, so put out concentrated body–building foods

Bulbs

April is frequently a cold month and yet bulbous plants can always be relied upon to flower. Narcissi of all types, both miniatures and standards, are in bloom now and as the flowers fade the stems need to be cut off. This prevents the plant's strength from being diverted to seed production. Instead it reserves its energy for ripening the bulb and replenishing it with food for its dormant season.

The plant's foliage should not be cut down but is best tied in a knot so that the ground around can be cleared for summer flowering plants. All the early bulbs, like galanthus (snowdrops), crocus, eranthis (winter aconite), muscari and chionadoxa can be left to seed. There is no need to remove the dead flowers.

By mid-April the early single and early double tulips will be coming into flower, and at the end of the month the paeony-flowered and triumph tulips. Keep the beds in which tulips are coming into flower hand weeded, though an autumn application of a residual herbicide should have inhibited weed growth to some extent.

Lilies in pots still need protection from frost, especially at night. If they are in a cold greenhouse they must be grown as near as possible to the light to prevent them from becoming etiolated and drawn. Spray with a systemic insecticide to control virus-carrying aphids. The lilies growing out of doors will need hand weeding and the young growth must be protected from frost and early morning sunshine. If any bulbs remain unplanted, this operation should always be completed before the middle of the month.

To plant lilies by themselves for display in raised beds is a good idea. The water drains easily from well-prepared raised beds, simultaneously providing the lily bulb with the depth of top soil in which it flourishes best. Some of the larger plants need staking. This can be done at the time of planting, but it is usual to provide a small stake or marker and to replace this with a larger one as the stem grows. Lily seed—a cheap way of increasing your stock—can be sown in pans or boxes out of doors now, or the pans can be kept in a cold frame. But allow four years before expecting flowers!

Continue to plant gladioli corms during the month to provide a succession of flowers. Unless the spring is exceptionally dry, refrain from watering gladioli and encourage the formation of secondary roots. Once growth shows above the soil, hoe carefully around the shoots. Towards the end of the month a light top dressing of fish manure will be beneficial.

Corms of *Tigridia pavonia*, tiger

Hyacinths, like this 'L'Innocence', and other bulbs take a year or so to flower in the garden after indoor forcing.

flower, are also planted out after mid-April. Put them in 3–4 inches deep and choose a sunny, well-drained spot because they shrivel from dampness in poor summers—but are exciting scentless flowers to try.

The bulbs forced for indoor decoration will all be over and can be planted out in odd spots in the garden. These bulbs cannot be forced again, but will provide the odd flowers for cutting in later years if left out of doors. *Cyclamen persicum,* the florists' cyclamen, will now be going out of flower, so one must discontinue watering gradually and let the leaves die down.

In the greenhouse the seed of this cyclamen sown in boxes last autumn will have formed tiny corms. Now that their 2-inch pots are full of root each corm should be moved into a 3–4-inch pot. Keep the plants shaded and in a humid atmosphere until they have recovered from the check, and maintain a night temperature of about 50–55°F (10–13°C).

Flowers for cutting

Many trees and shrubs open their buds to show a gorgeous burst of colour before they settle down to the routine of summer greens. These young shoots, with their bloom-bright leaves and silken textures, should be used immediately for flower arrangements. But beware! Immature growth, once cut, does not take water well. It is sometimes possible to harden the young shoot by immersing it in water, but usually this only serves either to discolour or damage the leaves.

Some preparation is essential and a method which seems to assist all young shoots in the quick uptake of water is to stand the stem ends in two or three inches of boiling water. The stem ends should either first be split upwards for an inch or two or cut on the slant. They should remain in the water until it cools, by which time they are usually turgid. After this they must be arranged in fresh, unboiled water.

When one tastes the sap of some of these plants, maple for example, and realises that it contains a great deal of sugar it follows that a little sugar in the diet of cut branches might also help, and it does.

You can use a small lump of sugar, a teaspoonful of glucose or a saltspoonful of honey to a pint of water. Alternatively, use one of the commercial preparations, most of which are largely made up of glucose and a bacteria inhibitor. All will help succour the young shoots.

Because they are so soft and tender, blossom and young leaves tend to transpire at a quicker rate than the stem tissues can carry water to them. Because of this they often wilt badly after arrangement unless some special preparations are made. Most need some,

The basal-rooting Lilies should be planted about 4 inches deep in well-prepared soil which has been enriched with well-decayed leafmould.

Sprinkle more silver sand around the bulbs before finally covering them with soil. It is important to remember that Lilies are best planted in groups.

1 If foliage shoots are removed from round the flowers, Lilac will not wilt. Harden soft foliage stems by standing them in hot water.
2 Seeds of Ornamental Gourds should be sown now. The fruits are highly attractive for winter decorations and autumnal flower arrangements.

1

2

if not all, of the leafy shoots removed.

Lilac is a classic example of how the flowers will die if the leaves remain. Cut the leafy shoots away early, harden them in hot water and then arrange them with the flowers and neither will flag.

Cut-and-come-again plants are a good investment for flower arrangers and dahlias probably give the best value. They are wonderfully varied, from tiny single flowers to handsome double ones, some with pompon blooms small and dainty, some spiky and cactus-flowered, other water-lily like, some with inner collars of tiny contrasting petals—and all in a fabulous range of colours. Although dahlias should not be planted out until frosts are over, they should be ordered now. Many kinds, including the strange and exotic orchid flowered varieties, can be raised from seed and this should be sown now.

Hardy annuals can be sown outdoors and at the very end of the month half hardy annuals can be sown where they are to flower. These will not, however, flower so early as those which were raised in heat.

If there was no chance earlier to sow everlastings get some in right away.

Plant corms of gladioli. These are divided into early, mid-season and late, but staggered planting of a few at fortnightly intervals gives one a succession of blooms instead of one glorious glut. The smaller flowered varieties are usually best for home decoration.

Anemones, chincherinchees, outdoor freesias, montbretias, nerines and ranunculus can also be planted.

Ornamental gourds are highly decorative in autumn, winter and Christmas decorations. They need plenty of room to grow because they are climbers and trailers. They will clothe an old low wall, clamber over and hide a compost heap or climb up trellis, poles or wire netting. Seed of ornamental gourds should be sown indoors now.

Fruit

This is a month in which the garden fruit-grower finds he has much spraying to do if he wants healthy, pest- and disease-free fruits. These operations should be timed by the growth of the trees themselves, varying with season and local climate. A calendar can only give approximate dates. One golden rule is never to spray with a pesticide when the blossom is open. That would kill bees and other insects that assist by transferring pollen from one tree to another.

If pears are only now reaching the green cluster stage, spray with captan to control scab disease, adding malathion or derris to kill harmful insects. Repeat this spraying when the early white bud stage is reached.

Spraying tactics for other fruits are as follows:

Apples Spray between bud burst and the green cluster stage with a combined spray of fungicide and pesticide—lime-sulphur or captan to control scab disease, and with malathion to deal with tortrix and winter moth caterpillars, aphids, apple capsid and apple suckers. At the pink bud stage (which may be late in the month or early in May) repeat the captan or lime-sulphur spray to control scab, this time adding BHC to keep down apple sawfly and woolly aphis and dinocap to check apple mildew.

Plums Between the bud burst and white bud stage apply malathion or derris or some other combination spray to destroy aphids and caterpillars.

Currants At the late grape stage (i.e. when the trusses of the unopened blossom buds look like miniature bunches of grapes) spray with 2 per cent lime-sulphur to kill the gall mites responsible for 'big bud'. Spray again in 3 weeks' time with 1 per cent lime-sulphur, on this occasion adding derris to control caterpillars and insects.

Gooseberries Before the blossom opens spray with dinocap to keep down American gooseberry mildew, an extremely troublesome disease. Late in the month or early May (just after the berries have set) repeat the dinocap spraying against mildew, this time adding derris to keep down gooseberry sawfly.

Raspberries At the bud burst stage, early this month, spray with 6 per cent lime-sulphur or colloidal copper as a precaution against cane spot disease.

Cherries Between bud burst and white bud stages spray sweet and sour cherries with pesticide to control caterpillars and aphids. Malathion, derris or a combination spray may be used.

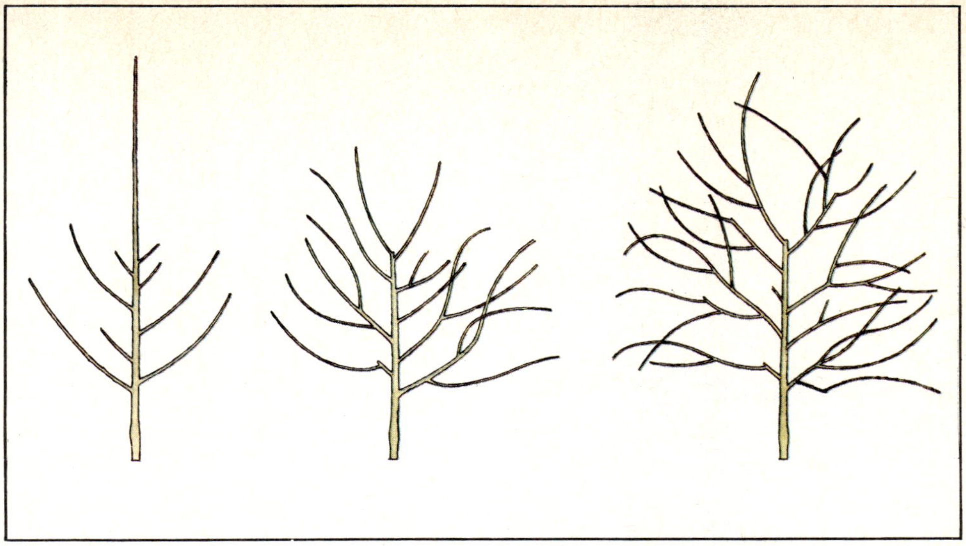

The maiden Plum tree is cut into a dwarf pyramid shape by pruning the leader, in the April after planting, back to about 5 feet. During the second and third years prune so that fruit-bearing branches are reasonably close to the ground. Remove laterals less than 18 inches from the ground. When strong growth has been formed, thin the tree during the summer months.

Peaches and nectarines As soon as all the blossom petals have fallen, spray with chlorbenside or derris to control red spider. Watch for this pest and repeat the spraying if necessary.

Strawberries Towards the end of the month spray with malathion to control aphids.

Because of the risk of infection by silver leaf disease avoid pruning plums, gages and damsons during the autumn and winter. Instead, pruning should be done in early spring when growth has begun or in late summer or early autumn immediately the fruit has been picked. At these times the risk is less because cuts heal over quickly. In any case, pruning should be minimal. Once the main framework of branches has been built up merely remove dead, diseased, crossing or damaged branches.

Where maiden plums have been planted to be grown as pyramids (excellent for the small garden), the leader should be cut back to 5 feet. Cut off flush with the central stem any laterals arising less than 18 inches from soil level and shorten others, if any, to half length. In subsequent years shorten the central leader each April by two-thirds of its length until a height of 9 feet is reached. Laterals will need attention in July.

Prune figs when the buds have begun to break and you can see which have survived winter frosts. Prune new trees fairly hard to build up a strong framework, then reduce pruning to a minimum to encourage fruiting. Tip young shoots, cut out dead or weak ones, but leave those showing embryo figs. With fan-trained figs, tip the leaders (the 'ribs' of the fan) in April and then pinch resultant laterals in mid-summer at the fourth leaf.

Start disbudding (removing unwanted growth) established fan-trained peaches and nectarines. Do not complete this task in one go but spread it over weeks, pinching off the sideshoots which grow out from the fruiting laterals until only two of these shoots remain on each lateral—one near the tip and one at the base. The latter will be next year's replacement shoot for fruiting—the sideshoot at the tip is simply a sap drawer.

When the peach and nectarine fruitlets reach marble size, start thinning, at first removing only sufficient to give those remaining space to grow.

Peaches and nectarines under glass should be syringed with clear water. This promotes healthy growth and keeps down red spider mites.

Keep down weeds, paying particular

1 Fan-trained Nectarines and Peaches must be controlled. Thin the laterals.
2 Pinch out sideshoots growing from the fruiting laterals, allowing only two to remain on each lateral.

1

2

attention to the soft fruits and young trees up to their first five years. Paraquat weedkiller may be used between trees and rows, but take care not to let any touch leaves or green shoots. This is only suitable for killing annual weeds easily. Perennial weeds, like bindweed, ground elder and dandelion should be given individual treatment with a hormone weedkiller applied with a brush.

If trees planted last winter produce any blossom, pinch it out—being careful not to remove leaves, too.

A fortnight after grapes have set, start thinning the berries in the bunches. Use sharp-pointed scissors and a forked stick to hold the bunch without touching the berries with the fingers.

Scatter slug pellets inside the rows of cloched strawberries.

Melons to be grown in an unheated greenhouse, cold frame or beneath cloches should be sown now.

All newly planted trees should be watered, as well as wall trees and soft fruit if there are drought conditions existing.

1

2

4

5

Greenhouse

April sees much faster growth in the plants in the greenhouse so make sure that all of them, including cacti, get increasingly more water now. If possible water them in the morning so that they are not wet and cold by night. In very hot weather avoid a dry atmosphere by wetting the floor and staging ('damping down') during the day.

Perpetual carnations in particular need frequent syringeing in hot weather, while those just coming into bud in cold greenhouses should be disbudded by removing all but the main central bud at the tip of each main stem.

Further sowings of summer bedding plants may be made now without artificial heat but they should be treated in the same way as the February and March ones, which must be pricked out as they become ready. Towards the end of April a sowing of zinnias may also be made in boxes or pots to provide plants for bedding or cutting. The much hardier antirrhinums, already sown and pricked out. can go into a cold frame, with plenty of air during the day and protection from frost at night.

If the frames are already occupied with pansies or violas these may be safely planted out, after they have first been hardened off.

Fuchsia and geranium cuttings can still be taken, while those rooted earlier will need potting up into 3½-inch pots of John Innes potting compost No 1. Geraniums need all the sunshine they can get but fuchsias are better in light shade on hot days. Fuchsias will need stopping at about 6 inches high if they have not already branched out.

Solanum capsicastrum, the Christmas cherry, is another plant that needs stopping—by pinching the young plants back to about 2 inches high when they have made 3–4 inches of growth. Some growers also stop the schizanthus, an operation which is usually advisable if the plants have not branched by the time they are about 6 inches high.

Begonias and gloxinias do not need

If Grapes are to grow large and succulent, they should be thinned two weeks or so after the fruit has set. When removing the crowded and small berries with grape scissors, hold the bunch with a forked stick.

3

1 John Innes No 3 potting compost should be placed in the base of a bottomless container that is standing on gravel.
2 First, the Tomato plant should be watered well, then allowed to drain before it is removed from the pot prior to being potted on.
3 The Tomato plant is stood on the potting compost and more is placed around the roots and worked in until the correct soil level is reached.
4 The old root ball and the surrounding compost should be of the same density, so the compost should be well pressed down and more added if necessary.
5 A stake is inserted at this point, well away from the root ball. Space is left in the pot for top dressings to be applied later in the season.

stopping but they must be potted on before they receive a check to growth, either into 3-inch pots of the J.I.P.1 from the boxes in which they were started, or into 5 or 6-inch pots if they are already in small ones. Both plants need shade from full sun and gloxinias also prefer a humid atmosphere.

As soon as cyclamen seedlings are about 2 inches high, with several leaves, pot them singly into 3-inch pots of the J.I.P.1 with the top of the tiny corm just level with the surface. Subsequent waterings will then leave it at the right level, with its upper half exposed. Water the seedlings in after potting but then keep them warm and fairly dry until growth starts again.

If dahlia tubers have not already been started, box them up immediately to provide cuttings. Cuttings can be taken from tubers started earlier as soon as the new shoots are about 2 inches high. Sever them close to the base and insert them in a warm, close frame.

Cuttings of the outdoor and greenhouse decorative chrysanthemum may also still be taken—the sooner the better—while those taken earlier must be potted up as they become rooted. Chrysanthemums for pot culture will be ready for their final potting early next month so make sure that pots, compost and crocks are all in hand.

In mild areas outdoor tomatoes should be sown now for June planting. Continue to prick out or pot up the earlier sown ones for greenhouse cultivation, then plant them out as soon as they are 6–9 inches high in deeply dug, well-drained soil, with plenty of compost or old manure well down and a dressing of a tomato base fertiliser in the top spit. Or ring culture can be carried out by planting in J.I.P.3 in bottomless containers on a layer of gravel. Make sure that the plants are moist at the root before putting them in, then water them sparingly. Do not allow the 'soil ball' to become dry.

Although not ideal companions for tomatoes, one or two cucumbers will yield enough fruits for domestic use. Sow the seeds $\frac{1}{2}$ inch down in $3\frac{1}{2}$-inch pots of moist J.I.P.1 and keep them in a temperature of 70°F (21°C).

Insect pests, such as greenfly, mealy bug and red spider mite, will be rapidly on the increase now. So spray or fumigate at the first sign of them.

Hedges

A hedge to a garden is what a frame is to a picture. As well as enhancing the beauty of what it encloses a hedge, when mature, will provide shelter, together with the privacy that is so important in the small contemporary garden.

The planting of a hedge, therefore, should have top priority when a new plot is being taken over. Coniferous and evergreen hedging plants can still be safely planted during April but unless they are planted ex containers and kept well watered for some weeks, deciduous shrubs are a riskier proposition.

Certain kinds of hedge will need trimming this month. Established hedges that bloom on the previous season's wood should have their flowering shoots cut out as soon as the blossoms have faded. This operation is best carried out with secateurs.

Clipping this type of hedge with the shears can result in an untidy, ragged look and may even inhibit its future

1

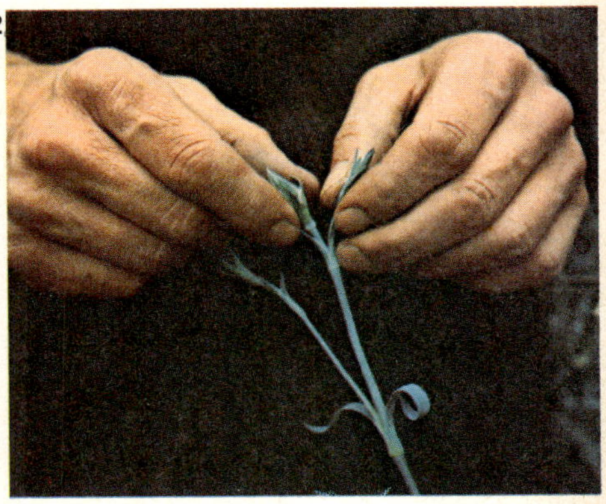

2

1 In very hot weather humidity can easily be provided by damping down the greenhouse floor and staging.
2 To produce fine blooms, Carnations should be disbudded. Remove all but the central, terminal bud.

RECOGNITION CHART

Weeds

Most weeds are common wild flowers, more welcome in hedgerow than garden. They are tough but can be removed by the right weedkiller

Sun Spurge, Euphorbia helioscopia, is an annual that flowers the whole season and is commonly found in both cultivated and waste places

Shepherd's Purse, Capsella bursa-pastoris, has distinctive seed pods. The roots can plunge deep. It flowers all year round. Probably the world's commonest weed

Common Speedwell, Veronica officinalis, is a weed found in dryish places. It flowers all summer

Groundsel, Senecio vulgaris, found abundantly all over Britain and Europe as a weed of cultivated places. The fluffy seeds blow away easily and germinate if the plant is not pulled up

Charlock, Brassica sinapis, is sometimes called Wild Mustard. A common weed of cultivation easily recognised by its bright yellow flowers and long seed pods

Mouse-eared Chickweed, Cerastium vulgatum, one of the commonest of weeds in the garden. Soft in growth and easily torn from the ground

Black Nightshade, Solanum nigrum, flowers in summer and autumn and produces black berries later. Sometimes the berries are green or a dingy red-brown

Lesser Bindweed, Convolvulus arvensis, has underground creeping stems and twines round flowering plants in the border and shrubs. It is hard to get rid of. Tearing out may spoil the 'host' plant itself

Dandelion, Taraxacum officinale, with bold yellow flowers, forms a rosette of leaves. Root plunges deep into the soil. Unsightly on lawns and grassy banks

Stinging Nettle, Urtica dioica, is a coarse-growing weed of waste places. It has a creeping rootstock and rough leaves that 'sting'

agwort, Senecio cobaea, a arse-growing eed of ltivated and aste land. It owers through-t the season, metimes until ry late in the ar

Creeping Thistle, Carduus arvensis, a weed with very prickly leaves. The commonest of all the Thistles found in Britain

Ground Elder, Aegopodium podagraria, is particularly persistent on heavy soils. Forking out small pieces of root repeatedly is the only way to eliminate it

Horsetail, Equisetum arvense, a weed that is difficult to eradicate, usually indicates waterlogged or starved soil. Best banished by improved cultivation

Curled Dock, Rumex crispus, is a tough growing weed of waste land and cultivated places which has a tenacious root that often snaps off when pulled flowering potential. Stems that have borne flowers should be cut back to new growths near their bases or to a conveniently placed dormant bud. The object of this exercise is to encourage fresh bottom growth and to maintain the hedge in good shape.

Among the hedging shrubs in this category that will need pruning this month are forsythia, chaenomeles (Japanese quince), *Kerria japonica* (Jew's mallow), *Mahonia aquifolium* (Oregon grape), and the popular flowering currant, *Ribes sanguineum*.

Shrubs that flower on their current season's wood need a different approach. With these, the procedure consists of cutting out wood that has flowered the previous season. With the majority of such shrubs, April is as good a month as any for the operation.

Buddleia davidii, the butterfly bush, varieties and species of cornus, hardy fuchsias, hypericums (St John's worts) sweet briar and tamarisk all need this kind of cutting back now.

Keep the hoe active on the sites of newly planted hedges in order to keep weeds in check. Mature hedging plants will act, to a large extent, as their own weed cover.

There is one species of weed, however, that is extremely difficult to eradicate once it gets a hold in the bottom of a hedge. This is ground elder, or bishop's weed as it is sometimes called. It spreads like wildfire by means of underground runners, some of which go down to depths of a foot or more and travel for very long distances.

In an open bed, ground elder can be got rid of by forking over and fallowing until every scrap of root and stem has been removed or has died from exposure. This treatment is hardly practicable where hedges are concerned. The only thing to do is to paint the leaves with a strong solution of selective weedkiller, taking care that none touches the foliage of the hedge itself. This is a long and tedious operation, but a very worthwhile one where serious infestation has taken place.

During April a careful look-out should be kept for caterpillar attacks. Beech, hornbeam and rose hedges are particularly susceptible to such attacks and the leaf-rolling caterpillars can be a serious menace to the young foliage of sweet briar and other hedging roses. They can be dealt with by squashing or, if the attack is severe, by the use of a systematic spray.

1

2

3

1 The hardy Fuchsias should be cut back, practically to ground level. This will encourage their new, strong shoots to grow better.

2 The shrubs that have flowered this spring must now be trimmed back to encourage the new growth that will flower next spring.

3 Buddleia davidii should also be pruned back now. Cut back all the long growths which flowered last year, ready for the dark lavender flowers.

Herbaceous plants

Dormant dahlia tubers can be planted outdoors towards the end of the month as long as they are protected by a cloche or polythene bags should the top growth appear before the frosts have passed.

Large roots may be divided where necessary, taking care that each piece contains growth buds. Plant in full sun, 3 inches deep, in ordinary garden soil enriched with well-rotted horse or cow manure, vegetable compost or spent hops. Apply a granular fertiliser high in potash content (potato fertilisers are suitable) about a fortnight before planting.

For garden display, space miniatures 12 inches apart, dwarf bedding plants and pompons 18 inches to 2 feet apart, all the medium types $2\frac{1}{2}$ feet apart, leaving 3 feet between the giants.

Medium and giant dahlia varieties need support. Stout stakes should be inserted at the time of planting to prevent damage to tubers. The dwarf bedding types—'Coltness Hybrids' ($1\frac{1}{2}$

Viola jackanapes is a good little plant for edging beds and borders. It needs to be planted 6–9 inches apart in rich, deeply dug soil.

An annual-filled border can be very gay. First, the soil should be well prepared, then marked off in areas for the different seed.

Make shallow drills for the seed and mark them with silver sand. Allow the drills to go in different directions so that the flower groups flow together.

feet), 'Dwarf Double Hybrids' (2 feet) and 'Mignon' strain with single rounded flowers ($1\frac{1}{2}$ feet) are delightful for massing near the front of a border, the plants continuing to flower from July until the frosts come.

As soon as the soil is friable and the weather favourable, hardy annuals should be sown where the plants are to flower. These quick growing plants are excellent for 'gapping' in a new herbaceous border where the perennials are still small. If the ground was not prepared last month, the area to be sown should be marked off with short sticks at once, the soil forked over and plenty of damp horticultural peat added to the top 2 or 3 inches. Soil for seed sowing needs to be very fine for good germination.

So the surface should be well raked down to a sand-like tilth before scattering the seed thinly, broadcast or in drills, just covered with soil. Twiggy sticks placed over the newly sown area will deter birds and prevent cats using the soil as a scratching ground.

Annuals that look well in a herbaceous border include larkspur 'Giant Imperial' (3–4 feet), malope 'Tetra Red' with trumpet-shaped flowers of carmine-red (3–$3\frac{1}{2}$ feet), godetia, tall varieties in shades of pink, carmine crimson and mauve (2 feet), dwarf varieties (9–15 inches), echium 'dwarf hybrids' in blue, pink and white—sometimes with all three colourings on one plant—(1–2 inches), clarkia (2 feet), agrostemma 'Milas', with soft lilac flowers that are beautiful for cutting (3–4 feet), clary *Salvia horminum* 'Colour Blend' ($1\frac{1}{2}$ feet), double 'Shirley' poppies ($2\frac{1}{2}$ feet), cornflower 'Blue Diadem' (2 feet) and the 'Tall Double' in blues, pinks, red and maroon (3 feet), calendula ($1\frac{1}{2}$–2 feet) and *Cosmos diversifolius* 'Goldilocks' which has golden-yellow star-like flowers and pretty fern-like foliage (2–3 feet).

Grey- and silver-leaved plants for colour contrast can be introduced into the border now: rosemary, lavender, senecio, *Cineraria* 'White Diamond' ($2\frac{1}{2}$ feet) with deeply cut white-felted leaves. *Santolina neapolitana* (2 feet), *Artemisia* 'Lambrook Silver' (3 feet), and for the front of the border lamb's ears *Stachys lanata*—12 inches.

Evergreens used as background hedging or dotted about the border provide an effective foil for the bright flower colourings, too: *Chamaecyparis lawsoniana* 'Green Hedger' or *Cupressocyparis leylandii* make superb hedging for a large border. *Lonicera nitida fertilis*, yew *(Taxus baccata)* and privet *(Ligustrum ionandrum)* are ideal for a medium-sized border. *Ligustrum delavayanum* is deep rooting so does not rob the soil of nourishment as much as most privets.

Newly planted evergreens should not be allowed to dry out during periods of cold wind. To prevent this happening the ground should be thoroughly watered and immediately covered with a mulch of bracken, rotting leaves or hay and the tops syringed regularly with a fine spray in heat or drought until the trees are established.

Plants that can be used as temporary background hedging are sweet peas trained over a thicket of tall twiggy sticks.

The seed can be sown this month now, 2 inches deep, 4–6 inches apart, in double rows 1 foot apart where the plants are to grow.

Violas and pansies can be planted out this month. Both make lovely edging plants spaced 6–9 inches apart in deeply dug soil enriched with rotted manure and bonemeal. Add a general fertiliser where manure is not available.

Belonging to the same genus *Viola* the sweet violet can be planted up to the end of April. Successful cultivation lies in planting the crowns 9–12 inches apart, in partial shade, in ground which has been liberally supplied with rotted manure, compost, peat and leafmould earlier in the year.

Paeonies should be given a mulch of

rotted manure or compost and bonemeal to encourage strong flowering crowns. When the buds turn brown and fail to open the trouble can usually be rectified by good cultivation together with a dressing of sulphate of potash applied at the rate of 1 ounce per square yard in spring or autumn. Shading them from strong sunshine after cold nights also helps. The plants benefit for feeding with liquid fertiliser or foliar feed from April to August.

Towards the end of the month you can plant pyrethrum *(Chrysanthemum coccineum)*, delphinium, lupin, cupid's dart *(Catananche)*—the flowers of this plant may be dried for winter decoration—*Scabious caucasica*, Iceland poppies *(Papaver nudicaule)*, the red-hot poker *(Kniphofia)* and *Tradescantia virginiana* in variety. The latter should be lifted and divided every three or four years if the plants are to bloom freely. *Scabious caucasica* does best in a sunny position, planted in well-drained soil with a high lime content. After planting, scatter slug pellets around—slugs and snails are a great nuisance at this time of year.

Given suitable weather, early-flowering varieties of chrysanthemums can be planted from the latter part of April onwards. Set the plants 15–18 inches apart in deeply dug and manured soil, watering the ground immediately afterwards to settle the soil around the roots. Hardy chrysanthemums wintered in the open can be lifted and divided now.

Finish weeding and forking over established borders as soon as possible, mulching the ground with rotted compost, manure or peat, together with bonfire ash if available.

1 Growth of herbaceous plants is rapid this month so finish weeding and mulching as early as possible to avoid damage to the fresh, young shoots.

2 Cacti need a fairly high light intensity to make them grow well and flower freely. They especially like very hot sunshine.

House plants

The days are now longer and warmer and as doors and windows are more frequently opened, indoor humidity is increased, so the house plants require less detailed attention and there is an opportunity of using them about the home with emphasis on their decorative value and less on their safety and comfort.

You can now group them wherever decor demands so long as the light is good enough. In general, tough leaved plants with dark green leaves can get along with the least light. These plants include aglaonema, araucaria, aspidistra, cissus, dieffenbachia, ferns, most of the philodendrons and sansevieria.

Flowering plants, cacti and succulents demand most light. The flowering plants should not as a rule be placed directly in the rays of a hot sun for long periods, but the cacti and succulents revel in as much hot sun as they can get.

This is also the time to begin increasing the number of your plants by propagating those you most like or those

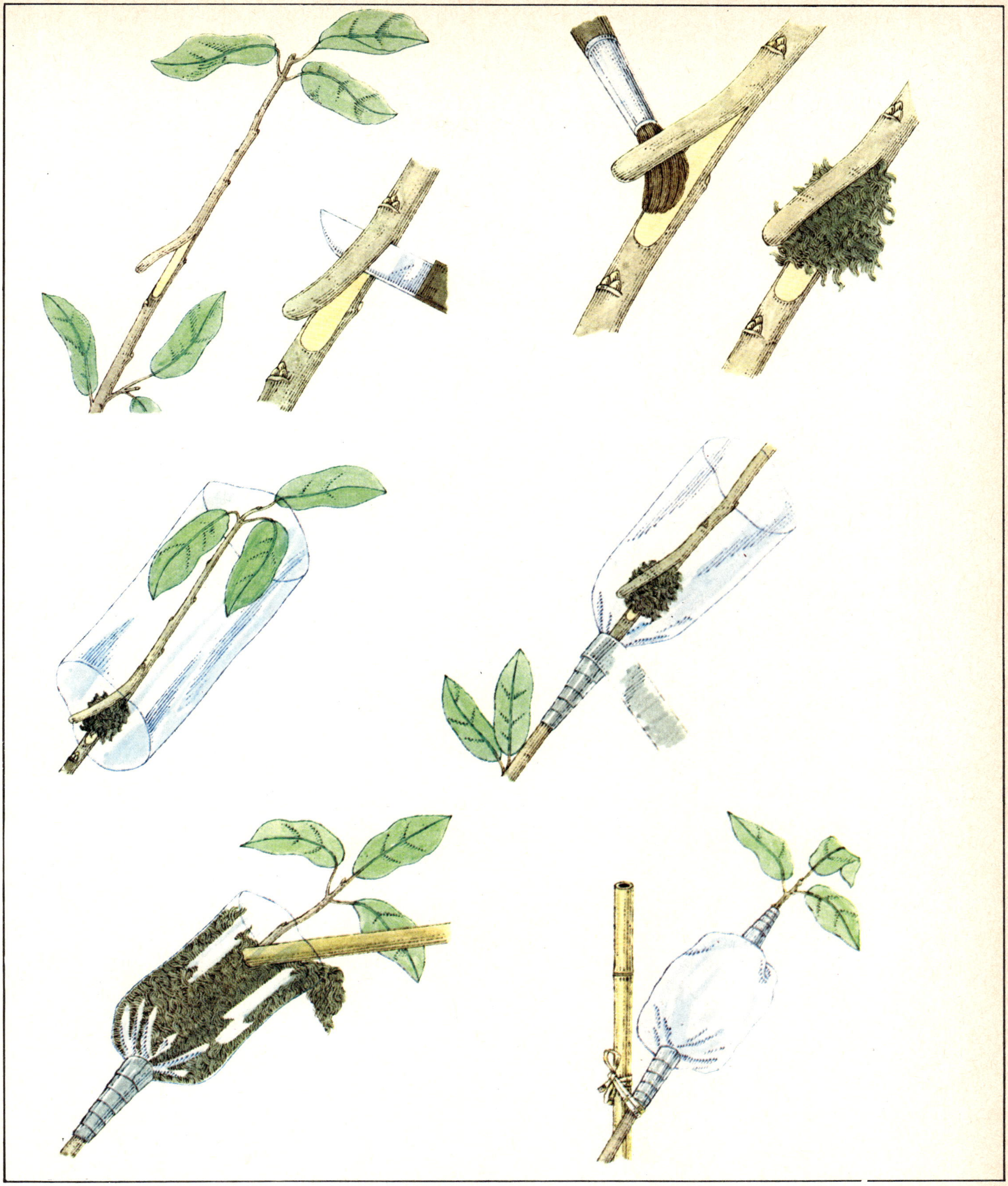

There is more than one method of air layering. Here is one that can be used to produce a new plant out of an old one. First, a tongue has been cut in the stem of the plant. The cut surface is then painted with a hormone powder to promote rooting. Then moist Sphagnum Moss is inserted under the tongue, against the cut surfaces. A tube of clear polythene is placed over the wound, packed with moss, then secured top and bottom. The plastic will keep the moss moist. New roots will grow into the moss and when they appear, or fresh growth starts, sever the new young plant from the old stem below the layer and pot it up in the usual way.

that do best with you. There are six basic methods of propagation; division, layering, air layering, stem cuttings, leaf cuttings and sowing seed.

Division is the easiest method, for it merely involves knocking the plant from its pot, separating the different sections, usually plainly visible, and planting each up in a separate pot in fresh soil or compost. If the roots cannot be separated by gently teasing them apart they may be cut carefully by using a sharp knife.

Plants with a growing habit most suited to this method of propagation include saintpaulia, sansevieria, aspidistra, practically all the many bromeliads, aglaonema, maranta and many of the ferns.

Once they have been properly divided and potted up, water them well and then leave them in a cool and slightly shaded spot out of all draughts until the plants are seen to be growing again, when they can be brought out and placed in their normal positions in the home.

Although layering is equally simple, only a very few common house plants are suited to this method of propagation. They include the chlorophytum, with its long arching sprays bearing baby plantlets at their ends, and *Saxifraga sarmentosa* with its hair-like runners. In each case the operation involves taking the baby plant and resting it in the centre of a pot of moist soil, pinning it down with a hairpin to increase the contact with the soil. Leave the baby attached to the parent until growth is apparent and then cut it away with a pair of scissors.

Air layering is a more complex business, but as there are frequently times when it is the only means of preserving an old plant past its best it is well worth learning. The most common use of this method is for restoring a rubber plant which has lost its lower leaves and is left with nothing but a tuft at the top. The plant may live quite happily like this for years but it is unsightly, so it is preferable to air layer it to obtain a fresh young plant.

At a spot on the main stem about 3 or 4 inches below the lowest leaves cut gently but sharply around the circumference of the stem, just sufficiently to penetrate the soft outer bark or skin. Then cut again a quarter inch below, so that you can remove the ring of bark between the two cuts. There will be a slight seepage or oozing of latex or sap. Dust a little hormone rooting powder into this cut and then surround it with a ball of very moist sphagnum moss, tying this very firmly into position with string.

As this moss will soon dry out unless it is protected and is difficult to keep moist, it must be protected with a piece of transparent plastic sheeting, closely tied around it at top and bottom to allow as little moisture as possible to escape

1 

2 

1 All the turves should be of a standard thickness and should be laid when the soil is reasonably dry. The turves are 'bonded'. This means that the joints are staggered, like the joints in a brick wall, and the turves should be laid in straight lines.
2 When applying a lawn fertiliser it is best to use a distributor. This ensures that the dressing is applied evenly as well as easily.

in the way of drips or evaporation. New roots will grow into this moss. When they appear through the plastic covering or are manifested by fresh growth at the top, the new young plant can be severed from the stem below and potted up in the usual way.

All the variants of the rubber plant and its relative *Ficus lyrata*, dieffenbachias and dracaenas can be propagated in this manner.

A point to remember: all these plants give off a poisonous sap, so always take care never to allow fingers moistened with it to come into contact with your mouth.

Propagation by leaf and stem cuttings and by sowing seed will be more successful under slightly warmer conditions, so it is sometimes better to leave them until May.

Lawns

The beginning of April is the time to complete preparing the soil surface prior to seed sowing or laying turves. Rough raking and consolidation should have been completed last month, and all that is necessary now is the final raking to create a good top tilth. An ordinary garden rake is suitable for turf laying, but a spring-tined rake is preferable for preparing the seed bed.

A light rolling will help to show up the obvious ups and downs of the surface and should ensure the ground is sufficiently consolidated to prevent an uneven lawn surface in future years.

To check finally whether the soil is as level as you would wish, a straight edged plank of wood moved over the surface will indicate any bumps and hollows that need levelling or filling. For a completely flat lawn area, a spirit level laid on the plank will tell you how accurate was your eye.

For sowing, the type of lawn seed mixture you have selected and the quantity required should now be to hand. The seed should be sown at $1–1\frac{1}{2}$ ounces per square yard and, for most lawn areas, the total quantity is best divided equally into two batches.

Choose a day for sowing when the top

1 inch of soil is dry but the soil below is moist, and when there is not a strong wind to blow the seed in all directions. Then, taking one of the two batches of seeds, walk up and down the lawn area scattering the seed from side to side. Follow this by walking at right angles to the first sowing, scattering the second batch of seed from side to side. Alternatively, a wheeled seed distributor can be used, again in two operations for transverse application.

When seeding large lawns, or for very accurate sowing, the area can be marked out in grids, and the appropriate weight of seed applied transversely to each marked out area.

A very light raking with a spring-tined rake should follow seeding. To keep birds and cats off the newly sown area, the best answer is the old-fashioned, but very effective method of criss-crossing of strong black thread supported on sticks and twigs.

Next comes a 2–3 weeks' respite, after which time the new grass should be 1–1½ inches high. The thread should then be removed and the whole area given a very light rolling in order to consolidate the soil surface lifted by the germinating seeds and to encourage the young grasses to produce new side shoots.

About one week later, the new lawn will be ready for its first mowing, which must be with the mower blades really sharp and set at least 1 inch above ground level. Thereafter, mowing should take place regularly, though the grass should never be cut too short in its first season.

Creating a new lawn from turves is popularly believed to be the easiest and quickest method of achieving a satisfactory green area; and so it is, if good quality turf is used. Unfortunately, this is usually in short supply, and it is advisable to purchase only British Standard Specification turf, which has to conform to a high standard. Poor quality turf can rarely be improved after laying, and will usually prove permanently unsatisfactory, never making a first-class lawn.

Starting a lawn from seed will give much better results in the long run, even though it takes longer to establish and involves rather more work. High quality turves should be of a good colour, uniform density, have a close texture, be in mown condition and free of weeds, diseases and stones.

Turves are normally sold in 1 foot squares or 1 foot by 2 feet or 3 feet lengths. They should be of standard thickness, usually 1¼ inches. If the turf varies in thickness, it pays to get all the pieces to the same thickness before laying. This can be done by placing them, face down, in a box of suitable depth and cutting off excess soil with a sharp, stout knife.

When delivered, the turves will be rolled and stacked. They can remain like this for 24–48 hours only. If a longer period is to elapse before laying spread the turves out in a shady place to prevent the grass yellowing and keep them watered in dry weather.

Turves are best laid when the soil is reasonably dry. The most satisfactory method is to start along the front side of the area, and to lay the turves in straight lines, working in a forward direction. The turves should be 'bonded', as when brick-laying, and should abut closely to their neighbours.

If any of the turves seem too high or too low, alter the soil level below the turf to get it level. If the turf has to be cut to fit awkward corners or curves, use a sharp knife. Planks of wood should be placed on newly laid turf for foot and wheeled traffic, to prevent marking or harming the grass.

When the area is completed, spread a 50/50 mixture of sand and coarse peat along the joints, and work this in with a broom. Follow by lightly rolling the turves to ensure their complete contact with the soil below.

As with new lawns from seed, the grass should only be 'topped' initially, and should never be mown closely during the first season.

Any spring-sown or -turfed lawn should be looked after with care during its first summer. It cannot be expected to withstand normal usage or hard wear and tear until its second year.

April is the time for giving an established lawn its first feed of the year. A reputable compound lawn fertiliser, applied at the rate recommended by the manufacturer, is the easiest method. It can be scattered by hand or applied with a wheeled distributor.

Moss is often a problem, particularly on damp, shady parts of the lawn. A proprietary mercurised or sulphate of iron lawn sand should be applied during the first week of April when the ground is moist. Take care not to apply lawn sands during drought and water the lawn thoroughly if no rain has fallen two days after treatment. Two or three weeks later, rake up the dead moss and apply a lawn fertiliser.

Grass should be cut often enough during April to prevent it growing too long but still not lower than ¾–1 inch.

Paths, fences and walls

As the spring progresses and the various colours, shapes, forms and textures of growing plants increasingly furnish the garden, the paths sometimes take on a somewhat bleak and stark appearance. In just the same way that an entire border of antirrhinums would be monotonous, so a length of unrelieved paving can be dull and uninteresting. However, there is much that can be done to give it added decorative value.

Although a crazy paving pathway is more difficult to lay well than one where all the slabs have easy right angles, its rustic air goes well in an informal garden. More practical is the path or paved area with edges or surrounds of formal paving, perhaps coloured tiles or

This area is to be laid with pebbles. These must be laid in concrete, so this needs to be spread over the base of the site and round the sides, too.

The pebbles should be laid as evenly as possible. The easiest way to achieve this is to lay a board over them and hammer it gently.

Finally, thoroughly wet the surface of the pebbles to make quite certain that every trace of concrete sticking to them is washed off before it sets.

bricks on edge, with a crazy paving centre. This avoids the difficulty of getting a straight and even line to the edges.

Differences in texture and colour add interest, so in a long path or a considerable expanse of paved area ring the changes. Where you have formal York stone paving insert a rectangle of cobble stones or pebbles, even a slab of a different colour. Lay a rectangle of concrete and before it dries brush the surface with a stiff bristled brush to expose the aggregate. Leave the occasional small space in the paving for a little plant of thyme or a miniature dianthus. In certain areas you can even sow a little grass seed in the cracks between the paving slabs to get straight lines of grass growing through. This can easily be clipped and controlled with shears.

Cobble stones or granite setts and pebbles are easily obtained from any good stone supplier and samples are usually to be seen at garden centres. Cobbles and granite can be laid directly into a sand or soil base, although this must be done carefully if they are not to move.

Pebbles must be laid in concrete. If they are not to be dislodged and so leave an unsightly gap they should be laid vertically rather than horizontally, with the greater part of their surfaces buried beneath and held by the concrete and only a small portion showing above. They should be as even as possible. A board laid over them and hammered gently so that the stones sink evenly into the wet concrete will achieve this.

Try to use contrasts of materials in logical places—at a corner or junction, as a border to a sitting-out area, as the surround of an island tree, on the edges of a pool. Use them with discretion, not with such frequency that they appear almost to be a stone merchant's catalogue.

Bricks, with their strong colours and rough textures, are an excellent contrast to paving slabs and are particularly good as edgings. Choose hard bricks of the engineering type, for some of the softer bricks absorb water and are apt to crack and break in winter frosts. Lay them always on their edges rather than flat and practise laying them in formal patterns of many available designs before you incorporate them in the pathway or the terrace paving.

Bricks frequently mellow with age and some will grow a special moss, attractive to the eye and comparatively safe under foot except in very wet weather.

Patios, balconies, roof gardens and window boxes

Because gardening on patios, balconies, roof gardens and in window-boxes demands for the greater part planting in containers, it is usually a little ahead of the normal garden and by now plants will be showing signs of strong spring growth.

The aim in April should be to have all preparations made and plantings completed so that the area, whatever it may be—even window-boxes—is clothed. Make sure that all wall surfaces are ready to receive and support the climbing plants that are already beginning to cling to the bases of the walls.

Patios and roof gardens depend largely on climbing plants for their effectiveness and most have some wall or railing on which to train the plants. It is surprising how many climbers can be grown in window-boxes to surround and frame the window and climb along the face of the building towards an upper floor. In normal circumstances the root space for these climbers will be confined, so select subjects that will grow well with a narrow and shallow root system, accept occasional hot and dry soil around the roots, climb with the minimum of support and give lavishly of some sort of vegetative colour.

Containers for patios can vary considerably. The only essential is that there is sufficient depth of soil to nourish the plants.

Many types of Narcissi make good pot plants and provide spring colour in odd corners out of doors. The variety 'Geranium' is bright and fragrant.

Wall surfaces for patios, roof gardens and balconies are usually comparatively accessible. Trellis or wires can be fixed to them for climbing plants and as the plants develop they can be given normal care and attention. But climbers growing in a window-box may sometimes have to be left almost entirely to their own devices once they have been planted, for it may be physically impossible to get to the outer wall to train them in the way that you wish them to grow. So subjects for window-boxes are considerably more limited.

One of the best subjects is ivy. It grows easily, clings to a wall without support, makes a comparatively small root ball, cheerfully accepts dry and hot roots for remarkably long periods, and is evergreen yet gives lavishly of its foliage, which can be gold, white, silver and in some cases a soft purple-pink. Almost as good is the Virginian creeper, *Ampelopsis* or *Parthenocissus*, which is deciduous but gives lavishly of its tender green foliage early in the year, later changing to fiery red. It is also a self-clinger. Jasmine and honeysuckle are two other climbers suitable for window-box culture, though both of these must have some sort of support. All the plants in this group will grow well in any aspect, not caring particularly whether they get sun or shade.

The question of sun or shade is important for many climbers and doubly important where they are to be grown under the artificial conditions imposed on them by special locations. In the open garden it is sometimes possible to provide shade for the roots of, say, a clematis, while letting the shoots climb up to the sun. But where the plant must grow in a container on a south-facing patio or roof garden there is little that can be done effectively to give a cool root run to the confined base of the plant, which may become warm and dry even though artificially shaded.

It is therefore best to choose plants carefully according to their aspect. On the other hand, if a special plant is desired (say a clematis again) despite a restrictive aspect it is worth trying to grow it in a large tub or pot, this being plunged inside a larger container holding moist peat or some other similar water-absorbent medium. Both inner and outer container may be protected from the moving sun by a leafy shrub or even a patio lounging chair, a table or, on really hot days, a strategically placed sunshade.

Where restrictions do not apply and there is a good south or west facing wall, there is a considerable choice of climbers that can be effectively grown on a patio or roof garden. They include such exotics as the passion flower, climbing roses, actinidia, coronilla, wisteria, bignonia and solanum as well as annuals such as *Cobaea scandens* and eccremocarpus. The latter is really a perennial but is so easily grown from seed that it is largely treated as an annual. These are all wonderfully attractive plants that flourish very well in artificial surroundings.

Given moderate protection, it is possible to grow the vivid orange trumpet vine, *Campsis grandiflora*, and on a longer term basis it is frequently worth trying the climbing hydrangea, *H. petiolaris*.

Both of these plants will, after initial training, cling to a suitable wall surface themselves without the need for additional support unless situated where winds whip around corners and prevent them getting a good hold.

Always take account of wind on artificial sites. On a patio it is usually possible to erect or grow some kind of a barrier or shelter, but this is seldom the case with a roof garden or a window-box on a balcony. Yet these are the sorts of site where winds are most felt because there are corners that they can whip around or their force is funnelled and therefore concentrated.

1

2

1 Even the very smallest rock garden can accommodate little conifers. Care should be taken, though, to ensure that these are properly sited, with the upright columnar types on the lower levels. The rounded forms should be in the middle levels and the prostrate types on the higher levels.
2 This beautiful blue Gentiana sino-ornata can be divided now. It looks best if it is planted in a bright, sunny position in the rock garden.

Rock gardens

All planting should be completed during April. Although the majority of rock plants are sold in pots and can be planted at almost any open period of the year, this is the best month. The plants are beginning to grow vigorously, the roots are active and they have the whole of the growing period to re-establish themselves.

Plants obtained from the open ground should also be planted this month. Early April for the herbaceous types and late for the evergreen. They should be well watered in and not allowed to dry out during the period of re-establishment. If cold drying winds are still prevalent, protection must be given, especially to the evergreens. Hessian erected on the leeward side of the rock garden will materially help.

A number of the easier grown plants can also be divided at this period. The following are representative of this group: *Anagallis tenella*, bog pimpernel; *Arenaria caespitosa* 'Aurea', *A. verna* (sandworts); *Asperula nitida* (woodruff); most dwarf astilbes; *Calceolaria tenella; Caltha* species (marsh marigolds); a few campanulas such as *C. carpatica* and its varieties; *C. 'haylodgensis* Fl.Pl.'; C. 'Kewensis'; *C. poscharskyana* and *C. raineri; Gentiana sino-ornata; Gypsophila cerastioides; Helleborus niger* (Christmas rose); *Hutchinsia alpina; Mazus reptans* and many others with tufted growth.

Dwarf conifers are a must in even the smallest of rock gardens and if properly sited enhance the scenic view. The upright columnar forms should be planted on the lower levels not, as often seen, at the apex of the rock garden. The rounded bun-shaped forms should be planted in the middle heights and the prostrate on the higher reaches. A word or two of warning. There are very few really dwarf forms and often the general public are offered specimens between 9 and 12 inches high that will become veritable giants in the course of a few years. When removed, and this will become inevitable, they create havoc in a well established rock garden.

A dwarf conifer on its own roots about 9 inches high could be in the region of 20 to 30 years old. So these are not cheap to buy. Two tips that will help. A visit during the first week of July to a nursery specialising in these plants will enable one to assess the annual growth quite easily. With a little mental arithmetic the overall average growth for a given number of years can be ascertained. Planting the conifer without removing it from its pot will restrain growth for a long period by root restriction.

The following plants can be relied upon not to outgrow their position for at least 10 years: *Abies balsamea* var. *hudsonia*, bun shaped; *Cedrus libani*, 'Comte de Dijon', dwarf tree; *Chamaecyparis obtusa* 'Caespitosa', *C. o. minima*, compact bun forms; *C. pisifera* 'Nana', blue/green bun; *Juniperus communis compressa*, the well-known Noah's ark juniper (columns of glaucous grey/green needle-shaped leaves); *Picea abies* 'Gregoryana', a dwarf spruce; *Pinus sylvestris* 'Beauvronensis', a dwarf form of Scots pine.

If a comprehensive collection of rock plants is being grown, labelling is a necessary evil. There are many types of labelling available and which is the most satisfactory type is open to question. One method that is simple and very effective is what, for a better name, is called the number system. A small book or pad is ruled up and numbered 1 to 100 (or more if necessary) and the name of the plant entered against each number.

The labels themselves can quickly be made by obtaining blanks of plastic or zinc about 2 inches long. The numbers corresponding to the names in the register are stamped out on a readily obtained machine that embosses the number required on an adhesive backed tape. The covering is removed and the numbered piece of tape is fixed to the label. A test carried out over a period of five years has shown no deterioration in this type of label.

Seeds of rock plants can be sown during this month, especially those of the easy species and varieties. The rarer are best sown when ripe, including all those that produce very small seed, for their viability is limited.

John Innes seed compost is suitable for the easy subjects. Seed pans are preferable to wooden flats mainly because they provide a more uniform temperature and moisture content. All pans must be cleaned before use, then crocked to a depth of 1 inch over which a thin layer of peat or leaf-mould roughage is placed to prevent the compost from filtering down and blocking up the drainage. The pan is then filled to within ½ inch of the top and made firm. The seed should be sown thinly, covered with a light sprinkling of coarse sand and firmed. The pans are then partially immersed in water and left until the surface darkens, when they should be removed and allowed to drain.

Unlike many of the rarer species the seeds will begin to germinate in 2–3 weeks. During this period the pans should not be allowed to dry out and if possible should be covered either with glass or asbestos sheeting to help retain moisture. They should be inspected at frequent intervals and once germination has taken place the covers should be removed.

Early spring flowering plants such as aubrieta, trailing arabis varieties and alyssum should be cut well back to help them retain a compact habit.

Roses

In Scotland and the northern counties of England rose pruning will often not be completed before the middle of this month, although this is normally late for the southern counties and the West Country. The prunings should always be gathered and burnt, the resulting ashes being sprinkled over the surface of the beds. Provided they are kept quite dry, these ashes have a useful potash content.

After each bed or border has been pruned it is labour-saving to consider combining the pricking over of the trampled down surface with feeding and mulching. How this will be tackled depends very much on the type of feed available. For the fortunate gardener who has access to a supply of farmyard or stable manure, it may be sufficient if a dressing of sterilised bonemeal or meat and bonemeal is applied at the rate of 3 or 4 ounces per square yard, together with a lighter dressing of hoof and horn at 2 ounces per square yard. These organic fertilisers are slow-acting, and will gradually release their nutrients over many months.

The fertilisers should be pricked in with a border fork. Take care not to penetrate the soil more than an inch or so to avoid injuring valuable feeding roots. The mulch of animal manure is usually best applied when the soil has begun to warm up, which may not be before the early part of May, depending on the district where the garden is.

After the strong winter gales, all Rose tree stakes should now be tested and the ties should be adjusted wherever necessary.

But the snag about leaving the mulch of animal manure until well into May is that, by this time, the new shoots following pruning will often be quite long and very brittle. However careful one may be in spreading manure at this stage, many shoots are bound to be broken. On balance, therefore, mulching is probably best undertaken about the middle of April in the south and early in May in the north.

Most amateur rose growers are unable to obtain supplies of animal manures, or else they find the cost so high that they cannot use them every year. Where this is the case, it will still be necessary to use organic material as a surface mulch. This may take the form of granulated peat, fortified hop manure, leafmould, garden compost, spent mushroom compost (except on alkaline soil) or even old chopped hay and straw.

With these materials it is normally advisable to apply a complete rose fertiliser, and it is convenient to apply this to the surface of the soil immediately before applying the mulch. Tonks' Fertiliser is recommended as being well-balanced for nearly all soils. It is clean to handle, being a fine, odourless inorganic powder, and it should be sprinkled evenly over the soil surface at roughly 2 ounces every square yard. The mulch of organic matter needs to be not less than 2 inches thick to be effective in conserving moisture. If granulated peat is used, this should be moistened thoroughly before applying it to the surface of the soil. Otherwise it would absorb any rain or cause it to run off, in either case preventing it from reaching the roots.

Some gardeners may prefer to buy the ingredients and mix their own inorganic fertiliser. This does work out cheaper than purchasing complete fertilisers. The following formula will be found satisfactory on most soils:

	Parts by weight
Superphosphate of lime	16
Sulphate of potash	10
Sulphate of ammonia	5
Sulphate of magnesia	2
Sulphate of iron	2

The ingredients should be thoroughly mixed on the day when it is intended to apply them. All lumps should be crushed to a fine powder. Uneven mixing should be avoided as this, of course, is tantamount to varying the formula. The complete fertiliser should be sprinkled evenly over the surface of the soil, but it should not be allowed to fall on the wood or the leaves of the roses. If the weather is dry at the time of application, the fertiliser should be pricked in with a border fork and watered well. When feeding rose beds it is always well to bear in mind that nutrients can only be absorbed in solution, which is why it is essential that dry fertilisers should always be watered in.

April is a suitable time of year to test for firmness the stakes and ties of standard roses and the supports of pillar roses before the plants are in full leaf, when they will offer much greater wind resistance and be more vulnerable to gale damage.

In renewing the stakes of standards, ensure that they are long enough, when driven well home, to come right up into the head. This will provide greater support and allow two or three of the main stems forming the head to be tied to the stake for additional support in exposed gardens. The ties should preferably be of tarred twine or insulated cable for durability.

A strip of felt—old carpet underfelt is suitable—should be wrapped round the stake and the standard stem in figure-of-eight fashion before securing the tie to protect the bark of the stem against damage from chafing.

Shrubs, trees and climbers

During the month of April things really begin to get under way in the shrub garden. Many beautiful shrubs will be in bloom, among them the early-flowering viburnums which are noteworthy for their flowers and fragrance.

Among the best of these are *Viburnum carlesii* and its named cultivars, all of which have a scent reminiscent of clove carnations. The pink buds of the type open to pure white. 'Aurora' and 'Diana' both have reddish buds, opening to apple-blossom pink.

Of the hybrids, the most widely grown is *V.* x *burkwoodii*. This is a strong-growing carlesii hybrid with clusters of fragrant white flowers on arching stems. *V.* x *carlcephalum* is another carlesii progeny. It produces its creamy-white flowers in globular clusters. Their scent is like that of heliotrope and equally penetrating.

The spiraeas, too, have several lovely April-flowering species. Early in the month the arching sprays of *S. thunbergii* will be festooned with tiny white flowers, while later the hybrid *S.* x *arguta*, the aptly-named bridal wreath, will put on a similar display.

Trees, too, will be starting to make their colourful contribution to the garden display. *Amelanchier canadensis*, the snowy mespilus, is a small ornamental tree with flowers like those of the gean, or bird cherry, which it displays against a background of coppery young foliage. Some of the earlier Japanese cherries will also be in bloom, including the well-known pink-flowered *Prunus sargentii* and *P. yedoensis* (Yoshino) whose arching branches smother themselves in pale pink buds that turn to white as they open.

Magnolias could be classified as small trees or large shrubs, but under either heading there are two species that are among the outstanding glories of the garden in April. The cultivars of *Magnolia soulangeana*, often incorrectly referred to as the 'tulip tree', bear their large flowers on bare branches. This seems to accentuate their beauty. The white form, *alba*, is one of the finest, but many gardeners prefer the purple-stained cups of 'Alexandrina' or the rosy-lilac petals, white on their insides, of *M. s. lennei*.

Clematis montana is one of the most vigorous climbers, growing to between 20 and 30 feet high. There are several varieties. This is 'Rubens'.

But perhaps the loveliest of all is *M. stellata*, the star magnolia, with its masses of whiter-than-white star flowers. There are two pink forms, *rosea* and *rubra*, but they lack the immaculate beauty of the type.

Magnolias greatly resent root disturbance and neither spade nor fork should be used in their immediate vicinity. Where cultivation is concerned, even hoeing should be avoided and it is best to play safe and suppress weeds with mulches.

Mulching is valuable for all trees and shrubs and the process can start in April and continue throughout the summer months. As well as conserving soil moisture, mulches add to the humus content and step up soil fertility.

To be effective mulches should be several inches in thickness. Lawn mowings make a good summer mulch, but they should never be used immediately after the turf has been treated with selective weedkillers. They must, in any case, be kept well away from the base of stems and branches. Grass mowings heat up rapidly in hot weather and could cause bark damage.

On walls and pergolas, the evergreen *Clematis armandii* will be opening its clusters of creamy white flowers. These will soon be joined by the vanilla-scented blossoms of *Clematis montana*. The best forms to plant are the rosy-pink *rubens* or the named pink variety 'Elizabeth'.

All clematis will be making vigorous new shoots and these should be carefully tied to their supporting wire or trellis. They should not, if possible, be allowed to tangle with the previous year's growth as this will have to be cut back hard after the earlier-flowering species have finished blooming.

New clematis plants from pots can still go in during April and early May. Clematis need firm planting with the top of the ball of soil (from the pot) two inches below soil level. Newly-planted specimens should be pruned to within 6–9 inches of ground level. A north- or west-facing aspect is the one that suits clematis best.

The aphids or greenfly and the dolphin or blackfly attack many shrubs at this time of year. They can cause serious damage to young shoots and can considerably weaken newly-planted specimens. There is, as well, an added hazard in the spread of sap-borne virus disease

Magnolia stellata is a glorious shrub and is one of the best of this tribe for the small garden. It really gives a striking display of blooms. The flowers are early to open and then follow one another in very quick succession after frost damage. This is a shrub well worth cultivating.

in the case of sap-sucking insects such as these.

Both greenfly and blackfly can be controlled by malathion sprays or one of the newer systemic insecticides. Red spider, another pest that causes much damage to certain shrubs in hot dry spells, is more difficult to cope with since the mites feed on the undersides of the leaves. Malathion or derris sprays give effective control but the spray must be directed at the undersides of the leaves where the red spider mites congregate.

Vegetables

The soil should be warmer and dryer now, receptive to many seeds that need kinder conditions than prevailed in February. Seeds that for some reason or another could not be sown then can now go in. Successional sowings should also be made.

To these add globe beetroot, quicker to mature than the long-rooted type. This can be made a still earlier crop by sowing some of the new varieties. All beet leaves are edible. Those who do not want the roots should grow spinach beet. If you object to the coloured leaves, which turn almost green when cooked, grow 'Cheltenham Green Top', a long-rooted storing variety with green spinach-foliage.

As the early maturing carrots should have been sown last month, the main-crop types should go in now and on until June. If you missed the boat sow some of the early maturing kind as well. Any seed remaining may also be sown at fortnightly intervals and pulled young. The other varieties are best left to mature in the ground and lifted later for storing.

Although endive is mainly sown in June and July for late use, enthusiasts may like to know that it can also be sown this month for a summer crop. Either sow it where it is to remain and thin out later to about 9 inches apart or, alternatively, start the crop in a nursery bed and transplant later. Endive must be blanched for up to 6 weeks when the plants are almost full grown or they will be indigestible. 'Broad-leaved Batavian' is a good variety for both salads and braising.

Kohlrabi offers change for summer menus, when the bases are boiled and leaves served as greens. The shredded 'roots' (really swollen leaf bases) are also delicious in salads. Sow in succession from the beginning of this month to the end of May.

Continue to sow peas at intervals. Early varieties can be sown early in the month but later, second earlies and maincrop varieties should be sown towards the end of the month. Any early seed left over can be sown in June or July. Sugar peas, or mangetout, should be sown now and in succession.

A succulent and delicious root crop is salsify and it has the advantage that it is hardy enough to remain in the ground all winter for spring use. Lift some and store in autumn for winter in case the ground is too frosted to dig. Sow now, 1 inch deep, and thin out later. When sowing, the soil should be light and well drained.

Chicory for forcing, for winter, should also be sown now. Rhubarb grown from seed sown now will be ready for pulling in two years.

Sow the brassicas, sprouting broccoli, summer cauliflower as well as winter ones. Use club root and cabbage fly preventive. Sow Brussels sprouts, cabbages for summer, autumn and some for winter, and also savoys. These may be left until next month if this is more convenient.

Radish is an excellent catch crop to sow in rows or broadcast among slow maturing crops. Alternatively, sow some seed thinly in the same drill as crops like parsnips, lettuce and parsley or in a drill only 1–2 inches away. In this way rows are defined early and hoeing can begin sooner.

Turnips can be sown between rows of peas and beans. Onions can still be sown and sets, if you can get them, can still be planted.

Peas sown earlier in the year will need supporting. Hazel sticks are becoming more and more difficult and expensive to obtain. Alternatives are mesh, wire, nylon, lustron or plastic. Another excellent method, and one strong enough for the normal crops, is to use bamboo canes and strong cotton or fine twine. Insert the canes firmly and vertically at 6-inch intervals on each side of the rows to make a double row. Hitch the cotton around each cane, beginning a few inches above ground to support the young plants and to deter the birds at the same time. Take the cotton first along the outside of the rows and then finally zigzag it across the centre. Make another line of cotton a few inches above this and successively as required.

Plant out any broad beans or peas that were sown earlier in pots. Transplant lettuce, onions, leeks, cauliflowers and

A good tilth soon forms once the soil is dry enough to rake. Using a line as a guide it is a simple job to draw a drill deep enough for all kinds of seed.

It is a mistake to sow seed too thickly. Pour a little from the packet into the hand and scatter it thinly along the drill.

Peas sown earlier will need supporting now. Where pea-sticks are used push these in firmly along the row but away from the pea roots area.

Lettuce raised in the greenhouse, frame or under cloches can now be transplanted outdoors, 9 inches apart. Stagger the plants in the rows.

other brassicas that are ready. Feed spring cabbage and sow kale.

Two-year-old asparagus roots, bought from specialists, can be planted this month to crop next year. These are best planted in special beds which may or may not be raised. Any existing beds should be top dressed in March. If you wish to raise your own plants, sow seed now after soaking them for 24 hours.

For early crops sow runner beans in boxes and grow on in frames until late May. Or, in mild districts, sow in warm soil under cloches. The main crop can be sown outdoors next month in the south. There are now dwarf varieties of runner beans that are ideal for small gardens. These are also good for early crops to be grown under cloches. Main crops of French beans should be sown from now at fortnightly intervals. Haricot beans need a long season. Grow as for French beans but in as warm and sheltered a spot as possible so that the pods mature and ripen early.

An excellent way of providing and generating heat out of doors is to make a much deeper drill or trench than seems needed. Line this with fresh lawn mowings (untreated with weedkiller, of course), cover with a layer of soil, cover this in turn with a thin layer of peat, sow the seed, cover with more peat and finally with soil. This is a good way to keep soil warm for French beans, radishes, sweet corn and other crops that need a high germination temperature.

Under glass sow capsicum, celery and celeriac (early in the month), outdoor and indoor cucumbers, sweet corn, tomatoes for outdoors, marrows, which include squash, courgettes and zuccini.

Earth up any early potatoes which may be showing and protect them against possible frost.

Sow seeds of both annual and perennial herbs.

Water gardens

The construction of new pools and waterfall systems should be completed this month. If plastic sheeting is to be used, choose a warm day and spread the liner in the sun before installation. If concrete is employed, be careful to protect the structure from any frost.

Established marsh gardens and waterside areas should be cleaned and old plants divided and replanted. The planting of new marsh and waterside features and the addition of dwarf conifers and alpines to the rockery can continue in April. Any iris and primula seeds saved from last July or August should be sown now in a cold frame or greenhouse, using a mixture of equal parts sand, peat and soil, plus 2 ounces of superphosphate per barrowload of mixture.

Water-lilies can be divided now. Select a plant with a good number of growing tips. Then, with a sharp knife, cut one of these tips away. It is important to make quite sure that it is complete with all its roots. This new plantlet can then be planted quite independently in its container.

A pool that has been established for several seasons will benefit from a thinning out of plant growth and a thorough spring clean. This operation can be carried out in any conveniently warm spell from mid-April to early June.

The water should be drained off—or pumped out, using the pump that normally serves the fountain or waterfall. All plants and fish are removed, the fish being very much easier to catch when only a small amount of water remains. Plants will survive for two or three days in a shaded spot under wet sacking.

It is best that fish are transferred to a large aquarium or an old zinc bath kept outside, again in the shade. Do *not* put any plants in with them and protect the container from cats. Let the water stand a day or two before transfer to avoid the abrupt temperature change that can be so harmful to fish. When the pond is empty, use a plastic dustbin to remove any mud. Then clean down with a stiff hand brush and clean water. *Never* use soap powder or detergent. When cleaning is finished refill with clean water (tap water is perfectly satisfactory) and leave standing for three days.

Now the plants can be divided and replanted. A water-lily should be a pad of tuberous roots with a number of growing tips. Choose a medium sized tuber and use a sharp knife to cut it away, complete with roots and strong shoot growth, from the parent, which can be discarded. Plant the tuber very firmly in stiff loamy soil, being careful not to cover the growing point. The top of the planting container should be finished with a layer of gravel or small pebbles. Marginal plants should be split up and two or three strong young divisions planted to a container, using a similar soil.

Most of the old tangled growth of oxygenating plants will be too damaged in the process of removal to be worth keeping and it is a good idea to buy a completely fresh stock of these and of floating plants such as *Hydrocharis* (frogbit), whose resting buds are usually lost in the cleaning operation.

Unless the fish are showing signs of distress, they can stay in their temporary quarters for a week after the plants are returned to the pool. If they appear unhappy they must be returned forthwith and any oxygenating plants which have not had time to get thoroughly rooted must be protected from their attentions with a rough dome of crumpled small mesh wire netting.

A pool which has been established a season or two, but does not need a complete spring clean, will benefit from half emptying and topping up with new water. Fish and plants need not be removed.

With no further danger of serious icing, the pool heater should be removed, cleaned and put away carefully for next winter. A submersible pump can be connected in place of the heater to provide a fountain or waterfall during the summer months—a feature appreciated by the fish as much as the gardener.

With rising water temperatures fish become more active and feeding should be resumed, giving as much food daily as they will readily clear in 5 to 10 minutes. The weekly addition of chopped earthworm and/or a pinch of Bemax will help them recover from the effects of winter and build them up to breeding condition.

Outbreaks of fungus infection are most likely to occur now. Fish may be treated in a shallow dish of water to which salt is added at the rate of two heaped teaspoons per gallon. Change the water daily for three days, increasing the salt content by one teaspoon each day. All water is likely to contain the spores of fungus, so there is no point in refilling the pool.

An adequate and varied diet is the

best protection against this common fish ailment.

Although most aquatic plants are not available from growers before late May—and some floating plants and pygmy lilies not until June—no time should be lost in placing orders for new stock.

Wildlife

In April the birds are still breeding and so are most of the mammals that use our gardens. So while in the hedges and shrubs the great tit and the wren are hatching their broods, the mammals in their various holes and burrows are rearing their litters.

Of all species of domestic wildlife the most common is the house mouse. It is, in fact, the most common of all British mammals and begins the first of its five litters this month.

The house mouse will build its nest in the floors, walls or ceilings of a house, barn or shed and in this nest gives birth to a litter ranging in number from 5 to 13. In about two months these young could be starting their own litters.

Under the hedgerows the rabbits are having their second or third litters, the first having been perhaps as early as February.

The young rabbits are born in special breeding stops made by the doe on the outskirts of the warren. She seals the opening for safety when she is not at home suckling her young. When the babies have grown sufficiently to leave the stop, it is enlarged and incorporated with the remainder of the warren.

All of the rodents that have not bred already may do so this month, so the garden is filled with a new generation of small animal pests. To make up for this increase the predators, too, start their litters and broods.

The weasel builds its nest in a tree trunk, wall or burrow and towards the end of the month gives birth to some five completely helpless and blind young. What a difference from the fierce little hunters they will be by the end of June! The mother weasel has the same philosophy as the mother cat: namely that if danger threatens her brood it is easier and probably safer to move than to defend them. The weasel and the stoat are Britain's most common carnivores, although both appear to be gradually disappearing, largely by accident, because of campaigns to eradicate the rabbit population.

Foxes are also building up their families in their deep earths, in a nursery lined with bracken dragged in earlier in the year. The vixen has perhaps four whelps which she keeps in the nursery until they are a month old. After this period they are let out at night to exercise and if they find a good place to rest during the day they may not return to the nursery. Even if they do not return to live they are still tended by the vixen until September.

Another predator that breeds in April is the kestrel, which plays a significant part in keeping down many garden pests. The falcon (for this is the name of the female; the male is the tiercel) lays her eggs in a nest built in a hollow tree or on a cliff edge.

Once the young birds have hatched, the parents' food-collecting efforts must be redoubled, for with hawks more than most birds the rule is the survival of the fittest. The weakest, often the youngest, only feeds on what his family leaves. If they are all hungry and leave nothing, it dies of starvation.

Through all of this month the garden sees the busy parents rushing to and fro finding food both for themselves and for their ever-demanding young. From the swallows scooping insects out of the sky to the foxes stalking a chicken in its coop, all the parents are searching for food.

The various attempts by parent birds to protect their young can be seen in a walk down the garden. Some birds give the alarm cry. Blackbirds lead you away from the nest by flying only short jumps ahead of you and many birds refuse to desert their nest even if their eggs are taken from under them.

Parent birds in April are so busy feeding their young that they need concentrated body-building foods themselves. Put out suet or a fat and flour dough pudding for the parents.

A Kestrel, Falco tinnunculus, brings a rodent to its young in a church belfry. Kestrels help keep down garden pests.

The Stoat, Mustella erminea, is one of Britain's most common carnivores. More of them visit country gardens than householders realise.

Unlike many other birds, the Kestrel builds no actual nest. These eggs just lie in the debris that has collected inside the hollow tree.

The Month of May

May is the month of celebrations, blossoms, cuckoos, warm sunny days and gardens bursting with colour. Suddenly, the whole of nature is busy preparing for summer. And it is a joy to watch the birds busily collecting food for their young.

1

3

2

4

1 Clematis jackmanii will begin flowering at the end of the month and will continue throughout the summer.
2 The mountain Clematis, C. montana, has many varieties, including this large-flowered tetra rosa.
3 The charming 'Mrs Cholmondeley' is a particularly free-flowering Clematis.
4 Clematis montana rubens is the most rampant of all, quickly growing to over 30 feet high. It is invaluable for covering walls and garages.

1 The Laburnum, or Golden Rain, is a neat and attractive tree and is ideal for the small garden. It is closely related to Cytisus. The seeds and, to a lesser extent, other parts are poisonous.
2 This really beautiful plant, with its mass of pale yellow flowers, is Cytisus praecox, or Warminster Broom, named after the nursery from which it originated.

1

2

3

4

3 Viburnum opulus sterile, the Snowball Tree, is a very adaptable shrub that does well in heavy, moist soil. All the flowers are sterile, so it does not produce berries as do the single-flowered kinds, but is worth planting for the beautiful colours of the foliage in the autumn.
4 Rhododendron 'Lady Cynthia'. This really lovely specimen was photographed in a Kentish garden. The colour and profusion of the blooms make it a magnificent shrub.

1

1 The delicate branches and leaves of the elegant Silver Birch make a charming background for flowering shrubs and rock plants. The 'silver' bark on the trunks seems to glow in certain lights.
2 Geranium farreri, the Crane's-bill, forms a neat clump of attractively shaped leaves and delicate white flowers. They are so named because the seed pod resembles a Crane's head and beak.

2

3

4

Rock plants really can be one of the gardener's joys. Given the right conditions they will produce a profusion of flowers. Most rock plants revel in the sun's warmth retained by a stone bank. This is proved by the glorious blooms here (3, 4).
The sparkling yellow of the Alyssum saxatile and the deep mauve of the Aubrieta harmonise and complement each other. Colour harmonies should always be kept in mind when planting.

1

3

2

4

1 Schizanthus revels in a rich soil. This is a really free-flowering plant and is very rewarding to grow.
2 Bougainvillea glabra is a strong climber which needs warm conditions in the greenhouse.
3 Like so many of our showy flowering plants, though strictly perennial, the Calceolaria is treated as an annual to ensure vigorous plants.
4 Gardenia jasminoides is a plant well worth growing. It is highly prized for its strongly fragrant pure white flowers. What can be more enjoyable than their lovely perfume on a warm May evening?

1

3

2

4

1 The Paphiopedilums are the most popular of the Cypripedium Orchids. This is a hybrid, P. x maudiae.
2 The Colvillei type of Gladioli responds very well indeed to gentle forcing. This variety is 'Spitfire'.
3 Here is a lovely group of spring flowers. Perennial Polyanthus, biennial Myosotis and Tulip bulbs combine to make an attractive spring border.
4 This picture makes a really beautiful collection. Trilliums and Erythroniums, or Dog's Tooth Violets, are mingled with Scillas and other little bulb flowers to make an informal patch.

1

2

3

4

5

1 The Common Daisy has proved a variable plant and has produced many charming border flowers, like the bright double Daisies shown here growing with Pansies.
2 This lovely pale yellow-flowered shrub is Rhododendron damaris 'Logan'. It grows best in warm gardens and near the coast.
3 The Bearded Irises are among the most handsome of garden flowers. This cultivar is 'Total Eclipse'.
4 These delightfully fresh and bright little flowers are Anthemis cupaniana. They form attractive cushions of soft grey aromatic leaves.
5 Tree Paeonies need to be in a partially protected position and in a deep rich soil to produce their beautiful blooms.

1 The Pulsatilla vulgaris, the Pasque Flower, flourishes in open situations where the soil is well drained.
2 Big Chief is one of the new race of Darwin hybrids. It has a gigantic flower produced on a tall stem which must be very strong to bear the bloom.
3 The sweet Lily-of-the-valley, Convallaria majalis, will grow in almost any situation, but flourishes in moist shade.
4 This is the elegant lily-flowered Tulip, 'China Pink'.
5 The Darwin hybrid Tulip, 'Dover', is one of the newest varieties. Like the others of its kind, it is outstanding both for its vigour and the brilliance of its colour.

1

3

2

4

5

Jobs of the month

Do not let the warmer days of May lull you into forgetting the tasks that must now be tackled. This is the time of year when plans for beds and borders should be put into action. Take cuttings, sow seeds of biennials and pay attention to pruning. All these jobs and the many others that are fully explained in the following pages will help you to get the best possible results

Bulbs

Lift lily bulbs from the garden for tub decoration. When tulips are finished, lift them and heel-in for bulbs to ripen

Flowers for cutting

Begin gathering materials for dried arrangements. Cut irises while they are still in bud. Sow many of the biennials and perennials for next year's flower arrangements

Fruit

Strawberries in flower must be protected from late frosts. Bark-ring apples and pears that produce no blossom. Continue spraying and pinching out

Greenhouse

Put some of the summer bedding plants out into frames. Damp down to maintain humidity and shade to prevent too much sunshine on the plants. A great deal of time will be spent potting on

Hedges

Fast growing formal hedges need their first clipping. Over-head – spray and mulch evergreens and conifers during dry spells. Last chance to plan ever-green and coniferous hedging subjects

Herbaceous plants

Stake plants. Feed delphiniums and phlox weekly with a diluted liquid manure. Plant out chrysanthemums that have been hardened off

House plants

Propagate by sowing seeds or stem and leaf cuttings. Move plants away from south windows. The May sun can be too hot for most house plants

Lawns

Pay careful attention to new lawns. Regular mowing is essential. Use a weedkiller on established lawns on which weeds have gained a hold

Paths, fences and walls

Check fence support posts and make sure that supports for climbing plants are strong enough

Patios, balconies, roof gardens and window boxes

Ensure that plants receive enough water. Fill window boxes now that there is little fear of frosts

Rock gardens

Spray to keep down pests. Watch for worms, which can damage cushion plants. An ideal time to construct a peat bed for dwarf rhododendrons

Roses

Eliminate multiple shoots. Take action against insect pests. Begin disbudding

Trees, shrubs and climbers

Remove rhodo-dendron flower trusses as soon as they fade. There is some pruning to be done. Still time to transplant evergreen shrubs

Vegetables

Have ground ready to receive plants that have been hardened off. Hardy outdoor tomatoes can be planted

Water gardens

Make preparations for new aquatic plants. Fish are ready to spawn

Wildlife

Bees and butterflies begin their travels. Encourage them into your garden by your choice of plants

Bulbs

1 The deep rich yellow Parrot Tulip 'Sunshine' grows to a height of 18 inches. It is a sport of the old Cottage Tulip 'Bouton d'Or'.
2 These bi-colour Tulips look well planted informally by the waterside.
3 Once Tulips have finished flowering take off the dead heads to prevent seeds from ripening and to direct the plant's activity to building up the bulb.

May is generally regarded as the month of the tulip. All the paeony-flowered and triumph tulips will be in flower during the early days of the month and will be followed by the cottage, Darwin hybrids and lily-flowered kinds. Then, by mid-May the 'Rembrandt', 'Bybloemen' and exotic parrot tulips will flower. Hand weed and hoe carefully before the flower stems grow to their full height, for it is virtually impossible to work between the plants later as the stems snap rather easily.

Once the flowers fade, pick off the dead heads and cut the stem from the base. The fading foliage is unsightly and the position is often needed for summer bedding plants. So the tulips can be lifted, shaken free of soil and heeled in immediately to allow the bulbs to ripen. If the spring is exceptionally dry, water the bed to encourage the bulbs to become firm.

The ornithogalums, star of bethlehem, will be in flower now—*O. narbonense* will not flower until the end of the month and no bulbs could be easier to grow. Each flower head produces dozens of individual white and green flowers. Some of the fritillarias will be adding a touch of purple-rust to the rock garden and troughs, but the larger *Fritillaria imperalis*, crown imperial, adds a dramatic touch of colour—yellow or orange—early in the month.

This plant, much associated with cottage gardens, has bulbs as large as 4 inches in diameter. If it is to be moved or divided this should be done at the end of the month, when the flowers have faded.

Lilies in pots, whether in the cold greenhouse, conservatory or on a patio, will need to be watered with care. Once the growth is really moving, and this should be happening now, they will require more water. Give them as much light and air as possible. This will help to keep aphids at bay. Pots can be moved around, providing interest wherever it is required, but are not a labour-saving device because to water them takes more time. Do not be tempted to put lilies in pots in the direct rays of strong sunshine or the flowers will be bleached. This is especially so in the case of *Lilium henryi* and *L. hansoni*.

It is possible during the early part of May to lift lily bulbs from the garden and transfer them to tubs for summer decoration, but this needs to be carried out with extreme care to avoid disturbing and damaging the roots. Stand the tubs in the shade for a couple of weeks until the plants have recovered from the move and do not let them dry out. The soft growth of lilies, especially those in beds in the garden, provides attractive targets for the slugs, especially during muggy weather. Keep these pests at bay by using a proprietary slug repellent. They are all made of meta plus some slug bait.

Gladiolus foliage will be growing erect during May, and towards the end of the month a mulch of peat or spent hops is beneficial to conserve moisture and smother weeds. Hand weed before applying the mulch. There is nothing to be gained by mulching earlier than the second half of the month (probably the last week in the north) because the ground will not have warmed up sufficiently and the mulch would then only serve as a barrier to prevent the soil absorbing warmth from the sun.

Flowers for cutting

It may seem early in the year to be gathering plant materials for dried arrangements, but all the same one should begin now. Grasses, for example, should be picked as soon as the inflorescence grows from the sheath. The younger they are the better colour they will be when dried.

In gardens where bulbs are allowed to

1

2

3

1 Sow Nigella, or Love-in-a-Mist, each year to provide seed heads for cutting. But use a few of the blue blooms now to fill posy bowls.
2 Poppies cut at this bud stage can be encouraged to last well if the bases of the stems are singed over a flame.
3 Foliage plants and green-flowered plants provide plenty of material for the early summer flower arrangements. Used in their green state they can be attractive and economical.

grow in grass that is not scythed until later in the summer there should be a real harvest ready to be gathered. Some grasses are better than others, but even those with indeterminate flower spikes may have stiff, stout stems which ought to be collected and kept for use as false stems for helichrysums, skeletonised leaves and other lightweights.

Make the grasses into fairly small bunches because it is important that the air circulates around them. Hang them upside down away from sun and strong light, which would bleach them. The place must be dry but not hot. An airy shed or garage would do. In a damp place they will become mouldy. Bind together tightly all stems of materials to be dried because as they dry they shrink.

Although the fading heads of most narcissi and tulips should be picked off, there are some varieties, and other kinds of bulb flowers, which should be allowed to go to seed so that they can colonise areas in the garden. Keep an eye on these seed heads—they can serve a double purpose. Many of them are very beautiful and dry well. They look lovely in arrangements of dried perpetuelles. Even the humble bluebell is not to be despised, but naturally one must wait until the seed is ripe before pulling the stems.

Nigella will soon be in flower and the blue blooms are quickly followed by the attractive fringed seed vessels. These are as useful, if not as colourful, as the flowers. They can either be cut from the plant and dried or saved from the vase when a flower arrangement is being discarded. Dry them in the same way as recommended for grasses and they will keep a good colour.

From now on watch all seeding stems. Some are useful to cut green and use in all-green arrangements. These can be both beautiful and economical. Aquilegia and poppy will soon be ready. Like the nigella, these can be used first fresh and then dried later.

Green flowers are always in demand by flower arrangers and the loveliest of them all is probably the *Molucella laevis* or bells of Ireland. Seed should be sown now in heat—65–70°F (18–21°C). The 'shell' studded stems can be dried but unfortunately they do not retain their lovely green. Instead they turn to beige and biscuit but the stems are beautiful all the same.

Often in early autumn one searches, without luck, for flowers to arrange with the dahlias and chrysanthemums. To ensure a continuation of the half hardy annuals sow some now in places where they are to flower. Coddle them a little in their early stages to hurry them along, watering them in dry periods until they are growing away well. Thin them out early, unless you have a leaning towards miniature arrangements, in which case let a few patches remain crowded. You will be enchanted at the lilliputian flowers which are produced. On the other hand, there are many tiny flowered annuals which may be sown for this purpose, such as ageratum, alyssum (in many pastel tints nowadays), asperula, ionopsidium, leptosiphon, linaria, lobelia, maroccana, tagetes and Virginian stock.

When you sow seed in the greenhouse for winter flowering pot plants remember that many of the flowers produced can be cut for winter flower arrangements. Cinerarias and primulas are examples. And do not forget foliage plants like *Begonia rex* and coleus, all of which last well in water and help eke out the cut blooms in lean times.

Border chrysanthemums should go out this month. Whether the gardener grows these flowers as specimen blooms or allows them to make natural sprays, no other flower registers the pungent appeal of autumn in quite the same way as chrysanthemums. There are enough kinds to suit all tastes. Pompons and Koreans bloom conveniently late and look lovely with autumn fruits, berries and foliage.

Many kinds of irises will be in flower now, the bulbous as well as the bearded kinds. Remember that they will last longer indoors if they are cut in bud and are not likely to become damaged and unsightly this way if transported as a gift to a friend.

Poppies of all kinds, so glorious in the garden, can sometimes be disappointing when cut. This need not be so. Gather only those which are either just emerging from the bud stage or which are so newly released that their petals are still crumpled and creased. Bunch with the stem ends level and, keeping the bloom portion well away from danger, singe the ends over a flame until they are black. Either arrange the flowers immediately in tepid water or place them in deep tepid water until they have to be arranged.

Many biennials and perennials for next year's flower arrangements should be sown now.

Fruit

There is still plenty of spraying to be done this month. Fruits to be sprayed are:

Strawberries With dinocap, immediately before the blossom opens, as a precaution against mildew. Repeat in a fortnight's time. Also spray strawberries with captan when one in five flowers have opened, to prevent botrytis disease (also appropriately known as 'grey mould'). Repeat the captan spraying when all petals have fallen and two or three times again at 10-day intervals until the fruit is ready to be picked.

Apples At petal fall (within 7 days of the moment when four out of five petals have fallen) with captan to control scab disease. It is better to rely on captan at this stage. Some varieties will not tolerate lime-sulphur as late as this and lose their leaves. Add BHC to the captan to control apple sawfly.

Pears At petal fall, with captan, to control scab disease.

Plums With BHC, against sawfly, at the cot-split stage. This is when the receptacles (or 'cots') of the fruitlets are beginning to open revealing the miniature plums within.

Cherries After blossoming, with malathion, if aphids are seen.

Gooseberries With dinocap against mildew. Add derris if sawfly caterpillars have been seen.

Raspberries Before the blossom opens, with colloidal copper, to control cane spot disease.

Blackberries, loganberries and other hybrid berries These are all liable to cane spot attack and should be sprayed with colloidal copper just before the blossom opens.

Peaches and nectarines With chlorbenside or derris if there is any sign of red spider.

When apples and pears being grown as dwarf pyramids have reached a sufficient height (7 feet is usually considered enough) the central leaders should be cut back by half of last year's growth. In following years cut back the central leader to half an inch in May.

Where plums are being grown as pyramids and a height of 9 feet has been reached, shorten the leader each May to within one inch of the new growth.

When cordon apples and pears reach the top support wire thay may be untied and lowered to a more acute angle. There comes a time, however, when they can go no lower and further extension growth must be stopped. The leader should then be cut back as necessary in May.

Prune bush peach trees. This task is left until now when the risk of silver leaf infection is less and when any die-back which may have occurred during the winter can be seen. Cut back to a visibly growing outward-pointing bud or new shoot. Cut out crossing branches and old branches which have been weighed down by fruiting. Try to encourage new growth from the centre of the bush to replace the old but at the same time avoid overcrowding by cutting to buds pointing outwards.

Continue the thinning of peaches and nectarines by easy stages. After the preliminary thinning wait until stoning has been completed, for there is often a natural discarding of fruitlets at this time. You can tell whether the stones have been formed by sticking a pin into a typical fruitlet. Then remove one fruit from each pair and any badly placed fruits (those that are, for example, pinched against a wall).

If you applied paper greasebands last autumn, cut these off now and burn them. If grease was applied to the bark, scrape it off.

Try bark-ringing apples or pears which continue to make vigorous growth but produce no blossom. Cover the wound at once with protective paint or insulating tape. This drastic treatment should not be given to stone fruits such

A clean pin can be inserted into ripe Peaches to ascertain whether or not the stone has started to harden. Great care must be taken in handling the fruit for this operation.

Cut away any runners from Strawberries that are not required for propagation and maintain as few as possible on any one plant unless the matted-bed system of cultivation is being followed.

Spread clean, dry straw around Strawberry plants early in the summer to act as a mulch to conserve moisture, keep the fruit clean and safeguard the crop from fungus disease and slug attacks.

as apricot, cherry, peach and plum.

Where large gooseberries are wanted for dessert or exhibition, they should be thinned down to 3 inches apart shortly after setting. Otherwise thinning may be left until some berries are big enough for cooking.

Keep an eye on the strawberries. If runners appear, cut them off (unless earmarked for propagation or the matted bed system is being followed) and, if aphids are present, spray at once with malathion or derris. The latter is non-poisonous and can therefore be used close to picking time.

In many parts of the country strawberries in flower risk being damaged by late frost throughout this month. An old but time-consuming dodge is to lay glass jam jars on their side with the truss of strawberry blossom inside. Late radiation frosts always occur on still windless nights, however, and a considerable degree of protection is afforded by laying newspapers over the plants. Gather the papers up first thing in the morning.

Do not be in a hurry to straw the strawberries as this increases the risk of frost damage as the light-coloured straw loses warmth quicker than the dark earth. Wait until the swelling berries are heavy enough to bring fruit trusses close to, but not yet touching, the ground. Scatter slug bait down the row and tuck the straw well in around plants. If straw is not available, little mats specially made for the purpose can be bought at garden shops. Alternatively you can prop up fruit trusses individually on forked sticks or bent wires—although this takes more time than strawing.

When grapes or other fruits are grown under glass prevent excessive temperatures building up during the day by increasing the ventilation and, if necessary, shading the glass.

Greenhouse

The greenhouse is likely to be bursting at the seams with young stock now but the position can be eased by putting many of the summer bedding plants out into frames to be hardened off. This should be done by increasing the ventilation at first during the day, then at night. Protect the plants from cold winds and, to avoid drying out which will occur more readily in the frames than in the greenhouse, give them copious waterings in hot weather. Dahlias in pots may also be hardened off now.

Hot weather will also mean shading and if this can be done by an automatic arrangement so much the better—otherwise slatted blinds, a proprietary shading solution or a mixture of flour and water will have to be used. Increased damping down, by wetting the floor and stagings, will also be needed to maintain a certain amount of humidity but the atmosphere must also be kept buoyant by generous ventilation.

Most of the main sowings have been made by now but three fine spring-flowering pot plants that should be sown between now and July are cinerarias, *Primula malacoides* and the greenhouse calceolarias. Sow the cinerarias just beneath the surface of the John Innes seed compost but merely sprinkle

Fuchsias grown from cuttings can be planted into hanging baskets during May. They give a profuse display of flowers over a long period. They look well on their own or mixed with other plants.

1

2

3

4

1 Take cuttings of Hydrangeas. Choose short noded non-flowering shoots from established bushes or pot plants.
2 Trim the base of the cutting with a sharp budding knife, making a straight cut immediately below a node. Remove the lower leaves.
3 Dibble in the cuttings around the edge of a small pot. Hormone rooting powder can be used before inserting them.
4 Several Hydrangea cuttings can be put into each pot.

the others on the surface and gently press them in. After sowing, soak the box or pot from underneath, then cover it with glass and paper and place it in a shady position at a temperature of about 50°F (10°C). The cinerarias, which germinate rapidly, will be ready for pricking out in a week or two.

Hydrangeas coming into bloom will need liberal watering and light shade, together with frequent feeding for all but blue varieties, which must not be given too much nitrogen or the colour will be poor. Cuttings of hydrangeas may also be taken now, using unflowered shoots taken off about 4 inches long and inserted in a peat-sand mixture in a close frame.

As the earliest hippeastrums pass out of bloom cut out the flowered stem, then keep the plants well watered and fed in full light for the rest of the summer. Cyclamen that have died down should be kept perfectly dry in full sun, while arum lilies *(Zantedeschia aethiopica)* should be given full light but gradually less water after flowering.

Schizanthus must be potted on before they become pot-bound. Move those in 3-inch pots on into 6-inch ones of the John Innes potting compost No 2 and autumn-sown ones, already in 5- or 6-inch pots, into 8- or 9-inch ones. Make sure that these plants get plenty of light, air and food.

By about the second week of May chrysanthemums for pot culture in the greenhouse will need their final potting into 9- or 10-inch pots, according to the vigour of the variety. The quickest way to do this is to stand the pots out on the standing ground where the plants are to spend the summer, fill each one with John Innes potting compost No 3 to about 2 inches from the top and then set the plant in the compost so that the base of the stem is just level with the surface. The plants should of course be hardened off before potting them outside.

Shoots appearing in the axils of the leaves of the Tomatoes need to be removed. This disbudding is done by breaking the shoot off sideways.

Tomatoes planted in the greenhouse will be making rapid growth now but do not encourage them too much by watering and feeding or the bottom truss may not set. Aim at slow, steady growth by adequate, but not excessive watering and use a feed containing a high proportion of potash. Make sure that all side shoots where the leaves join the stem are removed as soon as they can be handled without damage.

Cucumber seedlings in 3½-inch pots must be kept warm and moist and in a humid atmosphere until they are about 6 inches high, when they should be ready for planting out on the greenhouse bench 2 feet apart on mounds of rich humus soil with perfect drainage.

For greenhouse display, fuchsias and geraniums grown from cuttings will need moving on into 5-inch pots of the John Innes potting compost No 2, or the trailing kinds can be used in hanging baskets together with *Campanula isophylla, Lobelia tenuior, Begonia pendula, Nepeta hederacea (glechoma)* and similar trailing plants. To keep the baskets moist without heavy watering, line them out with moss, then with polythene sheeting, before putting the plants in.

Keep climbing plants trained in and to ensure that the passion flower *(Passiflora caerulea)* flowers well it should be kept fairly dry with no feeding.

Hedges

Fast-growing hedges that are trimmed to a formal shape will need their first clipping sometime during May. For the small to average sized garden a sharp pair of good quality hedging shears should suffice for this operation. In larger gardens, where there are long stretches of hedge needing frequent trimming, it would pay to invest in a mechanical hedge-trimmer.

The kind of hedges that will be in need of treatment this month are black-

The Capsid Bug is pale green in colour and feeds on many decorative plants, doing most of its damage during July. Affected plants show signs of distortion of flower and stunted growth

RECOGNITION CHART

Pests

To banish garden pests you must first identify them. On left-hand page: foliage and flower pests. On right: pests on or below the ground

Earwigs can do great damage to decorative plants by eating the leaves and flowers, particularly those of Dahlias and Chrysanthemums. The attacked blooms have a ragged appearance and leaves become skeletonised

The Thrip is yellow, blackish or brown in colour. The young are wingless and generally lighter in colour. These insects are carriers of virus diseases from one plant to another

The Flea Beatle directs its attack mainly against plants of the Cabbage family. The insect itself is almost impossible to see but the effect of its feeding is obvious. Most damage is done in May and June during dry seasons

Woolly Aphid, mainly a pest of Apples, Pyracantha and Cotoneaster is recognisable by the white woolly appearance of the colonies of insects. The vigour of the host plant is reduced and disfiguring pseudo-galls are sometimes formed

Greenfly aphids are probably the most easily recognised of all insect pests. They live in large colonies on the young growth of many decorative plants and cause deformity of leaf and flower

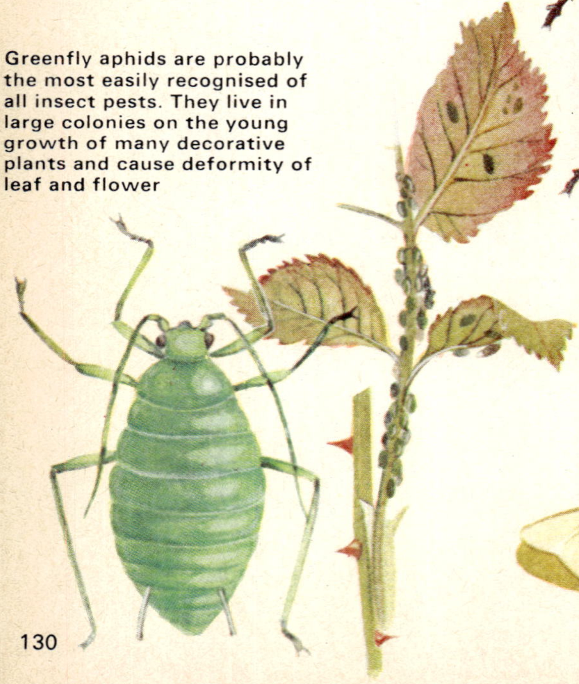

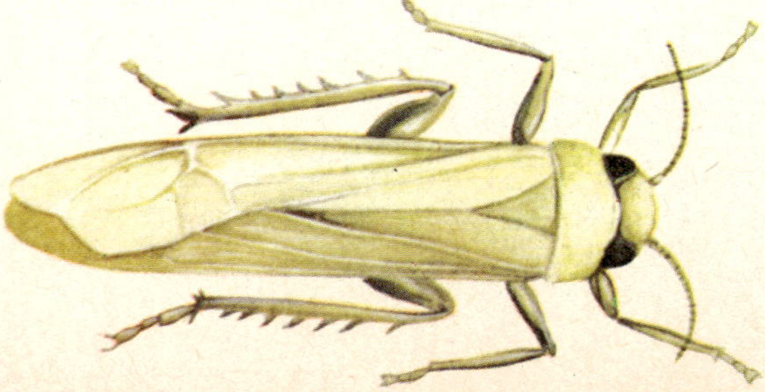

The Leafhopper, so named because it leaps from the plant when disturbed, is a yellowish green insect, particularly active in dry weather. Sometimes its moult skins are seen on the leaves of the host plant and mistaken for the insect itself. These are, in fact, called 'Ghost Flies'

The Common Black Ant is particularly a nuisance in frames and garden sheds, and can do considerable damage in the rock garden by loosening the soil around the roots and in soil pockets

Millepedes are sluggish grubs (the upper one is the Flattened Millepede) which do extensive damage to seedlings and the underground parts of established plants. Frequently they enter holes bored by other pests and extend the damage

The Chafer Grub is ugly and curved. It feeds all year round on roots of trees, shrubs and other ornamental plants, causing wilting

Woodlice creep about the ground, always hiding under seed boxes, pots, tiles. They are active mainly at night and can roll into a small ball if disturbed

The Wireworm is a serious pest of the underground parts of a plant. Potatoes and root crops are victims and are often badly damaged

The Black Slug attacks the foliage of a plant, particularly that of Iris, giving it a clawed appearance. It is a nocturnal feeder, leaving a slimy trail across soil and paths

The Leather Jacket eats on roots of grass, sometimes in severe cases causing dead patches to appear on the lawn. It is the grub of the Daddy Long Legs or Crane Fly

Snails are nocturnal feeders and of particular danger where Irises are cultivated. The Snail is familiar to most people because it carries its shell on its back when moving about

Golden Privet makes a firm hedge of good appearance. It responds well to clipping, a job to be done regularly and thoroughly to promote thick growth.

Because Holly is so slow growing, an established hedge is a source of pride to a gardener. If spring has been dry, Holly benefits from an overhead spraying.

and quickthorn, lonicera, myrobalan plum and privet.

Newly-planted hedges will need regular watering during dry spells. Watering with a can is more reliable than the hose. It is a more certain way of ensuring that each individual plant has had its proper ration—2 gallons each is not too much and is much better than 'little and often'. Where long stretches of hedge are being dealt with, it would be better to use a trickle hose or a reliable sprinkler.

In addition, evergreens and conifers may need overhead spraying during dry periods to offset moisture loss through leaf transpiration. Mulching, too, will help considerably by conserving soil moisture. Grass cuttings make an effective and convenient mulch that can be easily topped up each time the lawn is mowed.

The first two weeks of May will be the last opportunity for planting evergreen and coniferous hedging subjects. Even this is a trifle risky if a really dry summer ensues. But May is considered to be the best time to plant a holly hedge, although great care will have to be taken to give it sufficient water for the first month or so after planting.

Hollies make an attractive close-knit hedge that is especially good in shaded situations. *Ilex aquifolium*, native holly, is the species commonly used for hedging. It is very slow-growing at first, but puts on a considerable spurt after a few years. Hollies sometimes shed their leaves after planting but this should be welcomed, as it is a sign that they have 'taken'.

An unusual and interesting hedge that will double as a screen-cum-windbreak and is impenetrable by man, boy or beast can be made by planting one of the taller-growing bamboos. It would not be advisable where a formal type of hedge is required but is ideal for dividing the more ordered parts of the garden from a wild or woodland plot.

Bamboos planted in May have the best chance of survival. As well as being the best species for hedging *Arundinaria japonica*, or metake, is the kind most widely grown. The canes of mature plants reach heights of 10 feet or more. The arching tips display the fans of ribbon-like leaves to perfection. As well as performing an efficient hedging function, the old canes are useful as stakes and supports.

Bamboos can be difficult at first. Once established, however, they forge ahead with terrific vigour. They should be planted deeply and kept well watered during dry periods. They may take an entire season to obtain a proper footing and become established.

It can be very irritating when a hedge makes irregular growth so that it cannot be clipped to a uniform height. This can be due to several causes—lack of nourishment, faulty planting or pests and diseases. If the growth of a young hedge is not uniform after two seasons, it is probably due to the first of these causes. The slower-growing plants that have probably struck infertile soil can be persuaded to catch up by watering them with liquid manure once a fortnight during May and June. If animal manure is not available, one of the proprietary liquid feeds, used in accordance with the makers' instructions, will make an effective substitute.

Herbaceous plants

Most of us include a few spring bedding plants in a herbaceous border—wallflowers, forget-me-nots *(Myosotis)*, polyanthus, etc. These should be removed as soon as the plants finish blooming to make way for summer flowers. Although the old-fashioned wallflowers are perennial, the modern improved strains are treated as biennials and the plants discarded after flowering. The same applies to the forget-me-not.

Clumps of polyanthus can be lifted and divided, the rooted offsets being eased apart and planted 6 inches apart in rich, moist soil, in a semi-shady nursery bed, to grow on until bedded out again in the autumn.

Gardening is very much a matter of thinking ahead. If you want to raise spring and early summer flowering biennials for next year, seed of Canterbury bells, the sweetly scented Siberian wallflower *(Cheiranthus allionii)*, sweet William, forget-me-not, honesty *(Lunaria biennis)*, wallflowers and cynoglossum should be sown within the next few weeks. Cynoglossum is charming not only as a border plant; the vivid blue flowers borne on stems $1\frac{1}{2}$–2 feet high are also excellent for cutting.

Canterbury bells are available in dwarf varieties ($1\frac{1}{2}$ feet), double and single varieties ($2\frac{1}{2}$ feet) and the large semi-double 'cup and saucer' or 'Calycanthema' varieties ($2\frac{1}{2}$ feet) in rose pink, violet-blue and white colourings. Sweet Williams and wallflowers come in different heights, too. Wallflowers range

1 There are several ways of providing temporary support for plants. ***Below*** **a plant is given an individual supporting cane and tied to it at intervals.**

1

from 6–9 inches high to 1½ feet high, in pastel shades as well as the usual tawny colourings and sweet Williams from 6–12 inches high to 1½–2 feet high, in double and single strains.

Sow the seed in boxes, in a cold frame or in a finely prepared seed bed outdoors in rows 9–12 inches apart.

Given suitable weather conditions, antirrhinum, asters and ten-week-stocks can be planted out towards the end of the month, spacing the seedlings 9–12 inches apart, preferably in largish groups. Several half-hardy annuals—zinnias, asters, African marigolds, stocks and cosmea—may be sown where the plants are to bloom.

Continue planting gladioli for succession, setting the corms on a layer of silver sand, 4 inches deep, 9 inches apart, in deep, rich, well-drained soil. Corms of the deliciously fragrant freesias, which have been specially treated for outdoor culture, can also be planted 2 inches deep, 2 inches apart, in clumps of a dozen or more, in a moist, semi-shady part of the border.

Staking of tall and medium height perennials should begin now. Give the plants the first tie when growth is roughly 8 inches high.

A popular form of staking that requires no tying is the method by which plants are surrounded by strong, twiggy pea sticks. The foliage hides the sticks in time if the work is carried out while the growth is still short.

Certain perennials—delphiniums, Michaelmas daisies (perennial asters) and phlox, for example—are seen to better advantage when the stems are staked separately. The stems of the Michaelmas daisy, in particular, tend to crowd one another. This 'bundling' can be offset if the canes are driven in at an angle and the shoots are trained outward. Some thinning of shoots may be necessary after the first year. In general, three to five shoots to a root is sufficient if the Michaelmas daisy is to produce fine heads of bloom.

Delphiniums and phlox will benefit from a weekly application of diluted liquid manure, liquid seaweed feed or dried blood dissolved in water throughout May and June. Spread a dressing of sulphate of potash (2 ounces to the square yard) round delphinium plants in May to prevent the growth becoming too soft.

Both these plants need liberal watering in dry weather—a bucketful to a plant is not too much. The same is true of the astilbes, the flowers of which quickly shrivel or even fail to open when plants lack moisture.

After hardening off, early-flowering chrysanthemums can be planted, the ground for chrysanthemums should be deeply dug and manured in winter but, if this was impossible, rake in a dressing of superphosphate (4 ounces per square yard), hoof and horn (8 ounces per square yard) and sulphate of potash (2 ounces per square yard) about 2 weeks before planting. Or else you can make a mixture of bonemeal, sulphate of potash and hoof and horn in equal proportions by bulk and place a little under each plant.

Plant firmly, 15–18 inches apart, with as little root disturbance as possible. The holes should be large enough

After flowering Polyanthuses are lifted and divided, each clump making several good plants. Replant the pieces separately in a nursery bed.

2

2 Groups of plants that are going to make heavy growth are best supported by several bamboo canes driven obliquely into the ground.

3

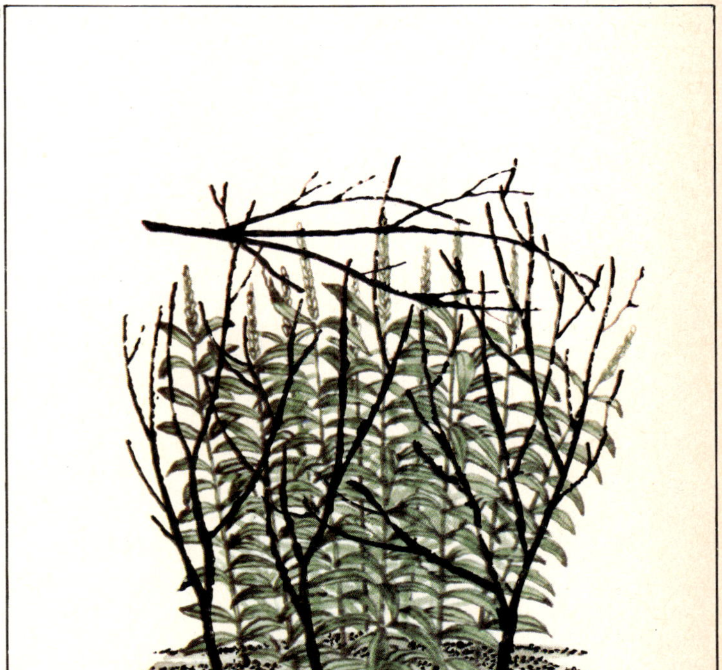

3 Plants of lax growth can easily be supported by twiggy stakes. As the growth thickens up, the stakes will soon be covered.

to hold the ball of root without cramping. Supports should be inserted before planting. Secure the young plant to the stake with raffia, always bearing in mind that the stems will thicken as the plant grows, make the first tie quite loose.

House plants

The May sun can at times be too hot for most house plants, so move them from south windows to positions in the home where direct sunlight will be on them for a few minutes only. Watering rates should be approaching the summer maximum and for some humidity loving plants it may be helpful to give a daily spraying with a mist of clean water.

This is the ideal time to propagate by sowing seed or by stem and leaf cuttings. Many house plants require high temperatures and humidity for their seeds to germinate. Unless you have the benefit of a greenhouse and a good propagating case you will be advised to stick to the easier seeds, such as those of cacti, coleus, impatiens and gloxinias. As you will not normally wish to be embarrassed with too great a number of young plants at one time it is best to sow just a few seeds in a pot and, if required, make successive sowings in the following weeks.

Use a good sterile soil mixture or a peat-based compost and sprinkle just a few seeds on the top, barely covering them with a dusting of the compost. Moisten the mixture thoroughly by lowering the pot into a bucket of water almost to rim level. Then remove the pot, when the surface compost is seen to darken, and leave it to drain. Lay a small pane of glass on the top of the pot to conserve moisture or slip the entire pot inside a transparent plastic bag and seal the opening. When the seeds have germinated and are large enough to be handled they can be pricked out and potted up individually or several to a larger pot.

Take stem cuttings from your plants just below a point where a leaf joins the stem. Cuttings should be about 6 inches long and have the bottom leaf or two removed to leave about 2 inches of stem bare. Dip this in a hormone rooting powder and then insert several cuttings around the rim of a pot filled with a peat based compost or moist sand. Water the medium well and keep the cuttings in a shaded spot until they have obviously started to grow. Remove one cutting and if the roots are well developed they can all be potted up in the usual way. Propagation by stem cuttings is suitable for ivies, coleus, cissus, rhoicissus, peperomias, syngoniums and several other plants.

Saintpaulias or African Violets are propagated by leaf cuttings. These are made by removing single healthy leaves from the plants and trimming the stem before inserting them into cutting compost. Let the leaves stand upright, usually in rows, one behind the other. Three methods of trimming the stem are clearly shown above—straight, nicked and V-shaped.

To propagate Begonia rex the leaf is laid flat on the surface of the compost and pegged down to maintain contact between the ribs of the leaf and the growing medium. If small slits are made across the ribs, new growth will spring from the incisions.

The leaf cutting method is suitable for saintpaulias, gloxinias, perperomias, *Begonia rex,* sedums and some others. Remove a good healthy leaf with its stem and insert the stem up to leaf level in the potting medium, preferably a well moistened peat based compost. Plantlets will grow from the base. Alternatively, insert the stem into a small phial or glass of plain water and when a good root system has grown pot the plants up in a soil mixture.

Begonias, with their larger leaves, can be propagated by another leaf cutting system. Lay a leaf on a pan or box of moist sand and cut through the main stems in several places. Pin down the sections with toothpicks or hairpins to maintain contact with the sand. Wherever a cut has been made a new plant or series of plants will grow, provided contact with the sand is maintained The sand should not be allowed to dry out.

House plants gradually deteriorate with age and if fresh young plants can be propagated now they will be able to make strong healthy growth during the summer months before the more difficult growing period of the winter descends on them.

Lawns

A new lawn raised from seed or turf will require careful attention this month if it is to become established and look good during the summer months. It will not stand hard usage until the following year, but at least it should be of an even green colour, weed-free and a pleasure to behold.

Beds or walls often make it impossible to mow the lawn in a different direction each time. Diagonal cutting can enhance the look of a lawn.

If the weather is hot and sunny for more than 2–3 days, and the surface soil starts to dry out, the new lawn should be watered—not by a quick light daily spray, but a thorough soaking every 1–3 days. Watering should be started near the beginning of a dry period, before the grass begins to lose its colour and turn brown.

The best and least laborious method of watering is with a lawn sprinkler. There are a number available, for attaching to a hose, in several sizes and capable of watering a variety of areas. If the water does not appear to be penetrating well, lightly spike the lawn with a garden fork or lawn aerator (a small wooden roller with spikes) to break the surface pan.

It is particularly important with a newly-turfed lawn that it should not dry out, otherwise the edges of the turf will die and shrink and never knit together evenly.

Care should be taken, however, not to overwater a newly-sown lawn, as this can give rise to a disease called damping-off, which may kill the young grasses. Sometimes the grass will recover from a mild attack of this disease, if weather conditions are favourable. If, however, the fungus appears to be getting a strong hold, it is advisable to make applications of a suitable fungicide, such as Cheshunt compound or a proprietary mercury product, either in liquid or dust form.

Any bare patches of lawn which result from damping-off, or any other causes, should be raked to a fine tilth, have any debris or weeds removed and be reseeded. Then cover the area with a thin scattering of sifted soil, firm the surface with a board and protect from seed-eating birds by a criss-crossing black thread or creating a 'cage' of twigs until the young grass has germinated evenly.

Although thorough initial preparation of the lawn site should prevent too many weeds growing among the new grass, inevitably some will appear. They should be dealt with promptly to prevent flowering, seeding and future weeding. Unfortunately, it is not advisable to use any form of weedkiller for the first 3 months of a new lawn's life, which means resorting to hand weeding. In these early stages, weed seedlings should be removed by one hand, while the other hand holds down the young grasses. Regular light mowing of a new lawn will also help to prevent weeds flowering and seeding.

Mowing of the new lawn should be done regularly to keep the height of grass between 1 and 1½ inches. The grass should never be allowed to grow too

To save time, water with a lawn sprinkler with the hose wound on a wheeled reel for mobility. Water before the lawn starts to suffer from dryness.

long, or the shock of cutting off too much leaf at once will reduce its vigour and delay its establishment. Whenever possible, it is sound practice to mow the lawn in a different direction each time it is cut. It is also advisable to collect the grass cuttings in the grass box on the lawn mower when mowing. They will make a useful addition to the compost heap.

A new lawn from seed will benefit from a light top-dressing of a 50/50 mixture of garden sand and coarse peat each month. This will help to create a smooth, level surface and encourage the growth of the young grasses.

Established lawns should be mown at least weekly between May and early September, sometimes twice weekly in good growing conditions. A really fine lawn, of first-class quality grass, should be cut to $\frac{1}{4}$–$\frac{1}{2}$ inch, a medium lawn is best cut to $\frac{1}{2}$–1 inch, while a rougher rye-grass lawn should not be mown closer than 1 inch.

If mowing is not carried out with sufficient frequency, the vigour of the grasses may be impaired by the shock of cutting too much at one time. In order to prevent worms and the spread of weeds, collect the grass cuttings and add them to the compost heap.

On a light, free-draining soil, watering may become necessary after 3–4 days of warm, dry weather. During very dry spells water should be given copiously every 2 to 3 days, rather than as a light damping over each day.

Where a weedy established lawn is an eye-sore, or the near-perfect lawn is marred by a few of these unwanted intruders, now is the time to apply a suitable weedkiller. A hormone selective weedkiller (which kills broad-leaved plants but not grasses) is suitable and can be applied in liquid form, either by a watering can with a fine rose or spray bar attachment, or from a sprayer. Whatever the means of application, always choose a mild, windless day, when the soil is moist. Take care not to allow the weedkiller to drift on to other plants. Apply it evenly over the lawn surface. Wash out the applicator thoroughly after use.

Resistant weeds may require 2 or 3 applications of the chosen weedkiller and it often helps to feed the lawn 10 days before the application to improve the kill of weeds.

A sulphate of iron lawn sand, applied evenly by hand scattering or with a fertiliser distributor, not only kills weeds and moss but also gives the grass a growth boost at the same time. It must be applied when the soil is moist, and watered in if rain has not fallen within 2 days of application. Dead growth can be raked up 3 weeks later and a further dressing applied if the first treatment was not successful.

Paths, fences and walls

By May the climbers against and over the garden walls and fences are really getting away and you must make sure both that the wall or fence is strong and undamaged and that supports for the climbers are secure and sufficient. Many climbers have been chosen largely because of their rampant habit of growth and this can be heavy and strong enough to show up any weaknesses.

Polygonum baldschuanicum, the Russian vine, with its creamy foam of flowers in the summer is so prolific with its growth that it should never normally be grown on a fence. Instead it needs a strong wall, a hedge or an old tree. It can lift the roof off a garage. Yet its yards of growth in a single year make it a most valuable subject where an unsightly surface needs to be covered or beautified.

A fence is only as strong as its support posts. If these rot underground, an entire length is likely to trap the wind and lean or fall, with consequent damage to the plants. So always make sure that fencing posts are strong, rot-proofed at the base and securely fixed into the soil. When erecting a fence a couple of extra days and a few extra shillings spent on bedding support posts into concrete can lengthen the life of the fence by up to 10 years. If this is impracticable for some reason, then dip the end which is to go underground in boiling pitch, soak it thoroughly in creosote or some other wood preservative or brace it with steel supports.

Always remember, however, that creosote is death to all plant life. Any portion of a plant coming into contact with fresh creosote will be killed and the fumes alone are sufficient to damage some plants. So if you have creosoted a fence, or the fencing posts, allow several months to pass before attempting to grow plants on or even near the newly treated surfaces.

There are so many kinds of fencing available today that it is impossible to

Fence posts that have been preserved from rotting will support the fence well for several years. They are preserved by dipping the ends of the posts in boiling pitch.

go into the virtues or drawbacks of them all. Always try to erect as low a fence as possible compatible with your requirements of privacy, screening and protection, for the higher the fence the more prone to wind damage. A low fence can have trellis panels fixed to the top to increase the height.

Trellis and plastic mesh can be both effective and inexpensive for many screening and disguising purposes in the garden. The oil tank or the dustbin area are easily hidden by a length of trellis on which is growing a clematis, a forsythia or an evergreen ivy.

With all fencing and screening problems, particularly where the object is to obtain privacy rather than shelter, remember always that a light screen is just as effective in keeping prying eyes at bay as a more solid block.

There is no reason today why timber should be used as fencing, or even trellis, for several excellent plastic materials are now on the market, which can be used for the same purpose. Some of these are translucent, admitting extra light into the garden and nearly all are long lasting.

Patios, balconies, roof gardens and window boxes

This is usually the first month when the facilities and pleasure of patios, roof gardens and balconies can be enjoyed. Window boxes can be filled with little fear that late frosts will damage or kill the plants that have been put out. Planning is all very well, but it is not until you go out to enjoy your 'outdoor rooms' that you discover what is missing.

As practically all plants in these situations must be grown in containers it is as well to consider what plants grow vigorously under the limitations imposed. The variety is surprisingly large and includes a number of trees and shrubs. Naturally for such large subjects the container itself should be large, but in all the cases mentioned here no container need be larger than a 12-inch diameter flower pot with roughly the same depth. Some of the trees mentioned will in time outgrow their situation, but they can then easily be transplanted into the garden. On the other hand, by keeping the root system confined many plants will tend to become dwarfed and will live for years in an unnaturally small home.

Trellis of wood or plastic is invaluable for screening purposes, but should never be taller than is required because it is apt to get blown over in strong winds. Use trellis to screen the dustbin and cover it with Ivy.

When fences are erected they are as strong as their supports and will last longer if the supports are put into the ground as firmly as possible. Sink posts to a depth of at least $1\frac{1}{2}$ feet. ***Left*** **concrete is poured on to a base of bricks or stones.** ***Right*** **a concrete post, which will never rot, is put firmly into the ground and the wooden fence is attached to it above ground level.**

Foliage plants give a sense of permanence to a patio or roof garden and provide the semi-formal background necessary to furnish this somewhat artificial form of gardening.

Some of the exquisite Japanese maples, *Acer palmatum,* with their soft green leaves in spring and their vivid autumn tints are among the best patio, roof garden and balcony trees, for they are slow growing, naturally dwarf and attractive both in shape and colour. Keep in light shade where possible and protect from strong winds.

The laurel, *Aucuba japonica,* is available in several varieties, some of which are suitable for all kinds of homes and situations even the window box. It is evergreen and can be gold spotted and berry bearing.

Camellias make marvellous container plants and no patio, roof garden or balcony should be without one or two examples. They flower early in the year, bearing flowers of a magnificent range of colours and complexity, apparently delicate yet actually tough and weather resistant. They should have a rich and slightly acid soil. Recent advances in camellia culture have presented us with opportunities of finding the widest possible range of varieties and colours at low prices. Keep roots always moist and on hot days give a light spray of clean water over the foliage.

The *Fatsia japonica* (extraordinary how many of these smaller trees and shrubs came originally from Japan) with its large, glossy, striking palmate leaves makes a tough and dramatic plant for the patio or roof garden. It is an easy plant to grow and although it gives no flowers of any consequence the size and shape of the leaves, together with the dramatic appearance of the berries, combine to make it a plant of emphasis. It is not fussy about soils, will accept sun and winds and may even be allowed to become dry at the roots for brief periods.

Hydrangeas, with their great mophead flowers, make wonderful container plants so long as they are never allowed to get dry at the roots. If they can be placed in semi-shade and watered regularly and lavishly in hot weather they are among the most strikingly beautiful and rewarding of plants for these contrived gardens.

In fact because the gardens are contrived and artificial it is wise not to try to make them appear naturalistic and a certain amount of formality and horticultural artificiality is a good thing. One of the best means of achieving this is to include a limited amount of topiary. Clipped box, privet, *Lonicera nitida* and the sweet bay, useful also in the kitchen, can look just right on an elegant patio, on a town roof garden or even on a high hung balcony. All these are easy to grow and all can be obtained with some degree of training already begun. Keep shapes formal rather than fantastic. Maintain cones or balls rather than the difficult and elaborate peacock or animal shapes.

Bulbs provide bold colours on the patio in spring and early summer. They can be lifted after flowering and replaced with summer flowering plants.

Almost all plants on the patio are grown in containers and these can be as simple as a barrel or far more elaborate, according to taste.

Bulb flowers suitable for growing in containers include all the normal spring flowering kinds, such as hyacinths, narcissi and tulips. Choose varieties which do not grow too tall, otherwise sharp winds can snap them off. Also try lilies, which are particularly successful in pots and available in a wide range of beautiful colours and scented. They will have to be staked, but this can be done inconspicuously so that the support does not offend the eye.

Many seeds of annuals can be sown directly into patio pots to give vivid colour later in the year and this is about the time to sow them. Seed is generally so inexpensive and readily available that a few failures are of no major significance. Alyssum, candytuft, nigella, campanula, mignonette, Virginian stock, wallflowers, forget-me-nots,

1 The rock garden is a living canvas of colour in May, and where there is water in the garden as well, the whole scene is alive with interest.
2 Banks and retaining walls or raised beds can be made of peat blocks. This is a good way of growing lime-hating plants in gardens on chalky soil.

pansies, *Anemone japonica,* London pride, armeria, arabis and many others are suitable and effective.

Choose low-growing plants rather than tall and make sure always that they do not get too dry at the roots. Some of these smaller plants can well go at the foot of trees and shrubs or be planted in containers separately at their bases to give greater concentrations of colour to the taller but less spectacular subjects.

Rock gardens

During this month the rock garden is at its peak and should present a living canvas of colour. But pests, too, are breeding prolifically and must be checked. These notes apply at any time during the growing season. But by taking early steps to prevent an infestation, you will help to keep pests to a minimum.

Unfortunately, rock plants are just as liable to attack as the larger occupants of the garden and, although small, the insects are the same as those which attack plants of a normal stature. Thus, what may be a slight infestation of a plant 6 feet in height is a major epidemic on one of only 6 inches.

The many forms of aphids, greenfly, caterpillars and other sap sucking insects can be controlled by the use of a systemic insecticide combined with Malathion, which is readily absorbed by the plant, either through the roots or leaves, and is taken up by the sap on which the pests feed. Another advantage is that the insecticide is persistent, remaining active over a number of weeks and is thus labour-saving, needing approximately only four applications during the growing season.

Worms can be a nuisance in the rock garden, their casts doing great damage to cushion plants, often killing the parts they come into contact with. Fortunately there is a chemical compound containing chlordane on the market and an application, according to makers' instructions, will kill off this pest. It is also persistent and will be effective for at least a year and a half. This compound also controls leatherjackets and the grubs of the vine weevil.

The ant is another pest which can cause a great deal of damage. Ants will destroy a plant in a matter of days by tunnelling through the root system. Where this pest is a nuisance a proprietary powder should be sprinkled liberally around the entrance to the nest.

Slugs are probably the only other major pest and these are more active during rainy and damp spells. They are nocturnal feeders and if possible a search after dusk with a torch will pay dividends. The best method of control is with a mixture of crushed methaldehyde and bran on pieces of slate, or commercial slug pellets near affected plants. These pests have a special liking for all the rare members of the campanula family.

A weekly feed of a good general fertiliser is beneficial during the flowering season of most rock plants. It is best applied at half the strength recommended for ordinary plants and should be discontinued once the plants have finished flowering.

During May cuttings can be taken from many of the plants. These will be from the new soft growth that is normally produced in abundance. Small pieces from 1–2 inches in length according to the size of the plants should be carefully removed and trimmed with a sharp knife or, better still, a razor blade. The cut is made at a node. This is the section where the leaves are joined to the stem. They can be rooted in a mixture of equal parts coarse sand and sieved peat ready prepared in a shallow pan. The cuttings are best inserted and made firm round the side of the pan, then well watered in. The pan is covered with a sheet of glass or, for the less delicate plants, a clear plastic bag is placed over the rim of the pan and fixed in position with a rubber band. Put the pan in half shade and do not allow it to dry out.

An integral part of the rock garden should be a section where a selection of dwarf ericacious plants can be grown. In a lime-free district this does not present any great problems—a site facing west is ideal. In the area chosen the existing soil is enriched with a liberal dressing of peat (3 inches is not too much) and well mixed. If necessary the section chosen can have a wall made from peat blocks. These are about

In May the rock garden looks at its best, bright with colour against fresh green foliage. Plants that produce hummocks of growth seem inflated when in flower.

3 inches thick and are laid as one would a brick wall, using the compost as a cement between each layer. Three courses will be sufficient and if birds are a nuisance the peat slabs can be pinned down with meat skewers. Any deficiency of soil is made good by using a mixture of four parts leafmould or peat, and equal parts of coarse sand and neutral loam. Should the indigenous soil be calcareous, this can be overcome by building the bed above the surrounding soil. A 2-inch layer of rough peat is placed over the existing soil and then a retaining wall of peat blocks, three courses deep, is constructed and the interior filled with the above mixture. Dwarf rhododendrons are used as dot plants to give height and underplanted with choice plants. The following is a small selection and there are many more: ***Andromeda polifolia nana, Arcterica nana, Calceolaria tenella,*** cassiope in variety, gaultheria, Asiatic gentians, phyllodoces in variety, Asiatic primula (this is best planted vertically in the walls of the peat bed), rhodohypoxis varieties, *Shortia uniflora.* A large number of these plants provide nearly nine months of decoration—flowers in spring followed by outstanding coloured fruits.

May is the ideal time to construct and plant a peat bed. Make sure that the plants do not suffer from drought during the first season after planting.

Roses

Early in the month it is advisable to go over rose bushes with a view to eliminating multiple shoots. Sometimes two or three shoots grow out from the eye just below the pruning cut. This may be due to frost having damaged the first shoot, so that two others appear, one on each side of the original one. Some varieties are very prone to producing multiple shoots even when there has been little or no frost damage. The correct procedure is to remove with the point of a penknife blade any shoots except the strongest one from each eye—otherwise there will be an over-crowded plant, and the shoots and flowers which develop from these eyes will not be of top quality. In addition, much thinning will prove necessary later on.

Pricking over and mulching the rose beds should be continued where this was not completed in April. The soil should have warmed up quite appreciably by about the middle of the month and, if a supply of well-weathered soot happens to be available, it it useful to apply a dressing to the surface at the rate of 3–4 ounces per square yard. This will be of two-fold value. First, it contains sulphate of ammonia in small quantities and, secondly, by darkening the colour, it makes the soil a better medium for absorbing sun heat. As a consequence it should warm up quicker than lighter coloured soil.

It is important to keep a sharp lookout for insect pests during this month. Aphids (greenfly) are sure to be in evidence on the young shoots to some extent. They multiply very rapidly so it is wise to spray before they are very numerous. Any of the well-known contact sprays such as gamma BHC, malathion and derris should be effective in keeping down the number of this sap-sucking pest. It is always a good plan to spray again after an interval of about three days, as aphids have the ability to give birth to live young after they have been killed by insecticides. Care should be taken to spray the underside of the leaves as well as the upper surface—otherwise large colonies of aphids will be missed. If a systemic spraying is preferred, formothion may be used.

During May, too, it becomes necessary to take action against other insect pests, including a wide range of caterpillars, the leaf-rolling saw fly, the larvae of the tortrix moth and the green capsid bug.

Everybody will be familiar with the 'shot-holed' appearance of leaves infested with caterpillars, although a few of them eat the edges of the leaves, where damage may not be so noticeable. For nearly all biting and chewing insects such as caterpillars, the remedy, apart from hand-picking, is to spray the foliage with malathion, since this is poisonous to the pest. This soon dries on the surface of the leaf as a fine white deposit, which may need to be renewed after heavy and prolonged rain. Alternatively, a trichlorphon spray may be used with some effect.

The leaf-rolling sawfly is becoming more widespread as a rose pest. The adult female lays her eggs in the margins of the leaflets and at the same time injects an irritant which causes them to roll downwards and lengthwise. The larvae, on hatching, are able to feed on the inner tissue of the leaf without emerging. The rolling also reduces the leaf area by over fifty per cent and so interferes with the process of photosynthesis. Spraying with trichlorphon four or five times between mid-May and mid-June has produced encouraging results. Otherwise there is little one can do to combat this pest except to pick off and burn any rolled leaves immediately they are seen.

Sometimes leaves are noticed folded together unnaturally, or a leaf may be seen adhering to the footstalk or even to a flower bud. Other leaves may be

1 Black spot, a fungus disease of Roses, and 'shot hole' which can be caused by caterpillars. The remedy is to hand pick and spray with an approved solution.
2 Paeony suffruticosa.
3 P. lutea x delavayi, a hybrid Paeony.

folded upwards and inwards. If these leaves are opened carefully, a small brownish maggot will usually be found. This is the larva of the tortrix moth, which can do a lot of damage in May and June. Hand picking of the folded leaves, after pressing them between the fore-finger and thumb, and then burning them, is the only certain way of dealing with this pest as it is extremely difficult to reach the maggot with contact sprays, protected and folded as it is inside the leaf.

The green capsid bug is a sap sucker and may be seen in May and early June, probably mounted on a small terminal bud, sucking its sap. It is a bright metallic green in appearance, not unlike a very much enlarged aphid, but with long legs and extremely active. If disturbed it will either drop down to the soil or hide underneath a leaf. This pest injects a poison when it sucks the sap, so the young leaves which are attacked, apart from showing puncture holes, have a curiously distorted appearance. Buds which are attacked turn brown and shrivel up, so that the shoot gives the impression of being blind. Spraying several times before the end of May with gamma BHC is recommended. Make sure to thoroughly drench both surfaces of the leaves, the stems and any flower buds.

It may not be too early to start disbudding later in the month. To be effective this job must be tackled in the early stages. It is pointless to leave it until the unwanted buds are as large as peas. Where there are more than three buds on a stem of a hybrid tea, it is advisable to disbud in two stages, first reducing to three and then to one, with an interval of a few days between the two operations. Normally the centre bud of a cluster of three will be left to develop, as this is usually the most advanced.

Trees, Shrubs and Climbers

At the beginning of the month, it will still be possible to transplant evergreen shrubs successfully. The secret of success with this operation is to have the new planting holes ready prepared, with plenty of leafmould or peat to hand for spreading round the roots. This will help to conserve moisture while the shrubs acclimatise themselves to their new surroundings.

When transplanting evergreens, it is advisable to retain as much soil as possible round the roots. With rhododendrons and azaleas this will be easy, since they make a close-packed ball of fibrous roots and soil.

These two last-named shrubs are particularly easy to transplant. Plants in bud can be moved at the beginning of May to flower in their new positions a few weeks later.

This is a good time to visit one or other of the great rhododendron gardens such as Leonardslee, Sheffield Park, Bodnant, or the Royal Horticultural Society gardens at Wisley where the magnificent display of rhododendrons and azaleas on Battleston Hill attracts many thousands of visitors during May.

Much can be learned from gardens like these even though one cannot hope

Rhododendrons can still be planted in early May, especially from containers. Ensure that the hole is big enough and that the shrub is in a central position.

Once the root ball is in position—take care it is not too deep—fill in around the roots with peaty compost, previously moistened.

The shrub is then firmed into position and the surrounding soil consolidated by the foot. The plant should not rock at all after planting.

to emulate their achievements. Before making one's choice of plants, it is advantageous to be able to see mature specimens growing in suitable surroundings. This is something that is seldom possible at nurseries.

Generally speaking, rhododendrons are among the most trouble-free of shrubs. During the coming weeks, however, there is one important maintenance task that will benefit the blossom display next season. It is vital that the flower trusses should be removed as soon as they fade. This prevents the plants from dissipating their energies in setting seed, to the detriment of next year's flower buds. When removing these spent flowers, care must be taken not to damage the group of leaf buds immediately below them. Apart from this tedious operation, rhododendrons will need no pruning.

Pests and diseases of rhododendrons are few and comparatively innocuous—in Britain, at least. It is, however, advisable to examine the plants during the latter half of the month for signs of their two major enemies, the rhododendron bug and the rhododendron white fly. The former has lacy wings and a black glossy body. It lays its eggs on the under-surfaces of the leaves in summer and early autumn.

The larvae start to hatch out in May of the following year. At this stage, they will still be in clusters and a mild infestation can be dealt with by hand picking. Heavier attacks will need a derris spray, vigorously applied to the undersides of the leaves.

For those who cannot, on account of their alkaline soils, grow these lovely lime-haters, *Paeonia suffruticosa*, the moutan or tree paeonies will provide ample compensation. They flower at the same time of year as the majority of rhododendrons and azaleas and although they do not attain the same majestic proportions as the larger rhododendrons, they yield nothing to the latter in the profusion and beauty of their blossom.

Tree paeonies can still go in from pots and two-year-old plants should produce one or two 'sample' blooms a few weeks after planting. They need a deep rich soil and a sheltered situation. Plants usually come grafted on to the rootstock of the herbaceous species *P. lactiflora*. This piece of rootstock should be several inches below the soil surface after planting to enable the tree paeonies to get away quickly on their own roots.

Tree paeonies are incredibly long-lived. Although plants seldom exceed 5 feet in height in Britain, they can have between 50 and 100 blooms, 9–12 inches across. A good selection would include 'Mrs William Kelway', a pure white, 'Duchess of Kent', a clear bright rose, 'King George V', a striking white-flecked scarlet and 'Lord Selborne', a pale salmon-pink, all semi-double.

Shrubs that flower on their previous year's wood, which finished blooming in April, will need to have their flowering shoots removed or cut back hard to encourage plenty of fresh growth for next year's flowers.

Clematis montana and its varieties which should have finished flowering by the end of this month will need similar treatment. Clematis gets into a shocking tangle so that it may be easier to leave the pruned shoots in situ for the new ones to scramble through rather than to risk damage to the plants by pulling them out.

Annual pruning of this kind will restrict this lovely climber to a limited wall space. If it is required to cover a more extensive area, pruning can be delayed until the desired space is filled.

Vegetables

Now that the days and nights are warmer those seeds needing a high

Hardy bush-type Tomatoes can be planted outside now, but these should be under cloches and must be protected in this way until June.

Sow Sweet Corn singly in pots. Keep the pots indoors or in the greenhouse or under cloches or frames to give them protection during the cold May nights.

germination temperature can be sown outdoors. Others already growing can be planted out at the end of the month when all fear of frosts is past. Meanwhile they should be hardened off; otherwise they will suffer a check and time saved by sowing them early will be wasted. Have the sites ready for them so that they can be planted out quickly and suffer as little check as possible.

Cloches, whether large or small individual types such as upturned jam jars and transparent food boxes, should be used wherever possible for the tender plants until the month is through.

Seed which can be sown includes many successional crops. French, haricot and runner beans can go directly into the soil where they are to remain so that they grow without a check. Otherwise they will not crop early. Guard them against slugs. Northern gardeners should sow runner beans indoors in pots or boxes. Plants become less disturbed if they are sown individually either in pots or soil blocks. Once growing, the beans should be watered freely in dry weather. Stake the climbing beans as early as possible. It is not essential that beans should be on very tall poles or in double rows. Some people may, for several reasons, find it more convenient to grow them in a single row up 6-feet bamboos well driven into the soil and each linked by twine at the top. The beans will then grow 5 feet or just over.

Sweet corn can still be sown singly in small pots in a greenhouse, on a sunny window-sill, in frames or outdoors in a sheltered place under cloches where the plants are to mature. A wall might seem to offer splendid protection from both wind and cold, but make sure that the plants will be far enough away from the wall itself to prevent the roots from becoming dry, for this results in poor crops.

Marrows and others of this family can be induced to germinate more quickly by using a seed box lined with moist peat, sand or moss and spacing the seeds on this. Cover them with several layers of tissue and moisten this with warm water. Slide the box into a polythene bag or cover it with a sheet of plastic. Keep it in a warm place—the airing cupboard will do if no greenhouse is available. Check after two days and then daily. Remove sprouting seeds and sow individually and grow on in the usual way. If they are to be sown where they are to grow, have the site well prepared with plenty of warm material rich in dug-in humus.

Any of the marrow family should be given protection until June, so these are best sown under cloches or even individual jam jars to help each seed get off to a warm start.

Sow New Zealand spinach, which will crop well should there be a hot, dry summer.

By planting Water-lilies and other aquatics in rot-proof plastic containers it is possible to keep the water in the pool clear and free from mud.

The only British true aquatic is the Water Fern, Azolla filiculoides. It floats on the surface, providing both pattern and colour in winter and summer.

Outdoor tomatoes of the hardier bush types can be planted, but these should be under cloches and must be protected this way until June.

In cold districts winter cabbage and savoys do not always survive and in this case kale is a good crop to choose. 'Hungry Gap' is the latest maturing and the hardiest of all, but 'Cottager's' and 'Tall Scotch' are also good for exposed gardens. Swedes, too, are very hardy vegetables and are both useful and delicious for winter meals whether grated as salads or used in a cooked dish. (Try a swede souffle—unusual and delicious.) Sow the seeds now and thin out as soon as possible.

Where there is space to spare, sow perennial broccoli early in the month. Plant out, 3–4 feet apart, on well-manured soil, remembering that the plants will yield for several years.

Some of the vegetables which for some reason were not sown last month can still be sown. These include chicory, cauliflower and cucumber.

At the very end of the month plant out celery and celeriac and be sure to water them freely in dry weather, for these are naturally bog plants. They can be planted in flat ground, but in trenches the ground will remain moist.

Garlic cloves can still be planted.

May is a good time to attend to herbs. Canister grown plants can be bought and planted at any time. Seed of many can now be sown. Chervil makes a pleasant change in sauces and soups from the ubiquitous parsley and unlike this herb can be grown in succession from fortnightly sowings.

Vegetables sown last month should be crowding through the soil. Start thinning them as soon as possible, going along the rows on several occasions, culling the weakest and gradually spacing the plants to their correct distances.

Not all thinnings need be discarded. Lettuce and young brassicas of all kinds can be combined with spinach to use raw in salads or to be cooked together if need be. Baby beets can be cooked whole, roots and all.

When transplanting remember that all brassicas must be planted really firmly on well limed ground. These crops suffer considerably if they are allowed to remain crowded. A good way to save time and labour, if there is room to spare, is to sow them by placing a pinch of seed in the drill at planting intervals. Then gradually thin out the groups until only the strongest plant is left.

Water gardens

With so many other garden jobs demanding attention in March and April, it is just as well that the planting of aquatics has to be deferred until the plants are actively growing. Some will not be ready until June, but many can be obtained in May and all necessary preparations should be made in good time to deal with them as soon as they are delivered.

There are two schools of thought on the best method of planting. One favours a continuous soil layer 6–8 inches deep all over the floor and shelves of the pool to encourage abundant plant growth. The drawbacks are the amount of soil needed, the inability to control excessive growth, the mud stirring caused by fish and the work involved in cleaning out. The more modern technique is to plant in rot-proof plastic containers. These greatly reduce both soil requirements and labour, prevent excessive growth and the intermingling of varieties, simplify positioning and re-arrangement of plants, frustrate mud-stirring fish (completely if the container is topped with pebbles) and make spring cleaning a very minor operation since there is no soil anywhere in the pool outside the containers. The objection that it looks 'unnatural' loses force as the container is hidden by plant growth. Suppliers of aquatic plants offer containers in sizes suitable for (a) individual water-lilies (b) one or two marginal plants and (c) four to six oxygenators. The broad-based containers are better than the flower-pot shaped types that are so liable to topple and spill out their soil.

The best medium for all aquatic plants is a really stiff soil with chopped turf mixed into it. The plants will grow well enough in this without manure, fertiliser, bonemeal or other additives and since they encourage green water they should be firmly excluded. Sifted soil composts, sand, peat and leafmould should never be used.

When the pond plants are delivered they must be unpacked at once and placed in a bucket or tub of water until they can be dealt with. Before planting trim off any damaged stems and leaves. The old fleshy roots of water-lilies are superfluous and can be removed, if the supplier has not already taken care of this detail. Lilies must be positioned so that the growing point is not smothered. All planting must be very firmly packed down indeed to compensate for an inevitable loosening of the soil as the container is lowered carefully and gradually into the water.

Containers holding marginals will stand on shelves, or a shallow end, so that there is one to four inches of water over the soil, according to variety. Submerged oxygenating plants (there should be one for every two square feet of water surface area) can be positioned at any level. Some in the shallows to encourage fish spawning, others in the deeper parts. Water-lilies, though destined later to stand in the bottom, should at first be supported on bricks so that new leaf growth can quickly reach the surface. When strong leaf growth has developed they can be lowered, though the depth of water over the crown need never be more than 12–18 inches. The idea that the stronger growers *need* a water depth of 3 feet is quite wrong, and only a few will even tolerate this much. Floating plants (azolla, lemna, hydrocharis, stratiotes etc.) do not need planting and are merely placed on the surface.

The seedlings of primulas and irises should soon be ready to plant out into a bed of good soil in a sheltered spot. The primulas must be well shaded.

Two ounces of bonemeal to the square yard will benefit the waterside area but do not allow this to fall into the pond.

A pond that has recently been filled (or re-filled) will probably by now be thickly coloured, as if the pond was filled with green distemper. This discolouration is produced by myriads of minute plants (algae) which thrive on light and mineral salts in the water, and may occasionally be red instead of green. This condition is normal and inevitable, a stage the pool must be allowed to go through. Changing the water only postpones the day when the water suddenly clears, as it will do once the plants are thoroughly established. Oxygenating plants contribute most to the transformation by consuming mineral salts. Water-lilies and floating plants assist by reducing the amount of sunlight that penetrates below the surface. This natural control is infinitely preferable to the use of chemicals that at best have only a temporary effect and at worst may be damaging both to plant life and to fish.

A fish being chivvied by others is a female near to spawning. Do not separate them. Such ministrations are necessary to stimulate the release of eggs among the dense growth of oxygenating plants.

Oval or sausage-shaped blobs of jelly on the underside of lily leaves are not 'slugs' but the egg clusters of aquatic snails which are likely, on balance, to do more good than harm.

Wildlife

The Red Admiral visits gardens in summer for the Nettles, Honesty and Buddleias.

May brings the very last of the summer visitors and pushes out the late winter residents. The earlier visitors are nesting in the north and in all the gardens the parent birds dash around frenziedly searching for food with which to quieten their young's everlasting demands. The animals that hibernated during the winter are back in their burrows and holes either rearing their young or preparing to do so.

A large number of summer visitors such as swallows, swifts and flycatchers are insectivorous. The garden insects on which they prey are many and fascinating to study.

Perhaps the best known of these insects are the bees. They have a very rigid class system, divided into three castes. The first is the queen. There is never more than one queen in each hive and her sole task is to propagate the race. The second type of bee is the worker. She is the infertile female and, as her name suggests, does all the work of the hive. The final member is the drone, the male, driven ruthlessly from the hive once he has fulfilled his function of mating with the queen.

Another garden insect with a highly developed sense of civilisation is the ant. The ant family is found and feared throughout the world. In South America and Africa ants can destroy great areas of crops when they are on the march, though in Britain there are no such worries. The garden ant, though a pest, does much good as a scavenger and clears the garden of carrion.

Any sources of water in a garden, from a pond to a water-butt, provide a breeding ground for the mosquito. This insect, like the ant, is harmless in northern countries. The larvae of this insect can be seen wriggling around in most stagnant water not occupied by fish that do a good job of pest control.

An insect seldom seen, but familiar from its excreta, is the froghopper or cuckoo spit insect. The nymphs settle on a blade of grass, lavender or other stem and build around themselves a protective shield of the frothy liquid they suck from the plant.

To have butterflies in the garden can be as colourful as having flowers. The most common of the butterflies are the whites, which include the pests known as cabbage whites because of their fondness for and damage to the brassicas. This butterfly, like the starling, is a semi-migrant and lays its eggs in the summer months in batches of 60–100 on the cabbage plants. When the eggs hatch out to caterpillars they have two months or so in which to devour the cabbage patch.

The red admiral is another common butterfly which is a semi-migrant. A great attraction to most butterflies is a buddleia tree and other good host plants are honesty and nettles.

Encourage butterflies and bees into your garden for the summer by planting, in addition to the hosts already mentioned, cotoneasters, lavender, lilacs, thymes, alyssum, mignonette, golden rod and verbascum.

Insects are preyed upon by many members of the animal and bird world—some birds basing their entire diet on winged insects. Closer to earth they are preyed upon by frogs, lizards and snakes, and the slow moving hedgehog.

In May nature's careful balance can be most easily observed. Not even man can significantly alter its delicate planning and in fact if man makes a mistake nature quickly corrects it. The animals, birds and insects of the garden manage to go on living much as they did before the first man walked upon the earth, despite pesticides, insecticides and other poisons.

The Month of June

Claiming her place, the rose, queen of garden flowers, reigns supreme from June right through the summer. The blossom has fallen and the herbaceous plants are at their best, but the wide range of rose colour, shape and form dominates the scene

Hybrid Tea Rose 'Hugh Dickson', one of the most fragrant varieties, is also a vigorous grower

1

1 The Hybrid Tea Rose 'Red Devil' is sweetly scented and is a good weather Rose. In seasons when wet weather predominates its performance is unfortunately rather poor.
2 The Hybrid Tea Rose 'Serenade' is a slightly fragrant flower. The plant has fine glossy foliage and is a strong grower.
3 The early blooms of Rose 'Super Star' grow in large clusters. The second blooms are large. Both first and second crops are sweetly scented.
4 Hybrid Tea Rose 'Ena Harkness' has been a favourite in our gardens for more than two decades. It is both a fragrant and free-flowering Rose.
5 The Hybrid Tea Rose 'Silver Lining' is very fragrant and has handsome deep green foliage which contrasts attractively with the soft hues of the blooms.

2

4

5

3

1 The Shrub Rose 'Kassel', raised by Kordes , flowers freely through the summer and is particularly good in the autumn.
2 Rosa spinosissima hybrid 'Fruhlingsgold' is a lovely shrub Rose producing fragrant blooms in long arching stems.
3 The Floribunda Rose 'Dearest' produces very fragrant large flowers on vigorous, yet neatly growing, bushy plants. It is an ideal Rose for bedding.
4 One of the many red HT Roses, 'Fidelio' is useful for cutting. Its neat deep green foliage furnishes both vase and garden attractively.
5 Rose 'Zephirine Drouhin' with thornless stems, is a Bourbon Rose, and can be either a climbing or a shrub Rose. It is free-flowering in summer and autumn.

2

4

3

5

1

1 Senecio cineraria, sometimes called by the name Dusty Miller, produces yellow daisy-like flowers. The plants make a better 'silver' display if they are picked off when in bud.
2 Ruta graveolens 'Jackman's Blue', the Herb of Grace, forms an extremely attractive shrub some 3 feet in height.
3 Stachys lanata 'Silver Carpet', the Lamb's Tongue, makes a dense mat of downy leaves. It is a dual-purpose plant, ideal both for edging and for ground cover.
4 Eucalyptus perriniana, the round-leaved Snow Gum, like most of its kind produces both juvenile and adult forms of foliage.
5 Senecio leucostachys grows much like S. cineraria, but it is distinguished by its finely feathered foliage.

2

3

4

5

Jobs of the month

For all its glories June makes its demands on the gardener. There are bulbs to be lifted, frequent lawn-mowing stints, house plants to be given a breath of fresh air, seeds to pot on and the kitchen garden to be tended. None of this can wait. June is an urgent month when growth and change are rapid and when you must act decisively or suffer the consequences

Bulbs

Overcrowded or deteriorating spring bulbs can be lifted and left to dry off in boxes. Drench gladioli during dry weather

Flowers for Cutting

Ensure that perennials, which like moist positions are watered before you arrange them. Delphiniums for arrangements should have hot water treatment.

Fruit

Spray apples early against red spider mite and repeat. Watch gooseberry bushes for hatching of sawfly caterpillars. Pinch out growing point of greenhouse melons as they reach top wire

Greenhouse

Now is the time for bedding out plants from cold frames. Pot-grown chrysanthemums now outside should be well staked against the wind

Hedges

Regular summer spraying of rose hedges against black spot, mildew and greenfly should begin this month

Herbaceous Plants

Remove May-flowering tulips to make room for half-hardy bedding plants. Destroy decaying petals. Fork fertiliser into soil before replanting

House Plants

Less delicate house plants should be placed out of doors to benefit from sunshine and showers. Give them protection against the wind. Some can be plunged into borders in their pots. Water well

Lawns

Mowing becomes a twice weekly job now Rake the lawn once or twice this month before cutting. This helps to control weeds. Time, too, for a summer application of fertiliser

Paths, Fences and Walls

Some flower borders can be improved by the addition of a perimeter path or edging which need not be more than six inches wide

Patios, Balconies, Roof Gardens and Window Boxes

Now the patio comes into its own and deserves to be well decorated

Rock Gardens

Seeds sown in April should now be ready to pot on. From now onwards seeds of the rarer rock plants should be sown as they ripen

Roses

Disbudding is an important job this month. Supplementary feeding will give very best results. Spray against mildew at first sign of the disease. Watch for insect pests

Trees, Shrubs and Climbers

Make sure that newly-planted climbers get the support they need. Tie main shoots of non-clinging wall shrubs to horizontal wires until they are strong

Vegetables

Careful planning now provides you with young crops for the rest of the summer. Use space between slow-growing plants for quick-maturing salads. Nip out broad bean tips

Water Gardens

This is still a good time to plant aquatics. New pools planted in May are now ready for fish. Watch new leaves on lilies for signs of midge attack and remove if affected

Wildlife

Warm June evenings bring out the insects and grubs, and their killers. The hedgehog, one of the most efficient, can often be lured from his hedge with a saucer of milk

Bulbs

Towards the end of the month, when the foliage has died down or turned yellow, the spring-flowering bulbs can be lifted. Lift tulips each year immediately after flowering and replant them in a sunny spot to ripen. Leave the tulip species bulbs undisturbed and lift them only occasionally when they need dividing. Other spring-flowering bulbs need only be lifted when they appear to be deteriorating or when the plants become overcrowded. Push a fork into the soil, well away from the clump of bulbs, and sufficiently deep to avoid damage to the plant's roots.

Leave the bulbs to dry off in boxes in a dry, freely ventilated shed. Burn any that are soft or affected by eelworm. When the bulbs are dry take off the dead leaves, remove the old roots and rub away the dried skins. Put the cleaned bulbs back into boxes or trays and leave them in a cool place. Keep the different kinds separate from one another and label the varieties.

Water gladioli during dry weather. A good drenching is far better than a few dribbles of water. Stake the plants now if this has not been done already. Otherwise, as the weight of the top growth increases, there will be some rocking in the wind, especially in exposed gardens. Mulch both gladioli and lilies with compost, peat or leafmould to conserve moisture, but ensure that no rotting material gets round the collar of the plants, for it will eventually cause rotting of the neck of the corm or bulb. Once flower spikes appear in either of these plants, keep a look out for aphids and use a preventive spray, especially in dry weather.

Bulb catalogues will be available late this month and the notes of requirements made during March and April will prove invaluable. Waste no time in ordering the supplies of spring-flowering bulbs which need planting this autumn, especially the narcissi, which do not like to be out of the ground longer than is necessary.

1

2

3

4

1 Tulip bulbs are lifted once flowering has finished and the beds are needed for summer plants. They should be heeled in until the top growth has died down and turned yellow. Choose dry soil in a sheltered place.
2 Narcissus bulbs can be lifted after flowering has finished and stored in shallow boxes or trays to allow the bulbs to dry off.
3 Rub the bulbs free of the dead outer coats and cut back all the foliage and old roots.
4 Store the bulbs loosely in trays and keep them in a cool dry place until they can be planted again at the end of the summer. Label each variety.

1

2

1 Hosta fortunei albo picta, one of the variegated-leaf Hostas which enjoy moisture at the roots when growing. So ensure that they have a long drink of water before arranging them in vases.
2 Vinca minor, the blue-flowered Periwinkle, with long trailing shoots.

Flowers for Cutting

Flower arrangers are as concerned with handsome and beautiful leaves as they are with flowers, and the ambition of interested people is to build up a collection of plants in the garden that will furnish it well and at the same time provide plenty of flowers and foliage for cutting.

Many of the perennials play an important role in the garden as ground covers and shade plants. The variegated periwinkle, *Vinca major variegata*, for example, has long, slender, trailing stems which hug the ground and root into it and which, when cut, hang gracefully from pendant or pedestal arrangements.

The Lamium species, the dead nettles, also with golden and silver variegated leaves, are again ground covering yet graceful and long-lived in arrangements. Heucheras, polygonatum or Solomon's seal, hostas and ferns are others. When you cut any of these you should remember that they like moist shade when growing.

Therefore you must see that they are well charged with water before they are arranged. Only mature ferns will drink. Gather those with well developed spores on the undersides and give them hot water treatment.

Among the bedding plants which should be planted out now, the ornamental-leaved pelargoniums are outstanding.

It is true that the leaves are small and short compared with hostas, for example, but being so bright they bring a valuable contribution to an arrangement. They have the advantage of being pot grown, which means that they can help in winter decoration as well. The ornamental-leaved pelargoniums are worth collecting for this purpose.

The true castor oil plant, ricinus, has large palmate leaves of bronze, purple or green according to variety. They look well if arranged outstretched at the foot of tall, smooth-stemmed flowers. These leaves are very soft and silky and must be given hot water treatment in preparation for arrangement.

Delphiniums are particularly valuable in dried arrangements because of their good blues which are not to be found among other perpetuelles. Take into account that the dried colours will be less intense than the fresh, so choose clear, bright colours. Deep purples become black and are unattractive, bringing a dead effect to a dried arrangement.

You must also avoid the grey-lavender types which dry a dirty hue. Those varieties with a good eye are particularly attractive. Clear whites are excellent. The annual larkspurs of all varieties may also be dried.

Although even outsize large spikes dry well (if one can find space to hang them) the shorter types of delphinium are really most useful for this purpose. Arrangers who do not wish to cut whole spikes and spoil the garden display should concentrate on the florets which grow at the bottom of the spike. These can be cut and dried individually. They are also useful in fresh flower arrangements.

Delphiniums—and any other flower which is not a true everlasting—should be dried quickly and in gentle heat. The most convenient method is to hang them individually in an airing cupboard, head downwards. Any other similar place, near a boiler for example, or any warm, dry place will do but it should be dark.

Delphiniums for fresh flower arrangements should be given hot water treatment. Like all the ranunculaceae these flowers can be very temperamental after cutting.

When shortening the cut flower stem for arrangement, after hardening, cut it while holding it under water to prevent the formation of an air lock.

Gypsophila paniculata should be cut at its best and dried at once.

Drying flowers by hanging them in a suitable environment is the easiest and least expensive way. Not all flowers will dry, however, and the arranger has to discover the best subjects by trial and error. Seasons, weather and time of gathering the flowers can make considerable differences.

However, with more trouble and at

greater expense, it is possible to dry sappy flowers by using silica gel as a desiccant. A great deal of this is sometimes needed because flowers have to be entirely buried in it, but it can be used time and time again. Stems may have to be removed from flowers and replaced later by florist wires or straws.

The desiccant and flowers must be in airtight boxes. Some flowers, such as daisies, are best placed in upside down, but others, such as pansies, are best laid flat, while cup flowers need to look upwards.

Arrange a bottom layer of silica gel in the box, lay the flowers on this so that they do not touch and pour the desiccant over until every part of the flower is covered. Test after two days. Some flowers, cornflowers for example, dry in about 48 hours.

Fruit

Anti-disease and pest measures must still have a high priority in the garden fruit-grower's programme.

Spray apples with malathion or derris in early June to control red spider mite. Repeat this twice at fortnightly intervals, or spray with a summer ovicide in mid-June and repeat three weeks later. It is advisable to ring the changes in spraying against red spider mite as these minute creatures soon develop a certain unfortunate immunity to one chemical.

The codling moth can be a very troublesome pest. The grubs are sometimes found inside the apples. They must be killed before they eat their way in by adding sevin to the second and third malathion or derris sprays or to both ovicide sprays mentioned above.

Two sprayings of malathion with a fortnightly interval will usually control any woolly aphid which may be present. (This is the creature which protects itself with a white froth looking like a tuft of cotton wool.) In bad cases, where the pest still survives these sprayings, or in isolated attacks the tufts of 'cotton wool' may be dabbed individually with a brush dipped in a strong solution of BHC.

Normally, a programme of anti-scab spraying carried out in March, April and May will ensure clean, disease-free apples and pears. Where this trouble has been exceptionally rife in past seasons, give yet another spraying of captan in June.

Red spider mite can be seen with a reasonably powerful magnifying lens. Examine the undersides of plum, gage and damson leaves and, if mites are seen, let the tree have the same control programme advised for apples.

The red plum maggot is to plums what codling moth is to apples. Trees sprayed in winter with tar-oil should not be troubled; otherwise spray in mid-June with sevin. Repeat two or three weeks later. Never apply DDT at any time—its use is strictly forbidden.

An old-fashioned but still worth-while way of controlling apple codling moth and red plum maggot is to trap the caterpillars when they hibernate. Take a piece of sacking, fold it to make a double thickness and wrap around the trunk of the tree just below the crotch and tie in position with string. The caterpillars will creep into the fold of sacking which can be removed and burnt in the autumn. If, in these days of plastic sacks, you have no sacking, use strips of corrugated paper: the birds will probably pull these to pieces hunting for the caterpillars before you can burn them.

Spray raspberries with derris ten days after full bloom to deal with the raspberry beetle and repeat ten days later. If cane spot disease has been very severe, add colloidal copper to these washes.

Keep an eye on gooseberry bushes for another hatching of sawfly caterpillars and, if any are seen, spray with derris.

Pinch off any blossom formed on raspberries or other cane fruits only planted during the last winter. Perpetual strawberries which have hitherto been deblossomed may now be allowed to develop the next trusses of flowers. Keep the weeds down among these late strawberries. A 2-inch mulch of lawn mowings or moist peat will assist in this and help to conserve soil moisture. See that cloched strawberries are well ventilated on warm days.

1 The 'king' or 'crown' fruit in a cluster of young Apples is the first one to remove when thinning the fruit. It may be the largest but it is of inferior quality and frequently misshapen. Remove it with sharp scissors.
2 The larvae of the Codlin Moth can be trapped by wrapping bands of sacking around the trunks of fruit trees, just below the crotch. Tie the bands of sacking firmly with string both top and bottom, and inspect the bands regularly.

Greenhouse or cloche-grown Melons are growing well at this time of the year. The growing points of the sub-laterals need to be removed and the remaining shoots trained to fill available space.

The unwanted canes of Raspberries can be chopped out with a hoe because the plants root very near to the surface. The job can be repeated as required throughout the summer months.

When greenhouse melons reach the top wires, pinch out the growing point to make side-shoots develop. Plant out melons in cold frames or beneath cloches. Pinch these plants, too, and train out four side-shoots to the corners of the frame or the length of cloche space available.

Pinch out laterals on wall-trained apricots. This will stimulate the production of fruit spurs.

Carry out the final thinning of wall-trained peaches and nectarines. The extent of this will depend upon the vigour of the tree. Usually it is reckoned that a tree can only support one fruit to each square foot of wall covered; but with very vigorous trees this can be extended to one fruit per 9-inch square.

Bush peaches are frequently left unthinned but the size of individual fruits will be improved and the prospects of regular cropping increased if very heavy crops are thinned until there is at least a handspan between the fruits along a branch.

Where heavy crops of apples, pears and plums have set, it pays to thin. The remaining fruit will be of better size and quality.

The following year's crop is less likely to be impaired by over-cropping this year and, as with plums, the risk of branch-breaking will be reduced.

In the case of apples and pears, start by cutting out, with a pair of scissors, the 'king' fruits. At each cluster of fruitlets you will notice that the one formed by the central flower is the largest: it is not as good as it looks, however.

The 'king' fruits often prove to be poorly shaped and indifferent keepers. Also remove any obviously blemished or misshapen fruit. Similar principles apply to plums. After this preliminary thinning of inferior fruit wait until after the natural 'June drop'.

Restrict autumn-fruiting raspberries to from six to eight of the strongest new canes. The unwanted canes can be chopped out with the hoe but always be very careful when hoeing in the raspberry bed, as these plants root very near the surface. This is why chemical weeding is the best method. See that newly planted raspberries are provided with canes or some suitable means of support as they grow.

Towards the end of the month prune back laterals on gooseberries and red and white currants to five leaves.

Greenhouse

Dahlias, zonal pelargoniums ('geraniums'), fuchsias, zinnias, *Salvia splendens*, cannas, *Begonia semperflorens*, heliotropes and gazanias may all be planted out now from the cold-frames if they have been well hardened off. If there are any surplus plants, some of them should be potted up into 5-inch pots for summer flowering in the greenhouse but a few of the pelargoniums will also come in useful for winter flowering if all the flower buds are removed until the end of September.

The empty frames can then be used for those pot-plants coming on for next winter and spring, such as cyclamen, *Primula obconica, P. malacoides*, cinerarias and calceolarias, as soon as these are in their final pots. Some of them will already be in 3- or 3½-inch pots, but others will still be in the boxes in which they were pricked out. In the latter case the plants must be moved on into 3- or 3½-inch pots just before their leaves meet in the boxes, when each one should be potted singly in the John Innes potting compost No 1.

Make sure their roots are moist before moving the plants on and see that they are potted moderately firmly with about half an inch left at the top of the pot for watering. Plants without an obvious stem must not be buried too deeply; just keep the base of the plant level with the surface of the compost.

Plants already in small pots will be ready for their final potting as soon as the roots can be seen in the drainage holes.

After making certain that the plants are moist at the root knock each one out of its pot and set it in a 5- or 6-inch one, filled with the John Innes potting compost No 2 over good drainage so that when the potting is done there will be a space of about three-quarters of an inch

1 Cucumber plants must be stopped when they reach the top of the supporting wires, and flowers on the main stem and male flowers need removing.
2 Give greenhouse space now to Gloxinias.

at the top of the pot for watering. Keep the plants shaded and slightly on the dry side for a few days after potting, then transfer them to the cold-frame.

Here they will grow better and need less water if they are 'plunged', or buried to the pot-rim, in a mixture of peat, sand and sieved soil; or peat and sand alone can be used. Do not overcrowd the plants as their leaves must never be allowed to touch. Give them plenty of ventilation and shade them from full sun.

Solanum capsicastrum, the Christmas cherry, is another plant that should be similarly potted and plunged, but add a pinch of Epsom salts (magnesium sulphate) to each pot of compost. Then, when the plants produce their small white flowers, keep them well syringed to ensure a good 'set' of berries.

If the late-flowering plants are in the frames, the greenhouse can be used for the summer-flowering ones, such as gloxinias and tuberous begonias. To produce large flowers start to feed these as the pots fill with roots, giving weak doses at frequent intervals rather than stronger ones at longer intervals, with the feed always being given when the soil is already moist. Keep these and other summer pot-plants shaded from full sun. 'Damp down' and ventilate the greenhouse on hot days.

Pot-grown chrysanthemums now outside must be securely staked against wind damage. Use 4- or 5-feet canes according to the height of the variety, with one or three canes to each pot. If one is used, stand it upright in the pot and secure it to a wire stretched between two firm end posts. If three are used, splay them outwards and fasten two to the supporting wire. Watering of these chrysanthemums will need very careful attention, with sufficient being given at each watering to soak the soil right through.

Plants of *Azalea indica* kept from last winter should go outside now. Plunge them to the pot-rim in peat or in a lime-free soil and keep them well watered and syringed with lime-free water—rain-water if necessary.

Tomatoes will need more water as they grow. See that all sideshoots are regularly removed and spray the plants overhead daily to help the fruit to set.

Greenhouse cucumber plants must be stopped when they are about 4 feet high or at the top of the supporting wires. Remove all flowers from the main stem and all male flowers (those without an embryo fruit). Then, as the fruits appear, stop all shoots two leaves beyond the fruit.

Hedges

June is the month when many flowering hedges are at their peak. Among those that will be making their colourful contribution are philadelphus, berberis, pyracantha, rhododendron and, of course, rose hedges.

Rose hedges are becoming increasingly popular and any opportunity of seeing roses grown in this way should be taken during the next six weeks or so.

Many types of rose make first-rate hedging plants and floribundas, with their great vigour and sturdy constitutions, are particularly well suited for the purpose. Three of the best of these are the deep crimson 'Frensham', a semi-double; 'Queen Elizabeth', with its profusion of pink, hybrid tea-type blooms, and 'Masquerade', whose large flower clusters make a patchwork quilt of reds, pinks and yellows.

Penzance briars, with their sweetly scented foliage and free-flowering habit, have been popular for hedging for many years. They are hybrids of *Rosa rubiginosa*, the sweet briar or eglantine, which were raised and introduced by Lord Penzance in the last decade of the nineteenth century. Although their flowering season is shorter than that of the floribundas, they make up for this by the abundance of their blossom.

RECOGNITION CHART

Natural Order 1

Within major groups of classification, plants are collected into families according to the arrangement of their parts

POLYGONACEAE
The genus Polygonum includes several decorative plants for the rock garden and border. Polygonum bistorta is both a wild and a cultivated plant and Polygonum baldschuanicum the Russian Vine a scrambling climbing plant. The Knotweed is a weed of cultivated ground and Sorrel provides food, as does Rhubarb

LILIACEAE
The multi-coloured Lilies are related to Tulips, Bluebells and the unusual shrub Butcher's Broom. Food in this family is represented by Chives, Leeks, Onions and Asparagus

CRUCIFERAE
The colourful and highly scented Stocks and Wallflowers are in the same family as as Cabbages, Cauliflowers, Brussels Sprouts, Kale and Broccoli. Watercress provides salad food while Shepherd's Purse is a weed

LEGUMINOSAE
Food in the form of Beans and Peas is part of this family, whose Sweet Peas provide colour and scent. The Brooms, in a wide range of colour, are shrubs and the Clovers are weeds

COMPOSITAE
All the Daisy-like decorative plants belong to this big family, the Shasta Daisies, Sunflowers, Chrysanthemums, Heleniums, Cornflowers, Rudbeckia and Cosmos. The Lettuce is food while Burdock, Dandelion and Thistle are weeds

PRIMULACEAE
The wide range of Primulas, including the Primrose of the hedgebanks, the Auricula and the Polyanthus are related to the cormous Cyclamen of woodland garden and greenhouse. The weeds in the family include the Scarlet Pimpernel

GRAMINEAE
Grasses, such as Rye Grass and Crested Dog's Tail, are often in the lawn seed mixture. Yet Couch Grass is a weed. Wheat, Barley and Oats are cereals used for food, as is Maize, and Sweet Corn. Some grasses such as Cortaderia, Pampas Grass, are used as decorative plants

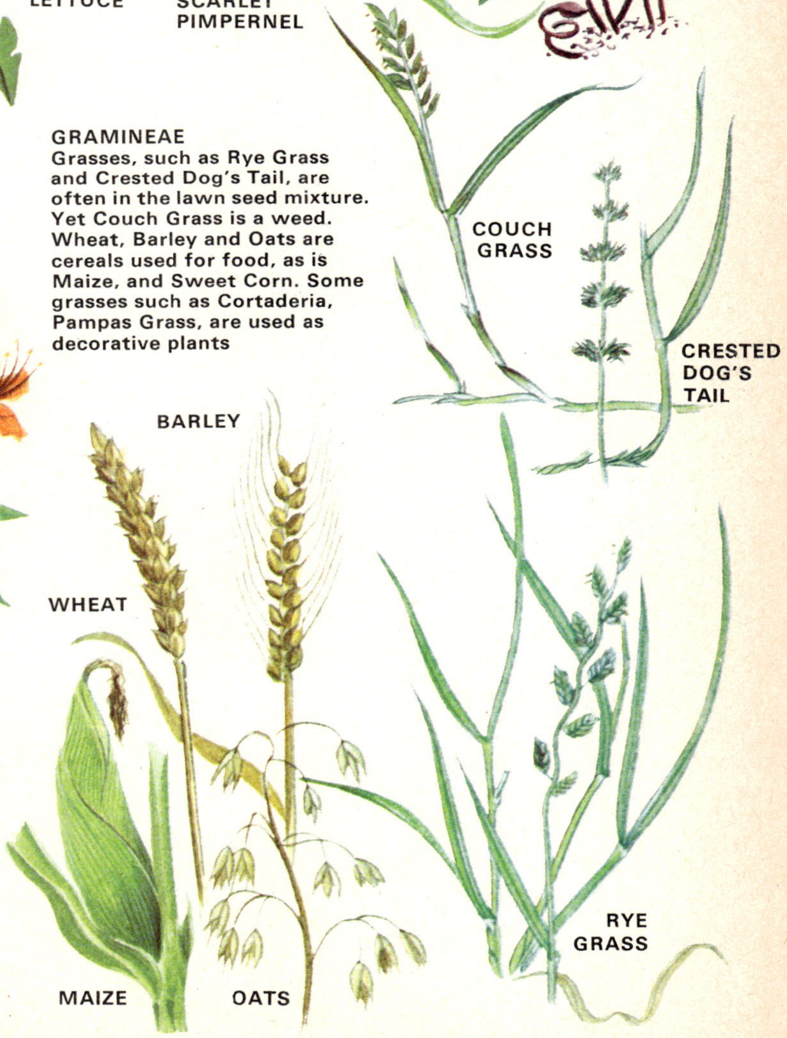

ERICACEAE
Rhododendrons and Azaleas are in the Heather family as shrubs. Many sub-shrubs like Heathers and Daboecia, Cranberry and Wortleberries are represented. The Strawberry Tree, Arbutus unedo, is also in the family

1

2

1 Ideally the dead wood should be removed from a Rose hedge in winter or when pruning is done in March. But all obviously dead wood can be removed at any time during the growing season.
2 A hedge of Rose 'Albertine'. Rose hedges are increasingly popular, and provide a decorative boundary.

The Penzance briars are a distinct improvement on their parent. Good named forms include the deep rose-pink 'Amy Robsart', crimson 'Anne of Geierstein' and the vivid red 'Magnifica', which has a white eye. All of these are semi-doubles. 'Lady Penzance', with coppery-orange flowers, is a single and one of the most striking members of the group. The flowers of all of them are intensely fragrant.

A large number of the old-fashioned species or 'shrub' roses also make excellent hedging material. Their free and often arching habit of growth makes them ideal for the job. For a brilliant hedge to flower this month, the early-blooming *Rosa xanthina* 'Canarybird' would be hard to better. It makes a magnificent hedge with elegant arching sprays that are massed with large yellow scented single flowers.

R. centifolia and its varieties come into bloom later in the month and continue throughout most of July. The flowers are more delicately coloured than those of 'Canarybird' or the Penzance briars. Those of 'Chapeau de Napoleon' and 'Fantin Latour' are both a delicate shade of pale pink.

R. rubrifolia will make a striking hedge whose leaf colour will provide the major attraction. The foliage of this old rose is beetroot-red, with a greyish bloom like that of a hothouse grape. The small pink flowers are relatively insignificant but the striking leaf colouring makes a hedge of *R. rubrifolia* an outstanding feature throughout the whole of the summer and autumn.

'Zephyrine Drouhin', the 'rose without a thorn', makes an easily managed hedge and 'Mme Pierre Oger', another lovely Bourbon rose, will display its lovely shell-pink blossoms to good effect when used for the same purpose. All of these bloom almost continuously throughout the summer and autumn. Exciting contrasts are provided by the grey-green foliage and scented blush-pink flowers of 'Maiden's Blush', a well-known variety of *R. alba* that was flourishing in English gardens more than five centuries ago.

Rose hedges will need only a *light* clipping, once a year in March. This annual operation should consist merely of trimming for shape, plus the cutting out of dead or diseased wood. Cutting back a rose hedge too drastically not only destroys its character—it also results in sparse flowering.

Regular summer spraying, starting in June, is advisable to combat black spot, mildew and greenfly. Systemic sprays are good for the last-named pest, but many gardeners prefer to use two or more compatible sprays and combine them to give protection against a wide range of pests and diseases with one application.

Herbaceous Plants

May flowering tulips should be removed as soon as the flowers fade to make way for half-hardy bedding plants. If the bulbs are not lifted, decaying leaves and petals should be destroyed at once as tulips affected by disease can contaminate the soil.

Having cleared the ground a complete fertiliser can be forked into the soil before re-planting. Zinnias, asters, African marigolds, penstemon, petunias, cosmos, tuberous and fibrous-rooted begonias, dahlias, ageratum, nemesia, *Salvia splendens,* lobelia, ten-week stocks, tobacco plants *(Nicotiana alata)* and cherry pie (heliotrope) are just some of the half-hardy plants that can still be planted.

The last three are richly scented and should be planted in the front of a border, but not together, so that their fragrance can be enjoyed in passing.

Tagetes, dwarf French marigolds and lobelia are also plants for the front of a border, their bushy habit of growth and bright flowers forming a neat and pretty edging to a bed.

Foliage plants that can be planted now include the castor oil plant (Ricinus, 2–4 feet) with its large decorative bronze, purple or green leaves, the silver foliaged *Cineraria maritima* 'Dwarf Silver' (9–12 inches) and *Senecio cineraria* 'White Diamond' which has whitish leaves cut in diamond fashion.

Zonal pelargoniums (geraniums) are

When Lilies in pots are staked, each stem needs to be supported individually and tied separately with soft twine. The twine needs to be tied first round the stake and then round the stem.

seldom grown in a herbaceous border, but a few dotted among the hardy perennials will provide colour through the summer and on into the autumn until the frosts.

Standard fuchsias look attractive in a border, too, the handsome heads of the flowers rising high above most other plants. Housed under glass until June, the pots in which the standards are raised can be sunk into the ground, enabling pot and plant to be lifted in autumn for wintering in a frostproof place.

Most perennials can be propagated by outdoor sowings this month, very fine seeds being sown in boxes in a cold frame. This is by far the cheapest way of stocking a new border or adding interest and variety to your present collection of plants.

Fork over the seed bed, raking the surface to a sandlike tilth, before sowing the seed thinly, in rows 6–8 inches apart, and labelling each row with name and height, bearing in mind that plants are often difficult to identify in the early stages.

Popular perennials that can be propagated by this method are doronicum (1½–2 feet), aquilegia (1½ feet), anchusa (4 feet), *Campanula pyramidalis* (3–4 feet), *C. persicifolia* (2 feet), border carnations (2 feet), shasta daisy (*Chrysanthemum maximum*)—the giant hybrids at 3½ feet or the variety 'Little Silver Princess' 1½–2½ feet, delphiniums (2½–3 feet and 4–5 feet), geum (2 feet), heuchera (15 inches).

Other suggestions are oriental poppies (papaver) in scarlet, pink and blood-red (2½ feet), the bright scarlet *Lychnis chalcedonica* (3 feet), lupins (dwarf strain, 2–2½ feet, tall 3–4 feet), double and single pyrethrum (2 feet), coreopsis (1½–3½ feet), hollyhock 'Triumph Supreme', a highly rust-resistant variety with frilled and fringed double flowers (5–6 feet), and Michaelmas daisy (*Aster*, 2½–3 feet).

Not all perennials are quick to germinate. Aquilegia seed sometimes lies dormant for as long as six months before germinating.

If you have taken delphinium cuttings earlier in the year, the first flower spike should be nipped out before transplanting the cuttings into an open border around the middle of the month. Continue feeding properly established plants with a liquid manure until the end of June, cutting down the blooms as they fade.

Hardy annuals should be thinned out at once now—left unthinned they become a prey to damping off disease which can run through the whole batch of seedlings. Allow room for each plant to develop; 6 to 9 inches is not too far apart for godetia and clarkia, 2 inches apart for annuals such as night-scented stock and scarlet flax (linum). Leggy seedlings of clarkia and godetia should have the tip of the main growth pinched out to encourage branching.

Lilies need plenty of water throughout the growing season. Water the soil, not the plants, damping the ground to a depth of 6 inches. A mulch of leafmould or damp peat will conserve the moisture between waterings.

Almost all varieties of lilies prefer a cool root run during summer. This can be achieved by planting dwarf perennials or shallow-rooted annuals nearby. Tall, heavy-headed lilies in an exposed position need staking; a single cane beside each stem, secured loosely with soft string, should give sufficient support. As a protection against pests, spray with an insecticide every 10 days or so.

Do not leave carnations to flop about. The stems should be secured to 2-foot canes with wire rings specially sold for the purpose. Plants will benefit from a dressing of soot, stored under cover for three or four months. Apply at the rate of 6 ounces per square yard.

Early-flowering chrysanthemums can still be planted, 15–18 inches apart. The chrysanthemum should never be allowed to suffer from persistent drought as this hardens the stems and this in turn checks growth. Plants can be stopped by the removal of the tip of the main stem shortly after planting out.

House Plants

Now that all risk of frost has passed and spring gales have lost their power it is time to think of giving some of the house plants a summer holiday in the open air. Most of them will benefit from the sunshine, the greater degree of humidity available and the cleansing summer showers, but in no circumstances should you attempt to place outdoors any really delicate or furry leaved plants such as saintpaulias.

Choose carefully where you place them, giving them all some protection against strong winds and allowing most only a little strong sunshine at one time. Only the cacti and succulents can be placed out in the full sun for the whole day.

Most plants are best placed on the north side of a house, fence or wall or in the shade of a tree or vine where they will catch the sun mainly when it is low on the horizon and not at its fiery peak.

Because the pots will dry out very quickly outdoors they should be watered

Many house plants can be put out of doors safely now that all fear of frost has passed. Find a sheltered position for them and remember that they will probably dry out more quickly and need constant attention to watering. Keep woolly-leaved or tender plants indoors.

much more frequently and if facilities exist it is even wise to use some type of trickle watering system to keep them constantly moist. Much worry and time can be saved if the plant pots can be plunged in moist peat, shingle or sand, preferably in some kind of purpose-made container which is both practical and decorative.

With a little careful planning and forethought it is possible to use many house plants on the terrace or patio to great decorative effect, for this is the time when the patio really comes into its own as an extension of the home—an extra room out of doors.

If it is possible or convenient to move some of your larger house plants kept in a more or less permanent place indoors because of their size, then remember that they will be particularly vulnerable to gusts of wind. They are probably trained to canes, so remember to tie these canes securely to a fence or tree so the top-heavy plants will not be blown over.

A particularly effective means of displaying the smaller house plants out of doors is to erect a series of shelves or open boxes along a wall and place the plants on these in positions where they blend or contrast attractively. This method saves space and masses the plants so that they form a living wall and gain in importance and dignity because of their number.

Smaller plants can also be placed in a line along the side of a pathway, particularly if the path is running roughly east and west so that they can benefit from the soft shade of the plants alongside. Another means of displaying them to advantage, and saving space at the same time, is to hang them by string or wire around their pots to a series of hooks in a fence or wall.

Some of the flowering plants normally kept indoors, such as pelargoniums and begonias, can be plunged, in their pots, in the flower borders, where they will give added colour and where they will require watering much less frequently.

Cacti and succulents are particularly effective and decorative in the garden if they are placed in formal and stylised patterns in large saucers or bowls.

These can, of course, be situated in the full sun and because the root system of these plants is normally so shallow they can come to no harm if they are knocked from their pots and planted into the soil. This takes a little extra time and is usually unnecessary, but sometimes much better effects can be obtained this way.

Plastic mesh or trellis can sometimes be fixed behind a climber or trailer so that the long shoots can be trained on this to form a living screen. If this gets too much sun, remember to spray over the foliage once or twice each day. This should be done in addition to watering the soil in the pots.

Lawns

Mowing of established and new lawns usually becomes a twice weekly operation during June, July and August. Weather conditions will have considerable bearing on how fast the grass will grow, and this must be taken into account when deciding on which day the lawn needs mowing.

It is advisable normally at this time of year not to allow the grass to grow much taller than twice its cut height. This means that fine grasses in lawns of high quality should not be allowed to grow more than 1 inch tall before being cut back to $\frac{1}{4}$–$\frac{1}{2}$ inch.

The normal average household lawn, which is cut back to $\frac{1}{2}$–1 inch, should be mown before the grass is 1–2 inches high, and a rougher, rye-grass lawn, which is never cut closer than 1 inch, should be mown when the grass has reached a height of 2–2$\frac{1}{2}$ inches.

Exceptions to these cutting heights may be necessary during drought conditions if the lawn is not being watered regularly. In which case, raise the height of cut of the mower a little, so there is no danger of the grasses being cut too short and so weakened. If this is not done, weeds and moss tend to inhabit, only too quickly, the areas where the grasses are thin on the ground through over-mowing or 'scalping'.

Although not usually to be recommended during drought periods, grass cuttings can occasionally be allowed to remain on the lawn to act as a mulch.

It is very important, too, that the lawn mower is kept in good condition, with the blades sharpened as regularly as necessary. Blunt blades only chew the grass and leave a rough finish, and often barely cut back weeds at all.

Raking the lawn once or twice during June before mowing helps to control creeping weeds such as trifolium species (clovers) and *Ranunculus repens* (creeping buttercup). The raking lifts up the creeping stems, and the mower blades will then make short work of cutting them off.

Any broad-leaved weeds which were

1

2

1 Clover, one of the commonest weeds of lawns, can be controlled to some extent by raking once or twice during June. The raking lifts the creeping stems and these are then more easily cut when mowing follows.
2 Isolated lawn weeds can be given the 'spot treatment' with weedkiller.

not killed off completely by weedkiller applied in May should receive another dose now. If the weeds are isolated, the simple, cheap and effective way to deal with them is to 'spot' treat the crown of each with one of the hormone weedkillers, diluted according to manufacturers' instructions. There are, on the market, several types of applicators for 'spot' treatment and one of these could prove a useful investment for the gardener who likes to see his lawn weed-free at all times.

If weeds are still a fairly general problem in the lawn, however, it will be quicker to cover the whole area with one of the hormone weedkillers applied from a sprayer or watering can with fine rose or spray bar. Care must be taken not to allow the weedkiller to drift on to cultivated plants and the spraying applicator should be washed out thoroughly after use. For best results, apply the weedkiller two to three days after mowing and do not cut the lawn for three days afterwards.

Most lawns will benefit from a suitable summer fertiliser application this month. The grass is usually growing strongly and being cut frequently, and so the soil nutrients tend to be used up fairly fast. There are a number of excellent proprietary compound lawn fertilisers available and these can be scattered evenly by hand, or by a wheeled fertiliser applicator, at the recommended application rate. Liquid feeds can also be applied via the watering system if preferred.

If weed-killing is to be part of the June lawn care programme, a better kill of weeds will be obtained if fertiliser is applied ten days prior to the weedkiller. This 'softens up' the weeds and they tend to absorb a larger quantity of the lethal hormones.

There are certain weeds that are notorious for being difficult to eradicate from lawns and against which the hormone weedkillers are not particularly effective. *Sagina procumbens* (pearlwort), *Trifolium* species (clovers), *Bellis perennis* (common daisy), moss, lichen and algae (black slimy areas) are the most common of these and, if you yearn for a perfect lawn, they need to be tackled regularly until they are completely eradicated. Now is a good time to start if you have not already done so.

The most suitable method of chemical control is with one of the proprietary lawn sands containing sulphate of iron. This must be applied when the soil is moist (either following rain or artificial watering) and it must be watered in if no rain falls within two days of application. Dead growth should be raked up three weeks later and further applications given every month during the growing season until the weed problem has been entirely removed.

Cultural operations also play their part in controlling these weeds. Mowing the lawn during the summer months with the grass box on the machine will prevent spread of weed seeds or spores. Moss, lichen and algae in particular are nearly always indicative of poor growing conditions, such as unfavourable soil drainage, lack of fertilisers, too dense shade, too close mowing, insufficient soil aeration, rain dripping from trees or excessive rolling.

Therefore, these factors must also be remedied if complete freedom from trouble is to be ensured. Clovers usually indicate shortage of nitrogen and soil moisture during drought periods and pearlwort generally infests areas which have been 'scalped' through mowing too closely.

Following the killing of these weeds, large areas should be raked clear and be re-seeded or turfed to prevent any further take-over by other weeds.

To the perfectionist, coarse grasses appearing in a fine, turf lawn are a nuisance. There is no effective chemical control of these and regularly cutting them out during the summer with a knife, re-filling the holes left with top soil, and re-seeding or turfing, is the only suitable answer.

New lawns from seed or turf sown or laid during the spring should still be treated with care. Watering and hand weeding should be carried out when necessary, and mowing must be done with the blades set to the right height, so that the grass is not cut too short or left too long.

It may seem hard, but if the new lawn is to be a special feature of the garden, it should not be used for picnics or as a children's play area in its first summer, however tempting these may be. By its second summer it will have become sufficiently well-established to withstand a fair amount of pleasure usage.

Paths, Fences and Walls

A garden path, like a road, should be functional, travelling in as straight a line as possible from one significant point to another. The minimum width should be 2 feet and, where space permits it will always be worthwhile to make this 4 feet or even 5, to allow two people to walk abreast or for a well laden wheelbarrow of long prunings, for example, to be pushed along easily without catching on projections from the sides of low walls, and so on.

In any new garden it will be found after a few weeks that there are natural paths made for travelling directly to one or two parts of the garden and paths should not be made until these natural walks have been discovered.

Obviously some paths must curve or bend to avoid a tree or bed, but pathways should not normally meander merely for the sake of the garden layout or you will find that short cuts are taken when carrying a heavy load or rushing to the house to answer the telephone.

Not all paving, however, consists of paths. All pools and water gardens, for example, should have a paved area around them, for this serves many purposes. It provides a clean standing area.

It prevents crumbling banks. It also keeps the water clear of debris falling in. And it gives an area increased dignity and importance. The only time when a paved area around a pool looks wrong is where the water fills a large expanse, though even here the most frequently used standing or sitting site can well do with a hard surface.

A newly planted tree in the lawn should always have its base kept clear of grass for the first few years. This means that the edges of the grass must be kept constantly clipped to keep the site looking neat. It only takes an hour or two to pave or brick a square or circle around the base of the tree and this will prevent for all time the chore of trimming these edges. At the same time it makes for ease of weeding, fertilising and tending generally. It once again adds significantly to the importance of what is sometimes a small and overlooked tree in its early days.

Some flower borders and beds are improved with a perimeter path or edging, both to neaten the edges and to provide a secure and clean place for standing while weeding or otherwise

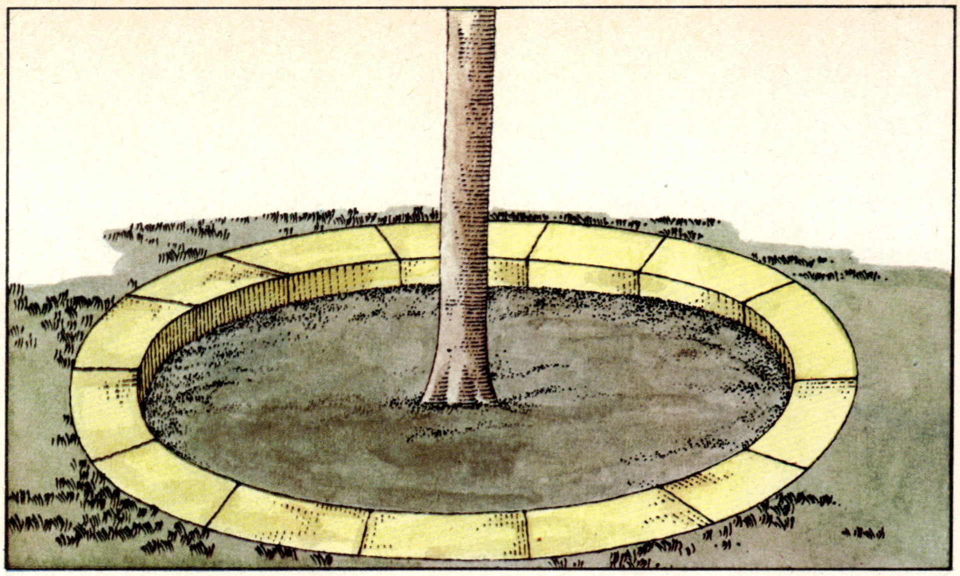

1

2

1 Keep the bases of newly planted trees free of grass by making a bed, with a surround of brick or paving.
2 All pools and water gardens should have a certain amount of paved area at the water's edge. The main utilitarian purpose of such paving is to provide a firm footing and prevent the bank from crumbling into the water and becoming soggy and unmanageable. Time spent on laying firm and durable paving in the vicinity of water is time well spent. A narrow edge to a pool is provided to divide the lawn from the water, making mowing easier and keeping the pool clear of soil and debris.
3 Further decoration can be added in the form of pebbles either set in the edging or loose, as here.

3

tending the flowers. This perimeter paving can be as little as 6 inches wide, so long as it is securely laid and will not rock when trodden. A paved portion like this can sometimes go actually into the bed where this is too wide for the centre to be reached from the sides. A single stepping stone or two is sufficient to ease the task of hoeing or weeding.

A stepping stone pathway through grass is sometimes attractive, but should not be carried to extremes and should never be the main or only garden path, for the grass around the actual stones will not bear heavy or continuous traffic.

Stepping stones leading through grass are most effective when they merely suggest the way, point ahead to the rose beds or pool or take one around a bend.

Patios, Balconies, Roof Gardens and Window Boxes

From June onwards until the late autumn the days will be warm and the evenings long. This is the time when outdoor living comes into its own, when patio, roof and balcony are really used and the window-boxes brighten buildings with their gay flowers. This is the time when you most want colour and gaiety, particularly in those parts of the garden that can be used almost as living rooms.

Almost theatrical effects can be achieved with a patio. You can change the scene literally overnight, to prepare perhaps for an evening party or for the arrival of a special weekend guest. Flower markets, some street markets and all garden centres will have many boxes and pots of flowers in bloom which can be planted out without fear of frosts and which can bring instant colour at little cost in time or labour.

As in the open garden, the greatest effect is to be obtained by planting colours in concentrated blocks rather than scattering them indiscriminately like confetti. Annuals are cheap and instantly effective, so here, according to colour groupings, are brief selections of low growing annuals suited to window-boxes as well as container plantings on patio, balcony and roof garden. Some flowers, of course, come in several different colours, so may be listed more than once.

White: alyssum, begonia, daisy, candytuft, *Celosia nana*, dianthus, echium, eschscholzia, forget-me-not, gazania, linaria, lobelia, mignonette, nemesia, nemophila, pansy, petunia, *Phlox drummondii*, polyanthus, portulaca, Virginian stock, verbena.

Yellow: *Celosia nana*, eschscholzia, gazania, leptosiphon, limnanthes, nasturtium, nemesia, pansy, polyanthus, *Tagetes signata*, wallflower.

Red: anagallis, begonia, *Dianthus sinensis*, eschscholzia, leptosiphon, mignonette, nasturtium, nemesia, petunia, *Phlox drummondii*, polyanthus, portulaca, *Silene pendula*, Virginian stock, verbena, wallflower.

Blue: anagallis, anchusa, echium, forget-me-not, lobelia, nemesia, nemophila, pansy, petunia, phacelia, polyanthus, Virginian stock, verbena, viscaria.

Choose boxes of plants which are showing colour but which also have many buds waiting to open. Inspect them carefully to ensure that there is no disease present and that the soil is moist.

1 

2 

1 In a window-box planted for summer flowering effect, purple and white Petunias are used in conjunction with deep scarlet Pelargoniums and white Oxeye Daisies. The yellow trailing Lysimachia nummularia hangs down to cover the box.
2 Assemble summer flowering plants that are just coming into flower.

When you get them home keep them in a cool and shady spot until you are ready to plant them.

Have your containers ready with soil, either John Innes potting compost or one of the proprietary no-soil mixtures. Water the boxes of plants again a few minutes before planting and then lift each plant out carefully with a good ball of soil adhering to the roots. Plant with a trowel, spreading the roots well and firming the soil over them. Water again thoroughly until water begins to trickle from the drainage holes. Leave the newly planted containers in shade for a day or two before bringing them to their final positions.

Once the plants are growing away well, examine them each day for disease, water regularly and pick off all dead flowers to ensure a continuity of bloom. Any plant that dies should be removed at once, both for the appearance of the container and in case the dead or dying plant spreads its infection to its neighbours.

There are many herbaceous plants besides annuals which are useful and colourful subjects for the patio but, unless the containers are large, perennials seldom give such good results or last as long as they do in the open ground, and for more or less permanent plantings trees and shrubs are to be preferred. Dwarf and slow-growing forms can be obtained of many trees and shrubs, but even normal growing kinds will usually last for several years in a container before they outgrow their homes.

As a general rule it is wiser to grow evergreens in containers for patio or roof garden than deciduous trees or shrubs, for there is little point in looking during the winter at an attractive container holding a stark and bare-branched tree.

Conifers are particularly effective evergreens for the patio or the roof garden. Many dwarf and slow growing types are available and their outlines—conical, fastigiate, globular or prostrate—give architectural form to what is in effect an architectural situation. They keep their shapes well and resist the strong winds that so frequently trouble other plants. But because they stand up to winds they can sometimes be top heavy in small or narrow based containers. Where possible choose heavy or broad based containers for any plant, particularly a conifer, that is in peril of being blown over. A good layer of pebbles for drainage at the base of the container will usually provide useful stability.

Because evergreen conifers shed their foliage gradually over the year, no dramatic change in their appearance is immediately apparent when they are sickening or over-dry. For this reason it is important always to keep young plants well watered and where possible to give them a thorough spray with clean water over their foliage when the weather is hot and sunny. The soil in which they are planted can well have an extra portion of peat added, both to retain the necessary moisture and because the majority of conifers prefer a slightly acid soil.

Rock Gardens

During this month the seed sown in April should have germinated and will be ready to pot on. Do not allow the seedlings to become overcrowded and drawn in the seed pan, but prick out as soon as the first true leaf can be seen. John Innes No 1 will suit the easy species and varieties, and small thumb pots, such as used for cactus seedlings,

1

2

1 Remove dead flowerheads from Rhododendron keleticum, as shown, and other dwarf Rhododendrons. This prevents the seed from setting and encourages flower formation the following season.

2 Dianthus provide good patches of colour in mid-summer in the rock garden. Here Diathus neglectus contrasts well with the soft sandstone of the rock work. Again, dead-heading is important.

are ideal. By the time they have filled their pots with roots, as a rule during August, the young plants are ready for their permanent position in the rock garden, and should have become fully acclimatized by the onset of winter. It is not practicable to plant out the seedlings direct from a seed pan into the rock garden.

From this month onwards, and during the rest of the summer and autumn, seeds from the rarer species of rock plants should be sown as they ripen. These require more sophisticated composts but even here two will suffice. The sun-loving species should be sown in equal parts fibrous loam and leafmould to two parts of coarse sand. Shade-loving plants, including dwarf rhododendrons and other ericaceous genera, are best suited to an open spongy mixture consisting of equal parts leafmould, peat and coarse sand.

In many instances germination is spasmodic and often a period of anything up to two years can elapse before the seedlings appear, so do not despair. Two tips that may be useful. One, Asiatic primula seed is best sown green—not allowed to ripen; two, seedlings of the rarer bulbous species should be allowed to remain in the seed pan for a whole year before transplanting.

A weekly check of the rock garden during June is necessary. Where possible remove the dead flowers on the dwarf rhododendrons. Allowing them to seed often prohibits the setting of flower buds for the following year. All trailing plants, such as the different varieties of the moss pinks, *Phlox subulata*, aethionema and edraianthus, among others, should be cut hard back once they have ceased to flower so that they retain a close, compact habit. In many instances this treatment will often induce them to produce a second crop of flowers in late summer.

The edelweiss, *Leontopodium alpinum*, in flower this month, is commonly believed to be a notoriously difficult plant.

Many gardeners just cannot believe that the plant grows readily from a packet of seed costing a few pence. fact all it asks is to be planted in a well-drained, lime spot—the emphasis is on the well-drained—where it will settle down and flower profusely.

The campanulas and pinks are now taking over the colour scheme of the rock garden, contrasting well with each other.

Among the many species of campanula which are worth growing, the following are representative of the genus and can be recommended. These are all easy species and only require a sunny, well-drained position in the rock garden. *C. carpatica* and its many varieties will flower from June to September; *C. garganica* has deep blue stars and its two varieties 'Fenestrellata' and 'W. H. Paine' have dainty stars of lilac and violet with a white eye; *C. hirsuta alba* is a prostrate white form; 'Little Marvel' is a hybrid with many dainty purple stars on slender stems; 'Pseudo Raineri' is a fine large form with violet, saucer-shaped flowers; and there are the many forms of pusilla, all with dainty roundish bell-shaped flowers of white to blue. These pusilla varieties are at their best in half shade.

The following choice specimens, if grown in the scree, will prove permanent occupants of the rock garden: *Campanula abietina* (Greece), funnel-shaped flowers, light violet; *C. allionii* (Western Alps), with huge purple bells—there are named forms of this species ranging in colour from white to reddish flowers; *C. arvatica* (Spain), dainty foliage, large violet stars; *C. excisa* (Italy), grassy leaves and hanging pale-blue bells, each petal perforated at its base; *C. raineri* (Italy), the true plant with open upturned flowers of china-blue; *C. saxifraga* (Caucasus), a tufted rosette with radiating stems and violet-blue bells.

There are a great number of dwarf dianthus, both species and hybrids. Most are easy, but to keep some of the difficult ones in good health for long will tax even the specialist.

All the following dianthus hybrids are good and reliable: 'Bombardier', scarlet-crimson, double flowers; 'Cavalier', fringed pink with chocolate zone; 'Grenadier', grey leaves, scarlet-maroon double flowers; 'Icombe', single, bright pink; 'Little Jock', double pink, deep eye; 'Mars'—still one of the best—highly scented double crimson flowers; 'Pauline', semi-double, salmon pink, and the white 'Bourbrille'.

Among the species the following are reliable: *Dianthus alpinus* (Europe), rose-pink; *D. caesius* (Europe)—the Cheddar pink—fragrant fringed rose pink; *D. glacialis* (South Europe), a real gem of large deep pink flowers on short stems; *D. microlepis* (Balkans), small foliage, clear pink flowers; *D. neglectus* (Europe), cherry rose-backed buff flowers and *D. simulans* (Bulgaria), with tufts of blue-green foliage and almost stemless deep pink flowers.

Roses

Disbudding will be one of the jobs requiring attention this month if the highest quality blooms are desired. It is not merely the hybrid teas which benefit from disbudding, contrary to popular belief. The removal of the centre bud of the truss in floribunda and modern shrub roses will often result in a better display, with more of the flowers open at the same time, but without these being overcrowded.

It will often happen during this month that soft side-shoots will start into growth before the terminal flower bud has opened. These side-shoots should be pinched out in the early stages while still soft. Otherwise they will divert the supply of sap from the main flower bud, which then will not develop its full potential. This form of de-shooting in the early stages is much more sensible than allowing the growths to mature and then cutting them back to relieve an overcrowded plant.

The grower who is interested in exhibiting his roses will wish to provide supplementary feeding during this month. There are numerous proprietary brands of 'complete' rose fertilisers and, if the instructions printed on the container are followed strictly, there should be no complications.

If home-made liquid feeds are preferred, these may be made by suspending

When disbudding Hybrid Tea Roses, the buds need to be removed cleanly quite early in their development. This will encourage the formation of better and fewer blooms.

By removing the central bud of a truss on Floribunda Roses a better display can be had with more of the flowers open at the same time without being too overcrowded for good effect.

a bag of animal manure in a water butt for a few days and then applying the liquid, diluted if necessary, so that it is never deeper in colour than a pale straw.

It is far better to apply two weak solutions of liquid manure than one of double strength, which may do more harm than good. Steps should always be taken to ensure that the soil is not dry when liquid manures are applied.

For inorganic stimulants, nitrate of potash—1 ounce dissolved in a gallon of soft water—is recommended, divided between two established bushes. Soot water may also be prepared by suspending a bag of soot in a butt of water, but as this is nitrogenous it should not be overdone, or soft growth may result which falls an easy prey to disease.

Mildew is the disease of roses which appears in all gardens, and spraying should be undertaken at the first sign of the powdery white or grey surface fungus appearing on the leaves. Under suitable conditions for its development mildew will spread rapidly. Preventive spraying is not the answer, but rather thorough spraying of both upper and under surfaces of the leaves at the first sign of infection.

Many growers use dinocap under the proprietary name of Karathane, but this is intended more for restricting the spread of the disease than for curing leaves which are already infected. Bouisol mixed with Volck is recommended by some growers; others find that 1 ounce of ordinary washing soda crystals dissolved in a gallon of soft water, with a little liquid soap added to act as a spreader, is as effective as most proprietary mildew sprays, as well as being considerably cheaper. Dryness at the roots seems to encourage an outbreak, so any roses planted near walls or fences should be watered liberally during dry weather.

Rose growers who live in pure air districts which are troubled with black spot disease should start preventive spraying against attacks at the beginning of this month and continue every 10 days or so in really bad areas. The curious thing about this disease is that growers in industrial and heavily built-up areas are seldom troubled with black spot, as the amount of pollution in the atmosphere acts as a fungicide. In pure air districts, on the other hand, the spores of the fungus are able to develop unless regular preventive spraying is practised.

The only way to control black spot disease is by this regular spraying as, once the black spots have appeared on a leaf, that leaf cannot be saved. Maneb 80 and captan (e.g. Orthocide) are the most effective preparations, and both are sold as a fine wettable powder. As the disease attacks the older leaves at the base of the plant first, particular attention should be given to ensuring that these are thoroughly covered on both surfaces.

Wisteria sinensis, a very sought-after shrub with lilac-purple colouring. All the wisteria, with their beautiful blossom and attractively cut foliage, are ideal plants for south or west walls.

Continue to watch for insect pests, particularly caterpillars and the leaf-rolling sawfly, both of which can do a great deal of harm in quite a short time. Hand picking, if undertaken in the very early stages, can save a lot of trouble later.

During the second half of the month, at any rate in southern regions, there should be quite a colourful display from the hybrid tea bedding roses. Even farther north some of the climbing sports of the hybrid teas will be in bloom, as these normally flower about three weeks earlier than their bush counterparts. As the blooms fade they should be cut off with several inches of stem, just above a leaf, so that the dormant shoot bud at the junction of the leaf and stem can develop and replace the stem that has been removed. These sub-laterals, as they are called, will often carry a crop later in the season. On no account should seed pods be left to develop on any of the climbers, as this will prevent any further display.

When removing faded flowers from bedding roses it is best to cut back the stem to about half-way. Cutting back harder will cause a longer flowerless interval. Equally, if merely the old flower head is removed, the bush will tend to become overcrowded with many thin shoots. During the first season after planting, however, it is best to remove the flower with the footstalk, as every leaf is helpful in establishing a strong plant.

Trees, Shrubs and Climbers

June is a month for relaxation; an opportunity to enjoy the beauty of the garden to the full. Many flowering trees and shrubs will still be at the peak of perfection and others will soon be providing continuity of interest. At the beginning of the month, there will still be the long golden tassels of the laburnums and the scarlet and white blossom of *Crataegus monogyna*, the flowering thorn, or 'May'.

These will give place to the rose-pink

1

2

1 Chaenomeles speciosa, the Japanese Quince, still known as Japonica, has finished flowering now and is ready for pruning. All growth needs to be shortened.
2 The soft growth of many wall plants needs to be tied in early in the season while it is still soft and flexible. Here Ceanothus is being tied in.

pea flowers of *Robinia hispida,* the lovely rose acacia, which starts to flower towards the end of the month. The foliage of this small ornamental tree is as attractive as its flowers—finely cut, pinnate and of a delicate clear green.

The wood of the rose acacia is extremely brittle and, when it is grown in standard form, the main stem can easily be snapped by summer gales. It is advisable, therefore, to keep specimens grown in this way securely staked at all times.

June, too, will see the flowering of the larger false acacia, *Robinia pseudoacacia,* in all its attractive varieties. These trees are grown mainly for the beauty of their foliage. Some forms, such as the mopheaded *R. p. inermis,* seldom flower here, while others give a striking display of white or pink flowers.

All of them will thrive in almost any soil conditions; they make ideal trees for town gardens. Some are armed with fierce spines, others are less vicious. One of the most popular varieties is *R. p. decaisneana,* a quick-growing tree with pink flowers. *R. p. frisia,* introduced recently from Holland, is noteworthy for the beauty of its golden foliage which is attractive throughout the summer and autumn.

June would seem to be the month of the *Leguminosae,* a family title that embraces all kinds of leguminous plants such as peas, beans and lupins, as well as a host of trees and shrubs, including the robinias.

One of the choicest members of the tribe is wisteria, whose magnificent blossom and attractively cut foliage makes it one of the most sought-after shrubs for a south or west wall. The kind most commonly seen is the lilac-purple *W. sinensis,* which has racemes of scented flowers 12 inches long. There is also a white variety and another with double flowers.

The most sensational of all wisterias is *W. floribunda macrobotrys* (syn. *multijuga).* The pendent lilac flower trusses of this variety are often as much as 3 feet long. (Note: newly planted wisterias often hang fire for a very long time. The buds may fail to break until late June or early July. Overhead spraying in dry weather will help to stimulate them into earlier growth.)

Most other newly planted climbers should be getting away well by now. It is important to ensure that each kind gets the sort of support that it needs. Non-clinging wall shrubs will want their main shoots tied to wires until their basic framework has been established. Lengths of galvanised wire, tightly stretched at horizontal intervals of about 9 inches is useful for this purpose. For smaller shrubs, wall nails, with their flexible lead strip, can be used to anchor recalcitrant shoots.

Wooden trellis, preferably of oak, makes an attractive support for choicer climbers. Rampant twiners and clingers like the clematis species and the lovely blue passion flower do best on squares or rectangles of wire netting attached to the wall surface.

Early flowering clematis species, such as *C. montana, C. macropetala, C. alpina* and *C. armandii,* should now be ready for their annual pruning. It is usually recommended that all shoots that have flowered should be cut out. However, with vigorous species such as *C. montana* and its equally rampant variety *C. m. rubens,* this need only be carried out if the gardener is a perfectionist.

With mature plants, there will be such a tangle of flowering and non-flowering shoots that it will be virtually impossible to separate them without damage. All that can be done is to go over the plants with a pair of secateurs, shortening all growths indiscriminately. This will produce plenty of flowering wood for the following season.

Another group of wall shrubs that will be needing attention now are the so-called Japanese quinces, chaenomeles, still often referred to as 'japonicas'. These shrubs have undergone more botanical name-changes than most. In their time they have been grouped with pears and quinces and borne such varied names as cydonia, pyrus and lagenaria. At the present time they are best known under the generic title of chaenomeles.

When grown as a wall shrub, chaenomeles respond well to a form of spur pruning similar to that practised for espalier and cordon fruit trees. Towards the end of this month new growths should be cut or pinched back to three or four buds.

The cutting-back procedure is repeated in July for the resulting fresh growth. Summer pruning of this nature will produce an abundance of blossom buds for the following year.

New plants should be allowed to extend their main shoots until a basic branch structure, extensive enough to cover the allotted wall space, has been built up.

Vegetables

While you are enjoying the first crop of the summer's early vegetables it is time to be sowing more for later on in the season. Careful planning means that you always have more young and succulent crops. It is worth while, if the ground seems fully occupied, to steal spaces by sowing near or between rows which will soon be finished, or which have just been sown or planted.

Crops like bush marrows and zuccinis, for example, need a wide strip of ground, some 3 to 4 feet, but not for all of the time.

You can avoid wasting precious space by using the areas between the young plants or between the seed stations for short rows of quick maturing salads. Many of these need rich and moist soil if they are to grow fast and succulent, and any food or water given to them will also benefit the longer standing vegetables. These areas may also be used as nursery rows for brassicas of all kinds and, as these should be planted out before they become drawn, the ever encroaching plants they are between will soon make their removal essential to the benefit of all.

'Shorthorn' or some of the other new, quick maturing varieties of carrots; globe and the new, cylindrical-rooted beetroot such as 'Housewives Choice'; kohl-rabi, radish, lettuces and peas are all successional crops which should be sown as early in the month as possible so that more can be sown later.

Leeks are ready for planting out this month and the 9-inch holes ought to be made with a dibber to ensure firmness in the soil. The seedling is dropped down into the hole.

When seedling Leeks are lifted from their seed bed, reduce the length of the foliage before planting out. Choose a level and firm site for the permanent planting positions.

Lettuce should be sown where it is to remain. It does not transplant well after this month because it then tends to bolt. Instead sow it thinly. If you have the patience, space pinches of seed along the drill at 4 or 5 inch intervals rather than fill the row with seed. If this is done, the intervening space can be used by sowing radish seed between the lettuce stations. This will germinate quicker and should be pulled and out of the way before the lettuce needs the space.

Look ahead and make provision for winter salads now. Sow chicory, the roots of which will have to be lifted for forcing in the winter. Also sow endive and parsley, Chinese cabbage, okra and French, runner and broad beans if you have not sown them earlier.

Earlier sown broad beans should now be forming thick and fast. These are good eaten young. Pods should be gathered when they are about 3 inches long and cooked whole. Only just cover the beans with water to which a knob of butter and salt to taste has been added. When they are cooked and strained add a little more butter and sprinkle chopped fresh basil over them.

Go along the bean row and nip the tips from the plants now. These can also be eaten, although they are usually taken out to prevent the plants from being infested with blackfly which will take over the top part of the plant if not prevented.

Any early spray with an effective insecticide will ward off attacks, but remember that if a systemic is used once the beans have formed they must not be eaten immediately. Read instructions on the insecticide packet or bottle carefully. An alternative is to spray with non-harmful soapy water.

All pests seem to be particularly active now and routine spraying is advisable. There are many good insecticides on the market which cater for all eventualities. Inspect peas for thrips and other vegetables for aphids and caterpillars which are to be found curled up snugly in the tips of some shoots.

Watch also for fungoid diseases. Spray potatoes against blight at the end of the month. Do not wait until next month if you know from past experience that it is likely to exist in your soil or locality. Watch for mildew on other crops, particularly peas. Pests and diseases can affect both the quality and quantity of your crops.

There is quite a lot of planting to be done now. Young plants are best moved as soon as they are large enough to handle. If their permanent site is not yet ready, then give them a move to 3 inches apart in a nursery bed and move them yet again when they begin to touch; anything to keep the roots in a fibrous mass, which is something transplanting helps to encourage. Once seedlings grow and find themselves crowded and in competition with their neighbours they will send down tap roots in search of food.

When the time comes to lift the drawn plants these tap roots become broken, the plant flags and remains wilted until the roots are able to re-adjust themselves, during which time they will have received a considerable check on growth.

Get out all the half-hardy plants which have been raised in the greenhouse or frame and remember that the care and attention given to them at this stage will make all the difference to them in their later stages.

Celery, for example, is a bog plant in its wild state, receiving not only ample supplies of moisture but of food in liquid form, so water the plants frequently and supplement the watering with liquid fertiliser—anything to get the plants growing away so that the stalks become thick and succulent.

Plant out leeks as soon as they are long enough to drop down into the 9-inch deep holes which should have been made with a dibber. Nothing further is required: the plants will grow up from the holes and the soil will gradually be washed down into them. The soil for leeks should be really rich.

Water Gardens

The last aquatic plants to start into growth—miniature water lilies, the floating plants *Azolla caroliniana* and *Lemna gibba*, and the marginal sagittaria (arrowheads)—are now fit to move and June is an excellent time for planting all aquatics. The stocking of new pools, or the spring-cleaning and replanting of established ones, can be continued throughout this month.

Plants installed in May should be well rooted and showing positive signs of development. Any leaves and buds present at planting time, particularly on water lilies, will probably be wilted, if not dead, but this is normal and new growth should be in evidence. The new leaves of lilies, especially the smaller

1

2

1 **The Great Diving Beetle, Dytiscus maginalis, is a menace in the garden pool and will even attack small fish. It is large, and flies from pool to pool.**
2 **Blanketweed, which grows on the surface of still water, can be removed from the pool with a stick. First draw it all to one side to form a solid mass.**

types, should be watched closely for signs of attack by the larvae of various midges.

The midge larvae, tiny and almost transparent, are very difficult to see, but if the leaves begin to disappear, skeletonised from the edges inwards, their presence can be assumed.

Affected leaves can be removed and destroyed, but if further leaf growth is attacked the only remedy is to lift and immerse the whole plant in a bucket of derris solution for an hour. It should be rinsed in clean water before replanting in fresh soil.

The bloodworm, the bright red half-inch larval stage of another midge, is often found in plant remains and blamed for any losses. As it is only equipped to attack decaying plant tissues, it is doubtful whether it can ever be solely responsible, though it may well finish off plants which are already dying back.

The most effective protection against insect attack is the presence of *small* fish. The energetic foraging of young goldfish or small golden orfe will work wonders in preventing any eggs deposited in the pool by mosquitoes or midges from reaching maturity. Insecticides must never be sprayed on, or even near, the pool because of their disastrous effect on fish.

A pool newly planted in May will soon be ready for the introduction of its quota of ornamental fish. A delay of a few weeks is essential, so that the submerged oxygenating plants have time to get well rooted and are able to withstand the tugging and mouthing they will suffer after the arrival of fish, which are partly vegetarian. If fish go in first and plants later, the oxygenators are destroyed before they root. This neglect of the right priorities lies at the bottom of most green-water problems.

The surface area of the pool (important in terms of oxygen-absorption) is the basis on which to calculate stocking limits. Either two or three inches of fish for every square foot of water surface area will be enough to start with, and will still leave ample room for growth and future fry.

The greatest virtue in a pond fish is visibility and a good red goldfish is hard to beat. The mottled colouring of shubunkins makes for variety and the long-tailed 'Comet' variants of both are fish of exceptional beauty. Golden orfe, slender, lively surface-feeders, should be present in any but the smallest pools. Silver orfe and rudd are hardly showy enough to be worthwhile, and such native fish as roach and gudgeon should never be accepted as gifts from ardent anglers since, apart from being designed by nature to be practically invisible in water, they are likely to bring with them a variety of parasites and diseases. Green tench, though seldom seen, do a useful job in scavenging neglected food fragments and drowned worms, but are not vital; the goldfish family, by nature bottom-feeders, will do this job pretty thoroughly themselves.

All the fish varieties mentioned above will live amicably together. The predatory fish which should never be mixed with them are catfish and the native perch and pike.

Among the fascinating insect life which turn up in every pool are a number of aquatic beetles. Most are small and harmless, but the great diving beetle, *Dytiscus marginalis*, is a voracious brute quite ready to attack fish as much as 5 or 6 inches long. The adult beetle, which flies readily and so may turn up in any pool, is 1–1½ inches long and about ¾ inches wide, dark brown or blackish in colour, the thorax and wing cases edged with gold.

If it is present, a quiet watch at the poolside is sure to reveal *Dytiscus* since it has to rise to the surface periodically to take in air at the tail end. The same is true of the larval stage, a creature with a curved tapering body up to 2 inches long, six legs and bristles at the tail end through which it breathes at the surface. Larvae and adults are easily netted when they come up for air and should be destroyed without hesitation. But remember that a small beetle does not grow into a large beetle and leave the little chaps to go about their harmless business.

There is an algal manifestation which may occur in the form of the slender green threads of various species of filamentous algae. Every pool has them to some extent and most are of little concern, making only a short furry growth on the pool sides and plant stems, which is grazed by water snails. Some types, however, grow so vigorously as to become a serious nuisance, making a choking web of long green strands. These are known as blanketweed, silkweed or flannelweed. Like the algae that cause water discoloration, the filamentous algae thrive on sunlight and the dissolved mineral salts in which the water of a new pool is usually rich, and the same methods of natural control are employed.

If blanketweed is out of control before these measures can become effective, manual control must be employed. Either a garden rake, or a rough stick twisted among the growth, will draw threads from all corners of the pool to a central mass that can easily be lifted out. There is no chemical treatment that can be recommended which would not seriously endanger the plant and fish life in the pool.

Wildlife

In June come the longest days with their early dawns and late dusks. In these twilights the nocturnal animals which, in winter hunted under cover of darkness, can be seen and heard.

In the early morning the night predators—foxes, owls and badgers—can sometimes be seen going back to their daytime haunts, their hunting finished for the night. A vixen may be seen teaching her cubs which, though they may have left the earth, still rely upon their mother for food and protection, or a dog fox may be seen passing through the garden, a young rabbit held high in his jaws.

In the summer twilight the owls are very noticeable, particularly the barn owl, whose creamy white plumage shows clearly in the half light. Another night hunter betrayed by his own camouflage is the badger, whose death-white mask shows him up while the rest of his coat merges into the undergrowth.

Warm June evenings bring out the gnats, midges and mosquitoes which, to the twilight gardener, are a nuisance. But these numerous insects attract the winged insectivores. The pipistrelle bat, for example, can be seen in most areas of the country flitting to and fro, silhouetted against the dying sun and the still light sky. The pipistrelle, though the smallest of native bats, is also the most common. Despite its small size it has a great appetite for winged insects, which it stores in pouches and eats while still on the wing.

The birds also play their part in keeping down pests. Swallows, swifts and martins all take their toll, all the more so now that they have broods to rear. Less common but equally effective winged hunters are the small falcons—the kestrel, merlin and hobby—who, though they do not eat only insects, base their diets upon this source.

The insects and grubs on the ground are kept in control by such animals as the hedgehog. In June this small but efficient predator can be lured from the hedgerow with a saucer of milk. As the animal becomes accustomed to his nightly drink he will become gradually more tame and the saucer can be moved a little nearer to the house and farther from the hedge each night. It might be just this tameness, or perhaps their slowness and habit of rolling themselves up into a prickly ball at signs of danger, that causes so many to be killed on the roads.

1 The Hedgehog can be encouraged to come into the garden by a saucer of milk in the evening. It feeds on grubs and ground insects.

2 The Barn Owl is often to be seen at twilight at this time of the year and its creamy plumage shows up well in the half light.

The Month of July

This is high summer. Porches and doorways now wear climbing plants. Trellis and walls are decorated with vivid blooms. Old trees are rejuvenated with flowers along their ancient branches. Bloom-covered pergolas shade paths from the summer sun

Passiflora caerulea, the Passion Flower, a hardy climber in the south and west, likes a warm wall

1

1 Clematis 'Ville de Lyon' is one of the large flowered Viticella group. It is in flower from July to September and responds best to hard pruning in February. It will flower on the old wood in May and June if left unpruned.

2 Clematis x lasurstern belongs to the Patens group, and has a long flowering period, sometimes blooming as early as May and continuing right through until September.

3 Clerodendrum thomsoniae, a vigorous evergreen climber for the greenhouse. There is also a variegated form.

4 Clematis 'Ap-pare', a newcomer from Japan, is in the Patens group. In addition to the vivid petals, the central sepals of this variety are very striking.

2

4

3

1 The lovely Morning Glory, Ipomoea rubro-caerulea, is a showy and most attractive annual climber.
2 The Tulip Tree, Liriodendron tulipifera is one of the most magnificent trees. Tulip Trees make remarkable plants, often reaching 100 feet in height.
3 Lonicera periclymenum, the Honeysuckle, has a number of very lovely varieties. These varieties are all climbers ideal for covering old trees as well as providing colour and interest to walls and porches. The delicate perfume of the Honeysuckle is enchanting.
4 Hibiscus rosa-sinensis can be grown in a tub in a greenhouse where a winter temperature of 60°F (16°C) is maintained.

3

4

1

2

3

1 Erigeron 'Festivity' is one of the most free-flowering of the daisy-like flowers in the herbaceous border.
2 Eschscholzia californica, the Californian Poppy, flourishes comfortably in any ordinary soil and produces flowers over a long period.
3 Lysimachia punctata is one of the many distinctive yellow Loosestrifes. They prefer a moist loamy soil and bloom in June and July.
4 Godetias are hardy annuals that can be sown in either spring or September preferring light soils and plenty of sun. From the September sowing they will flower in the early summer.
5 Hemerocallis aurantiaca major, the Day Lilies, grow in most soils including those that are heavy and usually rather unresponsive.
6 Roscoea purpurea procera is taller and has larger flowers than the type. All grow best in light turfy loam enriched with some leafmould.

4

5

6

Jobs of the month

High summer, which brings so many rewards to the gardener, is also a very busy time. Jobs abound. There are hedges and lawns to be cut continually, vegetables to be kept weed-free and copious watering to be done in shrubberies, rockeries and herbaceous borders. This is the gardening season in top gear

Bulbs

Lift and dry off tulip bulbs. Complete your bulb order now for autumn planting

Flowers for Cutting

Gather everlasting flowers for drying. Make sure they are not wet when you pick them. Helichrysums should be mounted on false stems

Fruit

Prune cordon pears early in the South and a fortnight later in the North. Melons will begin to need support now. Spray loganberries

Greenhouse

Chrysanthemums in pots need feeding from now onwards. Give perpetual carnations plenty of water and ventilation. Shade cucumbers from hot sun

Hedges

Mulch newly-planted hedges during dry periods. Leave spring-planted hedges untrimmed. Trim other hedges to a wedge shape. Wide at base, tapering to top

Herbaceous Plants

Gladioli need lots of watering in dry weather. Annuals should now be supported with twiggy sticks. Remove flowers from delphiniums, lupins, paeonies as they fade

House Plants

Look for aphid damage and spray immediately. Other pests attack house plants now including red spider mite, mealy bug and scale

Lawns

New lawns sown or turfed in spring are now old enough to take weed killer if necessary. Take care with the dose

Paths, Fences and Walls

Plants spreading over walls are at their best now but need close attention, especially climbing roses. Feed well. Remove dead flowers

Patios, Balconies, Roof Gardens and Window Boxes

This is a vital time to water all container-grown plants regularly, some as often as twice a day

Rock Gardens

Take stock of your rock garden now and note down mistakes in planting. All iris species should be lifted and divided now

Roses

Roses can be budded during this month. The job must be done quickly. Take great care not to damage the bud itself

Trees, Shrubs and Climbers

Shrubs like overhead watering on hot dry days. Continue pruning flowering shrubs that have finished blooming

Vegetables

Routine weeding is essential in the vegetable garden now. Attack with a hoe three or four times a week to prevent seedlings germinating

Water Gardens

Watch out for the great pond snail which eats healthy pond plants. This is fish-spawning time so make sure your pool is not starved of oxygen

Wildlife

Grass snakes are laying now, usually in a warm, rotting compost heap. Take care you don't step on their eggs

Bulbs

The tulip bulbs that were left to finish flowering, or were moved to another border to ripen in June, can be lifted now and dried off. Then store the bulbs with those lifted earlier.

Plant *Anemone coronaria* of the de Caen and St Brigid strains for winter flowering in mild districts and in frames for cutting. Set the corms 2 inches deep and 4–6 inches apart or in groups, allowing at least a foot between the groups for effect.

Also in mild districts *Amaryllis belladonna,* the belladonna lily, is regarded as hardy and can be planted in a sunny spot, possibly beneath a south or west-facing wall. Plant the bulbs so that the noses are about 2 or 3 inches below the surface of the soil, and the fragrant pink trumpet-shaped flowers will appear before the leaves. *Nerine bowdenii* and its cultivars also flower, on tall stems, before the leaves appear. These bulbs put in now just below the surface of the soil will produce some flowers this autumn.

Corms for planting now for flowering in the autumn, and in fact up to the end of the year, are colchicums or autumn saffron, and the autumn-flowering crocuses. Put both among shrubs or in rough grass because the leaves in spring look too mature for a tidy lawn and have not died down enough to be cut off. *Sternbergia lutea,* not unlike the crocus in flower, planted now, will also flower in the autumn, but the leaves appear at the same time as the flowers and so are ready for cropping in the spring when the lawn is first cut.

Hippeastrums will have finished flowering indoors and in the greenhouse by now. Gradually reduce the water and rest the bulbs once they are dry until they are ready for repotting in January.

Complete the bulb order for autumn planting bulbs without delay and resist the temptation to buy bulbs offered in lots at a reduced price. They are probably old or very small.

1

2

1 The bulbs of the tender Amaryllis belladonna can be planted out now in a sunny and sheltered spot. Try the base of a south-facing wall for protection.

2 The bulbs should be put in so that the noses are about 2 or 3 inches below the soil surface, and any growth that has been made is just covered.

Flowers for Cutting

As soon as the helichrysum, acroclinium, helipterum and other everlastings come into flower one should begin to gather them. The younger the flower the better will be its colour and those cut in good, dry, sunny weather will be best of all. Never cut any flower for drying when it is wet, either with rain or dew.

If any of the so-called straw-daisies are allowed to develop too far they will eventually turn to seed. The petals will turn backwards and instead of a lovely compact colourful centre it will be a dowdy, fluffy mess. So as soon as the petals expand enough to reveal the centre, cut the flowers.

Helichrysums can be gathered on long stems and tied in bunches after all the leaves have been stripped off, but this is a wasteful method because it sacrifices the buds in the leaf axils. There is also greater danger of the flowers becoming mouldy.

There are two better methods. Cut the flowers by beheading them. Lay them out in single layers on a mesh table. A large piece of small mesh wire netting with the ends bent table-leg fashion, so that air can circulate under the flowers, will do. When the flowers are crisp and papery they are dry enough either to store in bags or boxes or to arrange.

These flowers have to be mounted on

One way to support the dried heads of Helichrysums is to cut the stems to about an inch in length and insert florist's wire while the stem is still soft. The wire will then rust into place.

As soon as the 'everlasting' flowers come into bloom, gather them if they are destined for drying and winter flower arrangements, so that they will retain their colour and be of good texture.

false stems. The best way is to pierce the centre from the top with an awl or cuticle stick, then to pass in the end of a grass stem. This should be pulled through until the grass top nestles snug in the flower centre. It should then be cut level so that it becomes inconspicuous and seems part of it. Timothy grass is best for this purpose.

The second method is much simpler. Cut all helichrysums with about an inch of stem. Immediately they are cut, while the stem and flower are still soft, insert a 22g or 20g florist wire (22g is the finer gauge), according to the size of the flower and the thickness of the natural stem. Put this up the stem into the base of the flower and stop when it reaches the thick seed box. The 'stemmed' flowers may then be stood in a container in a cool, dry, shady place until they are dry, by which time the stem will have withered and the wire rusted firmly into place.

Accessories such as foliage, seed heads, flowers and grasses will hide the wires when they are arranged. The only drawback is that unlike the flowers with the grass stems, which are inclined to stand and hang gracefully, flowers treated in this manner are stiff, but otherwise it is a quick and excellent method.

Acroclinium stems, unlike those of the helichrysum, are tidy and dry stiff. Provided the flowers are cut young, they will need only to be made into small bunches and hung upside down. However, if there is a possibility that some of the flowers will have to go into really tall arrangements, wire them first. The wire can always be shortened if necessary. This will be much easier than trying to wire the flowers after they have become dried.

If helipterum is to be cut while young and of a good colour, some of the buds will almost certainly have to be sacrificed because of the way in which the flower grows. Strip the stem ends of as many leaves as possible and bunch, then hang to dry. Repeat this process with ammobium, lonas, statice, limonium, lavender and all the ornamental grasses.

Shoots of silver-leaved plants, such as the lovely *Cineraria maritima* varieties (incidentally, easily raised from seed), anaphalis, ballota, the senecios and atriplex, to mention only a few, are delightful with flowers in fresh arrangements. They look particularly lovely with the dianthus family. Many of these will also dry by simply hanging upside down in the usual way. But not all of them dry tidily, the leaves are inclined to curl inwards. These can be pressed with a warm iron and once pressed they stay in good shape. But this takes considerable patience. However, if the leaves are picked individually and pressed between newspapers under a weight until they are dry, they can then be mounted on false stems and used among dry flowers quite effectively. For drying and pressing gather the leaves while they are at their best and most silvery and attractive.

Fruit

Early this month the pruning of cordon pears may start in the southern counties, a fortnight later in the North. Cut back mature laterals growing from the main central stem to three leaves. Cut back mature shoots growing from existing laterals to one leaf beyond the basal cluster. Do not touch the leader. This pruning should be spread over several weeks and shoots still immature at the beginning of the month may be dealt with as they become mature. Mature shoots are usually 9 inches or more long and have a woody base. If this summer pruning results in secondary growth, deal with this in September or later in winter.

About mid-month (in southern counties) the cordon apples will be ready for pruning to begin along the same lines as for pears. It is unwise to start too early as this may cause an unwanted profusion of secondary growth.

Pyramids should also be pruned in summer, starting with the pears in early July (in southern counties) and a fortnight later with the apples. Do not touch the central leader of each tree but prune mature branch leaders to five leaves beyond the basal cluster, mature laterals arising from the branches to three leaves and shoots originating from laterals to one leaf beyond the basal cluster.

Early in the month start pruning wall-trained plums and sweet cherries—again, spreading the work over weeks so that there is not too much check to the tree at one time. Shorten all side shoots to five leaves, leaders remaining unpruned. Espalier and fan-trained pears should be treated in the same way and then, a week or two later, fan-trained apples. Dwarf bush trees may be given the same treatment, always provided that they are growing well.

If growing a plum as a pyramid, in the first summer after the initial heading back of the maiden shorten branch leaders to about 8 inches, making the cut to a downward or outward pointing bud. Do this towards the end of the month, when growth has ceased. Prune back any laterals to 6 inches. Repeat this pruning annually towards the end of July. If any branch grows vertically, to challenge the leader, cut it out.

Pinch laterals on fan-trained figs at the fourth leaf.

When melons have had their first stopping, pinch resultant side shoots back to one or two leaves beyond each fruit. Greenhouse melons will need support when they start to swell: make a sling of netting and hang them from the roof wires.

To keep down red spider mites on apples, if they are still persistent after the June spraying, either give a third spraying of malathion or derris or a second application of ovicide. Add sevin to control codling moth grubs.

Although plums were sprayed in June, to control red plum maggot give a second sevin spraying to plums which were not winter-washed with tar-oil.

Raspberry beetle also attacks blackberries, loganberries and other hybrid berries. Spray these with derris 10 days after full bloom, adding colloidal copper if cane spot has been in evidence, and repeat after a 10-day interval.

Complete the thinning of apples, pears and plums. As a rule, apples and pears should be reduced to one per spur, at the most two, and dessert apples should be allowed an average of 5 inches each—cookers 7 to 8 inches. Pears may be left a little closer. Dessert plums should be reduced to about 2 inches apart—and the cooking varieties a little less.

When the last berry has been picked from the summer-fruiting strawberries, the straw may be burned in situ provided it is dry enough to burn quickly. If mats have been used, gather them up and cut the old leaves off the plants with the shears. Weed the rows but do not hoe deeply.

Strawberries should be replaced after three years at the most. If you are quite sure your plants are healthy and yielding well, runners from the heaviest-cropping plants may be layered to provide replacement plants for setting out in August or September. Crock 3-inch pots, fill with John Innes or soilless potting compost and plunge up to four pots round each selected parent. Peg one runner down into each pot with a wire hairpin so that the little tuft of leaves will be kept touching the soil. Pinch out the growing point of the runner and keep watered if necessary. Spray with malathion as a precaution against aphids.

If you want more blackberries or loganberries, these may be propagated easily by bending a shoot to the ground so that the tip can be buried in the soil, keeping it there by tying to a stake or fastening with a large wire hairpin. Keep the soil moist and the tip will soon root. In autumn it can be severed from the parent and transplanted.

Dust outdoor grape vines with sulphur to keep down mildew.

Remove leaves shading melons ripening in the greenhouse.

1

2

1 Loganberries can be propagated by bending shoots over so that the tips touch the round. If they are pegged down with a hairpin, roots will soon form. Later they can be severed and planted out in new positions.
2 As greenhouse melons reach maturity and swell they will need to be supported with netting to prevent snapping.

1

3

2

4

1 Cuttings of Hoya carnosa are taken in the form of leaf-bud cuttings. Cut the stem into inch-long pieces so that each one contains a leaf at the centre.
2 Insert the cutting, in an upright position, singly in a pot containing a compost made up of peat and sand. Small pots should be used for this purpose.

3 Firm the compost around the cutting making sure that the sandy compost is level. In the background an alternative type of cutting can be made using a single leaf. These cuttings would also be inserted singly in small pots.
4 The pots then need to be kept in a close frame until rooting has occurred.

Arrange nets over soft fruits and early fruiting wall trees to protect from birds.

Greenhouse

Leaf cuttings provide a fascinating method of propagating certain pot-plants now, notably the popular gloxinias, varieties of *Begonia rex* and saintpaulias.

There are several effective ways of taking these cuttings but for gloxinias and saintpaulias a simple way is to cut off mature, but not old, leaves, each with a good inch of the leaf-stalk. Insert these upright in a mixture of peat and sand so that the base of the leaf-blade is just buried. After insertion keep them moist in a warm, close propagating frame.

For *Begonia rex* the simplest way is to use similar leaves but with the main veins cut through in several places on the underside of the leaf, which should then be laid on a peat-sand mixture so that the cuts are firmly in contact with it. In the warm, humid atmosphere of a close propagating frame new plantlets will then form at the cuts.

The popular 'busy Lizzie' *(Impatiens holstii* and *I. sultanii)* is even easier to root now. Cut off unflowered shoots 3–4 inches long and stand them in a jar of water in full sun. Saintpaulias too may be rooted in water, by using leaves as mentioned above and merely standing them in the water.

For the propagation of ivies (hedera), *Ficus elastica* (the rubber plant), rhoicissus and the beautiful climbing *Hoya carnosa* leaf-bud cuttings may be taken now. Cut inch-long pieces of the stem so that each piece contains a leaf at its centre. Insert the leaves upright in a peat-sand mixture and keep them moist in a close frame.

Tuberous begonias cannot be propagated by leaves, but the side-shoots that spring from the junctions of the leaves and main stem can be used. Take these off, 3 to 4 inches long, where they join the stem and leaf-stalk, so that each one has a solid wedge-shaped base. Insert them in a peat and sand mixture in a close frame.

Tuberous begonias will need staking now, or as soon as the flower buds form. When the buds appear they will be in threes, with a small one on either side of the large main one. In order to ensure extra large blooms remove these smaller side ones.

Cyclamen kept from last year should be repotted now. Shake them out of the old soil, remove any withered roots and repot in well-drained pots of the John Innes potting compost No 2, with the top of the corm just level with the surface. Give a thorough watering, then stand the plants in cool shade, where they should be given frequent overhead syringeing.

Further sowings of cineraria, calceolaria and *Primula malacoides* may be made now to provide a succession. Tuberous begonias and gloxinias may also be sown now to provide young plants for storing through the winter.

As hydrangeas pass out of bloom, cut the flowered stems back to 6 inches long. Repot into a size larger pot, using the John Innes potting compost No 2, and stand the plants in full sun outside, where they must be kept quite moist.

As regal pelargoniums finish flowering cut them back hard and rest them by laying the pots containing them on their sides outside. They will need little or no water for the next few weeks but do not let them dry out completely.

Chrysanthemums in pots will need feeding from early July onwards. Use a fertiliser with a fairly high nitrogen content. Either a liquid or a dry feed may be used, but always follow the maker's instructions.

Perpetual carnations need plenty of water and ventilation now, together with damping down and overhead syringeing to prevent a too arid atmosphere. Feeding, preferably with a proprietary carnation fertiliser, should be carried out regularly from now until the end of October.

As soon as tomato plants have set their fourth truss feed with a nitrogenous fertiliser, such as dried blood, to prevent the tops of plants bearing a weight of fruit 'running off' thin.

As cucumber roots appear on the surface of the soil top dress with an inch thick layer of well-rotted manure mixed with good loam. If manure is not available use garden compost with a little general fertiliser added. Shade the plants from hot sun and syringe regularly to keep down red spider mite.

Hedges

Evergreen and conifer hedges, whether spring or autumn planted, should be getting away well by this time. Evergreens may drop some or all of their leaves the first summer after planting. This is nature's way of reducing transpiration, the loss of moisture through the leaf surfaces.

There is, therefore, no need to worry if this happens. But if the leaves wither and stay put there is cause for concern. Any plants showing these symptoms should be watched and watered regularly until growth gets under way. Some will not recover and replacements will be needed in the autumn.

Newly planted hedges will still need mulching during dry periods. Summer mulches, however, can be a mixed blessing. As well as retaining soil moisture, they can keep rain from penetrating to the roots in wet weather. When rain comes, therefore, it is better to rake the mulching materials away from the base of the hedge.

Spring-planted hedges should be left untrimmed for their first season, apart from topping to give uniformity of height. This operation, as well as any other clipping, should be postponed until the second or third season for conifers.

Established formal hedges that flowered in June should have their annual cutting and cleaning this month. Among those likely to need trimming are the June-flowering barberries, cotoneasters, *Osmanthus delavayi*—which, incidentally, makes one of the loveliest of scented hedges—pyracantha, rosemary, tamarisk and hebe (shrubby veronica).

Beech, hornbeam, holly and yew, as well as dwarf hedges such as box and the green and gold-variegated *Euonymus radicans*, can also be given their first 'short-back-and-sides' some time this month.

Informal hedges will require less drastic clipping than those just mentioned. Shoots that have flowered should be cut back to within two inches of their point of origin as soon as the flowers have faded. *Philadelphus coronarius*, the mock orange and its varieties and hybrids, evergreen ceanothus and deutzias are some of the hedging shrubs that are likely to need this treatment at the present time.

It is very important to have the proper tools for the job. Quality counts in garden tools and it is always advisable to buy the best that one can afford. In the small to medium-sized garden, nothing could be better for hedge-cutting than a well-balanced pair of shears, preferably with a notched blade for tackling the thicker stems.

For large-leaved shrubs like laurels and rhododendrons, secateurs are better than shears. Leaves slashed in half with shears soon turn brown and die, giving the hedge an uncared-for look. Where such hedges are extensive, however, the use of secateurs will not be practicable.

Agricultural type hedges—hazel, quickthorn and *Acer campestre*, the hedging maple—are made of sterner stuff and can be trimmed with a sickle or bagging hook; once this month, with a repeat in the autumn. This cut-and-thrust method will do the job quickly and

In the average garden a good pair of shears is the best tool for tackling the hedge cutting. Lightweight sharp shears with notched blades are ideal for coping with the thicker branches.

In general, hedges should be trimmed to have a wedge shaped section, wider at the base and tapering slightly towards the top. This type of hedge is not so easily damaged by heavy snow.

RECOGNITION CHART

Natural Order 2

Plants within one Natural Order can vary widely in type. Edible fruits, weeds and shrubs may all be one family

RANUNCULACEAE
Decorative perennials like Hellebore, Aconitum, Pulsatilla, Aquilegia and Paeony are in the same family as weeds such as Buttercups

EUPHORBIACEAE
The evergreen Box, Buxus sempervirens is in the same family as the Euphorbias or Spurges, which genus provides decorative plants and weeds as well as the Caper. Weeds such as Dog's Mercury are in this family

ROSACEAE
One of the largest plant families includes all wild and garden Roses, edible fruit like Apples, Crab Apples, Strawberries and Blackberries. Trees such as Rowan and Hawthorn are also in this family together with Potentilla species some of which are shrubs and others weeds

UMBELLIFERAE
Decorative plants like Astrantia and Eryngium are in the same family as Celery, Apium graveolens and Carrot, Daucus carota and the ubiquitous weeds like Cow Parsley. Several herbs like Fennel and Dill are umbelliferous

CARYOPHYLLACEAE
The scented Carnations and Pinks, and other Dianthus species such as Sweet Williams are in the same family as Saponaria and the Chickweeds

LABIATAE
Aromatic plants such as Monarda and Salvia species and decorative plants such Lamium are in the same family as the unwanted Stinging Nettles

SOLANACEAE
The Deadly Nightshade, Atropa belladonna shares poisonous qualities with the above-ground parts of the Potato plant. The Tomato or Lycopersicon is in this family too, together with the Capsicum species which provide decorative plants as well as Peppers and Chillies

SCHROPHULARIACEAE
The decorative Antirrhinums and Musk are in the same family as the Veronica species which provide border plants and shrubs as well as the Speedwell weeds. The Foxglove species and the Verbascum species grow both in cultivation and in the wild

reasonably well but does not produce the same neat effect as shears or a hedge-trimmer. It is really suited only to the wilder parts of a garden, where formality and tidyness are not of paramount importance.

In general, hedges should be trimmed to a wedge shape, wider at the base and tapering slightly towards the top. This will enable them to shrug off heavy falls of snow and keep them well furnished at their base.

Two other useful accessories for hedge trimming are a strong pair of steps and a garden line. The former will be necessary for taller hedges and a level top to the hedge can be obtained by stretching the line tightly between two posts, an inch or two above the desired height.

Herbaceous Plants

This can be one of the most colourful months in the herbaceous border. One or two perennials that have given joy but are now fading, however, may need attention if they are to be seen in their full glory next year.

The bearded irises, for instance, should be lifted and divided every third or fourth year. These velvety beauties—often called the 'poor man's orchid'—move best immediately after flowering when the rhizomes are making fresh roots, though transplanting can also be carried out during August and September.

Flowering in May and June, they are easy to grow in a sunny position, planted in well-drained soil enriched with bone-meal and containing lime or old mortar rubble. On heavy soil, beds should be slightly raised to assist in drainage, adding plenty of coarse sand when digging.

When thinning out old clumps, use the outer rhizomes for replanting, cutting them off cleanly and discarding the worn out centres. Rhizomes should be planted 8–15 inches apart, partially covered or, in the case of light soil, just below the surface. The roots on the underside which anchor the plant should be spread carefully and made firm.

Bearded irises come in various heights—tall, from 2½–4 feet; intermediate, from 1–2 feet and dwarf, from 6–10 inches. The dwarfs start to bloom three to four weeks earlier than the taller varieties.

Suggested varieties for those adding to a collection or growing plants for the first time: 'Elmohr', ruffled reddish-mulberry blooms (3 feet); 'Fantasy', rose, orchid-pink and raspberry colourings with tangerine beard (34 inches); 'Cape Cod', pure white with purple falls (3 feet); 'Blue Denim', blue with white beard (14 inches); 'Tulare', golden yellow (24 inches) and 'Bright Eyes', lemon-yellow with falls splashed dark blue (16 inches).

1 Bearded Irises need to be lifted and divided every third or fourth year, in July, once flowering is over. Old portions of the rhizomatous stock can be discarded and the best pieces, usually from the outside, used for propagation.
2 Cut the stock into pieces.
3 Trim each piece so that there is a good bulbous piece of rhizome and a fan of leaves at one end. Trim the leaves.
4 When planting the new pieces put them all in the same direction, so that the rhizomes face the same way and all towards the sunny side of the borders.

Here is a list of dwarf varieties that are excellent for the front of a border: 'Blazon', maroon black with gold beard (7 inches); 'Negus', violet-blue with yellow beard (9 inches); 'Fortissimo', orange-yellow with orange beard (8 inches) and 'One Fine Day', blue-lavender overlaid red-purple with white beard (7 inches).

Another perennial that should be divided every three years, preferably in July or August, is the pyrethrum *(Chrysanthemum coccineum)*, a neat, pretty plant with fern-like foliage and double or single daisy flowers. In rose, salmon, crimson-scarlet and pure white, the flowers are invaluable for cutting, the plants thriving in full sun in rich loamy soil. The normal flowering period is from May to June, but this can be prolonged by cutting down the old flowered stems to the ground.

While still enjoying the blooms of border carnations, new plants can be propagated by layering non-flowering shoots. The ground surrounding the plants should be forked over and top-dressed with damp peat and coarse sand to provide a suitable rooting medium for the layers. The actual layering is simple.

Choose those shoots nearest to the ground, a cut about an inch long (not beyond a joint) is made up the centre of each stem where it contacts the soil when pegged down with a wire pin—old-fashioned hairpins are good for this job—bending the shoot upwards. Layers usually root in four to six weeks, after which time they can be severed from the parent, before potting up in 2–2½ inch pots filled with turfy loam, damp horticultural peat and silver sand.

Of the same family (dianthus) are the deliciously scented pinks—'Mrs Sinkins', 'White Ladies Improved', 'Dusky' (dusty-pink), and so on. These old favourites can be increased by 'pipings' (cuttings) now—healthy non-flowered shoots being pulled from a joint. They root readily in a cold frame, planted 1½ inches apart in a bed of peat and coarse sand, after the lower leaves have been stripped with an upward pull. Where no cold frame is available, shoots can be rooted in the same medium in the open provided the soil is kept damp, but the percentage of 'takes' will not be as high as when rooted in a frame.

Whether rooted indoors or outdoors, the plantlets must be lifted and potted on in the same compost as suggested for the border carnations as soon as they have made roots (roughly 8 weeks) as the plants become weak and drawn if left to grow in peat and sand.

One of the showiest of garden plants—the crown imperial fritillary *(Fritillaria imperialis)*—can be planted towards the end of the month or in early August. These tall (2–3 feet) elegant plants with their huge heads of clear orange, yellow or rusty red drooping bells, crowned with a tuft of bright green leaves, produce their distinctive flowers in April when there is little else in bloom. The bulbs, planted 5–6 inches deep, 8 inches apart, do best in heavy ground where the surface is rarely disturbed, the soil being firmed round as the shoots appear. They should not be replanted more often than once in four years but repay for an annual top-dressing of rotted manure during summer.

Although gladioli are sun-lovers they need copious watering in dry weather. Surface watering is useless and can be harmful; the moisture must penetrate the roots if it is to be beneficial. After watering, a protective mulch of straw, rotted manure or moist peat will help to prevent evaporation. The large-flowered type may need support in windswept areas, but this can sometimes be dispensed with by mounding the soil up round the lower part of the stems of the plants.

Where necessary, support annuals—clarkia, viscaria, cornflowers, godetia, echium, malope, larkspur, *Lychnis flos-jovis*, and Shirley poppies—with twiggy sticks, placing them round and in between the plants. Check dahlia and chrysanthemum stakes, giving an extra tie as the plants grow.

Flowers should be removed from delphiniums, doronicum, anchusa, lupins and paeonies as soon as they fade, leaving the foliage; leaves, while green, are an essential part of the plant mechanism.

If the individual blooms of geum—both the variety 'Mrs Bradshaw' (red) and the rich golden yellow 'Lady Stratheden'—are nipped off as they die, the plants generally continue flowering until October. The same is true of petunias.

House Plants

On the whole house plants suffer from few pests and diseases. This is due partly to the fact that most have been grown and distributed by commercial growers who cannot afford to allow any such troubles among their plants lest they be decimated, but mainly because the plants receive individual attention indoors and are maintained in a comparatively clean and sterile atmosphere compared with the great outdoors.

But at about this time of year pests sometimes appear on house plants, particularly the ubiquitous aphids which are trying always to attack roses and so many other garden plants. Some of these pests may be brought indoors unknowingly on flowers cut for decoration and others may fly in through open windows or even be brought in on the clothes or in the hair.

Fortunately aphids find many other plants in the garden more succulent than house plants, so those house plants that are sunning themselves in the garden will seldom be attacked and those indoors become infested only because there is little else for the pests to feed upon.

Plants in the home can sometimes be attacked by just one or two greenfly which escape notice for a day or two and, because of the extraordinary speed of their breeding, the plant suddenly appears to be covered with them. So in the summer months it is well to look for the signs of aphid attack—a curling of the young foliage, a yellowing of the leaves, a sticky film on some of the leaves.

Waste no time in cleaning affected plants and checking any others in the vicinity. Spray with any good garden insecticide, if necessary taking the plant outside to do so, for the spray can stain or damage furniture and walls. Do not attempt to clean an infected plant by wiping or washing alone, for some of the pests are almost certain to escape. Systemic insecticides can be watered into the soil containing the plants and will gradually enter the sap to kill all insects but, although this is helpful for plants which do not appear to have been affected yet, it is too slow a method for a badly infested plant.

As a precautionary measure it is helpful during the summer months to include a dose of systemic insecticide in the watering of most house plants at monthly intervals. For nearly all plants it can do no harm and it may do much good.

Another pest which usually appears only in the summer, but can sometimes attack in the winter, is the red spider mite, always occasioned by atmospheres which are too arid—lacking in humidity. The mite is so small that it is almost impossible to detect with the naked eye, but its presence is suggested by the appearance of distorted leaves, curled and twisted young shoots and the evidence of fine hairs like a tiny spider's web. Powder or even cigarette ash

Mealy Bugs can be a pest on indoor plants. The best way of removing them is to apply white oil to the end of a match-stick or paint brush. Then pick up and kill the mealy bug.

sprinkled on a suspect part will, if caught in the web, soon prove a red spider mite attack.

If possible immerse the entire plant in a solution of white oils to kill red spider mite. It is difficult to kill by any other means. If infestation is limited it may be possible to clean the plant by painting the affected portions with white oils.

If a plant is too large to remove to a bucket of the solution, then it may be possible to prune away and burn any infected parts, but if this is again impossible you will be wise to remove the plant as quickly as possible and discard it before the pest spreads to other plants.

The only two other pests likely to be encountered are mealy bug and scale. The first is shown as a fluffy white growth almost like cotton wool on a leaf or in a joint. It can be scraped away with a matchstick dipped in white oils and the surrounding area should then be painted with the solution.

Scale is more difficult to remove. It looks like a small, hard-shelled wood louse sticking to a leaf. It should be prized away with a penknife or some similar instrument and the area painted with white oils.

Of diseases, the only one likely to be encountered is damping off, a fungal disease, also known as stem rot. This is soil borne, rarely found and incapable of being cured. Discard the plant.

Lawns

Some people say that the lawn is only as good as its edges! Crumbling, uneven and untidy edges certainly give the lawn an unkempt appearance, but this does not necessarily indicate that the lawn itself is not in excellent health in every other way. However, to prevent visitors saying, or even thinking, your lawn is neglected, a little time spent tidying up the edges will not come amiss.

At this time of year all that should be necessary is to cut overhanging grass. A pair of hand shears can be used, but this means awkward bending, which can become very tiring. Special long-handled lawn shears are much easier to operate from an upright position. For really long lengths of lawn edges, wheeled and power-driven edgers are available.

Even when given regular attention, the actual soil edges of the lawn will probably require straightening now and again. This can be done this month with a straight bladed spade, one of the proprietary lawn edgers, or special half moon turfing iron.

Unless your eye for estimating a true line is particularly good, for straight lawn edges it pays to peg out a length of string as a guide line. The pieces of chopped off turf should be removed from where they fall, otherwise the grass will

Lawn edges can be kept trim or recut to a better line with the automatic types of lawn-edging machines. Here the Spintrim powered edging machine is being used for the job.

When an edging iron is used to give a fresh, clear-cut edge to the lawn it is advisable to put out a garden line as a cutting guide. Otherwise you may get a wavy edge to your lawn.

start growing in the wrong place and increase your weeding problems. Any drastic changes of lawn outline are best left until later in the year.

Many lawns are never troubled by pests or diseases, but it is as well to keep an eye open for their possible appearance.

Ants can sometimes be a bit of a problem during July and August, and anthills can be a nuisance. They disfigure the lawn, make mowing difficult and offer a suitable place for weed seeds to germinate, free of competition from the grasses. Also, of course, ants can be a biting and most disturbing nuisance when the family wishes to use the lawn for recreation.

There are a number of proprietary ant killer products on the market and these should be applied according to the manufacturers' recommendations. Once the ants are killed, flatten the 'hill' with the feet and remove any surplus soil. Then re-seed or turf the area.

The results of leather-jackets (daddy longleg grubs) may be seen now or even earlier in the season, especially on sandy soils near the seaside. The indication is smallish brown patches of grass, where the grubs have fed on the grass roots. Unfortunately, nothing can be done at this time of year, but in autumn the lawn should be dusted with malathion or aldrin. The grass usually recovers of its own accord if well-watered and fed with fertilisers.

Another 'pest' which can be a problem is a bitch who makes a habit of urinating on the lawn. The result of urine is to kill a small area of grass, while the circle of grasses round the dead patch turn a vivid deep green colour. If the affected area is noticed quickly enough, heavy watering will help to reduce the discoloration. The only satisfactory answer to the problem is to train the bitch to go elsewhere.

On large lawns in country areas moles can occasionally be a nuisance, in the same way as ants, in that they create unsightly 'hills' of soil. There are various anti-mole devices and products which can be used but, if the moles really become a problem, a call to the local rodent operator is advisable. Then, as with anthills, the soil should be flattened and the area turfed or re-seeded.

Of diseases, fusarium patch disease (snow mould) is the most common. It shows up at any time of year, though usually July to October, as reddish-brown patches, on which a white mould appears in moist weather. It is particularly common on over-fertilised damp soils.

Corticium disease (red thread) can make its appearance also from July to October and is most common on lawns which have been underfed and are particularly short of nitrogen. It shows itself as large patches of sandy coloured grass, often with a reddish-tinge caused by the minute red 'needles' of the fungus growing on the dead grass. In both cases, a mercury based fungicide should be applied at the first sign of dying grass patches.

Mowing of the lawns should continue to take place regularly. Lawns should be watered thoroughly during drought periods, by means of a sprinkler, if the grass is to remain a healthy green and not take on a scorched appearance.

Any odd weed that offends the eye can be given 'spot' treatment with a hormone weedkiller. Equally, if a number of weeds are still around, an overall hormone weedkiller application may be made, although preferably not when the weather is very hot and dry. Raking before mowing will help to lift up stems of creeping weeds, so that the mower blades can cut them off effectively.

A new lawn, which was sown or turfed in the spring, will now be old enough to withstand a weedkiller application if this is necessary. Under no circumstances, however, should the manufacturers' recommendations be exceeded, as the grass will still be young enough to be scorched if an overdose is applied. In fact, it is sound commonsense to stick rigidly to the manufacturer's application rates.

Paths, Fences and Walls

In July it is immediately evident how good walls in a garden, including the walls of the house, can significantly increase the garden area. They should be covered with rampant growth, rich with colour. Many of the plants growing on the walls will be deciduous and some may even be annual climbers.

As so many climbers and scramblers will mingle happily with each other, it is well when planning wall plantings to think first in terms of winter and to provide permanent evergreens which will give some colour in the dark days yet not be dull, oppressive and overpowering during the summer. One of the best plants for this purpose is the ivy, and although the many forms of the common green ivy, *Hedera helix*, are helpful and attractive, there are better and more brightly coloured varieties.

Two good variegated ivies are *Hedera canariensis*, so frequently seen as a house plant, with leaves irregularly blotched, streaked and mottled with white, silver, grey and even hints of pink, and the golden and cream variegated *H. colchica dentata variegata*. These plants normally need no attention whatsoever. Ivies have the additional virtue of growing happily in any aspect and will clothe a north wall that might otherwise be left naked.

Other non-flowering plants include many of the vines, most of them deciduous. Many give lavishly of their foliage, which frequently turns to magnificent and glowing colours in the autumn before the leaves fall. Some of these vines will also give grapes and gardeners must decide whether they wish to give up good south or west wall space to a plant which produces only insignificant flowers but later bunches of fruits, or whether they would rather keep the area for the richer colours of prolific flowering plants. Vine foliage is usually too dense to allow flowering plants to mingle with it, yet it is sometimes worth trying to grow a climbing rose or a honeysuckle together with the vines.

Honeysuckles, many of them strongly

1

2

1 Hedera colchica dentata variegata is one of the Ivies with attractively marked leaves. It will provide colour and more interest in winter than the ordinary green-leaved form of Hedera.

2 Vitis coignetiae is one of the Vines that provides attractive colour to its foliage in the later part of the year. It is, however, too dense-growing to allow other plants to mingle with it.

scented, are wonderful climbing plants for walls. Most of the climbing varieties are deciduous, though of these some, such as *Lonicera japonica halliana*, retain their leaves so long as to be almost evergreen. They are usually rampant growers and do not object to shade.

Other rampant growers which frequently look lovelier sprawling along the top of a wall than climbing up its face are the clematis tribe. There are so many of these in such rich colours and with such a long season of flowering that it is normally difficult to decide which to grow, so a specialist's catalogue should be consulted before making the perhaps more obvious choices available through the general nurseryman.

Jasmines make good wall plants with their sweetly scented flowers and, although only *Jasminum primulinum* can be considered evergreen, other varieties include silver and golden variegated forms which are a constant delight for their foliage alone. They are carefree plants, growing quickly and strongly, requiring little or no attention and careless of aspect.

Climbing roses, of which there are many, demand certain attention if they are to give of their best, but with care given to their initial training and with good support wires they need little more than annual pruning, feeding and mulching and the regular removal of dead flowers to ensure continuation of bloom.

1

2

1 Container-grown plants dry out quickly in summer and every trick possible must be used to retain moisture at the roots.
2 When potting up, a rag can be placed over the crocks and beneath the compost to retain some moisture in the compost at the base of the pot.

Patios, Balconies, Roof Gardens and Window Boxes

The next few weeks should bring the hottest periods of the year. Apart from the sheer heat of the sun there is also both the brightness of the light and the length of time each day in which it shines.

All these necessities of plant growth lead to respiration. On a warm, bright day, many plants can respire more quickly than they can absorb moisture from the soil. This leads to wilting and eventually to death through exhaustion. A single plant can absorb and breathe out enough water for its root system to be suitably wet in the morning and dry at night.

Normally in the open ground plants have an underground reservoir of moisture on which they can draw, although in summer months even this is sometimes insufficient. Plants grown in containers are severely limited in moisture availability and as a rule the smaller the pot or container the less water available.

So for all container grown plants on the patio, roof garden or balcony, and for all plants growing in window-boxes, it is vital during the summer months to ensure that adequate supplies of water are available. Although there are several means of supplying this demand, nothing can replace the need of all plants to have a certain amount of moisture available to the roots, for these are primarily the most vulnerable parts of all plants. It is basically through the roots that plants draw up their vital moisture, basically through their roots that they absorb their plant foods, available to them only in the form of a water-based solution of minerals.

Plants in containers may require lavish manual waterings as often as twice a day. This is sometimes impossible so some means must be discovered of avoiding the necessity. It is helpful to use containers which are large, holding considerable quantities of soil. It is helpful to make this soil as water-retentive as possible by the addition of extra peat or other absorbent materials. It is advisable, where possible, to have containers sheltered to some extent from the sun, possibly in the shade of a wall or in the shade of other plants. In some circumstances it is possible to plunge containers inside a quantity of moist peat.

When they are carried out, manual waterings must be thorough. The root soil must be completely soaked, so that any excess moisture is trickling out through the drainage holes. Where a number of plants in containers are involved it is almost impossible to do this by means of watering cans and a hose must be brought into play. Yet even with a hose watering must be gentle, for if too much water is applied at one time it frequently has a tendency to rush away too quickly without being slowly and gently absorbed by the soil.

The ideal in summer months is to install some kind of drip watering mechanism, whereby each plant in each container receives a slow and steady supply of water from some central reservoir.

Unfortunately this method is seldom practical and always hideous to the eyes—to be used only when the family is away from home for some time.

Respiration rates are slowed if the foliage of the plants is thoroughly wetted as well as the soil at the roots, so each thorough watering should aim at drenching the entire plant from tip growth to root ball. It is also helpful to provide additional humidity by watering the nearby floor. This is possible on a patio, usually possible with a roof garden and sometimes possible on the balcony, but of course this aid cannot be practised with window-boxes.

It is possible at times to see steam rising from a patio or roof floor when watered and for one section to be almost dry again before the other end has received its wetting. This indicates quite clearly the necessity for water.

It also shows that if watering is carried out during the hottest part of the day you are sure to waste a considerable part of both your water and your effort through immediate evaporation, whereas if water is applied to plants before the sun has reached its peak the plants will have been enabled to enjoy and absorb water for some hours. So watering early in the morning and late in the afternoon is more beneficial.

Under no circumstances must the drainage system of plants in containers be interfered with to slow the flow-through of water, for air is as necessary to the roots as water. Yet it is sometimes helpful to add between the drainage crocks and the soil a layer of absorbent material, such as a piece of old rag or a close fitting wad or strip of absorbent flower arrangement plastic. Both of these will hold moisture and slowly release it to the soil.

As plants in the situations under discussion are not as compacted together as, for example, is grass, automatic sprinkler systems are of little real value and can sometimes be a real nuisance to neighbours. It is sometimes possible, however, to set such a system working at low level to wet continuously one side of a patio for an hour and then to remove it to another part.

Sprinkler systems can also be helpful for climbers which may be growing in the soil at the foot of a wall. As all walls are slightly absorbent and as they frequently shelter from the rain plants growing at their base, many climbers fail to put out their full potential simply because most of the time they are kept dryer than they ought to be. A good and thorough soaking in the hotter days can be invaluable to climbers in this situation.

Rock Gardens

Under normal circumstances the rock garden rarely needs watering by artificial means. The top dressing of chippings provides a suitable mulch and prevents water escaping by evaporation. During a prolonged dry spell, however, artificial watering will be more beneficial on the rock garden than in other parts of the garden. The open texture of the soil allows easy ingress and there is no doubt one gallon of water here is better than ten elsewhere.

Naturally the best time to carry out this operation is after the sun has set, but if this is not possible early morning will do before the sun has climbed to any height. An oscillating sprinkler with a fine mist-like spray is ideal and should be used for a period of at least two hours.

It is far better to give a thorough soaking at one period—not a little and often. A constant supply of small amounts tends to bring the fine feeding roots to the surface, to their detriment when the soil dries out.

Scree gardens, when well established, rarely suffer from drought. The plants produce long roots which quickly penetrate the loose gravelly compost down into the natural soil below where there is always a sufficiency of moisture. On the other hand, troughs and sink gardens —especially those raised above their surroundings—will need a great deal of water during hot dry spells. Here again a little goes a long way and all that is necessary is to water overhead until this percolates through the soil and out of the drainage holes.

July is the month when you should take stock of the rock garden and its occupants. You may find mistakes in planting: perhaps too vigorous species adjacent to the more delicate plants at the expense of the latter, colour clashes and tall plants blocking dwarf plants from view.

Notes can be made concerning plants which give a long flowering season and those which tend to be shy flowering or, as sometimes happens, do not flower at all; of silver foliage plants and their association with their neighbours; of flowering plants which go well together.

Everybody makes mistakes and glowing descriptions in nurserymen's catalogues often tend to lead the unwary to purchase plants that are a menace in the rock garden, often becoming pernicious weeds impossible to eradicate once they have obtained a foothold. The following list will help gardeners to avoid this trap: *Achillea millefolium; Asperula odorata; Calystegia pubescens; Campanula rapunculus; Cerastium tomentosum;* snow in summer, the nurseryman's favourite that will grow anywhere and everywhere—(but who wants a rock garden of one plant only?)—*Cerastium biebersteinii; Convolvulus althaeoides,* if grown in chalk; most *Cotula* species; *Helxine soleirolii; Veronica filiformis; Oxalis corniculata* and its forms; *O. repens; Allium moly; Ornithogalum umbellatum; O. nutans; Acaena microphylla,* in a small garden; *Hieracium aurantiacum; Coronilla varia; Sedum album; Sedum spurium* and *Chrysanthemum arcticum.* This list is not exhaustive by any means, but it contains a good number of the plants one can do well without.

Miniature roses have come to the fore in recent years and, although the rock garden purist will have none of them, they can be very attractive in either a small rock bed of their own or as occupants of an old stone sink or trough. Ranging in height between 6 inches–1 foot they seldom outgrow their allotted space. All need an open, well-drained soil with a fair percentage of humus worked into it.

Planting can be carried out at any time for they are pot grown and buying these when in flower not only helps in choosing good flowering forms, but also enables you to pick the correct colours. When planting they need watering-in well and a light dose of liquid manure given weekly during the flowering season.

Their one real deadly enemy is greenfly which seems to be attracted to these dwarf roses from miles around. Here a periodic spraying with a systemic insecticide will keep the pest in check. As a guide the following varieties will go towards making a collection; it is a far from complete list but it is a selection of the best kinds; 'Baby Gold', orange and gold, scented; 'Baby Ophelia', salmon-pink, scented; 'Bit o' Sunshine', yellow, scented; 'Cinderella', white tinged pink, scented; 'Eleanor', coral-pink, scented; 'Grenadine', scarlet-crimson; 'Jackie', pale yellow, scented; 'Josephine Wheatcroft', dark yellow, scented; 'Little Flirt', interior red, yellow reverse, scented; 'Little Princess', white; 'Little Scotch', cream, centre yellow; 'Maid Marion', tight scarlet flowers; 'Mr Bluebird', semi-double, lavender-blue, 'New Penny', semi-double orange; 'Oakington Ruby' (one of the oldest, but best) crimson, scented; 'Peon Crimson', crimson with white eye; 'Pink Heather', pink shaded white, scented; 'Pixie Rose', deep pink, scented; 'Robin', carmine-crimson; 'Rouletti', pink; 'Silver Tips', buds deep pink opening to light pink with silvery shade; 'Tinker Bell', open deep pink and 'Yellow Doll', pure yellow.

There is no doubt that a bed or trough confined to dwarf roses looks bare when out of flower. To give a longer flowering season it can be planted with dwarf tulip, daffodil or scilla species—the tulips in November, the daffodils in August and the scillas in June. Only the smallest of these plants should be used and those with a maximum height of six inches are best.

All iris species, such as *I. pumila*, which make rhizomes, should be lifted and divided during this month. The divisions are replanted with the rhizomes resting on the surface of the soil —they must not be covered.

Roses

Many rose shows are held during the last week in June and the first week in July. As a matter of fact this fortnight represents the peak of the year for rose shows.

There is more to showing roses than going into the garden on the morning of the show, cutting whatever blooms may be available and arranging them in bowls or vases. The consistently successful exhibitor will almost live with his roses for the two or three days prior to the show. Even if he decides not to 'tie' young blooms in order to increase their size and length of petal, there is much to be done in arranging the conical bloom protectors to shield them on the plant from sun and rain and excessive heat.

The blooms are cut during the evening before the show and the stems are plunged immediately into cold water in deep containers, so that the water almost reaches the base of the bloom. Only those with perfect centres are suitable for exhibiting, i.e. where the centre forms a perfect cone or spiral, free from clefts or other irregularities. Most beginners tend to show their blooms well past their best, or even blown. Once the centre has opened out, revealing the anthers, the flower is useless for exhibiting as a specimen bloom, whatever its size.

When arranging a decorative bowl of roses, brightness and freshness are more important than size alone, especially when, as often happens, size goes hand in hand with insipid colours. There is scope in such an arrangement for skilful colour blending and contrast.

It is only by actually exhibiting his own roses that a gardener can compare his with the standard reached by other growers, and it may well act as a spur to further effort if his best blooms are not among the prize-winners. While experience in 'dressing' blooms will help to some extent in disguising faults, it cannot convert a bad flower into a good one.

The keen amateur will not be satisfied until he has tried his hand at budding and July is the month when this is normally undertaken. The rootstocks should have been planted in their budding quarters between January and mid-March, about 8 inches apart in the rows and 18 inches between the rows. The most popular rootstock is the seedling briar *(R. canina)*, or one of its many selected strains, to ensure greater uniformity.

Many beginners go wrong because they take far too long over the job. It should be borne in mind that this is in the nature of a surgical operation on a plant, so that speed and cleanliness are essential to success. In budding, the cambium layer of the bud, i.e. the tissue between the wood and the bark, has to unite with that of the rootstock, and if

Roses are budded in July.
1 The bud is removed with a sharp knife.
2 The scion is trimmed.
3 The pith is removed from the bud.
4 A T-shaped cut is made in the stock.
5 The bud is inserted into the cut.
6 The union is firmly bound with raffia.

this is allowed to dry out by taking too long over the job, the operation is bound to fail.

Apart from this, the essentials to success in budding are threefold: first, a really fresh bud in good condition; second, the removal of the wood behind the bud, without damaging the bud itself; third, the sap to be running freely in the rootstock, so that the bark will lift cleanly on both sides of the 'T' cut, without forcing or bruising.

In order to ensure the correct condition of the bud, a stem of the chosen variety on which the flower is just fading should be cut off just above the fourth leaf down from the flower. This will leave three buds on the stem—one at the junction of each leaf with the stem. The third one down from the bloom will normally be just right and maybe the second one also, depending on the variety. The leaves should be cut off apart from half an inch of the stalk, to facilitate handling the bud.

When removing the bud from the 'stick', as the stem is called, a really sharp budding knife should be used. Starting half an inch above the bud, make a cut on the slant, gradually penetrating deeper behind the bud and then becoming shallower, so that the blade emerges half an inch beyond it. This severs a boat-shaped piece of bark with the bud and leaf stalk in the middle and a thin slice of wood behind. It is the removal of this wood without damaging the bud that causes most trouble, especially when too much wood has been left by cutting too deeply. The simplest method is to remove the wood in two operations. If the shield is held between the forefinger and thumb of one hand, with the thumbnail pressed hard against the wood behind the bud, and the top of the slice of wood above the bud is held between the forefinger and thumb of the other hand, a sudden sideways snatch will remove this wood without damaging the bud, which is protected by the thumbnail of the other hand. The shield of bark should then be reversed to remove the piece of wood below the bud in a similar manner. The base of the shield should then be trimmed straight across, prior to inserting it behind the flaps of bark raised in readiness on each side of the 'T' cut in the bark of the rootstock at soil level. As to whether moist raffia or the more modern rubber or plastic ties are to be preferred is a matter of opinion, but the beginner will probably find raffia easier to use. It should be bound round the entire cut in puttee-fashion, but leaving the dormant bud itself exposed.

Lawn mowings can be used to mulch the soil around most shrubs at this time of the year. The mulch will retain moisture and at the same time help to smother weeds. Here lawn cuttings from the grass box are being used around Roses.

Trees, Shrubs and Climbers

Mulching and regular watering should still continue in the shrub border during dry periods, especially where there are new plantings. Although the rhododendron and azalea display is over, these shrubs appreciate overhead watering on hot dry days. Hydrangeas are another race of shrubs that cannot flourish properly in conditions of drought. The best sprinklers for this kind of watering are those that produce a mist-like spray at about shoulder height.

Lawn clippings from the grassbox of the mower make an effective moisture-retaining summer mulch that will also smother weeds. They should be spread out to a depth of about two inches round, but not touching, the base of the plants. Regular 'topping-up' at intervals of about a fortnight will keep the mulch effective.

It is not advisable to use grass clippings from the first few cuts after a lawn has been treated with a selective weed-killer. Traces of the latter can have a harmful effect on the growth of many garden plants.

The pruning of flowering shrubs that have finished blooming should continue throughout the month. Restrict the operation, however, if the shrub flowers on the previous year's wood. Such pruning should start from the first year of planting and continue regularly. This will produce a shapely shrub, well furnished with flowering shoots.

Certain shrubs increase in size so slowly that it would be foolish to practise any but the most moderate pruning. The pruning of rhododendrons and azaleas, for example, is normally restricted to the removal of dead flower trusses to enable the new leaf shoots to develop more rapidly.

More drastic pruning should be restricted to plants that have exceeded their allotted space. The rough-barked types of rhododendron can be cut back hard; even thick branches can be removed without harm. With the smooth-stemmed kinds greater caution is advisable. In any event, drastić pruning of this kind should be carried out during the dormant period from November to March.

July is a good time to take stock of future planting needs and for placing orders with nurseries for autumn delivery. These busy individuals like to be given plenty of notice and those who are sensible enough to order early usually get the pick of the nursery stock with the added advantage of delivery before severe weather causes planting problems.

Whenever possible, it is a good idea to

Although the flowering period of Rhododendrons and Azaleas has passed, these shrubs appreciate an overhead watering during the dry summer days. This will prevent the plants from drying out, with the consequent dropping of foliage.

visit the nursery to see the shrubs growing. Many nurseries set aside areas where the trees and shrubs that they offer can be seen growing in ordinary garden conditions. A more recent innovation is to supply the customers with labels and turn them loose in the nursery grounds to choose and label the trees and shrubs that they like.

Any orders for a new garden should include some winter-flowering trees and shrubs. As well as providing interest during the dullest days of the year, these act as a constant reminder of the colour and beauty that is to come.

Not many trees flower in winter, but *Prunus subhirtella autumnalis* is a small flowering cherry that produces its blossom at intervals from November to March.

There could be few more cheering garden sights, on a gloomy November day, than a specimen of this shapely tree, spangled with white or pink blossom that seems to gain in beauty from a background of bare brown earth and leafless branches.

There are plenty of winter-flowering shrubs that will bring both colour and fragrance to the garden in winter. *Hamamelis mollis,* the Chinese witch hazel, starts to open its scented yellow spidery flowers in December.

Both the cherry and the witch hazel will give a display in their first winter. A longer wait is needed for the fragrant blossoms of *Chimonanthus praecox* (syn. *fragrans*) and the scented flower trusses of *Viburnum fragrans*. As they may take several seasons before they produce any appreciable amount of bloom, it pays to plant them as early as possible.

The flowers of the winter sweet are waxy in texture and pale yellow with a purple blotch at their centres. There are some named cultivars with larger flowers than those of the type, but they lack the intense fragrance of the latter.

Viburnum fragrans gets ready for the winter display by massing its branches with unopened clusters of pinky-white buds in October. These open in succession during spells of warm winter weather and a well-grown specimen can scent the air for many yards around.

The evergreen *Viburnum tinus*, known as laurustinus, is a good all-rounder to follow on after the shrubs just mentioned. The flowers, pink in bud, open in February and March and remain attractive for many weeks.

There are several interesting named varieties, but most of them are unsuited to colder districts. Two exceptions are 'Eve Price', a form with carmine buds and pink flowers, and 'French White', an outstanding white-flowered variety.

Vegetables

Unless you take precautions your vegetable garden can become bedevilled by weeds this month. The best way to prevent these becoming a real nuisance is to make a routine task, three or even four times a week, of quickly scuffing the soil between the rows with a hoe or hoe-type tool so that any germinating seedlings are immediately killed.

To save labour it is also possible to use the 'chemical hoe', a modern weedkiller which affects the plants when it comes into contact with the green tissues but does not affect bark. This chemical also becomes completely inactivated when it touches the soil, a convenient factor. It is expensive but remarkably economical when used correctly with its special applicator.

It also helps to mulch vegetables with lawn mowings, although on heavy soil one might be advised to put down some slug pellets first. Fresh lawn mowings are excellent, but make sure that the lawn has not been treated with weedkiller. However, lawn mowings are inclined to mat unless they are tossed from time to time. Gardeners with large gardens (and possibly also large weed problems!) can mix nettle, turnip and radish tops with the grass, thus providing an ultimately nutricious manure. Mulching is particularly favourable where there is to be considerable traffic along the rows, between pea rows ready for picking, for example.

When the peas are finished, or other crops pulled up, the mulch can either be forked into the soil or merely raked away. The soil underneath will be found to be in an excellent condition. Once the surface is allowed to dry out a little it will quickly make a good tilth and seed can be sown with little extra trouble involved.

Although it is now midsummer there are still many seeds which can be sown, some to end a succession, others to begin the round. Some vegetables will be finishing, early potatoes and peas for example, and the ground on which these have been grown should be used immediately if the best value is to be drawn from the garden. No extra digging will be necessary if the plants have been lifted out by a fork, so sowing should not take long nor entail extra labour.

Carrots are good to follow crops of this nature because they can be pulled when young, in autumn or early winter, thus releasing the ground for digging or, if it is to be intensively cultivated, for

1

3

2

1 In an effort to conserve as much moisture as possible at the roots of Runner Beans, grass cuttings can be used as a mulch around the base of the plants. The mulch should be kept well away from the collar of the plant.
2 The small Onion 'Silverskin', so useful for pickling, can be sown now. Crops already growing will be almost ready for lifting and drying off.
3 Courgettes are ready to gather as soon as the flower has withered. Gather them regularly from the plants in order to obtain an abundant supply.

the sowing and planting of other crops. Use varieties such as 'Champion Scarlet Horn' and 'Amstel'.

Potatoes soon to be lifted can be interplanted with brassicas in between the furrows made by the earthing-up process. These offer the young plants shade and moisture while they are becoming established. Once the potatoes are lifted the ground is easily levelled.

Turnips are often overlooked as a vegetable crop yet they are well worth growing both for the succulent and spicy roots and the tops which can be eaten as spring greens. Like the radishes to which they are closely related they grow quickly; 'Early White Stone', for example, is also known as 'Six Weeks'.

Even so, and perhaps surprisingly in view of this, no dung or compost should be used. The best soil is that which has been thoroughly manured for the crop before the turnips. Soil which is too rich results in lush tops and no turnip root. At the end of the month sow some for winter use. 'Golden Ball', a small-topped variety, has yellow flesh, very appetising in appearance, and is the hardiest for this purpose because it need not be lifted. 'Greentop Stone' is a good variety for turnip tops.

The small and attractive onion 'Silver Skin', perfect for pickling, can still be sown. Seed should be sown thickly and the plants left unthinned so that the onions are kept small.

Other crops which can still be sown are broad and runner beans in the south, and spring cabbage, parsley and winter radish anywhere. The latter are very different in appearance from the neat little roots of summer. They are much coarser in appearance, but when sliced or grated are just as delicious. The varieties most often grown are 'China Rose', which is red, and 'Black Spanish', both the round and the long varieties. The new 'Japanese All Season' is also suitable. The roots are white.

Sow American or land cress which much resembles watercress both in appearance and taste and is an excellent substitute for it. It is easily grown and ready eight to ten weeks after sowing.

Spring cabbage can be sown in nursery beds now and transplanted later. Meanwhile other brassicas will need planting out. Remember that brassicas, especially broccoli, need a firm soil, never soil which has been newly dug or freshly manured. Broccoli does best on heavy yet well-drained loam which had been manured for a previous crop.

Be sure to keep an eye on marrows and marrow-type plants. Frequent waterings with feeds of liquid manure at intervals will make all the difference to the growth and the crop.

Cut courgettes and zuccini regularly or they will not produce well. Gather them as soon as the little flower has withered, by which time they will not only be a few inches long but succulent and tender.

If for some reason or another they cannot be gathered young they may be left to grow, develop and ripen. They can then be stored in the usual way, but in this case only a few will be produced.

Water Gardens

Although the splendours of the aquatic and waterside iris are now past, there is still a lot of colour to look forward to in the water garden, with the water-lilies reaching the peak of their long season and pontederia and lobelia still to come.

As the individual water-lily blooms finally close (usually to sink and rot) it will be noticed that there is hardly ever a sign of seed being set. A notable exception is the dainty white miniature lily, *Nymphaea pygmaea alba*, one of the very few lilies which regularly matures pods of fertile seed. Stock can be easily increased if the pod is removed as soon as the seeds become dark green—almost black—in colour.

Sowing should be carried out immediately, the seeds being left in the jelly-like covering that surrounds them, and spread carefully on a pan of wet sterilised soil and thinly covered with soil.

The pan is placed (very gingerly to avoid soil disturbance) into a shallow tank so that the soil is covered by ½–1 inch of water. Kept in a constant temperature of 55–60°F (13–16°C) the seeds usually germinate in four to six weeks, and should be allowed to grow on until the following June when they can be planted out with about 6 inches of water over them.

The great majority of hardy hybrid water-lilies produce seed so rarely that if a pod is ever seen the opportunity should not be missed to collect it and attempt to raise seedlings, using the technique already described. Success in this will be something to boast about and there is always the outside chance of raising a superior new variety.

Lobelia fulgens 'Bee's Flame', a bright red flowered cultivar that enjoys moist conditions at the edge of the water garden. Except in the mildest localities they ought to be lifted in October and overwintered indoors.

Further opportunities for stock increase by seed raising are provided by the iris and primula members of the pool community. They should be watched during this month and next, and the seeds collected when they are clearly ripe and ready to be released from the pods.

The seeds may be sown immediately after collection if you have a frost free cold frame or greenhouse, or alternatively stored dry for sowing under glass in March, or outdoors in late April in a well prepared, sheltered seedbed. The depth of the soil covering should be twice the thickness of the seed which means, for the iris, about ¼ inch and the thinnest sprinkling of coarse sand for the primula seed.

Water snails normally do a very useful job in consuming decaying plant (or animal) remains and browsing on algal growth. There is one species, however, the great pond snail, *Limnaea stagnalis*, which will turn his attention to healthy pond plants (and particularly the succulent growth of submerged oxygenating plants) if other food supplies fail. This is most likely to happen, of course, in small pools with a limited food supply, when the pool has been established long enough for the snail population to build up and when snails are reaching full size (the pointed conical shell may be as much as 2 inches long).

If there are signs that this situation exists it can soon be remedied by picking off visible large snails and laying bait for any others in the form of the stumps or bruised leaves of lettuce left on the water overnight. Dropping the snails in boiling water is probably the most merciful method of disposal of unwanted snails.

With snails there seems to be no middle course: either they are over-abundant or they steadily disappear. If thrushes take them the shells will be smashed. If empty shells are found in the pool, suspect the

1 Pontederias in the pond at the Royal Horticultural Society's Garden at Wisley, Surrey. Known as Pickerel Weed it is a north American plant with blue flowers in summer. Water-lilies spread over the surface of the water in the background, their flowers floating.
2 Water Snails generally are beneficial in the pond. The Great Ramshorn Snail, Planorbis cornelus, is seen here feeding on Frogbit under water.

activities of leeches, which are occasionally introduced as eggs on plants. These unattractive creatures are harmless to humans but deadly to defenceless snails.

A very severe infestation would call for a thorough cleaning of the pool and all the soil in it, but the need for such extreme remedies is rare. A small piece of raw meat suspended in the pool will do the same for undesirable leeches as lettuce stumps for surplus snails.

If your pond contains goldfish or shubunkin varieties more than 5 inches long they are almost certainly sexually mature and, given the right conditions, they can be expected to spawn. The right conditions include a well-planted, well-oxygenated pool and proper nutrition, but these are not the whole picture.

Water temperature and daylight length play a part, but precisely what combination of factors triggers off the spell of frenzied activity that leads to spawning remains uncertain. It may happen in May, even in April; if it did not, do not give up hope—it can still happen as late as August. Early spawning is best because the fry have a chance to grow to survival size before the onset of winter.

The transfer of spawn to special tanks, and the hand-rearing of fry, are techniques for the dedicated fish-fancier. The gardener who simply wants to see some 'home-grown' fish in his pond is strongly recommended to spare himself the frustration and disappointments entailed in attempting these techniques without expert knowledge.

If a gardener feeds his fish well and provides thick plant growth in which they can spawn, the fish will do the rest, and eventually the pool will be stocked with as many small fish as its size will be ready to support.

At this time of the year a spell of hot sultry weather may produce a crisis of oxygen-deficiency which causes fish to gulp frantically at the surface, as if they were standing on their tails and trying to push their heads out of the water. A prompt response to this distress signal will avert casualties. Agitating the surface violently with a jet from the garden hose will bring relief and even leaving the hose to dribble steadily into the pool for a few hours can help. A pool equipped with a fountain or waterfall has nothing to fear because the plunging

cascade and every droplet from the fountain spray carries life-giving oxygen to sustain the fish during the thundery spells when the work of the oxygenating plants suddenly and briefly becomes inadequate.

Wildlife

An above average rainfall, coupled with hot weather can make July seem a heavy, sticky month. In this kind of weather rivers, ponds and garden pools offer a cool, fresh haven, and a wonderful opportunity to watch the activities of the animals and birds that use the waterside for their hunting ground.

A good example of this waterside activity is the pied wagtail. This useful little insectivore gives the impression of being for ever in a hurry; he rushes from stone to stone in search of flies and ants, his tail bobbing up and down.

A close relation to this bird is the grey wagtail. Though similar in appearance to the pied, the grey wagtail has a yellow breast instead of the white one of his cousin.

The grey wagtail's habitat also is a little different, for he prefers fairly out of the way fast-moving streams, while the pied is found in areas near human habitations, not necessarily close to water.

Another active and familiar bird is the house martin. This member of the swallow family is nesting this month and can be seen constantly flitting to and fro between eaves and the bank of river or pool collecting mud for building his dome-shaped nest.

The grey, branch-like figure of a heron can often be seen standing motionless beside a pond or ditch, waiting for some small water creature to venture too close to his thrusting bill. One such creature is the frog and his family. This little waterside animal is also preyed upon by the grass snake, who about this time of year lays a clutch of several dozen eggs in some warm heap of rotting vegetation—perhaps the garden compost heap. By the end of the month these eggs will have hatched out and will be facing the threat of death—

The Grass Snake, which preys upon the waterside Frogs, lays a clutch of several dozen eggs in July. Usually it chooses the garden compost heap or other similar rotting vegetation where the warmth will ensure hatching.

crushed under the gardener's heavy boot because the little grass snakes have been mistaken for their distant cousin the viper.

Another well-known but little seen water animal is the otter. This creature, too, falls victim to man's lack of knowledge and understanding, for no animal does more to keep down fish disease by killing the sick and the old inhabitants of rivers and ponds.

In these warm, wet July nights many different animals may well come to the garden pond in search of prey or water. They are likely to leave their distinctive prints in any soft earth in the vicinity. By looking at these areas the watcher can tell exactly what animals and birds have visited his territory and it is surprising to learn of their numbers and range.

The Month of August

Many of the summer-flowering bulbs are still thriving in August, and the garden is particularly enhanced by the majestic gladioli. Birds and animals are already preparing for the cold winter days and the squirrel will be a frequent visitor to the garden.

Kniphofia 'Royal Standard' is just one of the many lovely varieties of Red Hot Poker

2

4

3

1 Phlox paniculata (sometimes called P. decussata) 'Aurore', like all the garden varieties of this plant, needs a good moist soil.
2 Kniphofia galpinii is a dainty species. In common with many others it appreciates a blanket of light litter in winter time.
3 Mignonette, Reseda odorata, has a sweet, distinctive fragrance. It flowers until autumn and may also be grown as a pot plant.
4 Petunias of all varieties are both sweet-smelling and free-flowering. Like all bedding plants they thrive and bloom so much better when their faded flowers are regularly removed from them.

1

2

3

1 Variegated maize, Zea gracillima, with African marigolds and mixed Antirrhinum tetra. An excellent summer bedding collection. The Maize is a short variety growing to about 3 feet and its foliage makes a foil for the flower colour.

2 Many annuals and bedding plants enjoy basking in the sun. In such a position it is important that Begonias should be watered freely, and a light mulch of peat is also helpful.

3 Most bedding plants can be grown in all kinds of containers. Here Pelargoniums, Petunias and Fuchsias are mixed together with Tagetes and Bellis. A greenhouse will always extend the seasons.

4 Tagetes signata pumila, a compact variety with Nicotiana 'Crimson Bedder'

2

3

4

5

1 Fuchsia 'Mission Bells', one of the lovely American introductions which is a welcome addition to the already large range of these brilliant flowers.
2 The evergreen Hypericum patulum forrestii from Nepal has large flowers which will go on blooming until October.
3 Hibiscus syriacus is sometimes called the Bush or Tree Hollyhock. This has many lovely varieties and is hardy in all mild districts.
4 One of the berry-forming St John's Wort, Hypericum elatum, 'Elstead Variety'. This is a highly decorative garden plant and has many uses.
5 Erica tetralix, the Cross-leaved Heath. It flowers from June until October and has many varieties to choose from.

Jobs of the month

As summer begins to draw to a close August becomes a month of tidying up and thoughtful preparation for the winter and for next spring. Jobs done now provide the basis for future Joys - from planting strawberries and herbaceous seeds, to laying paths and taking shrub cuttings. This is also an important time in the kitchen garden

Bulbs

Plant narcissi of all kinds from the miniature ones up to the big daffodils. Start preparing bowls of bulbs for indoor winter flowering

Flowers for Cutting

Gladioli can be cut now and kept for several days. Hollyhocks and clematis, with hot water treatment, will both last well in an arrangement

Fruit

Early apples and pears can be picked and eaten. Suitable rootstocks can now be budded. Plant summer-fruiting strawberries

Greenhouse

Cyclamen may be sown now, and cuttings of heliotrope and fuchsia may be taken. Arum lilies may also be started into growth. Ventilate tomatoes well

Hedges

Take care when pruning your lavender hedge. New growth only should be lightly trimmed now. Old wood cut back will not shoot again

Herbaceous Plants

Dahlias may need extra staking by now. Sow calendula, godetia, candytuft, cornflowers, sweet sultan, larkspur, echium, alyssum and agrostemma for early bloom next summer

House Plants

Plants left alone during holidays like to be grouped together to provide humidity for each other. They can be left inside a plastic hood forming a miniature greenhouse

Lawns

Frequent mowing is still the order of the day. If going away leave the box off for the final cut. The cuttings will help soil moisture to be retained

Paths, Fences and Walls

This is a suitable time to lay paths. Always treat base soil with weed-killer first. Remember to give paths a camber to drain off heavy rain

Patios, Balconies and Roof Gardens

Make sure outdoor living spaces are not too cluttered. Plants should be removed to the edges to make room for people and furniture

Rock Gardens

Take cuttings of dwarf rhododendrons. Plant spring-flowering bulbs and corms. Divide and replant bulbs already in the ground

Roses

Spray against black spot at intervals. Stop feeding with nitrogen. Start cutting out old wood from established ramblers. Suckers are numerous now. Trace them to root and pull them off

Trees, Shrubs and Climbers

Deutzias, buddleias, philadelphus, berberis and many evergreens will root easily this month. Remove leaves from lower half of stem. Dip end of cuttings in hormone rooting powder

Vegetables

Shallots and autumn-sown onions are now ready for lifting in dry weather. Lift and store beetroots. Sow brussels sprouts for next year, and the last batch of lettuce for this year

Water Gardens

Be ready to spot aphids. Blast them from foliage with a hose jet. The fish will then eat them up from the surface of the water

Wildlife

Animals of all kinds are already beginning to prepare for winter so step up the quantity and variety on your bird table.

Bulbs

1 2 3

Some Narcissi such as 'Bridal Crown', 'Paper White' and 'Cragford' can be grown on pebbles and water instead of in compost of bulb fibre.
1 Shingle or rough sand is bedded at the base of a shallow bowl and the bulbs are set upright on this. Do not put the bulbs too close together for this method.
2 Pebbles are packed around the bulbs, to hold them in position while growing.
3 Water needs to be poured over the bowl to about half way up the pebbles.

Many of the summer-flowering bulbs are still in flower during August, notably vallota, zantedeschia, zephyranthes, acidanthera, nerines and lilies. Once the flowers are over, those in pots can be dried off very gradually as the bulbs approach their dormant period.

The two major tasks this month are to plant narcissi of all kinds—including daffodils—and to start on preparing bowls of bulbs to flower indoors early in the winter. By planning a few bowls now, and more later, you can make sure of a succession of flowers throughout the winter months.

Narcissi range from miniature flowered kinds to the largest daffodils and are grouped into eleven divisions (Div I–Div XI) according to the formation and size of flower and the way in which the flowers are displayed on the stem. Catalogues usually list narcissi according to the Division to which they belong. By selecting the appropriate variety and method of cultivation it is possible to have them in flower from Christmas to April or early May. Always plant narcissi bulbs as soon as they arrive, because they hate to be out of the ground and have a long, slow growing season.

Where bulbs are to be left in for several years, among shrubs for instance, plant them 7–8 inches deep so that they will not be damaged by cultivation. In this position they look best planted in clumps. Daffodils lend themselves to naturalising better than any other bulb and look most attractive in large drifts in rough grass or at the edge of woodland. They are not a plant to use for a formal setting, although a bed of a single variety closely planted can look very effective. The miniature kinds like *Narcissus bulbocodium*, the hooped petticoat daffodil and *N. cyclamineus* are best used in an alpine meadow situation or in the rock garden or troughs.

Indoors, pots or bowls of most of the trumpet varieties from the Divisions will make a cheerful and worth-while display. The jonquils and pheasant-eye narcissi are the most fragrant and dainty, but they are not the best of bulbs for pot culture. The leaves tend to become drawn and grassy and need staking—always a tricky business in a pot. They are really best grown in a cold frame or cold greenhouse and then brought into the living-room just as the buds are swelling.

These bulbs and all other kinds of narcissi for bowls should be planted as close together as possible in prepared fibre and using, for the best results, the large heavier bulbs. The main essentials are early and shallow planting, in bowls deep enough to allow for a mass of root formation. This strength of root growth sometimes lifts up the bulb out of the fibre, and a deep fibre can help to prevent this.

Wrap the bowls in black polythene to keep them clean and put them into a deep plunge bed. After 12–16 weeks narcissi will be ready to bring out of the darkness and are best put into a cold frame or unheated room until the buds are showing. Keep them in a good light but not in direct sun. Only when the buds begin to colour should they be forced to flower.

It is possible to grow some narcissi on pebbles. Such varieties as 'Bridal Crown', 'Paper White' and 'Cragford' are best for this type of cultivation. The bulbs are planted firmly on top of clean pebbles or shingle and water is added to the level of the base of the bulb. The bowl is kept in a dark cool place, inspected from time to time and the water level maintained by adding cold water. Once growth has started bring the bowls into the light but always keep them away from direct sunlight. It is essential to top up the water level from time to time.

The white Roman hyacinths may be set on pebbles in the same way and brought into flower by Christmas; but such varieties of Roman hyacinth as

'Autumn Surprise' (pink), 'Fairy Blue' (pale blue, fragrant) and 'Rosalie' (deep pink) need to be planted during late August or the first weeks of September to ensure December flowering.

Out-of-doors gladioli and lilies will be in flower and can be cut for indoor decoration, but remember to let some of the leaves remain on the plant otherwise the bulb is robbed of its above ground chlorophyll-making parts.

Flowers for Cutting

Gladioli will last very much longer indoors if the spikes are cut when the lowest floret is only just about to open. The florets will continue to open in water. Sometimes the large varieties tend to snap when they are in water and this is usually because they are taking up too much water too fast and have become too lush. It is best to pour only a little water in a deep container so that very little of the stem is under the surface.

Save any gladioli leaves stripped from their stems and stand them in a glycerine solution. They will be preserved in a good tan colour for winter decorations.

Often a gardener finds that all the gladioli are ready at the wrong time. These can be cut and kept for 10 to 14 days if the following points are observed. Cut spikes with the florets just coloured and with the lowest one just ready to open. They must be dry when cut and must not be given water. Place about six in a bunch in plastic bags or roll them in thick paper which can be made almost airtight.

Lay the flowers on the floor of a cool, dark but dry cellar, shed or pantry. Remove them two days before the date they are required, cut a little off the stem ends and stand them in deep water for 24 hours.

Glorious ipomoeas, or morning glories, live only for a day both on the plant and when cut; because of this one tends to reject them for flower arrangement. Yet so wonderful is the blue that many a flower mixture is made distinctive by a centre knot of these pretty things. It is possible to use them this way: pick the coiled buds early in the morning and stand the stem ends in a half inch of boiling water. When it cools arrange the flowers among the others and they will soon open, but they will have to be replaced the next day. Any type of convolvulus can be treated this way.

Clematis, too, are often overlooked for flower arrangements, for the same reason. Hot water treatment is the only way to ensure that they become turgid. Hollyhocks, an important exhibition flower in Victorian times, are seldom seen as a cut flower today, yet given the same hot water preparation they will

There are several herbaceous plants that can be pulled up and the flowers dried off now. Here, Achillea is hung in bunches to dry in an airy place, to provide material for winter decoration.

last well in an arrangement. If you have experienced disappointment with any flower except those grown from bulbs it is worth trying this treatment. But if you cut hydrangeas, first split their stem ends before standing them in water.

Now that the fruit is swelling and ripening, arrangements can be made more attractive by using all kinds with blooms and foliage. Most fruits and flowers go well together, but there are exceptions. Green apples seem to have no effect on flowers, but ripe ones can cause certain flowers, carnations mainly, to die.

The flowers curl their petals even if they are freshly cut. The cause is one of the gases given off by the ripe fruit. The same thing happens if a pail of flowers is stood in a shed where the fruit is stored, so in case of difficulties of this kind keep flowers away from apples and pears in the store. Cut carnations are also sometimes affected by thundery conditions. Avoid cutting them until the weather changes.

Many umbelliferous herbs have good seed heads now. These should be cut and hung upside down to dry. They can later be used in 'perpetuelle' arrangements and they also look delightful at Christmas time if they are lightly painted and dusted with frost glitter. These firm heads with seeds still attached are much more attractive and easier to handle than the skeleton umbrella left after the seed has fallen.

If you have grown honesty for winter decoration cut the stems now and hang them upside down to dry enough to enable you to pull away the outer cases and reveal the lovely shining moons inside. Let some plants stay to decorate and lighten the garden in winter.

Plants may also be pulled up by the roots and hung and they are certainly less trouble this way. The earlier these seed cases are gathered the whiter and brighter the moons will be. The seeds which are inside can be sown, and even when gathered early they are usually quite viable.

Fruit

Prune pyramid apples and pears as young shoots reach maturity.

Pick early apples and pears as they become ready and as you can use them. The earlies will not keep for long once they are picked. The test for readiness is to lift a fruit in the palm of the hand

1

2

1 Arrange some kind of support for heavily laden branches of Plum trees. *Left* a maypole effect is achieved with a stout central stake to which each branch is tied. *Right* forked stakes are driven into the ground around the tree and individual branches supported.
2 Established Black Currants are pruned once the fruit has been gathered. Cut away about a third of the old shoots from the base in order to encourage new growth to break at ground level.

until it is horizontal and then give it the slightest possible twist: the ripe apple will then part company from its spur quite readily. Never pull an apple or pear off so that the stalk is left on the tree or whole or part of the spur breaks off with the fruit.

If in the past years you have been troubled by early apples falling before their time, try spraying with a pre-harvest drop inhibitor. Apply according to the maker's directions about 10 to 14 days before the usual picking time. Make sure the stalks of the apples are thoroughly wetted and remember that although this spray makes the apple stay on the tree longer it does not interfere with ripening. Once the fruit has ripened, quality will begin to deteriorate if the fruit remains unpicked.

Keen enthusiasts who want to raise their own fruit trees can now bud suitable rootstocks at a point about 8 inches above soil level. The bark of apple rootstocks will usually lift easily, as required, until the end of this month. No growth will be visible until the spring when you will be able to see whether your bud has 'taken'. If it has, the unwanted snag of the rootstock may be cut off a year from now.

Plant summer-fruiting strawberries in well-drained soil rich in organic matter. Space the rows 30–36 inches apart and allow 15–18 inches between plants in the row: the richer the soil, the more space the plants will need. If this is to be treated as an annual crop, however, and the plants are to be covered with cloches or a polythene tunnel to give early berries in the first year, a closer spacing is permissible—12–15 inches in the row.

Take special care to plant at the right depth, with the base of the crown level with the soil surface. Make quite firm, rake the bed over and water. Provide temporary shade when there is hot sunshine. If there is no rain, more watering will be necessary. Drying out in their first few weeks can be fatal to strawberries.

As soon as the summer crop of raspberries has been picked the fruiting canes can be cut down to soil level to make room for their replacements to be tied to the wires. Allow six to eight new canes per plant, according to vigour, and cut out any surplus.

Established black currants may also be pruned as soon as all the fruit has been gathered. Retain this year's shoots growing up from the base and cut out about a third of the older shoots, the aim being to encourage new growth from the base.

Arrange some kind of support for heavily laden plum branches: either individual stakes for branches or a central pole from which branches can be suspended maypole-fashion. The great danger of broken branches is the risk of silver leaf infection of the wounds.

Wasps can be a serious nuisance with plums and other fruits now. Destroy the nest if possible or sprinkle insecticide in the entrance. Hang wasp traps baited with beer and syrup among the trees.

To keep wasps out of a greenhouse in which grapes are ripening, fit muslin over the ventilators. Where greenhouse grapes have been cut, ventilate freely now and syringe the vines with clear water to deter red spider mite.

1
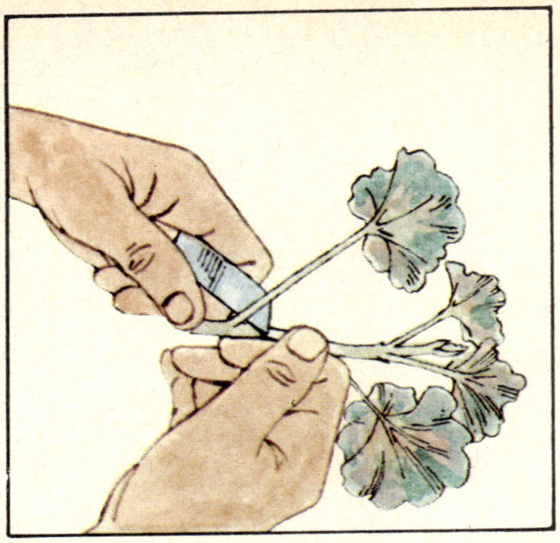
2

3

4

1 Cuttings of Pelargoniums are made from non-flowering shoots at this time of the year. Make the cutting 3 or 4 inches in length and remove the lower leaves with a sharp knife.
2 Cut straight across the base of the cutting, with a clean knife, through a node or leaf joint, because the growth cells are most active at this point.
3 Prepare pots filled with sandy compost and make holes with a small dibber to receive the cuttings.
4 Put in only three or four cuttings around the edges of a pot, firmly and upright. The cuttings must be potted-on once root formation has started.

Greenhouse

One of the most useful plants to sow now is the cyclamen, to provide plants for flowering in 12–15 months' time. The seed, which is large enough to handle individually, is best sown an inch apart and about $\frac{1}{4}$ inch deep in a seed-pan or tray filled evenly and firmly with either the John Innes or one of the soilless seed composts.

Following sowing, soak the compost from underneath until it is wet right through and then stand the pan or tray in a warm part of the greenhouse, where it should be covered with glass and paper. If the compost is kept quite moist germination should take place in 4–5 weeks.

Another invaluable plant that may also be propagated now, but this time by cuttings, is the zonal pelargonium (geranium). Use unflowered shoots that are half-ripe (those with a distinct reddish tinge), trimmed immediately beneath a joint to about 4 inches long. The cuttings may then be inserted round the edge of a pot of sandy soil or, for large quantities, in a bed of similar soil made up in a cold frame; or more simply, they may be merely dibbled into a piece of light, sandy soil in a sunny place in the garden, where they should root well but rather more slowly. Whichever method is used make sure that the base of each cutting is firmly in contact with the soil, 1–1$\frac{1}{2}$ inches below the surface.

Other cuttings that may also be taken are those of heliotrope and fuchsia. For the former use unflowered shoots 2–3 inches long trimmed off beneath a joint, and insert them fairly close together in a seedbox filled with sandy soil, finally placing them in a close frame.

Fuchsia cuttings to produce bush plants are not normally taken in summer, but for 'standard' fuchsias they should be put in now, using unflowered shoots about 3 inches long. These will soon root if inserted round the edge of a pot of light, well-drained soil kept just moist in light shade on the greenhouse bench.

Of the bulbous subjects for late winter and spring flowering one of the first that should be put in is the freesia, invaluable for both its beauty and fragrance. Use the John Innes potting compost No 2 made quite firm over good drainage in 5- or 6-inch pots. Each pot will take from 6 to 8 corms respectively. Set the corms with their tops about 1 inch beneath the surface, then make the compost just moist and stand the pots in a cold-frame, where, if shaded from the sun, they should need no further water until growth starts. If no frame is available they may be stood in the open and protected from the rain.

Lachenalias, another useful plant for spring flowering, may also be grown from corms in exactly the same way now.

Arum lilies *(Zantedeschia aethiopica)* may also be started into growth now, using either newly purchased 'crowns' or old plants, which should be repotted if they have been in their present pots for more than a year. Alternatively, these old plants may be divided. One young plant or division will go into a 6-inch pot or three into an 8- or 9-inch pot, in either case using the John Innes potting compost No 2 over good drainage. After potting keep the plants in the open and water sparingly until growth starts.

Mid-season chrysanthemums growing in pots normally start to produce their flower buds during August and for large blooms the plants must be disbudded by removing all but the main central bud on each stem. Any sideshoots appearing where the leaves join the stem should also be removed, together with longer sideshoots and suckers appearing near the base of the plant. Continue to feed the plants and guard against inseet pests by spraying with approved sprays.

As the flowers fade on the greenhouse climber *Hoya carnosa* cut off the dead blooms but leave the actual flower-stalks intact, as these should produce further blooms for your pleasure next year.

Feed pot-plants such as cinerarias, caleolarias and primulas for winter and spring flowering with a complete fertiliser about once a week as soon as their roots can be seen in the drainage holes. The later batches, now in 3- or 3½-inch pots must be potted into 5- or 6-inch pots before they become pot-bound.

Ventilate tomatoes freely from now on to guard against leaf-mould *(Cladosporium)* and make sure that the atmosphere is kept fairly dry and buoyant.

Hedges

Grey- and silver-leaved shrubs, by reason of the contrast they provide, are always an interesting feature of the garden. Many of them, thanks to their dwarf character and compact habit of growth, make ideal subjects for low interior dividing hedges. Most of them, too, will be in flower this month.

The most popular of these is, of course, lavender. A lavender hedge associates well with almost any garden surroundings but is particularly suited to paved areas of stone or mellow brick. For a really outstanding display, few species are better than *Lavandula spica*, the old English lavender of our cottage gardens. This grows 3–4 feet high and has a magnificent display of flower spikes at this time of year. Its only drawback is a greater tendency to legginess than most other species and varieties.

'Munstead', a dwarf form of very compact habit, makes an ideal low dividing hedge since it does not exceed 1–1½ feet in height. 'Folgate', a more recent introduction, is similar in character and is considered by some to be an improvement on the former.

The flowers of both these varieties are of a deeper and more intense violet-purple than those of the old English lavender. 'Gwendolyn Anley' and *L. spica rosea* are both distinctive forms with a decided pink tinge to their flowers.

The pruning of a lavender hedge needs special care. It is fatal to cut back into old wood, since this will not shoot again. Only the current season's growth should be lightly trimmed and this operation should take place this month, immediately after the plants have finished flowering.

After a few seasons, any lavender hedge tends to get decidedly leggy and it is a good idea to have replacements on hand when it needs renewing. Young shoots that have not flowered root easily at this time of year. They should be inserted in sandy soil in a sheltered part of the garden where the soil does not dry out readily. The foot of a north wall is ideal.

On heavy soils, it may be necessary to take out a shallow V-shaped trench with a spade and fill it with sharp sand in which to insert the cuttings. These can go into a nursery bed the following spring and will be ready as replacements by the end of summer.

Lavender hedges will benefit from occasional dressings of lime and the site of a new hedge should always be limed before the plants go in.

Another useful August-flowering dwarf hedging shrub is *Santolina chamaecyparissus nana*. This is the best form of the popular cotton lavender and the ever-grey foliage of this variety is beautifully frosted with silvery-white. It will make a fine hedge, growing only 1½–2 feet in height.

Unlike its namesake, lavender proper, the cotton lavender thrives on drastic pruning. Plants should be cut back really hard—to the base of the previous year's growth—every spring.

S. virens, a species with vivid green foliage, is in complete contrast to the grey-leaved kinds. Both bear clusters of yellow flowers in August and both are easily propagated from cuttings taken in early autumn.

Where a slightly taller ever-grey hedge is wanted, *Olearia haastii*, the New Zealand daisy bush, makes a good choice. This is a shrub that is particularly suited to seaside districts, a characteristic shared by many other grey-leaved subjects.

Although the plant's fragrant white flowers make little impact, they provide a certain interest in August, where shrub blossom is relatively scarce.

1

2

1 Lavendula spicata is an ideal plant for a low interior hedge. The grey foliage contrasts well with the mauve flowers borne in spikes, in summer.
2 Once flowering is over the Lavender can be clipped back, but care must be taken not to cut into the older wood because this will not break again.

RECOGNITION CHART

Seeds and Fruits

Seed heads of plants vary in form, but they are distinctive features, especially in autumn and winter Many are used in arrangements

A DRUPE is a fruit with a fleshy outer part and a hard central stone containing a seed. Examples are Cherry, Plum and Sloe

SLOE

PEA

A POD splits open from top to bottom in two places to release the seeds. Examples are Broom, Vetch, Laburnum and Pea

HORSE CHESTNUT

WALNUT

A NUT is the hard seed, usually with a softer protective outer coat. Examples are Hazel, Horse Chestnut and Walnut, though the latter is botanically a drupe if the whole 'green Walnut' is considered

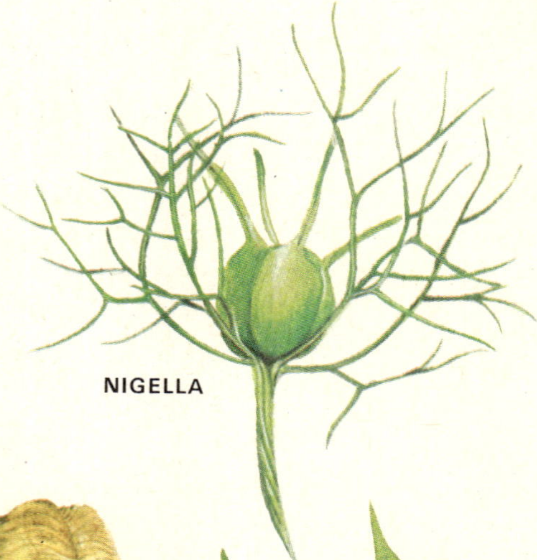

NIGELLA

A CAPSULE is a dry fruit, usually formed from several united carpels. Examples are Nigella, Poppy, Pansy, Hemerocallis and Hellebore

POPPY

HEMEROCALLIS

HELLEBORE

PANSY

A BERRY is a soft fruit usually globular, and containing seeds. Examples are Privet, Gooseberry and Viburnum

PRIVET

VIBURNUM

GOOSEBERRY

HONESTY

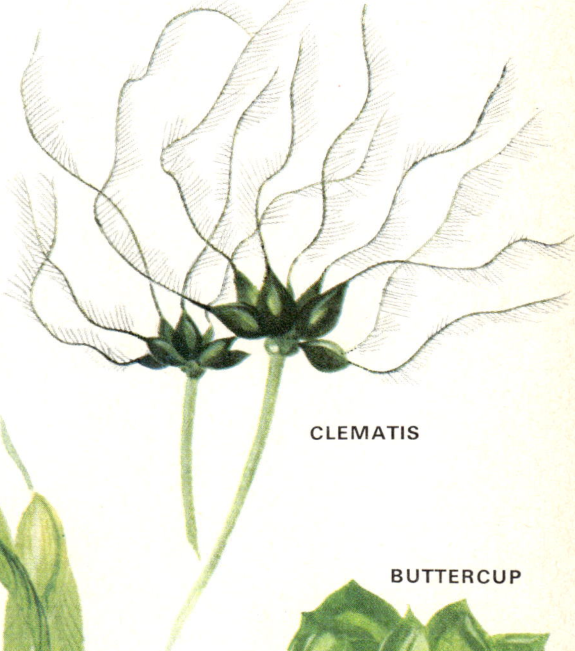

CLEMATIS

A SAMARA or winged fruit is dry and light. Examples are Honesty, Sycamore, Ash, Lime and Elm

ASH

SYCAMORE

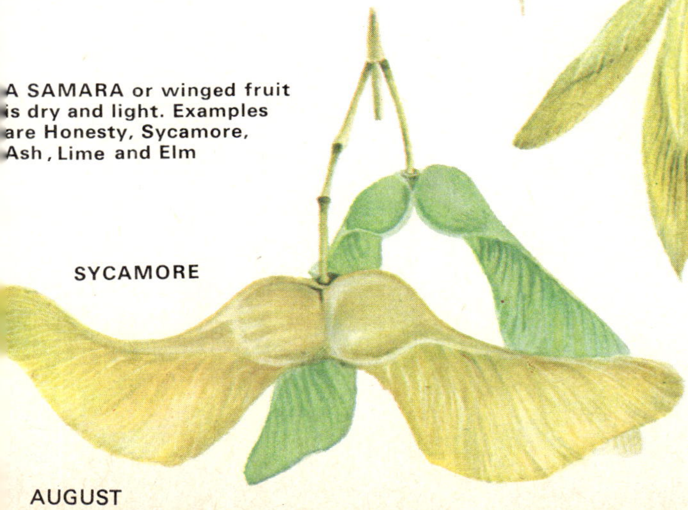

BUTTERCUP

An ACHENE is a dry fruit containing a single seed which remains with its case entire until germination. Examples are Scabious and Clematis. The Buttercup head is a collection of achenes

1

Herbaceous Plants

Most hardy lilies are not planted until October or November. Bulbs of the Madonna lily *(Lilium candidum)*, however, should be planted from August to early September if they are to bloom well next year.

This old-fashioned favourite is often seen in its full beauty in cottage gardens, where it grows undisturbed in a sunny corner in medium loamy soil containing lime.

Bulbs can also, however, be grown in heavyish soil provided the ground is conditioned with plenty of leafmould, sand and a little mortar rubble. This lovely sweetly scented lily looks delightful planted in groups close to bright blue delphiniums. The pure white flowers of the lily seem to intensify the colouring of the delphiniums.

Unlike the majority of lilies, the bulbs planted on a tee of silver sand 6 inches apart, should be covered with only 1 inch of soil—2 inches if the soil is very light.

Fresh manure should never be added to ground intended for lilies but poor soil can be enriched with well-rotted manure, provided it does not come into contact with the bulbs. Add bonemeal to the top spit.

Another lily that should be planted now is the tall, stately Nankeen lily *(Lilium excelsum)*—a lily that grows 5–6 feet high, bearing up to 12 richly fragrant nodding apricot blooms with brilliant scarlet anthers. This is a gorgeous variety for grouping at the back of a large border. Plant them 4 inches deep, preferably in part-shade. These two varieties of the lily benefit from liberal watering in dry weather together with heavy mulches of leaf-

1 Towards the end of the month some plants may be sown for flowering next summer. Some, like Larkspur, will need protection from the frost in the form of a cloche or some brushwood. Left to right: Lychnis, Godetia, Cornflower, Alysum and Marigolds. Sow in drills; thin or plant out in nursery beds later.
2 Some disbudding may be needed on Dahlias as the buds form, to encourage the formation of larger blooms. Take the side buds leaving the crown bud to bloom. Remove the bud stalk as well.

2

mould or damp peat to conserve the moisture.

Other bulbs to be planted this month that look attractive in a herbaceous border are the snowflakes (leucojum) and the belladonna lily *(Amaryllis belladonna)*. The latter, which bear umbels of pale rose-scented flowers from September to October, are only really suitable for growing in a border backed by a south wall, fence or hedge, for the plants need this protection if they are to flower freely. Planted 5–6 inches deep, they do best in fibrous loamy soil enriched with leafmould, adding a little sand if the soil is on the heavy side.

Snowflakes are similar to the snowdrop but with much larger flowers borne on stems 14–18 inches high, according to variety. The bulbs thrive in well-drained, rich moist soil and should be planted 4 inches deep, 4 inches apart.

If you want quality rather than quantity, Michaelmas daisy (aster) growths should be thinned now, leaving three to five heads of bloom.

As a precaution against mildew—a disease that attacks some varieties of aster—spray with lime-sulphur or dust or spray with Karathane, repeating the treatment at 7–10 days intervals. The same sprays will control mildew on delphiniums. Delphiniums that seem particularly prone to this disease should be scrapped in autumn. Replant mildew-resistant varieties such as 'Blue Tit', 'Charles Langdon' and 'Daily Express'. Lack of potash can encourage mildew and excessive use of the nitrogenous manures. Where these conditions are suspected, cut down on manures and apply a dressing of sulphate of potash at the rate of 2 ounces per square yard. Chrysanthemums can be kept free of mildew by watering weekly with Gris-feed, a product that contains the antibiotic systemic fungicide griseofulvin and also feeds the plants.

Dahlias may need extra staking as the plants grow. In light soil plants may require watering in dry weather, applying liquid manure as the buds begin to show.

For large blooms some disbudding may be necessary, leaving the centre bud. With the exception of blackfly and earwigs, dahlias suffer from few pests. Blackfly is easily controlled with a systemic insecticide watered over and

One method of self watering when house plants have to be left unattended, is to group the plants on the floor around a chair. Wicks of long bootlaces, hung from the water in the bucket to the compost in the pots, will act as syphons to keep the plants sufficiently moist.

around the plants, while earwigs can be controlled with Gamma-BHC dust, dusted over the ground as well as the plants, or earwigs can be trapped in flower pots inverted over the plant stakes and filled with straw or crumpled paper. Inspect the pots each morning and destroy the insects.

Towards the end of the month several hardy annuals—calendula, godetia, candytuft, cornflowers, sweet sultan, larkspur, echium, alyssum and agrostemma—can be sown for early bloom next summer. Larkspur make splendid bushy plants when sown at this time if the seedlings are protected with a cloche or twiggy sticks in severe weather.

Most background hedging—privet, beech, hornbeam, *Lonicera nitida*, thuya, holly and yew—can be clipped during the last half of August. Box can also be trimmed at this time.

Pansies and violas are readily propagated by basal cuttings, removing shoots 2½–3 inches long just below a joint and planting them firmly in sandy soil, in a cold shady frame. These delightful flowers are grand edging plants flowering as they do for months on end if the faded flowers are kept cut.

Spent blooms of sweet peas must also be cut daily if the plants are to continue flowering. Feed them with liquid manure once or twice a week.

In hot, sunny weather fuchsias repay for overhead spraying. These plants can take an almost unlimited amount of water from May to October, given well-drained soil. Bulbs of the crown imperial fritillary *(Fritillaria imperialis)* should be planted by the middle of the month. Choose heavy ground where the surface is seldom disturbed if possible, planting the bulbs 5–6 inches deep, 8 inches apart.

August is a good month to take stock of borders, making a note of colour clashes and other short-comings so that mistakes can be rectified in autumn.

House Plants

House plants are often left to their own devices during August. Some local nurserymen will accept plants into their care for short periods, and it may be possible to get neighbours to water plants—but in most cases steps should be taken to ensure that the plants do not deteriorate when their owners are away on holiday. This is not so difficult as it may appear, and there are several methods.

Remember that more house plants are killed by over-watering than by any other cause and that nearly all can be allowed to get slightly dry at the roots quite safely—provided this period is not too prolonged. They will almost certainly pick up quickly when given a good watering again.

Obviously the most important thing to do (but one of the last before the plants are left) is to ensure that all plants are in good health and well-watered. Pests can spread rapidly when plants are not regularly inspected, so examine all house plants carefully and treat any of them about which you may have suspicions.

All house plants are gregarious, they like to be grouped together, for this way they give off a micro-climate of humidity and each plant helps its neighbours. So if possible group all or many of your plants together in one spot, perhaps in the centre of the floor with a large waterproof sheet under them.

Some plants can be entirely enveloped inside a large transparent plastic bag which is sealed at the top. This makes in effect a miniature greenhouse generating its own humidity and root moisture. Other plants can have their pots only enveloped, the plastic bag being tied just over the soil and around the stem of the plant. This will allow the plant itself to breathe but will retain all the moisture at the roots.

It may be possible to plunge large or difficult-to-move plants inside an even larger container, with the space between pot and container filled with moist peat. This peat will probably give off sufficient moisture to the pot it holds to last the plant for a fortnight or more provided the foliage of the plant is not in direct sun nor subjected to any draughts, the latter should always be avoided.

Still another method of keeping the roots of house plants moist for long periods is to stand a number of them in the kitchen sink or in a domestic bath. If the plug is inserted and the tap left to drip very slowly the base of the pots will be able to absorb just enough moisture to keep the plants from drying out completely.

Several types of self-watering pots are on the market and some of these can be employed for plants such as the impatiens which demands that its roots are constantly on the wet side. These pots usually are of two types, either those in two sections with the base of the pot holding the plant resting in a lower reservoir containing water, or with the pot holding in its base a cloth or fibre-glass wick which leads down to a water-filled reservoir.

Both these self-watering devices can be useful and will maintain a plant in good condition for up to a month, depending on the size of the reservoir.

Another means of self-watering can take care of a number of plants at one time if they are grouped together in the floor on top of a large plastic sheet as outlined above. Place a bucket of water on a chair or stool beside them and from this lead a number of wicks down to selected plants. The long, thick football boot laces are excellent. One end can be fixed and weighted into the bucket and the other end can be pushed into the soil of the pot. A slight seepage of water will keep the plants moist.

Not all plants need constant watering. Cacti and succulents and others such as most bromeliads, sansevieria and a few others will last perfectly well for a fortnight and sometimes even longer if they are given a good drink and then allowed merely to get dry. So group your plants carefully according to their needs and you may very well find that there are fewer requiring special attention than you had imagined in the first place.

When plants are to be left for any length of time, or when they are newly divided and repotted, a miniature 'greenhouse' can be made by fastening a plastic bag over the pot and plant and securing it firmly.

Lawns

Lawn care this month is essentially the same as during July. The grass should be cut regularly, generally about twice a week, and any new lawn from spring turfing or sowing, or a lawn on a free-draining soil, should be watered thoroughly whenever the ground dries out during drought. If the ground dries out so much that cracks appear, these will prove perfect sites for weed seeds to germinate, and thus create a weed-killing and grass recolonisation problem later in the year. It is also a pointer to the fact that the soil will require top-dressing with humus matter in the autumn and spring, to assist moisture retention in future summers.

As August is traditionally the family holiday month, the garden often has to look after itself for a fortnight or so. All too frequently during the pre-holiday preparation rush, insufficient time is allowed to prepare the garden. If you do not give it some attention before you go —particularly the lawn—you are likely to come back to overgrown chaos, frequently depicted by gardening cartoonists who illustrate the family fighting their way through the jungle of overgrown grass and weeds to reach the front door.

The obvious job to be done, preferably the day before you leave, is to give the lawn a final mowing. The blades of the mower should be set as low as is possible without 'scalping' the ground, i.e. cutting off the grass plants completely, so leaving a bare patch of soil. If this happens, it gives any weed seeds about an excellent opportunity to germinate and colonise the patch without detrimental competition from the grasses. The average suitable cutting heights are: $\frac{1}{4}$ inch for a really level lawn of fine grasses; $\frac{1}{2}$ inch for a medium lawn of mixed grasses; and $\frac{3}{4}$ inch for rougher lawns where rye grass is predominant.

It is not normally advisable to cut the lawn without collecting the grass cuttings in the mower box or bag, because of the danger of spreading weed seeds and encouraging worm activity. However, on this pre-holiday occasion, if the cuttings are allowed to lie on the surface, they will act as a mulch and retain soil moisture.

The question of watering the lawn is a more tricky problem. If the area is not already moist from rain, it should be given a thorough soaking after the final mowing and before you leave. The water should be applied evenly and copiously, preferably via one of the proprietary lawn sprinkler devices available.

After this heavy watering the lawn should, with luck, survive without further water for the next fortnight. If your soil is very free-draining, however, or the lawn was only sown or turfed in the spring, it would be advisable to find out whether a co-operative neighbour could water your lawn, should this become necessary during a drought.

The final pre-holiday lawn task may be to 'spot' treat any weeds that have escaped previous weedkiller applications.

The easiest method of doing this is to use a proprietary applicator, filled with a hormone weedkiller diluted to the recommended rate; an aerosol weedkiller, or a weedkiller powder in a puffer pack.

Failing this, a weedkiller solution made up in a small container can be 'painted' on to the crown of individual weeds with a paint brush.

If a new lawn is to be created, the end of July or the beginning of August is the time for soil preparation for grass seed

1 Isolated lawn weeds can be given spot treatment by applying weedkiller to the leaves with a paint brush.
2 During the summer months a lawn needs to be cut regularly to maintain its good appearance. Pay special attention to watering to prevent the lawn from drying out, with the consequent appearance of cracks in the ground.

sowing between mid-August and mid-September. Seed sown this month has the advantage over a spring sowing, in that the soil is warm, weeds are less troublesome, and there is generally less likelihood of water shortage. The lawn also has a chance to become well-established before the arrival of the following summer.

The site should be selected and prepared. Following the digging and general levelling stages, regular hoeing and raking up of weed seedlings will assist in creating a weed-free seed bed for later on. Equally, treading or rolling after each hoeing will help consolidate the area and indicate any final levelling that will be necessary.

The correct grass seed mixture should be purchased, according to whether the lawn is to be in sun or shade, and of fine grasses or more hard-wearing species. Always buy from a reputable source, and get a mixture which does not contain too many different species, or you may end up with a patchy lawn.

A high grade mixture for a showpiece lawn usually consists of 4 parts of 'Chewings' Fescue' and 1 part of 'Browntop Bent' (American origin). A good, general-purpose, hard-wearing lawn will be obtained from sowing a proprietary mixture of some of the following grasses —'Chewings' Fescue', 'Perennial Ryegrass', 'Browntop Bent', 'Creeping Red Fescue', 'Rough-Stalked Meadow' and 'Crested Dog's Tail'. For a shady lawn area, grasses such as 'Creeping Red Fescue', 'Wood Meadow' and 'Rough-Stalked Meadow' grass should be included in the mixture.

When buying the seed, for applying at the rate of 1–1½ ounces per square yard, it is a wise investment to purchase an extra few ounces. The seed will not deteriorate fast and it is always useful to have in reserve the same mixture as sown originally, in case any bare patches occur or thin areas need a second seeding.

Paths, Fences and Walls

The hot and lazy days of August may give us time for path laying. But long stretches of the necessary good weather are not conducive to heavy work, so let us examine the possibilities of easy path making.

Probably the easiest garden path to

1 Neatly maintained grass verges give a well groomed appearance to a path, but require a lot of regular attention. Rolls of aluminium, steel or plastic edging material can be obtained at reasonable prices. These edges are hammered into the soil once they have been laid.
2 Many permanent plants lend themselves to decorating the edge of a path, such as Zephranthes candida.

1

2

make, and one that fits very well into the garden scene, is a gravel path. It may be wise to excavate the site thoroughly, put in a solid base of well-tamped stone, broken bricks, clinker and so on before adding the surface gravel, but it is not really necessary for a simple garden path. Instead, merely remove the top surface of grass or weeds and put down the gravel, preferably rolling it in although even this is not necessary. Maintain a slight camber on the pathway to allow heavy rains to drain away at the sides rather than make puddles. A gravel path made like this will need top-dressing every three or four years and an annual weedkilling treatment.

To estimate quantities required, remember that a load of gravel contains 1 cubic yard or 27 cubic feet. A ton contains about 20 cubic feet. A load will cover about 15–17 square yards 2–3 inches deep and a ton will cover about 10–12 square yards.

Gravel well-rolled and firm makes a good base for a cold laid bitumen path. Usually black or brown, frequently supplied with white or grey chippings, these paths may not fit happily into every garden, but they are excellent for garage drives or for working areas around frames or the greenhouse. The bitumen is usually supplied in plastic bags, requiring merely to be tipped out on to the firm prepared surface, raked smooth and level and then rolled. The tarry material will tend to cling to shoes, rake and roller, particularly in warm weather. Sprinkle the roller with water as it is used to discourage this. Allow these paths a day or two to harden before using them, particularly in hot weather.

For a concrete or similar firm surface that has been broken and repaired over the years—smooth and solid but disfigured and unpleasant to the eyes—there is a new material available which quickly and easily transforms the surface.

This is like a chipping-impregnated self-adhesive roofing felt which comes in rolls, can be cut to shape and stuck down. It is surprisingly long lasting but the under surface *must* be smooth and firm.

Any garden path is only as pleasant as its verges and although nothing can look better than a neat and cleanly trimmed grass edging, this needs regular attention if it is always to be seen at its best.

Rolls of aluminium, steel or plastic edging materials can be obtained at reasonable prices. These edgings are merely hammered into the soil at the sides and will keep grass more or less under control. Make sure that the surface is level with the grass to allow a mower to pass over it without bending or breaking the material or damaging the mower blades. Other edging materials include timber, concrete and bricks, all of which require careful fixing if they are to have a long life and to look always at their best. There are several ways in which they can be used and all will help to cut maintenance time and labour.

In laying any type of path, other than one of solid concrete or paving slabs set in concrete, it is always helpful to treat the base soil with weedkiller before adding the gravel or bitumen or other path surfacing.

Even if all the visible weeds or grass have been skimmed from the surface there are still many weed seeds dormant in the soil and these are likely to force their way through. Use sodium chlorate or one of the long lasting symazine-based completely effective weedkillers. If weeds appear through gravel or bitumen treat with sodium chlorate as soon as they are seen.

Patios, Balconies, Roof Gardens and Window Boxes

This is the normal holiday month, the time when you will wish to make the most use of outdoor living space. It is sheer waste to have a patio, roof garden or even a tiny balcony and not use it for an extension of living whenever weather conditions allow. Yet if the area is badly planned and inconvenient, or if the labour of organising living space is difficult or time consuming, this space is too apt to be neglected, to lie wasted and unused.

The greatest essential for all outdoor living space is a clear area of well-paved floor. Once there is room to move comfortably, then tables and chairs can be set in position, sun shades fitted, the barbecue employed, the drinks trolley wheeled out and the cushions occupied. In the outdoor room, just as in the home, plants and plantings should have a decorative function only. They must not be so dominant or obtrusive that they occupy the space designed to be filled by human activity.

So, therefore, in all outdoor living space relegate all planting to perimeters, except for minor features such as paving plants or plants in decorative containers which can easily be moved when the occasion demands.

Where space permits, and if money allows, it is always worth while to install permanent furniture for the patio or roof garden. Modern designs and materials are such that weather can do them no harm and they can be cleaned of dust or moisture by a quick wipe over. Aluminium furniture is rustless and lightweight. Many pieces today are nylon coated for cleanliness. Yet even timbers such as oak, elm and teak will come to no harm if left outdoors in all weathers. Cushions and coverings should normally either be brought indoors while not in use or placed safely under special covers. Yet even some of these are now produced in materials which will not suffer from the effects of cold and wet weather.

If space is simply too limited for permanently installed furniture, try to store this and all other pertinent pieces of outdoor living together in one place so they can be collected for use easily and quickly. Try to keep special eating and drinking materials for outdoor life rather than raid the normal home store —this often causes disorganisation and occasional temporary losses.

It will be found well worth the expense to have an electric lighting point installed on the patio or the roof garden. This can be employed for lighting, for a barbecue cooker, for running a small water pump or even for using a vacuum cleaner to clear the floor area before (and after!) a party. This electricity point, because it is outdoors, must be of a special weatherproof type and should be installed by a qualified electrician.

A patio party can be spoiled by a cool breeze and both for special occasions and for normal outdoor living it is helpful to arrange some kind of semi-portable screening or shelter. It is quite possible to grow a mobile hedge, beech, box or privet for example, in wheeled troughs which can be moved according to the position of the wind. Lighter and more practical is a three-sectioned screen, hinged at the two inner joints, of heavy grade transparent plastic set in a timber frame. This can be positioned as required to deflect any breeze and will be found a great comfort when sun bathing.

1

2

1 To furnish the patio for pleasure a mobile hedge is made, so that it can be wheeled about and used as a screen against the prevailing wind. Beech, Box or Privet can be planted in troughs and made mobile in this way.
2 Much outdoor furniture is light in weight and is weatherproofed with some plastic-type coating material.

On occasions when the sun is too fierce and some protection is required it is helpful to have some sort of shade. A gay sunshade may be sufficient on certain occasions, but this must be moved to follow the sun and gives only a limited area of shade. A useful fitment for the patio and where possible even for roof garden or balcony is the shop-type canopy blind, fixed to the wall and capable of being pulled down when required. This occupies little space, can be obtained in gay striped materials and will give shelter both from sun and light summer showers.

The pleasures of the patio, roof garden and balcony can be much increased by the sight, sound and atmosphere of water, particularly when the day is hot and sunny.

A roof-garden pool can be no more than a basin and the water if possible should be moving. A drip, gurgle or trickle fountain is better and more practical than a jet, for with the latter there is always the danger that gusty winds may spray people nearby. All these types of fountain are simple enough to install provided facilities exist for making use of a water supply and electricity. The water is merely circulated by a small pump and as quantities required will be small there is no necessity for a permanent water outlet. The basin can be filled by hand and merely topped up as necessary.

Where these areas of the garden are going to be used frequently, always make sure that there are some containers for cigarette ends, pieces of paper, tissues, drifting leaves, etc. All these can find their way into corners or on to the lawn or borders and in a surprisingly brief time the area around the sitting-out place can look untidy and take time to clear.

Ashtrays should be deep and heavy. Tables should be solid enough not to be tilted or shaken by passers-by. Provide each person with some convenient and solid horizontal space where food or drinks are served, otherwise there is likely to be a mess.

Rock Gardens

Cuttings of dwarf rhododendrons—this includes the evergreen azaleas which are now classified under the one botanical genus of Rhododendron—can be taken during the first week of this month. Short laterals of the current year's growth, with a heel of the old wood, are detached from the parent plant and rooted in a closed propagating frame. Normally the cuttings root successfully in a short period, but one often finds difficulty in growing these on when they have been transplanted, either to the garden or into pots.

Provided only a limited number of plants is required, the following method cuts out the necessity of potting on from the cutting frame. They are rooted singly in small thumb pots in a mixture of equal parts coarse sand and flaked leafmould to which is added a half part of soil from the bed in which these dwarf plants are growing.

There seems to be a beneficial association between a mycorrhizal fungus, present in the soil where these plants are grown, and the plants themselves. It attaches itself to the root cells and the rooted cuttings thrive on it.

The small pots are plunged to their rims in a cold frame containing either damp peat or coarse sand. The frame must be kept closed and should face north, as shade is essential.

August, in the minds of most gardeners, is the time when flowers in the average rock garden are no longer prolific. Possibly this is due to overplanting with spring flowering species that provide a grand display from April to July and very little else afterwards. Some gardeners plant annuals to prolong the season. This entails a lot of work in raising and setting them out in the rock garden, as a number do not

1

2

3

Cuttings of dwarf Rhododendrons and evergreen Azaleas can be taken during the first week of August.
1 Short laterals of the current year's growth are detached with a heel of the old wood. Several can be obtained from one branch of the shrub.
2 The cuttings are inserted singly into small pots, into a compost of equal parts coarse sand and leafmould plus some of the soil from the bed in which the parent plants are thriving.
3 Make the cuttings firm in the pot.

transplant well. Many are also too formal and look out of place. In a well-planned rock garden it is possible to have a good succession of floral decoration from April to the end of October at least.

A list is given here of some of the rock plants which bloom during these normally flower-starved periods. The plants noted here should, where practicable, be interplanted with the early flowering species so that as the one finishes the others take over.

Achillea x *jaborneggii* and *A.* x *kelereri*, two aromatic white daisy-like plants, the latter with grey frosted foliage; *Aethionema* 'Warley Rose' and *A. coridifolium*, pink flowers; *Allium platycaule*, an onion with pretty pale pink heads, and *A. neopolitanum*, white flowers; *Anagallis collina*, orange-scarlet flowers from May to October and *A. willmoreana*, cobalt blue with red eye; *Androsace lanuginosa*, June to October, red-eyed lilac flowers and *Lapageria cruenta*, iris-like bulbous plant salmon pink with crimson spots.

There are a number of campanulas such as *C. carpatica* and its varieties, *C. cochlearifolia*, *C.* x *haylodgensis* fl. pl. *C. isophylla* and *C. raineri*; Ceratostigma, deep blue; *Claytonia sibirica*, pink; some of the autumn crocus, where they can be placed so that the foliage is not too unsightly; the autumn flowering crocus —there are a good number which will provide colour from now until December; all species of cyananthus are in flower from July to October; there are several species of cyclamen of which *C. neapolitanum* is outstanding with its dainty pink flowers and crimson central zone; a few of the erigerons from N. America such as *E. aureus*, *E. compositus* and *E. uniflorus*; erodium is another genus which provides colour from June to October; all the gaultheria species are decorative with their different coloured berries; most of the Asiatic gentians rarely come into flower before the end of this month, the classic being *G. sino-ornata;* an underplanting of rhodohypoxis with this species, which enjoy similar conditions, will give a constant succession of flowers from May till the frost comes; mimulus species and varieties; platycodon, the balloon flower; a number of the shrubby potentillas; the autumn flowering *Scilla autumnalis* and many sedum species. There are many more, but enough examples have been given to prove that the rock garden can be almost as colourful in late summer and autumn as in spring.

August is the month when many of the spring flowering bulbs or corms should be planted, as they not only require a good season of growth but also deteriorate if left out of the soil for any length of time. Naturally one is now writing about dry bulbs, not those which are bought in pots to be planted at any time of the year. In this respect a note of warning.

Some genera, such as *Nomocharis fritillaria* and cyclamen, should not be bought as dry bulbs for if exposed to air they quickly lose their viability and take a long time to recover—if at all. Tulip species are an exception. These should be planted in November.

A general rule when planting bulbs or corms is to plant roughly two to three inches deep. Some, like the crocus, will adjust themselves once in the ground. Cyclamen need shallow planting—one inch below the surface is sufficient. If the soil has a tendency to be heavy the bulbs should rest on a small amount of sand. After covering with soil and making firm, you should lightly fork in bonemeal at the rate of four ounces per square yard. No other form of manure is needed or desirable.

This is also the time to divide and replant bulbs, with the exception of snowdrops which are best divided when in leaf.

Any bulbs or corms too small for flowering the following season can be potted up in John Innes No 1 compost and kept in a cold frame until the following year.

Roses

Any rootstocks not dealt with in July should be budded as early as possible this month, as there is a strong tendency for the sap to stop running sufficiently to give a good 'take', unless regular artificial watering is undertaken, in dry weather.

In general, standard stems, whether English briar or *rugosa*, should be budded early in the season to obtain a satisfactory 'take'. On the other hand, both cutting and seedling rootstocks of *R. polyantha multiflora* (syn. *R. multiflora japonica*) will usually bud reasonably well into August, as they continue to grow, even in dry weather. This rootstock has a very thin bark, so it will be necessary to tie the maiden growth to a short cane in the first season to avoid accidents from blowing about in high winds.

Spraying against black spot disease should continue at 10-day or fortnightly intervals, and if mildew is troublesome the bushes should be sprayed to keep the disease under control.

All the disagreeable insect pests do not usually prove unduly troublesome in August, but if aphids (greenfly) show signs of multiplying rapidly, a compatible insecticide could be added to the black spot spray to deal with them both in the same operation.

The second crop of hybrid teas and floribundas should be opening during the second half of the month, at least in the southern counties, as well as new shoots from the base. In general it is inadvisable to feed roses with nitrogenous fertilisers after the end of July, as these would encourage the production of soft wood which would probably become badly infected with mildew. On the other hand, it is recommended that the rose beds receive a dressing of sulphate of potash, at about 2 ounces to the square yard in mid-August, to encourage the ripening of the wood.

It is not too early to start cutting out the old wood which has flowered from established plants of Wichuraiana ramblers. A few of them which continue to bear flowers later in the season, such as 'Crimson Shower', should be left for another month or so, but most of them, especially those that flower early in the summer, such as 'Alberic Barbier', 'Albertine', 'Dr W. Van Fleet' and 'Francois Juranville', may now be tackled.

New basal shoots will already have appeared, and to avoid damaging these when drawing out the old canes, you should cut the latter into several pieces and pull them out separately. If there is doubt as to whether sufficient new canes will be forthcoming to replace the old wood, one or two of the flowered canes may be left to be on the safe side. All the new canes should be tied in as soon as possible, spacing them out evenly to avoid any overcrowding, which can encourage mildew. These rules also apply when cutting out the canes which

1

2

1 Fresh growth on Roses needs to be tied in now. Whippy growths of considerable length can be made during the summer and should be tied in now while they are still soft and manageable.
2 Similarly, young growth may have arisen from below the ground in the form of suckers. These must be severed.

have flowered from the heads of weeping standards.

In the case of the stiff-stemmed climbers, it is a wise plan to tie in the new canes as they grow and while they are still soft and pliable. This is the only really satisfactory way of training these canes in the right direction, as they harden in the desired position. By leaving the job over until the wood has hardened there is always a danger of the canes breaking off at soil level when they are being tied in, as some just will not bend.

Suckers from the rootstock must be dealt with as soon as possible after they appear above the soil. On no account should they be allowed to grow tall, as they will then flourish at the expense of the cultivated rose. Suckers can appear any time during the summer and autumn, but they are often fairly numerous in August. With a little practice it is quite simple to distinguish between suckers and basal shoots of the cultivated variety, as the leaves, prickles and stems are normally quite different. The leaves of suckers tend to comprise narrower and more numerous leaflets. These are pointed, whereas the leaflets of the cultivated rose are much broader and rounded. In the early stages the leaves of suckers are mostly green, whereas those of cultivated roses are often crimson, bronze and coppery tints. The prickles of suckers are numerous, narrow and pointed, whereas those of most cultivated roses are much broader, but fewer. The stems of suckers are usually pale green, compared with the red or bronze stems of young basal shoots of the rose.

Occasionally there may be some doubt as the the identity of a shoot in the early stages, and the only safe measure is to trace it carefully to its point of origin with the aid of a small trowel. A sucker will spring from either the root system or the main stem, below the budding point, whereas a true rose shoot can only emerge from the budding point or higher. It is important to remove all suckers by tracing them to the point from which they emerge on the roots or main stem and then pulling them off. Cutting will only encourage them to multiply.

Suckers will also sometimes appear on the stems of standard roses, and may even develop from the stem between the two budding points, so that the sucker becomes entangled with the head. It is necessary to pull it off before it attains any size, when it will be much more difficult to remove.

Before you go on holiday remove all flowers from your roses. These will only have died and may have set seed pods before your return. If the weather is dry, climbers against walls or tall fences should be given a really thorough soaking—say three large bucketsful per specimen.

Catalpa bignonioides, the Indian Bean Tree, flowers somewhat late in the season, unlike other flowering trees. The white purple-flecked flowers stand in upright spikes rather like the Horse Chestnut flowers.

Trees, Shrubs and Climbers

Many shrubs can be propagated with ease from half-ripe cuttings of the current season's shoots, taken in late summer. The ideal material for this purpose will be relatively firm and woody at the base.

Half-ripe cuttings root more readily if they are taken from the parent plant with a 'heel'. Dipping the ends of the cuttings in a hormone rooting powder also hastens the process.

Among the shrubs that can be successfully and easily increased by this method are deutzias, buddleias, philadelphus, berberis, cotoneasters and heathers. Many evergreens, too, root easily. These include escallonias, santolinas, lavender and rosemary.

The cuttings should have all the leaves removed from the lower half of the stems—i.e. the part that will be below soil level. If the tips are very limp and wilted these, too, can be cut off.

There are various suitable rooting mediums for cuttings and most experienced gardeners have their favourites. A mixture of equal parts of sharp sand, loam and peat is as good as any although pure sand, peat, vermiculite and other special rooting compounds are used successfully.

If just a few cuttings of any one shrub are required—and the average gardener seldom wants to reproduce his existing stocks in large quantities—they can be inserted in a suitable medium round the edges of a flower pot. Holes should be made with a small dibber or the point of a pencil.

The shrub cuttings are inserted into the holes and firmed in carefully. The last operation is essential to success. If the base of the cuttings is not in contact with the rooting medium, roots will fail to develop.

After insertion, the cuttings should have a good watering—with a fine rose —and the pot should be allowed to drain thoroughly. The pot is then

Many shrubs can be propagated in August from cuttings taken with a heel. Here, a conifer cutting is being made by pulling the new growth away from the old wood with a strip of the wood, or heel, attached.

encased in an upside-down polythene bag—the kind without holes in—and stood in a sheltered part of the garden, shaded from the sun.

At the end of a month, the cuttings should be starting to make roots. As soon as this happens, the bag can be removed. They will need protection from severe frosts and a cold frame serves this purpose best. At the same time they will require sufficient ventilation to prevent them from damping off. Therefore, the frame should be open during the day, whenever weather conditions are fine enough to permit this.

Larger numbers of cuttings can be inserted, in a suitable medium, direct into a cold frame. They should be fairly close together, not more than 2 inches apart, as togetherness is supposed to encourage rooting.

The frame should be kept closed for the first four to five weeks, being opened only for a very short period each day to disperse moisture from the inside of the glass. Overhead spraying or syringeing will prevent the cuttings from flagging and encourage rapid rooting.

In spring they can be planted out in a nursery bed. Most should be ready to go into their permanent positions by the following autumn.

A number of interesting climbing shrubs and wall plants come into flower, or are still flowering, during August. Two of the most exciting are exotics: *Clianthus puniceus*, a tender New Zealander that needs the protection of a south wall, and the self-clinging trumpet vine, *Campsis* x *tagliabuana* 'Mme Galen' from North America.

The former gets its popular name of lobster claw or parrot's bill from its curious scarlet flowers, which bear a strong likeness to a parrot's beak or the business end of a lobster. The trumpet vine has salmon-red tubular flowers borne in clusters. It is one of the most striking of late-flowering summer creepers.

Jackmanii group clematis will also be making a brilliant showing. Although a north or east wall is generally recommended, they will flourish on any aspect provided that their root run is cool and moist.

Since most present-day houses have some kind of paved or concrete surround it is only a matter of time before the roots of plants growing on the house walls find their ideal conditions under this paving.

In the meantime, the plant roots can be protected by tiles or large flat stones laid on the surface at the foot of the plants or by planting a low-growing shrub such as lavender or *Viburnum davidii* to shade them from the hot rays of the sun.

Another lovely clematis that is seen at its best in August is *C. flammula*. This is a species that is grown as much for its penetrating fragrance as for the attraction of its flowers. Although it produces its small white flowers in great profusion, these are not outstandingly eye-catching, but their scent will fill the garden, particularly on still summer evenings.

Although honeysuckle seems to associate itself naturally with June and the season of roses, there are several kinds that do not come into bloom until July and continue in flower until the beginning of October. The late Dutch honeysuckle is one of these. The flowers are a striking reddish-purple with a yellow throat.

Two interesting hybrid honeysuckles, 'Dropmore Scarlet' and the rosy-purple and buff 'Goldflame', both flower from July to October and are at their peak during this month.

Few trees have a great deal to offer during August, although that lovely Japanese cherry, *Prunus sargentii*, sometimes blushes a premature scarlet at the end of the month to remind us that autumn is not too far away.

Catalpa bignonioides, the Indian bean, a choice tree from the United States, is an exception. During August it will be displaying its large spikes of white purple-flecked blooms, very much like those of the horse chestnut. These are quickly followed by long pods like outsize scarlet runner beans.

At 30 feet plus, with a spread of similar dimensions, this is rather a large tree for the small to average-sized garden. It does, however, make a magnificent lawn specimen where there is sufficient space for its proper development.

Vegetables

In the average season harvesting begins now, although in some years, when the season is early, certain tasks may have to be carried out earlier.

Herbs still in flower should be gathered for drying and storing. Gather them only when they are dry and hang them in

1

2

3

1 Endive can be blanched by putting a plate or large flower pot over the plants once they are nearly fully grown. Inspect the plants from time to time.
2 Shallots are ready for harvesting when the foliage dies down, and should be dried off before storing for winter use.
3 Onion 'Ailsa Craig' being pulled when mature. Other Onions can be sown at this time, and overwintered.

small bunches upside down in a cooling oven or, alternatively, protected from dust by polythene bags, over a stove. When brittle to the touch the leaves may be stripped from the stems and rubbed between the hands before being placed in airtight jars. For herb powders use an electric coffee grinder. So that one herb scent does not affect another, wipe the inside of the container with a piece of lemon skin before proceeding to grind a different herb.

Shallots and autumn-sown onions may be ready for lifting—the indication is when the foliage has faded completely. Do this when the weather is dry. However, if the season is wet and the bulbs are obviously ready, lift them and spread them on polythene sheeting in single layers and cover with cloches. They will not then be in contact with the soil and are not likely to begin to root. They can remain there until they are quite dry. They should then be cleaned of soil particles and loose skins. Store them either on trays, in string bags or bound in ropes. The bulbs must be kept in a dry and frostproof place until the winter.

Onions can be sown in the autumn as well as spring. Good varieties for this purpose are 'Autumn Triumph' and 'Reliance'. They are best left unthinned (and some gardeners say unweeded!) until the spring when they can be used as spring onions or transplanted. Some autumn sown onions are suitable as green or spring onions only and certain of these must be pulled before Christmas because they are not hardy enough to stand the winter. 'Lisbon' and 'White Portugal', two of the best spring onions are examples. 'White Spanish' is an excellent true spring onion.

Lift and store beetroots that are large enough, although globe beets can be pulled as required and left in the soil until frost threatens. Gardeners who have a deep freeze need not waste the leaves of the lifted beets. They can be frozen and served in the same way as spinach.

Winter spinach makes a pleasant change from the seasonal brassicas. 'Prickly' or 'Winter' (the term refers to the seed and not the leaf) can be sown from the beginning of August to the middle of September. It grows best in a sheltered place, even between rows of large growing brassicas if no border near a wall or fence exists.

Often more than one job can be done at the same time. When one earths up potatoes, leeks or celery it is inevitable that small weeds and seedlings are eliminated also. Earthing up is a simple method of blanching stems and it should be started this month. However, it must be remembered that celery makes little growth once it is earthed up, so make absolutely sure that the plants have attained a good size first.

Endive, which also should be blanched, or the deep green leaves are apt to be indigestible, is not treated in the same way.

The simplest method is to cover the plant with an inverted plate, laid flat on the leaf rosette, which must be quite dry. Blanching takes about five to six weeks. Again it should not be attempted until the plants have reached a good size. Inspect the plants carefully from time to time.

Another method of blanching is to use cloches covered with black polythene to show no crack of light and placed over the rows.

Gardeners with room to spare might consider sowing Brussels sprouts now for use next summer and autumn. The young plants should remain in the seed bed all winter and then transplanted to a few inches apart in spring. Later they can be planted to their permanent positions. Plants treated this way make fine, strong specimens and 'butter-up' early.

Sow the last batch of lettuce to be grown outdoors this year, but be prepared to cover this with cloches should the frosts or cold nights come early. Sutton's 'Spring Beauty' is a good crop to sow now, being extremely mildew resistant. 'Continuity', with a darker leaf, is another. At this season do not transplant. Sow thinly instead and thin out soon. Endive, land cress and corn salad or lamb's lettuce should also be sown for late winter and spring salads. In a small garden it is possible to sow these close enough to each other to enable them to be covered by a single row of cloches.

Water Gardens

This is the month to enjoy the pleasures of the water garden. With no urgent jobs demanding attention, you should be able to settle down to long relaxing spells of pond-watching.

These activities can be justified on the grounds that you must keep an eye open for undesirable visitors such as the great diving beetle.

While thus engaged it is likely that you will notice other insect visitors such as dragonflies, ranging from the slender beauties known as damselflies which rest with the wings together over the body, to the sturdier looking typical dragonflies of darting powerful flight, which usually rest with wings spread. As they hawk for small insects over the pool, their shining wings and metallic body colours flashing in the sunlight, you can enjoy their beauty and admire their remarkable aerobatic skill, secure in the knowledge that they are completely harmless to humans.

You may see some pairs flying 'in tandem', the 'neck' of the female clasped by the tail end of the male, dipping repeatedly into the water to deposit eggs. These hatch into goggle-eyed, six-legged larvae, or nymphs, which live in the pool from one to five years, depending on the species, and stalk and devour small aquatic creatures in the underwater jungle.

If you are observant, or lucky, you may see one of these ugly creatures climb up a plant stem out of the water. You can watch the dragonfly struggling to free itself from the pupal skin and see the body begin to glow with colour, the crumpled wings straighten and harden, until the perfect insect sets off to begin the few weeks of its adult life.

1

2

1 In August there is little to be done in the water garden but enjoy the cool pleasures of the pool side. It is always wise to keep an eye on the amount of debris collecting on the surface of the water and remove it frequently.
2 The female Eashnid Dragonfly rests on a sedge with its wings outstretched. Its metallic body shines in the sun.

Less welcome winged visitors may begin to appear now, in the shape of blackfly (aphids). Since the danger to fish rules out the possibility of spraying with insecticides, they must be dealt with by brute force. With the thumb positioned across the end of the hose to produce a powerful fine jet, the aphids can be blasted off the foliage of water-lilies and marginal plants to float on the pool surface at the mercy of the fish.

This works very well except in the case of old-established water-lilies with crowded foliage standing well above the surface so that the aphids can attack the undersides of the leaves. These then become curled and deformed, making it difficult to reach the pests. If this situation exists, it is a clear indication that the plants are overdue for lifting, dividing and replanting, a job which should be noted in the garden diary as needing attention next May.

Fish fry lead hazardous lives. Nature

has arranged for them to be produced in very large quantities so that they provide food for a variety of insects and other predators (including adult fish) and still leave enough survivors to ensure continuation of the species.

These survivors are the fry that have been most successful in hiding in corners, skulking in plant growth and generally making themselves inconspicuous.

So it is usually quite a few months, or even a full year, after spawning has occurred that the pond watcher first spots baby fish venturing into the more open stretches of water. When one has been seen it suddenly becomes easy to spot more, very slender but already bright with goldfish red or the mottled livery of shubunkins. And there are very likely to be some that are just a dull bronze. They may or may not develop colour.

All the varieties of goldfish have been developed, over the centuries, by selective breeding from coloured sports of an originally bronzy brown species. In every generation there is likely to be a percentage of throwbacks to the dull-coloured ancestor. So the dull-looking fry need watching. They may develop the characteristic goldfish or shubunkin colour during the first two seasons. If they have not done so by the time they are three inches long, they should be weeded out and not allowed to grow to breeding size, and so perpetuate more uncoloured progeny.

If you are going to be away on holiday, do not worry about the fish. They will survive. If you ask someone to come and feed them while you are away they will, with the best intentions, be almost sure to overdo it, and overfeeding can be very dangerous. Starvation, in a well planted pool, is impossible.

Holidays provide the opportunity to study other people's pools, in private gardens, public parks and stately homes. They may or may not be examples worth copying but are always worth studying, particularly with an eye to the effective use of plants. One must always, of course, be conscious of scale, and realise that the dramatic effect of lakeside gunneras and weeping willows cannot be attempted beside a garden pool of a hundred square feet surface area.

But during this month every patch of ornamental water should have something to show in the way of water-lilies. This will give you the chance to compare varieties. Most public parks show little imagination in this respect, being content with the old reliables, *N.* x *marliacea albida* or 'Gladstoniana' (white), *rosea* or 'Colossea' (white flushed pink) and 'Chromatella' (yellow), with an occasional bright red 'Escarboucle'. Visit a growers nursery and see such magnificent varieties as 'Gonnere' (double white), 'James Brydon', 'Gloriosa' and 'Newton' (reds), 'Sunrise' and *odorata sulphurea* (yellow), and 'Lustrous' and 'Mme W. Gonnere' (pinks), and see what possibilities the public parks neglect, and perhaps get some ideas for your own pool.

And if you visit the splendid RHS Gardens at Wisley, do not be misled by the blue water-lilies *(Nymphaea capensis)* growing in an outdoor pool. The pool is heated by pipes from an adjacent greenhouse and there is definitely (and unfortunately) no blue water-lily suitable for unheated garden pools.

In August the Grey Squirrel begins to collect nuts and other food for his winter hoard, and hides them away.

Wildlife

By the beginning of August the swift and cuckoo are already beginning their winter's stay in warmer lands. The swallows and martins are lining the telegraph wires and setting their bearings for the long flight to Africa, oblivious of the rhythmic clatter of farm machinery echoing through the valleys.

In the corn that the machines are so efficiently gathering the harvest mouse is in peril of his life. Since the advent of the combine harvester the mouse has drastically decreased in numbers and now at harvest time is forced to flee the corn for the open field or the garden, where he begins to attack the crocus bulbs and gather nuts fallen from the bird table.

As the machine claws its way through the golden stalks it destroys the harvest mouse's nest. It is a sphere about 5 inches across, off the ground and built of shredded blades of corn, or grass. There is no regular entrance, but the inhabitants wriggle their way in through the top of the nest. This habit, and the growth of the vegetation, results in the need to build several nests during the summer in which the four or five litters are born.

Into the fresh cut stubble fields come those starlings which brought up their young in northern lands. The young birds can easily be distinguished from the older members of the flock by their brownish, immature plumage. The autumn fruit and insects provide plentiful food for these new arrivals, common throughout the country. There are few houses, particularly, though not necessarily in country areas, which at one time or another have not been inhabited by this colourful migrant.

In the lush hedgerows the squirrel is busying himself collecting nuts to store for the winter ahead. He will even raid the bird table if he is particularly attracted. A once common resident of our woodlands, the red squirrel has unfortunately become rather rare, his habitat having been taken over by the grey squirrel. The latter species was first introduced from North America nearly a century ago, since when it has been quickly spreading and is now well-known all over the British Isles.

Though August is a month of harvest and plenty, the cold winter days ahead should not be forgotten. Birds and animals of many kinds are already preparing for this bleak time and food on the bird table should be slightly increased in quantity and variety to attract passing migrants as well as residents. The migrants may thus be encouraged to stay awhile in the garden before carrying on their long journey into the southern sun.

The Month of September

September is a month when the garden seems to glow with colour. Apples are ready to be picked, berries on trees and shrubs have ripened, leaves are beginning to take on their autumn tints, herbaceous perennials are still flowering. It is, perhaps, the most rewarding month

Platycodon grandiflorum, the Balloon Flower or Chinese Bell Flower, has inspired many painters and fabric designers.

1

1 Sedum spectabile 'Meteor' is one of the newer cultivars of this perennial plant that can be relied upon for a really good and lasting display of flowers in the late summer and early autumn. It attracts butterflies.
2 Aster x frikartii is a good perennial of medium height for effect in the late herbaceous border.
3 Rudbeckia 'Goldsturn' is a sturdy perennial with starry, daisy-like golden yellow flowers which bloom well on into the autumn.

2

3

1

2

3

Much of the attraction of many trees and shrubs is in the brightly coloured berries they bear in the autumn.
1 Of all berry-bearing shrubs, the Berberis species probably carry the most profuse crops, and Berberis x rubrostilla is undoubtedly the finest of all fruiting Barberies. Its transluscent amber-red berries are carried in very heavy crops.
2 Crataegus oxycantha, the Hawthorn, bears berries in profusion.
3 The Mountain Ash, or Rowan, has clusters of orange-red berries.

1

2

Apples, both ornamental and edible, ripen during the month of September and car. be gathered.
1 Malus 'Golden Hornet', a Crab Apple with a golden-yellow skin.
2 Apple 'Laxton's Fortune', an early ripening variety which is a heavy cropper. It makes a compact tree, useful in smaller gardens, and the fruit is remarkably resistant to scab.
3 Many Crab Apples or Malus species are grown for their ornamental appearance, but can also be useful in providing fruit for preserves to put into the store cupboard at this time of the year.
4 Ceanothus 'Gloire de Versailles' flowers continuously during the late summer and autumn, with soft powder-blue flowers.

3

Dahlias of all types are probably at their best in late August and September, and will flower until the cold frosty nights come. If the month remains frost free, they can be expected to make a good late show. Some late spikes of Gladiolus are still available for cutting.
1 Dahlia 'Red Cheer', a formal decorative Dahlia with bright red quilled petals.
2 Dahlia 'Sincerity', a collarette type with white flowers.
3 Gladiolus 'Assam'.

1

2

3

1

2

Dahlias and Chrysanthemums, often grown together, are the most colourful of late summer and autumn flowers in the garden, and provide a wealth of material for cutting.
1 Dahlia 'Lucky Fellow' a shell pink flower of the cactus type.
2 Chrysanthemums, gay, decorative and very sturdy will make a first-class show in the garden until the frosts come.

Jobs of the month

September is the main month for bulb planting to ensure a good spring display. This is also a busy month for flower arrangers who should gather materials for pepetuelle arrangements. There is work in the greenhouse to provide blooms for Christmas. Jobs to be done this month are summarised here. Over the following pages they are covered in detail

Bulbs

Plant spring-flowering bulbs, with the exception of tulips. Always use fresh fibre for bulbs planted in bowls.

Flowers for Cutting

Preserve seed heads and foliage. Make quite certain that foliage for this job is chosen and cut at the right moment.

Fruit

Ripening melons should be kept very dry and exposed to the sun. Complete the planting of summer-fruiting strawberries. Prepare the ground for November fruit planting.

Greenhouse

Plant bulbs for Christmas flowering. Winter- and spring-flowering pot plants should be brought into the slightly heated greenhouse. Sow schizanthus and mignonette for early summer flowering.

Hedges

Complete the annual trimming of mature hedges. Plant evergreen hedging shrubs and conifers towards the end of the month. Prepare the site in advance.

Herbaceous Plants

As soon as dahlia tops are blackened by frost cut back to within a few inches of the ground. Lift tubers, clean and store. Clear ground, prepare and plant spring and early summer biennials.

House Plants

Reduction in the watering and feeding rates should now begin gradually, until the winter minimum is reached.

Lawns

Mower blades should be raised and the lawn raked to remove excess fibre and runners of creeping weeds. Top dress with a slow-acting organic fertiliser.

Paths, Fences and Walls

Now is the time to consider constructing raised beds, which should have strong, firm walls.

Patios, Balconies, Roof Gardens and Window Boxes

Plan ahead for winter colour. Heathers are an ideal choice for winter flowers. Walls can be clothed by berried plants.

Rock Gardens

Shrubs are the backbone of a rock garden, but care should be taken when making a choice. Now is the time to carry out the transplanting of evergreen rock garden shrubs.

Roses

Continue spraying to control black spot. Remove all small buds that are unlikely to open before the early frosts begin. Shorten extra long shoots that can be damaged by autumn gales.

Trees, Shrubs and Climbers

This is the month when so many shrubs are showing their glowing autumn colours Trees planted now will get away to a good start.

Vegetables

Produce still to be harvested should be gathered before it is touched by frost. Haricot beans should be brought indoors to dry.

Water Gardens

Clear the pool of decaying vegetation and take measures to prevent leaves falling into the water.

Wildlife

Carry out repairs to the bird table and ensure that there is a constant supply of food so that birds will continue to visit your garden during the barren winter months.

Bulbs

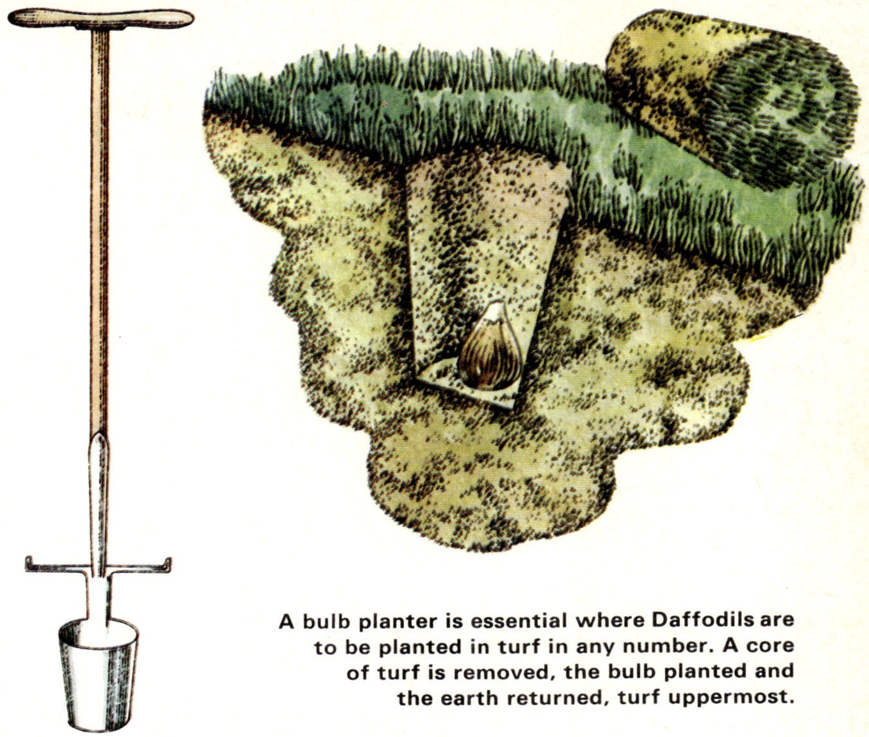

A bulb planter is essential where Daffodils are to be planted in turf in any number. A core of turf is removed, the bulb planted and the earth returned, turf uppermost.

Plant most of the spring flowering bulbs this month. Tulips are the main exception, and they can be left until November if necessary, to relieve the work during September and October. As soon as the bulbs and corms that were ordered in July are received, open the bags and keep the bulbs in a cool place until they can be planted.

Narcissi and erythronium, in particular, do not like to be out of the ground and need to be planted as early as possible in the autumn. So attend to these first. Narcissi are among the best plants for naturalising in shade or full sun, but crocuses, snowdrops and *Fritillaria meleagris* also look well when naturalised. When planted this way a reasonable quantity of bulbs is needed to give a good effect, but the number can be added to over several seasons to spread the initial expense.

When naturalising, handfuls of bulbs should be thrown over the area to be covered, with the hand and arm low, and with a swinging movement. The bulbs will fall haphazardly in drifts and should be planted where they fall. The resulting effect when the flowers appear will be natural—and informal. Bulbs can be planted in this way beneath shrubs or trees, in borders or in grass.

It is advisable to use a bulb planting tool, especially for planting in turf as this will remove a core of earth and allow the bulb to be planted sufficiently deeply. The core of earth can then be returned and the surface of the turf is affected as little as possible. A trowel can also be used for most bulbs, but it is a slow and difficult job to plant deeply enough, especially on heavy soils. There is an easy method for putting in tiny bulbs like scillas and snowdrops. It is to make holes with a crowbar or stout stake, drop the bulb in and cover it over.

Bulbs to be planted in September include camassia, leucojum, chionodoxa, snowdrops, hyacinths, narcissi, scillas, muscari, fritillarias, erythronium and cyclamen.

As a general rule the depth at which various bulbs and corms are planted is relative to the size of the bulb and the nature of the soil—always plant a little deeper in light soils. Fritillarias and snowdrops need to be about 3–4 inches below the surface and the large bulbs of *Fritillaria imperialis*, crown imperial, can be put 6–7 inches down and in wet soils can be planted slightly on their sides. This will prevent the water from lodging in the necks which would cause the bulb to rot. (The pronounced foxy odour of this plant means that it must always be grown well away from the house.)

Plant narcissi 4–6 inches deep, the miniature varieties 2–3 inches deep; crocuses and chionodoxa 2–3 inches deep and always put in more than are needed because mice will remove some. Plant the smaller scillas 3 inches deep and the larger bulbs 5–6 inches, muscari and erythronium 4 inches down.

The little hardy cyclamen need only be 2 inches deep, although some, like *Cyclamen europaeum* and *C. neapolitanum,* root from the top of the tuber. They do best on limy soil, to which some leafmould has been added, and they prefer a shady place. Soak these corms in water for twenty-four hours before planting them.

Bulbs for cultivation indoors should be put into bowls or pots this month or next, though the tulips can be left for a little while longer. By preparing a few bowls now and a few in three or four weeks time a long period of display is assured early next year.

Hyacinths and daffodils and the bulbous iris, like *I. histrioides,* lend themselves best to this treatment, and bulbs specially prepared for forcing should be bought. Beware of the cheap offers. Order from a bulb merchant of good repute, or select the bulbs yourself at the local store. Choose the firm heavy bulbs rather than the papery light ones.

John Innes potting compost can be used, in which case the pots will have to have adequate drainage material at the base. But specially prepared bulb fibre is the easiest to deal with in decorative bowls that have no drainage holes. This fibre is not so suitable for use with clay pots as it dries out far too quickly, and is the cause of irregular growth.

Buy fresh bulb fibre—do not try to re-use the fibre which was used last year—and soak it in a wheelbarrow, bucket or old tin bath before using it to fill the bowls. The soaking will take several hours and the fibre should be sufficiently moist to hold together in a loose ball when squeezed in the hand, but not wet enough for the water to ooze between the fingers.

Always use clean bowls. Pack a layer of fibre at the bottom and then stand the bulbs on this, packing them as close as possible, for effect, and because once growth starts they will shrink in size. Pack fibre around and between the bulbs, making it firm and level and leave only the noses of the bulbs showing. For this reason shallow bowls are best, and economical on fibre, because the final level of the fibre should be about an inch below the rim of the bowl.

When John Innes potting compost is used in pots or seed pans, put large crocks over the drainage holes and cover them with a layer of rough material to ensure sharp drainage. Plant the bulbs in the same way as for the bowls.

Whether pots or bowls have been used, put them somewhere dark and cool—indoors or out of doors. A plunge bed is the most satisfactory way of ensuring the low temperature necessary to allow the strong roots to form before the bulbs are forced, and such a bed can be made of peat or soil of sufficient depth to cover completely the bowl of bulbs. Put each bowl into a polythene bag before covering it with peat. This will ensure that the pots are clean when they are removed from the bed.

Label the bowls with not only the names of the bulbs but the date of planting, and put the bowls in the plunge bed roughly in order of planting. It will be interesting to take note of the time that has elapsed before each bowl is ready to be brought out into the light later on.

Flowers for Cutting

Many leaves, branches of foliage, seed stems and seed heads, even silvery or woolly ones, can be preserved by standing their stem ends in a solution of glycerine and water. Few are likely to retain their original hues and some become unexpectedly handsome. As the solution spreads through the stems and leaves the colour of the subject changes, usually to a tone of brown, tan or purple-bronze.

Treated early this month green beech changes to something which looks very much like copper beech and becomes an attractive component of perpetuelle arrangements of all kinds. Helichrysums look well contrasted with the beech leaves while the wooden materials—cones, seed heads and fruits—harmonise with it beautifully.

Preservation of this kind is very much a matter of experiment on the part of the flower arranger. This is a worthwhile venture because it helps to build up a useful collection of floral accessories which can be used in beautiful arrangements of many different kinds at all times of the year.

Many evergreens take the treatment well, although these must be mature—at least a year old. Eleagnus, laurel and olearia, for example, become very much like brown polished leather, the last retaining the silvery-grey undersides to the leaves.

Fluffy seed heads of clematis and pulsatilla can be fixed so that the clusters of styles will not disintegrate.

Three things are essential for success: foliage must always be mature; everything must first be hardened in the usual way preparatory to arrangement, to determine whether or not the stem tissues are conducting the water, and finally, the stems must be stood in the solution while it is hot.

Boil two parts of water to one part of glycerine. Pour two or three inches of the hot solution, according to the length of the stems to be treated, into a tin or some other container which will not crack. They should stay in the solution until it is apparent that the glycerine has spread through the network of veins. If materials stay in too long the solution may be exuded from the leaf surfaces, which could then become unpleasantly sticky.

Many leaves and seed heads take on a silvery appearance when dried or preserved with glycerine and water, and can be assembled to create attractive long-lasting arrangements. Teasel, Clematis, Achillea, Acer and Irises have been added to this arrangement of preserved foliage.

It is not possible to say how long this process will take, for it depends on the state of the material, its type and the relative heat and humidity of the room. Eucalyptus, for example, need be stood only two or three days, which is long enough to 'fix' the leaves and prevent them from curling. If they stay longer they lose their attractive colour. Ferns, mature and well covered with spores, can be given one or two days and then put into water. This way they will last for weeks.

Generally speaking most tough, smooth-leaved subjects can be preserved this way. For example, beech and hornbeam are easy while elm and hazel are not. On the other hand downy and silvery leaves often take the solution surprisingly well and with remarkable effect. Verbascum, woolly leaves and stems, after the flowers have faded, can be preserved this way.

It is sometimes possible to fix fruits and seed cases. Beech branches with the unopened mast on them will take the solution and then open the four-valved cups to reveal the nut cluster. They then look like little wooden flowers. Hazel and cob nuts and fruits of almost any tree or shrub, maple keys for example, can be treated this way, but the fruits should not be too mature.

This is also the case with coloured leaves. Usually once the foliage of trees begins turning colour the arranger thinks about preserving them, but preparations should begin long before this. Leaves expected to turn as near as possible to their natural autumn tints must be gathered at the right moment. This is before the sap is drawn from them by the tree. Unless the branches still retain the mechanism to draw up water they cannot take up the solution. This month is usually the best time to gather autumn coloured foliage. A good guide is to watch a shrub or tree and the moment you see the odd branch or leaf cluster changing colour, cut the branches for preservation.

If materials are not to be used immediately after preservation, they should be stored in polythene bags or in boxes.

Fruit

Look over the cordon apples and pears which were summer pruned. If secondary growth has since been made, cut these new shoots back to one bud beyond their point of origin. If, due to high rainfall, there is much secondary growth, defer this task until the trees are dormant.

If in previous seasons your apples have rotted in store, spray the trees of 'keepers' now with captan to reduce fungus infection.

Melons ripening in frames or beneath cloches should now be kept drier. Certainly do not syringe any more. Lift the fruits on to upturned flower pots to expose them to the sun and be ready to cover with mats, sacking etc., on clear, cold evenings.

To assist the ripening of the wood, peaches or other fruits growing in an unheated greenhouse should be given more ventilation and less water.

Prepare ground intended for planting with fruit in November. Heavy soils need digging to improve drainage and to allow well-rotted compost to be worked in. Pick out the roots of any perennial weeds encountered as you proceed. Top fruits seldom require the addition of any manure but soft fruits need richer conditions and, while still needing good drainage, are helped in summer by the incorporation of plenty of moisture-holding organic matter. It is best not to dig actual planting holes in advance of planting.

Continue planting summer-fruiting strawberries. Wherever possible this should be completed this month. Make certain that recently planted strawberries never lack for water. Strawberries of the perpetual fruiting type (also known as remontants or ever-bearers) may be planted now if available.

Autumn weather is often favourable for the spread of mildew. Look out for white, powdery growth developing on fruit leaves—apples, plums and gooseberries are particularly susceptible—and if seen, spray at once with Dinocap.

Once the fruit has been picked from fan-trained peaches, nectarines and Morello cherries, the fruited shoots should be cut out and the shoots which have been allowed to grow to replace them tied in in their stead. If there are still bare areas of the wall waiting to be 'clothed', a few of the fruited shoots may be retained and the replacement shoots used to fill the gaps.

The sweet cherries, fruiting on both old and new wood, need slightly different treatment. Cut out any dead wood and prune shoots previously pinched to three or four buds. Also attend to fan-trained plums and gages as soon as the crop has been harvested, cutting shoots previously pinched back to half their length. Cut out any dead wood.

Sacking bands put on in June should now be cut off and burned to destroy their catch. It is now the turn for another type of trap—the greaseband. You can buy a special preparation of vegetable grease that does not harm the tree and smear it directly on the bark or you can buy paper-backed greasebands for tying round the stem. The purpose of the grease is to catch the wingless females of the winter group of moths as they climb up the trunk to lay their eggs. Direct greasing is much less trouble than tying on paper-backed bands but never use animal grease, which can be very harmful.

Prune loganberries as soon as the fruit has been picked. Cut the fruited canes at soil level and tie in the new growths to replace them, spreading them out so that each will enjoy the maximum of sun and air.

Pick early and second-early pears as they become ripe. Do not pinch them to see whether they are ready: lift gently in the palm of the hand until the fruit is horizontal and then give it the slightest possible twist.

Greenhouse

Hyacinths and narcissi, including daffodils, make a valuable contribution to the greenhouse display at Christmas or soon afterwards, so, to ensure these early blooms, get the bulbs planted in pots or bowls as early in the month as possible. For Christmas hyacinths use 'prepared' bulbs, one to a 4-inch or three to a 6-inch pot and plant them in the John Innes potting compost No 1 if they are to go into pots or in bulb fibre if they are to be grown in undrained bowls. The 'noses' of the bulbs should finish just above the surface. After planting soak the potted ones well, then bury them beneath about 4 inches of sand or weathered ashes in the garden. Those bulbs planted in bowls, however, are better in a cool, dark and airy place under cover. The main thing then is to make sure that the compost or fibre is kept quite moist.

Daffodils and other narcissi are similarly treated, except that they can be planted rather closer together. Small bulbous subjects such as snowdrops, crocuses and muscari (grape hyacinths) may also be potted up quite close together now and plunged beneath sand or weathered ashes outside.

Winter and spring-flowering pot-plants now in frames must be brought into a slightly heated greenhouse before there is any risk of severe frost. But they should be quite safe in the frames until at least the end of the month if the frames can be covered with mats or sacking on cold nights. But do not bring in hydrangeas yet. These plants must be left outside until all their leaves have fallen.

Most plants will need rather less water

Grease bands are put around the trunks of fruit trees, well above the ground, in September to trap the wingless females of the winter Moths as they climb up to lay their eggs.

Chrysanthemums in pots that have been standing out of doors during the summer are brought into the greenhouse now, as soon as there is a threat of frost at night.

1

2

3

1 When planting Hyacinth bulbs in bowls first put a layer of fresh fibre at the base of the bowl.
2 The bulbs are set upright on this and the fibre is filled in around them.
3 The fibre should be made very firm.

now, particularly hippeastrums, which should be gradually dried off. Achimenes, too, should be similarly dried off after they have flowered. Cacti also need less water now but keep them in full sun to ripen their growths properly.

Regal pelargoniums, on the other hand, will already have had their resting and ripening period so these can be started into growth again. Cut them back to about 8 inches high if this has not already been done, then re-pot into the John Innes potting compost No 2, using pots one size larger than the present ones. After potting keep the plants in the greenhouse, where they should be frequently syringed but at the same time watered sparingly until growth starts.

Two useful plants to sow now are schizanthus and mignonette for early summer flowering under glass. The schizanthus is best sown in a pot or seed-pan to provide seedlings for pricking out and potting on later. Mignonette, however, is best grown in the pots in which it is to flower. For this plant a rich, well-limed and very firm soil gives the best results, with the seeds being sown very thinly just beneath the surface. When the seedlings are large enough to be handled safely thin them out to leave the strongest ones about an inch apart.

Towards the end of the month a start will have to be made on bringing the pot-grown chrysanthemums into the greenhouse, so make sure that this is cleared out and cleaned in readiness for them. Make sure that the chrysanthemum pots are as clean as possible and the plants themselves free from pests before housing them just close enough together to prevent one plant from touching another.

As soon as frame space becomes available a start can be made on the propagation of bedding plants from cuttings. The main ones to be taken are of violas, pansies, bedding calceolarias, antirrhinums and penstemons. For violas and pansies use strong young shoots springing from the base of the plant trimmed off beneath a joint to about 2 inches long, but for the others use unflowered sideshoots similarly trimmed. The cuttings of all these plants should then be firmly inserted about 3 inches apart in a firm, level bed of good sandy soil in the frame, where after a good watering-in they should be kept close until new growth indicates that rooting has taken place.

Early roses for cutting or greenhouse display may be obtained by growing the plants in pots with or without artificial heat, although in the latter case the flowers will obviously be later. Suitable varieties to use are 'Lady Sylvia', 'Talisman', 'Madame Butterfly' and 'Ophelia', all of which should be ordered immediately for potting up in October.

Dormant plants of the extremely beautiful but tender *Azalea indica* should also be ordered now for potting next month.

Hedges

The annual trimming of mature hedges should be completed as early as possible during the month. When an established hedge is being clipped, the base should be left wider and thicker and the sides should taper slightly towards the top This helps to prevent damage after heavy falls of snow.

Newly-planted conifer hedges should not be clipped until the plants have reached 6–7 feet in height. This is generally in their second season after planting. After this, conifer hedges can be lightly clipped each year. Care must be taken not to cut back into mature wood or bare patches are liable to develop.

Most evergreen hedging shrubs and conifers can be planted towards the end of the month. Generally speaking, autumn is preferable to spring planting, first because there is less likelihood of long spells of dry weather and secondly because the plants have a chance to make new roots that will help them on when top growth makes its appearance again in spring.

Box, yew and holly are three of the most popular evergreen hedging subjects. Yew is actually a conifer, in

An effective plunge bed can be made by putting the bowls out of doors and covering them up completely with a few inches of moistened peat.

Where bowls are to be kept indoors, covering them with several sheets of newspaper or brown paper will serve to keep the light away from them.

1

2

Many gardeners prefer to put in evergreen hedging plants in September, rather than in the spring. This ensures that the young plants do not suffer from drought.
1 Measure stations for Holly plants.
2 Stagger the plants for thickness.

which the small coral fruits—which are poisonous—take the place of the more orthodox cones. They can all be planted now. The planting site should be well prepared in advance of planting by digging it at least two spits deep and incorporating as much humus as can be spared, finishing off with a dressing of coarse bonemeal at 2–3 ounces to the square yard.

For hedging purposes all these three should go in at intervals of $1\frac{1}{2}$–2 feet. For a denser, thicker hedge, the plants can be in two staggered rows.

Yew has been justly acclaimed as the finest hedging plant we have. It is also the longest-lived, as the centuries-old yew hedges of some of our famous gardens so clearly testify. *Taxus baccata*, the common or English yew, makes the best hedging form. Yews have a reputation for very slow growth but this is undeserved as far as the early stages are concerned. It can put on between 6 inches and a foot in height and spread every year for several years. It is only at maturity that the yew really slows down. This is an advantage since it reduces maintenance of the hedge to an absolute minimum.

Buxus sempervirens handsworthensis, a strong-growing variety of the common box, will make a tall compact hedge up to six feet in height that will need only light clipping annually. For edging, the dwarf *B. s. suffruticosa* is used. It can be restricted to as little as a foot in height. This must be one of the few garden plants that is sold by the yard, current quotations being in the region of seventy-five pence a yard.

Another of our native plants, *Ilex aquifolium*, the English holly, makes a superb hedge, impenetrable by man or beast. It will remain densely clothed from top to bottom even when allowed to grow to heights of 12 feet or more and its only drawback is its habit of dropping its dead leaves during the summer months.

Named varieties, including the gold- and silver-variegated forms can also be used for hedging, but apart from 'J. C. van Tol', a less spiny kind with distinctive olive-green foliage, their cost could well prove prohibitive.

Herbaceous Plants

Night frosts often finish many of the half-hardy bedding plants in September, especially in low-lying areas, although the days may still be warm.

Some bedding plants—begonias, geraniums (pelargoniums) and heliotrope—can be potted up *before* the nightly frosts begin to form, placing them on a window-sill or in a greenhouse to continue flowering for another month or so.

Dahlias, however, should be cut down to within a few inches of the ground as soon as the tops are blackened by frost, lifting the tubers and cleaning off the surplus soil with a pointed stick before storing in boxes of sand or peat in a cool frostproof shed.

Once the ground is clear, the soil can be forked over, working in a good scattering of bonemeal in readiness for planting spring and early summer biennials (or plants treated as such)—wallflowers, sweet William, Canterbury bells, polyanthus, double daisy *(Bellis)*, forget-me-not *(Myosotis)*, foxgloves *(Digitalis)*, and so on.

Wallflowers look attractive in a herbaceous border growing in groups of three or more, or as an edging in a carpet of blue forget-me-not. The little dwarf double daisies form a pretty, neat edging, too, particularly when mixed with coloured primroses, the dainty blue chionodoxa, violas and forget-me-not.

As the name suggests, wallflowers thrive in ground containing mortar rubble or lime. The same is true of the sweet William which belongs to the lime-loving dianthus family. Planted 9–12 inches apart, both enjoy full sun, the colouring of the sweet William becoming intensified when the plants are grown in loamy soil manured for a previous crop.

Polyanthus *(Primula)*, primrose *(Pri-*

An island bed can be quite small and still be most effective in a lawn, provided it is built in proportion to the rest of the garden and in proportion to the lawn itself.

RECOGNITION CHART

Cones

Cones are the seed cases of conifers. They differ within a genus and are a distinguishing feature of the species

Picea sitchensis, the Sitka Spruce, has cones 4 to 5 inches long, which hang downwards.

Picea abies, the Norway Spruce or Christmas Tree has cones that are distinctively long and cylindrical and always hang downwards.

Picea breweriana, not a common tree, is known as Brewer's Weeping Spruce. The slender branches hang to as much as 8 feet with the long pointed cones drooping from them.

Pinus pinaster, the so-called Cluster Pine bears clusters of the largest cones of any European pine. The cones are very slow to mature, often remaining hard and unopened on the tree for some years.

Pinus holfordiana bears its cones in pairs, and they fold back along the branch.

Pinus sylvestris, the Scot's Pine, carries its cones behind the fresh growth at the tip of the shoot. The pointed form of the cone is a distinguishing feature.

Abies procera, the Noble Fir, has upstanding elliptical cones the bracts of which are bent downwards, giving the cone a somewhat feathered outline.

Abies concolor has hard, rather large heavy cones that stand upright singly on the branches, and look like candles on the ends of the branches.

suga heterophila the Western
emlock carries small cones at
ie end of the drooping branches.
he cones are narrow at first, but
roaden as they ripen. They
emain on the tree after
leasing their seeds.

Pinus cembra, the Stone Pine, has a somewhat square cone that stands alone. upright, on the branches

arix decidua, the European
arch has small cylindrical cones
which expand slowly, and often
ersist on the tree through the
winter. The Larch is a deciduous
onifer – a rare plant, and the
ones are easily recognisable on
ie bare branches in the winter.

Chamaecyparis lawsoniana, the Lawson Cypress has very small globular cones tucked at the base of the leaf sprays in autumn.

Pinus nigra, the Corsican Pine, the cones of which shine when ripe and are yellow-brown in colour. They are rigidly held in a spreading attitude around the shoot.

Pinus strobus, the Weymouth Pine, has gracefully arched cones which hang and are markedly sticky with resin.

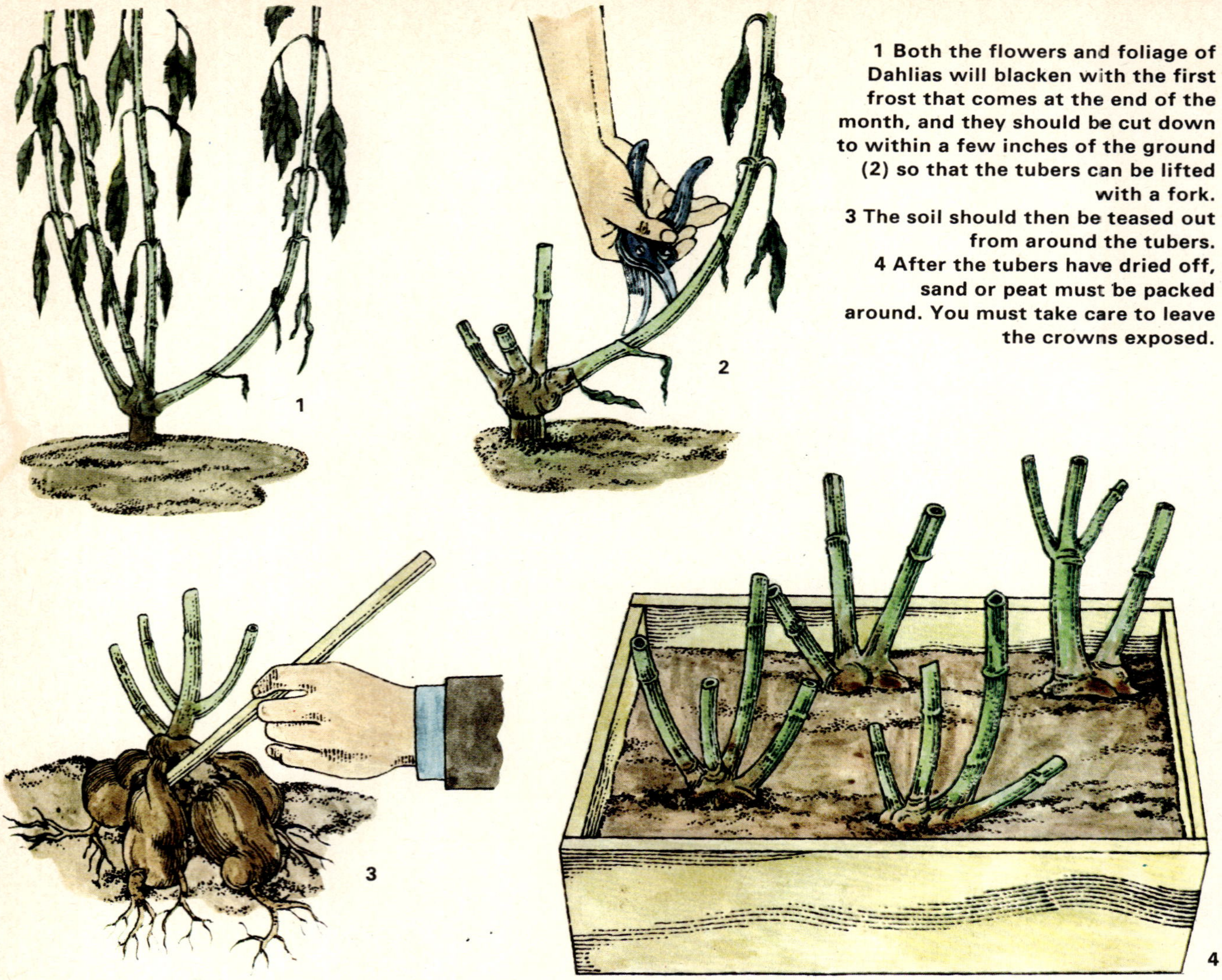

1 Both the flowers and foliage of Dahlias will blacken with the first frost that comes at the end of the month, and they should be cut down to within a few inches of the ground (2) so that the tubers can be lifted with a fork.
3 The soil should then be teased out from around the tubers.
4 After the tubers have dried off, sand or peat must be packed around. You must take care to leave the crowns exposed.

mula), and foxglove—the 'Excelsior' strain bears the flowers horizontally all round the stem instead of drooping to one side—are happiest in shade or partial shade, the polyanthus and primrose planted 6–9 inches apart preferably in moist, rich, heavyish loam, while foxgloves 9–12 inches apart, are happier in ordinary rich soil.

Canterbury bells *(Campanula)* do well in partial shade or sun, planted 9–12 inches apart in sandy soil mixed with plenty of leafmould. These old-fashioned favourites are excellent plants for a herbaceous border for if the individual bells are picked off when they fade, without damaging the embryo bud behind the bell, they often flower two or even three times.

Another plant that will grow in part shade or sun is the herbaceous paeony *(Paeonia)*. This lovely bushy perennial moves best in September or March, planting the roots 3–4 feet apart with the crown no more than 2 inches below the surface, in deeply dug neutral or slightly limy loam enriched with rotted manure or hop manure. These beautiful plants can be propagated by division but, in general, it is best that they should not be disturbed more than necessary as the plants flower better when left to grow into large clumps.

Recommended varieties: 'Sarah Bernhardt', apple-blossom pink; the richly scented bright red variety 'Felix Crousse' and the fragrant soft salmon pink 'Madame Calot'.

The popular sweetly-scented lavender blue *Iris unguicularis* (used to be known as *Iris stylosa)* which flowers from November to March when established, should be planted this month, too. This iris only blooms freely when almost starved in poor soil, in a dry, sunny position.

Other irises to be planted now are the bulbous Dutch, Spanish and English iris. Of these, the early June blooming Dutch are the most vigorous of the three, flourishing in all types of soil, planted 3–4 inches deep, 5–8 inches apart in groups of half a dozen or more. The varieties 'Blue Champion', 'Lemon Queen', 'Orange King' and 'White Excelsior' are outstanding, as beautiful for cutting as they are decorative in the garden. Flowering slightly later, planted 3–4 inches deep, 4–5 inches apart, the Spanish iris take over from the Dutch. They are not quite as large but equally lovely, the varieties 'Cajanus' (golden) and 'Summer Time' (white flushed lavender with canary yellow falls) being especially in demand as a cut flower.

The long-stemmed English irises are not as hardy as the above. The bulbs require covering with litter in winter as protection from frost. In a wide range of colour, flowering from June to July, they should be planted in ordinary garden soil, 3–4 inches deep, 6 inches apart, in full sun, lifting and replanting the bulbs every third year.

Although most established borders are still bright with flowers, September is the month to begin planning new borders, deep digging and manuring the soil so that it has time to consolidate before October planting.

Herbaceous borders can be almost any shape or size—single-sided with curved or straight edge backed by a wall, fence or hedging; or 'island' beds—oval, oblong, arc-shaped etc.—whichever is most in keeping with the garden layout. Sufficient room should be left in front of background hedging to allow space for clipping. Island beds are more satisfactory, as a rule, than very narrow single-sided borders, the plants tending to become drawn in the latter unless the bed faces due south.

Once the shape is decided, preparation of the ground can begin. Where the site is turfed, the grass should be skimmed off and stacked in a heap to rot down into valuable compost for use as top-dressing. Alternatively, double dig the ground, burying the turf in the bottom of the trench after treating it with Gamma-BHC dust to destroy wireworm. The soil should be tested for lime content using one of the simple lime testing outfits available at any garden shop—the majority of herbaceous plants prefer neutral soil.

Subsequent treatment depends on the nature of the soil but most soils are improved by the addition of rotted manure compost, hop manure or peat worked in at the time of digging.

House Plants

House plants really come into their own during the autumn when flowers are becoming scarce. Zebrina pendulina (syn. Tradescantia zebrina) is a particularly popular example.

Conditions in the home do not always reflect those outdoors, so for house plants you cannot always follow exactly the seasons as you would for plants in the garden. In September, for example, hours of daylight outdoors are beginning to diminish, yet indoors the period of light is extended by switching on electric lights earlier in the evening and perhaps even supplementing daylight during the day. Outdoors the days are beginning to get cooler and we must even look forward to night frosts during the next few weeks, yet indoors the central heating may be switched on again, which not only gives unseasonable warmth but a dryer and less humid air than the plants have been enjoying during the warmer months.

All of this complicates the matter of the care necessary for the long life and health of indoor plants. A naturally shorter day and naturally cooler temperatures would normally slow the growth rate of plants and you would subsequently give them less water and food. Naturally moister conditions outdoors because of the winter rains would increase relative humidity and release us from the task of providing this artificially.

So a nice judgement is required at about this time of year in deciding which plants should have their watering and feeding rate reduced, which plants are getting sufficient humidity and which require placing nearer to the windows to give them better light. Unfortunately it is impossible to give hard and fast rules because so many varying elements are involved. Light will be better in the country than in town and better in a house with large windows than in one with small windows. Temperatures can vary by as much as ten degrees or even more depending on the efficiency of the heating system, the thermal insulation of the house and even the personal warmth requirements of the inhabitants.

In time you gain an almost instinctive knowledge of the requirements of different plants, but to begin with it is best to play safe and in September begin gradually reducing the amount of food and water given to almost all plants. More house plants die from over-watering than for any other reason and while it is always possible to increase the amount of water a plant receives it is more difficult to abstract the amount of moisture lying around the roots of a plant. This reduction in the watering rate should be a gradual one, continuing for a few weeks until the winter minimum is reached. This should then be maintained until the days begin to lengthen and warm up again.

The feeding rate should also be proportionately reduced at this time and for some plants, such as the cacti and others which make no growth at all during winter, feeding can be stopped entirely. If feeding is continued while the plant is making no growth there is a danger of a build-up of chemicals in the soil that will damage or even kill the sensitive root system.

Because of the reduction in both length and power of daylight it is well to place nearer to the windows any plants which demand good light—this applies particularly to all flowering plants. Make sure, however, that they are brought farther back into the room at night in case of frost damage through the glazing.

With the artificial heating on, the relative humidity in the home will be reduced and it is important for the plants that the air should not become too dry. Ceramic humidifiers hung on the radiators will release several pints of water into the air each week and special electric humidifiers are now available which carry out this important task automatically. Without either of these aids it is helpful merely to place about the house a few shallow pans of water. This will have the effect of increasing the humidity.

Some plants will benefit by having their pots plunged inside a larger container, the space between the two being filled with peat or some similar moisture-retentive material which is always kept just moist, but not sodden.

Lawns

September is the time to start preparing the lawns for the winter months ahead. It is also the best period for remedying any deficiences that became apparent during the summer months.

As the grasses will gradually cease to grow as fast as during the summer months, the lawn will not need to be mown so frequently. The intervals between cuttings can generally be increased by a day or two each time. Obviously, however, the intervals between mowing will be dependent on the height of the grasses, as these should never be allowed to grow much longer than the usually accepted height.

This is also the month when the mower blades should be raised by about ¼ inch from the usual summer level. In other words, fine grass lawns should now be cut to ½–¾ inches, medium grasses to ¾–1¼ inches and rough lawns to 1¼–1½ inches.

This is the best time to rake or scarify the lawn to remove excess fibre and the runners of creeping weeds, and to keep the grass growing vertically to retain a nice green carpet-like appearance.

Light raking with a spring-back lawn rake will usually be sufficient, and the rubbish collected in the prongs should be removed to the compost heap, or burnt if it contains weed runners.

If the lawn has been badly neglected, it will probably require very vigorous raking to remove the old fibres, and a mechanical scarifier would be an advantage. It would also be useful for large lawn areas. In this latter case, the rubbish lifted must be swept up, either with a lawn broom or a wheeled lawn sweep. If this raking or scarifying is carried out prior to lawn mowing, the cutter blades will then chop off any raised weed growths which remain.

Following this raking or scarifying, sometime during this month or October will be the ideal period to spike the lawn, to improve aeration and drainage, to compensate for over-compaction due to wear or machinery, and to enable suitable organic dressings to be applied most effectively.

The amount of spiking necessary will depend very much on the state of the lawn. A well-maintained area will probably only require light spiking each autumn, either with a spiked roller or by pushing in the tines of a garden fork 3–4 inches deep at 6–8 inch intervals. A neglected lawn, or one on soil which either lies water-logged for overlong periods or dries out too fast, is best spiked with a hollow-tined lawn fork, which draws out cores of soil. (The soil cores should be discarded away from the lawn, to prevent unsightly soil patches and potential weed germinating areas.)

Top dressing of the lawn should then follow. At this time of year, no quick-acting, growth-stimulating fertilisers should be used. It is best to use an organic, slow-acting fertiliser such as bonemeal, bulked up with coarse gritty sand and a good grade of coarse peat. The bonemeal should be applied at the rate of 2 ounces per square yard, with the sand at about 1 lb per square yard and the peat at 4–6 ounces per square yard. Alternatively, one of the proprietary autumn lawn dressings may be applied at the rate recommended by the manufacturer.

After scattering it evenly over the surface, the top dressing should be brushed well into the spiked lawn, so that it fills the holes left after spiking. Not only will this treatment encourage a healthy grass root system, but the condition of the soil, the drainage and moisture retention will be improved.

Should the grasses appear thin in any areas light seeding, ½–1 ounce per square yard, of matching species is advisable at this time of year.

If a new lawn area was not seeded last month, the grass should be sown before the middle of September. Equally, September is the time to start final soil preparations prior to laying turf during October or early November.

A new lawn area from seed sown last month will probably be ready for its first brushing, light rolling and 'topping' during this month. After a gentle brushing over with a lawn broom to remove any surface debris, a light rolling will help to compact the surface soil a little and encourage the grasses to produce new shoots. The first 'topping', with a mower with very sharp blades or a pair of hand shears, should follow when the grass is about 2 inches high. Thereafter, the grass should be mown whenever necessary during the following autumn and winter months, so that it never grows taller than 1½ inches or 1 inch if the species are very fine-leaved.

Hand-weeding on new lawns should be carried out as necessary, and care taken to firm back any grass roots which may be disturbed by pulling out the weeds.

Mild moist weather encourages earthworms to work near the soil surface, and they are frequently most active from September to November and in the spring during April and May. Worms are most valuable in the garden generally, for aerating the soil, but as far as a lawn is concerned they are nothing but pests. Not only do they disturb the surface soil structure, but their casts are unsightly, make the lawn surface untidy and slippery, smother the grasses, and create ideal seed beds for weed seeds.

The best way to discourage earthworms is to use a grass box when mowing, avoid any form of liming, and reduce the quantity of organic dressings. Where they are a real problem, worms are best killed chemically during September.

There are a number of good proprietary wormkillers on the market, usually

1

2

1 Earthworms are most active during the period from September to November. Use a proprietary worm repellant to rid your lawn of them.
2 Spiking the lawn helps in surface aeration and improves both the drainage and the texture.

A formal raised bed, constructed of brick, has been made to decorate this patio. The plants which are growing in it can be seen especially well from the living-room.

based on mowrah meal, derris, chlordane or lead arsenate. These should be applied as recommended, and will probably need to be well watered in, unless heavy rain follows treatment. Any worms which come to the surface should be brushed up and destroyed. Care must be taken when using these wormkillers. The first two are harmless to children, pets and birds, but poisonous to fish if you have a garden pool. Chlordane and lead arsenate, however, are harmful to human beings and animals but not to fish.

This is a good month to start renovating overgrown neglected lawns. The tall grass and weeds should first be cut down to 2–3 inches, either with a rough grass rotary cutting machine, billhook or handshears. Then rake the area to remove the cut vegetation. A few days later, mow the grass with the blades set $1\frac{1}{2}$–2 inches high. Repeat mowing, as and when required, to keep the grass to this height.

Spiking and top dressing, as described previously for this month, should follow, and a hormone weedkiller applied overall if the area is very weedy. Really persistent weeds are best dug out and the bare patches re-seeded or re-turfed.

Paths, Fences and Walls

For the elderly or the partially disabled gardener who enjoys growing and tending plants but finds normal gardening too much of a strain, raised beds are the answer. These are, in effect, waist high walls enclosing a raised mound of soil.

The minimum of bending and stooping are required for their maintenance and they have the added attraction that the flowers and other plants they contain are so much nearer the eye and nose and their sight and scent can, therefore, be enjoyed more freely. A raised bed can even include a little sink pool, on the small side but still large enough to sustain a miniature water-lily and a fish or two.

September is the ideal time to make raised beds, for the considerable initial labour involved can be spread over some days and when the walling has been completed and the vacant interior filled with soil there is time for this to settle during the winter before planting in the spring.

One of the major benefits of raised beds is that they can be tailor-made for the plants they are to grow. They can be filled with acid soil for rhododendrons, azaleas and ericas, or with alkaline soil for pinks and dianthus of all types.

Raised beds can be studded with rock and sharply drained for alpines or bleached and sandy for cacti. They can grow anything from trees to tiny annuals, in each case the soil being specially designed and imported. Raised beds are, in fact, nothing more than very large and static containers or pots and can be treated as such.

As already indicated, a raised bed demands considerable time and trouble to make in the first place, but once properly constructed it is extremely labour saving. It can be made in any shape or size, but in practice, a rectangle is usually found to be best, about six feet long and no more than four feet wide.

A raised bed of this size enables the gardener to reach any part of the surface without reaching or stretching unduly. For his additional ease and comfort it is well to pave around the circumference.

The retaining walls for a raised bed must be both strong and firm, so unless large and heavy stones are to be used the stones should be bedded in concrete. As the walls will be heavy a good foundation is required. The bed will be an important feature in the garden so it must look attractive and therefore demands good stone rather than the bleak regularity of brick or precast concrete.

To avoid the considerable task of filling the completed area with soil when the walls have been built to waist height it is advisable to fill as you go. The base should have a good layer of drainage material and weep, or drainage holes, should be left in the walls as work proceeds.

Directly over the drainage layer, which can be a foot or so in depth, it is helpful to lay a strata of fresh turf, grass side down, and to place the final soil on top of this. The type of soil selected for the raised bed will depend on what it is wished to grow, but as the bed will be comparatively sharply drained it is well to incorporate a proportion of water-retentive material such as peat in the final planting soil.

The raised bed suggested here is, of course, a purpose-made feature, but raised beds can be dual purpose. A much slimmer bed, for example, can act as a patio wall or as a division in another part of the garden.

If a raised bed is to hold a tiny pool an old kitchen sink will suit admirably if sunk in the soil and the edges suitably disguised and softened with overhanging rock or sprawling plants. If the entire area is to be made into a raised pool, then it is essential that it should be made of concrete.

Patios, Balconies, Roof Gardens and Window Boxes

Although the days still seem to be comparatively long and warm the winter is approaching and it is time to plan ahead for winter colour on or near the patio, on the roof garden and balcony and even in window-boxes. Nothing adds so much to the bleak aspect of winter than to look out of the windows from the warmth of the house and see before you the dead stems of frosted flowers and the grey twigs of deciduous trees and shrubs. So begin now to look critically at the more intimate sections of the garden and to decide on what new plants you must order.

Remember that outdoors it will be quite impossible to achieve anything like summer's blaze of colour and that you must make the most of evergreens and the few shrubs and trees which open their brave blossoms while snow and frost surrounds them. Remember, too, that evergreens can be gold, silver, grey and blue as well as green.

Many of the dwarf and slow-growing conifers make excellent plants for pots and tubs. Choose for shape as well as colour, for during the winter they will often be seen in silhouette against snow or mist. They can be conical, upright, rounded, weeping or prostrate. Plant for contrast of outline and colour to bring as much interest as possible to the winter scene. Some dwarf conifers are small enough to go into window-boxes and there are many for balcony and roof as well as the larger areas of the patio.

Juniperus communis compressa makes a slim, blue-grey pillar seldom more than two feet tall, while *J. procumbens nana* spreads itself over the soil to make a fresh green carpet only a few inches high. *Chamaecyparis minima aurea* is cone shaped with elegant twisted soft gold foliage. *C. lawsoniana pygmaea*, shaped like a cushion, has fanning foliage which turns red at the tips in winter, while *C. l. thyoides andelyensis* turns almost plum coloured.

If you want winter flowers that will blossom even while covered with snow, look to the heathers or ericas. Plant in an acid soil, for even though *Erica carnea* varieties will tolerate a little lime in the soil they will serve you better without. Ericas can be obtained which will give flower colour throughout the entire year and many varieties have rich tints of gold and red in their foliage as well which makes them quite as colourful as flowers. They grow well in tubs and mix effectively with dwarf conifers.

A stone plant container houses a fine collection of evergreens—Hedera and conifers. The value of such plants is readily appreciated once the summer flowering plants have finished.

Camellias, also splendid tub plants, are much tougher and hardier than they look and, although it is possible to obtain greenhouse varieties, there are many that will flourish out of doors, particularly with a north aspect, and produce a profusion of flowers as early as January. When newly planted they may require a little coddling in their first couple of winters, so heap warm peat over their roots when the frosts are hard. *Camellia japonica noblissima* and *C. williamsii* will both flower in January and go on until about March or even April. Try not to plant against an east facing wall, for morning sun on frozen flowers can burst the tissues and cause them to brown and fall earlier than necessary.

A large tub will take a rhododendron, again in acid soil. 'Christmas Cheer' really will flower for Christmas and this can be followed by *R. mucronulatum* and *R. praecox* and others to give flowers of vivid and cheering hues at a time when all else is grey and spiritless.

If early flowering bulbs have not yet been planted they should go into the soil as soon as possible for early bloom. Snowdrops and crocus species are the first to flower, but they are quickly followed by aconites, other crocuses, the earliest narcissi and tulips and so on into the season. All are suitable for trough and tub planting and most can be underplanted among heathers or taller conifers to add their more vivid colour to the greys, golds and greens. All bulbs, because of their more vivid colour, should be used as lavishly as possible to bring a brightness otherwise unobtainable in the earlier parts of the year. Many may be grown on in boxes to be ready to replace those which have passed their best. The idea is to lift those that have finished and plant those coming on so that there is a constant succession. This need take no more than an hour or so a week.

Walls can be clothed in winter by berried plants such as the useful *Cotoneaster horizontalis*, which will so often carry its berries through to spring, and by the unfailing and tolerant *Forsythia intermedia spectabilis*, first of this family to show its bright stars of bloom.

If there is any space against a wall or even out in the open it is always a good plan to plant one or more magnolias. The first of these will not begin to bloom until about March, but the trees are always impressive and the blooms, when they do appear, are so

1 A rock garden of warm sandstone. September is the time to plan the display for next season and to move plants from one place to another.
2 Evergreen shrubs in the rock garden can be transplanted now. For some weeks before moving them you should thrust a spade down near the roots to sever them and prepare the plants for a self-contained move.

magnificent that they are worth waiting some time for.

Rock Gardens

There is no doubt that shrubs must be considered the backbone of a rock garden. They lend form to what would be a meaningless whole if all the space were devoted to herbaceous perennials and evergreen cushion plants. Care must be taken in selecting suitable specimens for, like so many of the so called dwarf conifers, a number will outgrow their allotted space.

Like most other rock plants the shrubs, with few exceptions, are pot grown so do not present any great difficulty in planting. A point to remember is that a number cannot be transplanted. To cite a few: all daphne, genista, anthyllis, astragalus, berberis and cytisus are extremely intolerant of root disturbance so once planted they should remain undisturbed.

This is the month when transplanting of evergreen rock garden shrubs from the garden can be carried out successfully as there is still plenty of warmth in the ground and they will have settled down before winter takes over.

There are a few tips to remember when transplanting evergreens in the rock garden. Warm moist weather is ideal for the job but it is advisable when the shrub has been planted to spray it with water both morning and evening until root action has recommenced. This will do much to prevent transpiration and excessive loss of moisture which is not easily replaced until the roots are active again. If a rare or old specimen needs to be moved, this would include a conifer, which has been in the rock garden for some years, a great deal of care is needed. About two months before removal, periodically thrust a spade vertically into the soil to its full depth near the plant. Repeat until a circle equal to the spread of the branches has been cut. This is similar to root pruning. The plant must not be allowed to dry out during this period. Provided that the overall bulk is not too unwieldy, all soil within the circle should be retained when lifting.

The position in which it is to be replanted should have been well prepared and a hole made which will allow the ball of soil containing the roots of the plant to be accommodated comfortably without any undue squeezing. A compost comprising equal parts leafmould, loam and coarse sand is then forked in round the edges of the soil and roots of the plant, making the whole firm. Until well established once more plenty of water should be given and it will be of great assistance to the plant if the foliage could be syringed daily with water during this period of rehabilitation. There is a plastic spray on the market specially prepared for use on both the foliage and exposed roots. This helps considerably in reducing transpiration during the transplanting and resettlement.

There is still time to sow seed of the rarer species of rock plants and if these do not germinate quickly, the seed pan should be exposed to all frost and snow during the coming winter. This tends to encourage germination the following spring.

A general tidying up of the rock garden helps in preventing hiding places for such pests as slugs and woodlice that like nothing better than dead or decaying material as shelter.

During dry spells at this time of the year mildew is sometimes encountered and is best controlled with a fungicide spray. On the other hand if the weather has been wet and humid moulds often attack the plants—especially cushion plants. The moulds can be controlled with a fungicide spray, but should the fungus attack be severe remove the damaged growth.

For gardeners who would like to try some of the more difficult rock plants, whether one gardens in a few square yards or an acre or so, try growing the plants in tufa. Tufa occurs naturally in a few places in this country and is not as heavy in weight bulk for bulk as ordinary stone. It is composed of deposits formed from crustacea in rivers and streams, is highly calcareous, porous and easy to work. Pieces from 1–2 feet square up to several square yards may be used—the larger the rock the greater the number of plants that can be grown. Holes large enough to take plants should be made in the tufa with a hammer and chisel and the size of the hole will depend on the type of plant. Small well-rooted specimens are best and the soil is washed off the roots which are then placed in coarse dry sand. This allows them to be inserted in the hole made in the tufa without cramping them into a tight mass. The compost to use is made up of equal parts coarse sand and flaked leafmould to which is added the chippings of the tufa taken when making the hole. The plant is then inserted and the compost worked down amongst the roots and the whole well firmed. Small pieces of tufa are then placed round the neck of the plant and a good watering given with a fine-rosed can.

Once they have taken hold the plants will remain dwarf, compact, exceedingly floriferous and have a long life. It is not possible to list all suitable plants but the following are suggestions: all saxifragas of the *engleria* and *kabschia* groups are ideal; the rare Aretian androsaces; choice rock-loving primulas; the crevice campanulas and cushion drabas. Nurserymen who specialise in rock plants will be only too pleased to advise you.

Roses

Weeding will take up much time in a country district, especially where open fields are adjacent to the garden. The only satisfactory way of coping with this problem is to keep the weeds under control while they are still small. In a wet season, however, this is extremely difficult in a large garden. Weedkillers based on paraquat may be tried, although it is not claimed that these will kill perennial weeds, which are the ones that give the most trouble in a permanent planting, such as a rose bed. In applying the weedkiller it is best to use a special dribble bar which will fit on a plastic watering can. As it is non-selective in its action, this weedkiller must not fall

Above **Rose cuttings are made from ripened wood, about 9 inches long. First the tip is removed and then a straight cut is made at the base.** *Below* **The cuttings are inserted in a grip out of doors.**

on any soft young growth springing from the base of the roses.

Spraying to control black spot in pure air districts should be continued well into the autumn, as this is when the disease can spread very rapidly. Always see that the base of the plant is sprayed really thoroughly, as the disease attacks the oldest leaves first. Heavy autumn rains will wash much of the protective spray off the foliage so it may be necessary to spray more frequently than in summer to give adequate protection.

It will still be desirable to remove dead blooms, which can spoil the whole effect if left on the plants, but at this time there is no point in cutting the stem back half-way. It is sufficient merely to remove the dead flower with it attached to a piece of the footstalk.

Early frosts may occur in the first week of October, so some disbudding is strongly recommended. Remove all small buds which are unlikely to be open by then. It is far better to mature about one-third of the buds than to have all of them frosted before they can open.

Any extra long shoots which appear on bedding roses should be shortened about the end of the month. Autumn gales tug at these long shoots, causing great strain on the roots. The shoots, which are battered against the thorns of adjacent growths, become lacerated and the soil around the base of the plant is loosened, causing a cavity in which water may freeze. This will cause the roots to break.

It is a sound plan to examine all forms of support in late September, before the autumn gales start in earnest. In really exposed gardens windbreaks may be necessary, and tripods will be a sounder proposition than single upright pillars.

The edges of beds cut in lawns should continue to be trimmed, to set off the autumn display of roses which, in a well-maintained garden, will often almost equal the early summer display.

Towards the end of the month cuttings may be taken of the more vigorous groups of roses. It is questionable whether this is worth while with most of the hybrid teas in shades of yellow, apricot, orange, flame and bicolours, but many of the floribundas will root quite easily. Of course, groups like the Wichuraiana ramblers and many of the shrub roses will grow vigorously on their own roots, and may also be propagated from layers. The miniature roses are usually propagated from cuttings in order to retain their dwarf habit of growth.

Cuttings, except of miniature roses, should be about 9 inches long and prepared from well-ripened wood of the current season's growth. The wood produced immediately following spring pruning is best, as it is sure to be ripe enough. When preparing the cuttings the pithy growing tip should be rejected. All leaves except the top two should be removed and a cross-cut made to form the base of the cutting just below an eye or dormant shoot bud. The bottom inch of each cutting may be dipped in water and then in hormone rooting powder to hasten root formation.

A V-trench should be taken out in a sheltered part of the garden, making it about 6 inches deep and mixing coarse sand and moist granulated peat into the soil forming the base. The cuttings should be spaced about 4 inches apart and the soil firmed moderately as the trench is filled in. Only the top 3 inches of the cuttings will be above soil level, and it will help to conserve moisture if the surface is covered with granulated peat to a depth of 2 inches. The cuttings should then remain undisturbed for at least a year, and should never be allowed to dry out.

When cuttings of the miniature roses are taken they have, of necessity, to be very much shorter and are more conveniently inserted round the circumferance of a 4- or 5-inch pot filled with a porous potting compost. Because of their diminutive size they are perhaps more conveniently kept in a cold frame or a cool greenhouse.

Advantage may be taken of any fairly flexible long shoot of a climbing or shrub rose to increase it by layering. Here the technique consists of making a slit in the lower side of the shoot, so that when it is bent to the soil level the slit opens to form a tongue, which is usually anchored to the soil by a wooden peg and a small pebble inserted in the tongue to keep it open. By heaping gritty soil over the tongue, rooting is encouraged, but the shoot is not severed from the parent plant until it is seen, by the new growth emerging from the point of pegging down, that the roots are active and able to support the shoot independently.

The foliage of Euonymus alatus adopts the most brilliant hues in the autumn. The overall effect of the coloured leaves is a vivid coral pink.

Trees, Shrubs and Climbers

The season for blossom on trees and shrubs is at an end, but this lack is compensated for by the large number of trees and shrubs that start to develop brilliant autumn leaf colouring towards the end of the month.

Many of these will already have given good value for money with the beauty of their spring or summer blossom. With these, autumn leaf colours come as an acceptable bonus. *Viburnum opulus sterile*, the popular snowball bush, is just as attractive in its striking scarlet autumn livery as it is in May and June when the globular flowers are slowly changing from pale apple-green to creamy white.

The leaves of *V. lantana*, the wayfarer's tree, native to our chalk downs, take on a similar colouring in autumn, but its flowers are less attractive and it is rather a commonplace shrub for the smaller garden.

Cotinus coggygria, the smoke or wig bush, is as noteworthy for its autumn leaf colour as for the curious inflorescences that give it its popular name *Cotinus coggygria* has clear green foliage that turns a bright yellow, but this does not compare with that of the variety *atropurpurea* (syn. *foliis purpureis)* which is a deep rich purple, or the even more intense hues of 'Notcutt's Variety'.

The deciduous barberries, too, include many forms that are conspicuous for the bright colours of their leaves in autumn. *Berberis thunbergii* has vivid crimson leaves at this season. The leaves of the variety *atropurpurea* start off coppery-red in the spring, retain their colouring throughout the summer and end up in a blaze of crimson-scarlet.

Some of the most outstanding coloured leaves are produced by *Enkianthus campanulatus*. This oriental shrub is one of upright compact habit with bell-shaped spring flowers that are followed by attractive fruits. Its main attraction, however, lies in the magnificence of its autumn leaf colouring. This is a striking medley of scarlet and amber. The shrub is a lime-hater and likes a peaty, fairly acid soil.

But perhaps the richest colouring is provided by *Euonymus alatus*, whose curious corky winged branches are an additional attraction during the winter. The leaves of this moderate-sized shrub turn a brilliant coral-pink, quite unlike the autumn hues of any other tree or shrub. It grows very slowly, seldom exceeding 6 feet at maturity.

Among the few shrubs to make a colourful display of blossom in September are the so-called 'tree' hollyhocks which, far from being tree-like in character, grow only to an ultimate height of 5–6 feet. Like its perennial relations, *Hibiscus syriacus*, formerly known as *Althea frutex*, likes a position where it receives the rays of the full sun.

H. syriacus will thrive well in any good garden soil. This shrub is one of the latest to come into leaf, often delaying the opening of its leaf buds until mid-June or early July.

There are both single and double flowered forms and among the best are *coeleste* (purple-blue), 'La Reine' (rose-pink) and 'Woodbridge' (pink with a maroon blotch), all of which are singles. Good double forms are 'Admiral Dewey' (pure white) and 'Lady Stanley' (pink).

Another shrub with the unwarranted prefix 'tree' to its popular name is *Romneya coulteri*, the Californian tree poppy. This, in fact, is really more of a sub-shrub, as the stems normally die back to ground level in winter.

Romneyas need a well-drained soil and a sunny situation. The large poppy-like flowers, which appear from early August to October, are five inches across, satiny in texture, creamy-white with a central boss of golden stamens. They are among the loveliest of late-flowering subjects for the shrub or mixed border.

Flowering freely, too, in September

will be *Perowskia atriplicifolia,* the grey-leaved Russian sage, which makes a fine shrub for the edge of the border or for the rock garden, together with hardy fuchsias and the shrubby veronicas which are now known as hebes. Some of the last-named will flower right through until Christmas, but many are fairly tender and are suited only for sheltered positions or milder districts.

It will soon be time for autumn planting and orders should be given now for delivery in October and November. The examples that follow are of small specimen trees, compact enough for planting in the garden of small to average size. Planted in autumn, they will get away to a good start.

Thorns, crabs and cherries all make an excellent choice. Varieties of *Crataegus oxycantha* make the best all-round garden specimens. These include the well-known 'Paul's Double Scarlet Thorn' and *C. o. alba plena,* one of the finest white double forms.

Malus floribunda is the best of the flowering crabs. In May it is literally smothered in pinky-white blossom that makes a magnificent show for several weeks.

There is of course a very wide choice of Japanese cherries, including *Prunus sargentii* which provides striking autumn leaf colour as well as a wealth of spring blossom, and two lovely weeping forms, *Prunus subhirtella pendula* and *P. serrulata rosea.*

Weeping trees and shrubs always make first-rate lawn specimens and Young's weeping birch, *Betula pendula youngii,* has a particularly elegant form. Others well worth growing are *Pyrus salicifolia pendula,* the willow-leaved weeping pear and *Cotoneaster hybrida pendula,* which makes a large shrub or a small tree, according to whether or not it is restricted to one main stem.

Where gardens are still under construction, preparation of the planting sites for autumn-delivered trees and shrubs can begin towards the end of the month. This will save delay when the plants arrive. Double-digging or trenching and the incorporation of plenty of humus-rich material are the two cardinal considerations.

Vegetables

Although summer seems to linger on one must not forget that frosts are in the offing. Produce still to be harvested should be gathered before it is touched by frost or it will not store well. This applies particularly to marrows, pumpkins and squash, which should keep to the following spring if handled correctly. Not only do these change colour when really ripe, but the skin also changes in texture. When properly ripe the vegetable should be wood-hard. Even so it should be treated gently; 'like eggs' is good advice. A hard knock or careless handling can cause bruising which will result in rotting.

The Californian Tree Poppy, Romneya coulteri, flowers late in the season. It bears large, rather floppy white flowers.

When the fruit is picked allow it to retain a portion of stem. It will be necessary to use a sharp knife or a pair of secateurs to sever the stem. Handle by these stem ends.

One good and simple method of storage and one which saves space is to hang marrows in string bags suspended from hooks. This way air circulates all round them. Smaller squash can be stored in trays. Pumpkins can be stood on a cushion of paper on a shelf. In each case make sure that the location in which they are kept is not only frost proof but dry. The temperature should be roughly 55–65°F (13–18°C). So these vegetables are often best kept in the house rather than in the garden shed or garage.

Haricot beans should be brought indoors. It is best to pull the entire plant and let this dry. Remember that while the beans are inside their pods they are in a sterile pack. Once they are shelled they are more likely to become mouldy if they have not been properly ripened. Hang the plant head downward in the sun until it is quite dry, but should the weather be wet keep it in a cool airy shed. Later, when the pods are crisp to the touch, they can be shelled and the dried beans stored in airtight jars, drums or polythene bags.

Vegetables should be lifted for storing. Choose a dry, sunny day if possible. In every case the roots should be lifted and laid on the surface of the soil in the sun until they are dry and any large soil particles can easily be removed. Potatoes must be gathered up quickly once dry, because long exposure to sunlight turns them green. These are easily stored in sacks which should be kept in a temperature of about 40°F (4°C). Again the building must be frost proof. One should also take full precautions against mice and rats.

Maincrop carrots should be dug about the middle of the month. If left after this the roots usually begin to toughen and to crack. The same applies to maincrop beetroot.

Tomatoes should be gathered. The best way to get green fruits to turn red is to store them in the dark. Simply lay them on a bench or in trays and spread dark paper or black polythene over them. Alternatively, gather the bunches and hang them up in a dark place—not in the sun.

Where there are rows of successional crops not quite ready, it helps if these can be covered with cloches once the nights become cool. Salads, globe beetroot, carrots, radishes and others can be kept safely and used young this way.

Although most of the discarded vegetable tops can be composted, one should take special precautions with potato haulms to avoid blight in future years. Burn these and carefully rake and clean the ground on which the potatoes have been grown. Where the ground can be left unoccupied plan ahead for next year and, having decided where the potatoes are to be planted, dig it really deeply as soon as possible and let it stay rough through the winter. If other crops are to follow the potatoes it may not be necessary to dig farther than the disturbance caused when lifting the potatoes, but it will be advisable to feed or otherwise treat the soil according to what crop is to follow on. It will certainly need liming if brassicas are to be grown. The ground will also need to be firmed for these.

Much of the routine work this month follows last month's pattern. Seed to be sown includes Brussels sprouts, lettuce and endive, which must be removed to a frame later. Early varieties of cauli-

1

2
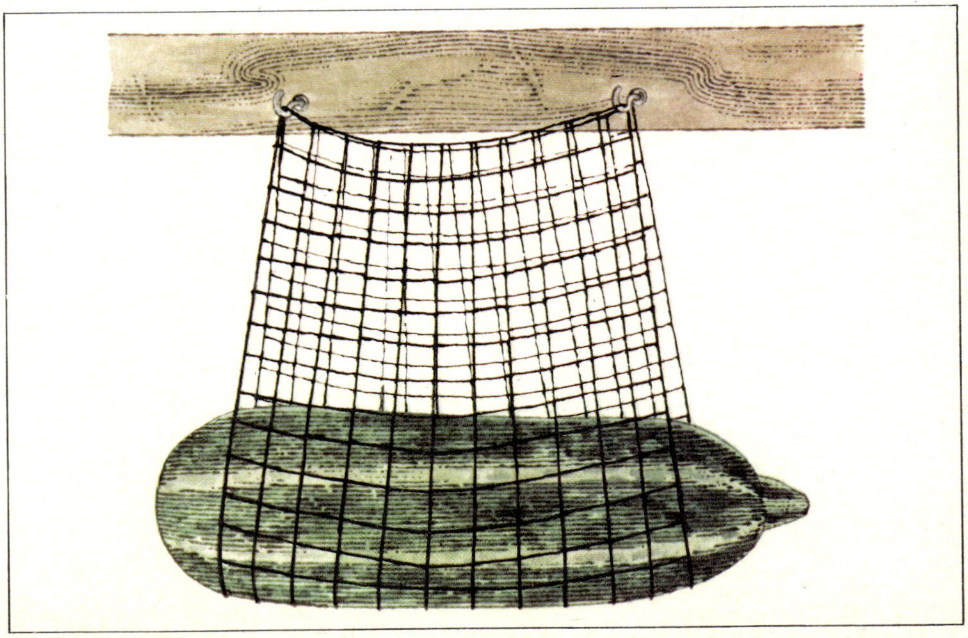

3

1 Tomatoes should be cleared of the crop and brought in for ripening before the frosts start. Put them in a dark place to ripen or cover them with black polythene. These Tomatoes are ready for covering, now that they are dry.
2 Marrows will keep in store until the spring if they are handled carefully. Suspend them in a string bag or piece of netting for really safe keeping.
3 Lift Carrots now for storing.

1

2

3

flower to mature next summer can be sown under glass now and early next month. They should either be planted in the open ground and given some protection with cloches, or alternatively potted individually and stood in frames until spring.

Winter radish, onions, land cress, corn salad and prickly spinach can still be sown in the open.

It is quite a busy planting month. All the late winter and spring cabbages, late kales and savoys, ought to go in this month so that they can become established by winter.

Water Gardens

The season's tide of growth is on the ebb now and the blue flower spikes of pontederia and the continuing blooms of water-lily and water hawthorn have a background of foliage that will become progressively more worn and tattered as the month goes on. Only the dark green foliage of *Cyperus longus* looks as lush as ever, emphasising the value of this outstanding marginal foliage plant.

With the certainty of frost now only weeks away, it is vital to ensure that any covering of the surface by ice does not find the pool loaded with decaying vegetation. It is essential, for the sake of the fish, that every dead leaf or bloom in or around the pool should be removed. The blown flowers and blackening leaves of water-lilies and aponogeton, the sagging foliage of calthas, the collapsing stems of rushes and the trailing fronds of parrot's feather will, if allowed to sink and rot in the water, produce gases which can be lethal to fish if a layer of ice prevents them from escaping into the air.

Although a heavy leaf-fall from trees and shrubs is not likely to occur before the end of the month, or even well into October, now is the time to take steps to keep them out of the pool. One-inch mesh netting spread over the pool will do the trick.

The netting can also, with advantage, be extended to cover the adjoining rockery, where great damage can be done to some alpine plants by soggy layers of dead leaves, particularly of such trees as chestnut and sycamore.

The netting can be removed after a few weeks, except in areas where seagulls or herons abound and fish may be taken in large numbers during a severe winter.

So the process of tidying must continue through the month, the stems of marginals being cut back when they turn brown, to three or four inches above water level, and the growth of oxygenating plants being drastically reduced.

Oxygenators are very often more of a

1 Most of the autumn work in the water garden is directed to clearing away excess growth. Leaves falling from the trees and shrubs should be kept out of the water by close mesh netting. They will only add to the decaying matter in the water.
2 The white flowers of the Water Hawthorn, Aponogeton distachys.
3 A small formal water garden in south Devon is built into the terrace.

A rock and water garden constructed of Westmorland stone, makes an informal setting for alpine and water plants. Clear surface debris before it decays.

nuisance than a help to fish in the autumn and winter. They become virtually inactive as oxygen-producers, but contribute to the production of toxic gases as the bulk of their growth decays. The fish need far less oxygen during the sluggish winter months, and will get all they need from absorption through the water surface.

This necessary tidying up and removal of dead or dying vegetation must not be confused with the renovating process of lifting, splitting up and replanting. That, for aquatic plants, is essentially a late spring job and it must never be done in the autumn. It will certainly do no harm to aquatic plants *in containers* to be lifted out of the pool or moved about *in their containers* if this makes it easier to get at decaying material—disturbance of the roots and soil must be avoided at this season.

It will not be long before falling water temperatures make fish less active, less willing to feed, and less capable of digesting food. This makes it all the more important that they should be given now, while they still have hearty appetites, as much food as they are ready to accept. But it must be good nutritious stuff to build them up for the cold months. The high-protein type of floating pellet food, chopped earthworm, and a weekly pinch or two of Bemax, will do far more good that bread, biscuit meal or 'ant's eggs'.

With winter approaching and fish fry in the pool, it is tempting to suppose that it would be safer for them to be carefully netted out and kept through the cold weather in an indoor tank. It is doubtful if this is worthwhile except for the dedicated fish-breeder who knows the pitfalls.

Apart from the extreme difficulty of netting fry, the operation will only be successful if the fish suffer no abrupt change of temperature when transferred from—and eventually back to—the pool, and experience no considerable change in the chemical content of the water; if the tank is well oxygenated (the higher temperature maintained in an indoor tank through the winter means both that the fish will be active and need oxygen and that oxygenators will grow and oxygenate); if the fish are fed with sieved hard-boiled egg yolk or other fry food and if the tank is not overcrowded and is kept scrupulously clean.

Even with all this care, fry have been known to die wholesale for no very obvious reason. If this sort of thing is going to happen, it is probably better that it happens in the pool where it will not be so distressingly obvious. If fry are $1\frac{1}{2}$ inches or more, leave them in the pool where their chances are pretty good, particularly if there is a pool heater to take care of the ice. If they are smaller than $1\frac{1}{2}$ inches, and you are devoted to them, then try the indoor tank—but do not expect too much.

Wildlife

With September comes the change from summer to autumn. In the garden, reds and browns dominate the lush summer greens. Not only do the trees' leafy coverings change colour in autumn, but so do the coats of many animals and birds.

Many mammals grow a winter coat, thicker and warmer than that necessary in summer. Two interesting examples stand out, the first more common in many gardens than rare sightings would suggest. It is the stoat, the big cousin of the weasel. Despite vicious persecution this animal is still a shy but common inhabitant of woodlands and a useful resident of stone walls, keeping down the

The Stoat's summer coat is rusty brown with a white chest. But during the autumn it begins to turn pure white—the perfect camouflage in the snows.

1

mouse population. His coat of rusty brown, with white belly and black tipped tail, turns to one of pure white in autumn, though retaining the black tipped tail.

The 'blue' or 'Scottish' hare, as camouflage against the highland snows, also changes to a white coat in winter. This change of coat colour is not confined to animals alone, for the common starling's plumage is tipped with white in winter.

The badger, whose coat merely thickens, is preparing for the winter in another way. Into his deep underground chamber he drags fresh bracken as bedding. A trail of this bedding can often be followed to his earth.

As if to show, however, that winter is not yet with us, the adder gives birth to its brood of vipers. Its young, unlike most other reptiles, are born alive, covered only by a thin membrane that is usually broken at birth.

In September any repairs or replacements for the bird table should be carried out. Probably the best type of table is one with a roof, and an area about 18 inches square. This table has the advantage that it can be mounted on a pole or suspended from a branch and thus moved about the garden. It should always be placed high enough to be out of the reach of cats, rats or other predators of birds

Food on the bird table should be increased in quantity and contain added fats to give warmth and energy to migrants using the garden as a resting place before their long journey. A constant food supply on the bird table will both draw birds to the garden during winter and keep them fat and healthy in the harder days that are to come. Early supplies create the habit of regular visits.

2

1 It is at this time of the year that the Adder gives birth to its brood of Vipers. They are born, not laid as eggs.
2 September is a good time to introduce a bird table into the garden.

The Month of October

Autumn, season of falling leaves and faltering sun, is a time of copper tints and subtle colours. In October, shrubs and trees take on a new look. Their last fling before winter's onslaught is one of the most attractive aspects of the gardener's calendar

The glowing autumn colours of the Beech tree are some compensation for the faded brilliance of the summer garden.

1

2

3

1 The autumn colours taken on by the foliage of Acers are as gay and bright as those of any tree or shrub. Here the Acer Glade at Westonbirt Arboretum, Gloucestershire, displays the wide range of leaf tints.
2 Parthenocissus tricuspidata veitchii, the Virginian Creeper, a prolific clinging climber that can seemingly change the colour of a building in the autumn.
3 Vitis amurensis, another deciduous clinging climber that is enriched by its glorious autumn colour.

1

2

3

1 All the Cotoneasters are invaluable for garden decoration in the autumn. Cotoneaster aldenemensis carries its berries in bold bunches.
2 Rose hips of varying form and size can be seen on bush Roses in October. Many of these make attractive and useful additions to floral arrangements indoors. Rosa canina, the fruits of the Wild Rose, are shown here.
3 Berberises are still bearing colourful berries in October, mostly in shades of red, orange and purple. Here the Common Barberry, Berberis vulgaris, has beautiful orange-red berries.

1

2

3

1 Horse Chestnut, Aesculus hippocastanum. This is a tree which most people can recognise by its distinctive 'conker' fruits. The nuts are of polished brown, encased in thick, spikey coats which split to reveal the fruit.
2 The bright red globular and shining fruits of Rosa sherardii follow the single pink summer flowers, and last on the bush quite well.
3 Later, these fruits of Arbutus unedo, the Strawberry Tree, will turn red.

1

2

3

1 Nerine bowdenii, a bulbous plant from South Africa, blooms throughout the late summer, and also well into the autumn when protected under glass.
2 Schizostyllis coccinea gigantea, the Kaffir Lily, or Crimson Flag, another South African bulbous plant which flowers out of doors in Britain during September and October.
3 Nerine undulata, a good plant for the cool greenhouse, where it flowers during October and November.

1 Maranta erythrophyllum has striking oval leaves which have pink veins and pink stems.
2 Maranta leuconeura kerchoveana is an attractive plant with dark purple-black blotches on its slightly glaucous green leaves.
3 The Crotons (their popular name) are really Codiaeums and here Codiaeum variegatum, of which there are numerous forms, shows the wide range of leaf colour.

1

2

3

1

2

3

1 Of all the ornamental grasses the Cortaderia is the most handsome and the large silver plumes of flower are at their best in October. Cortaderia argentea is seen here at Sheffield Park, Sussex.
2 Among the herbaceous perennials Physalis alkekengi (syn. P. franchettii), popularly known as Winter Cherry, or Chinese Lantern, is most colourful in autumn. Its papery lantern-like fruit case encloses an orange berry.
3 Cortaderia 'Sunningdale Silver'.

Jobs of the month

Many jobs begun last month should be completed now. Ensure that the fruit store is in good condition, ready to receive apples and pears. This is the time of the year, too, for overhauling the herbaceous borders—and for constructing paths, patios and terraces. Summer may be over, but there is still much to be done before winter sets in

Bulbs

Lift half-hardy summer-flowering bulbs, clean and store. Gladioli foliage should be cut down as it begins to turn yellow. Lift, clean and store the corms.

Hedges

New spring-planted beech, hornbeam, quickthorn and privet should be drastically cut back to encourage a hedge with a well-clothed base.

Paths, Walls and fences

When choosing paving materials always bear in mind that a terrace or wall should complement the house.

Shrubs, trees and climbers

There are many shrubs, trees and climbers that can be planted now to provide autumn and winter colour for years to come.

Flowers for Cutting

Polythene bag 'sleeves' will protect branches laden with berries. The berries will then stay plump for Christmas decorations. Gather gourds as soon as they are ripe.

Herbaceous Plants

If the herbaceous border is ready for an overhaul, remove all plants, divide them, then dig deep and manure the ground. Label plants with their height and colour before lifting.

Patios, Balconies, Roof Gardens and Window Boxes

Take steps to minimise the effect of rain, frost and snow on your plants. Protect plants against winter winds Clear all drainage holes.

Vegetables

The main work this month is preparing the soil for next year's crops. Think about rotational cropping. Finish lifting and storing all roots. Protect cauliflower heads from sharp frosts.

Fruit

Make preparation for the fruit planting. season. When all blackberries have been picked, cut fruited canes down to soil level.

Houseplants

Now is the time to consider what colour you can bring into your home during winter months. African violets for instance, given the right conditions, will flower almost continuously.

Rock Gardens

Now is the time to construct troughs and rock-beds. Clear peat gardens and walls of all dead foliage.

Water Gardens

October is a good time for planting waterside perennials. Remove leaves from pond. The job of extending water gardens or constructing waterfalls and cascades should ideally be done now.

Greenhouse

Remove tender pot plants from frames into the greenhouse. Allow gloxinias and tuberous begonias to die down after flowering until stems and foliage can be easily removed. Store the tubers.

Lawns

The last mowing this month should be no more than a light 'tipping' of the grass blades. Treat the lawn against worms. Sort out the bumps or hollows now.

Roses

Test and, where necessary, renew stakes and ties. Prepare ground for delivery of new roses. Allow soil to settle and consolidate before planting.

Wildlife

Hedgehogs still wandering abroad can be taken home, fattened up and encouraged to spend the winter in the garden if provided with a box for hibernation.

Bulbs

The bulb planting continues this month for forced flowers both indoors and in the greenhouse and out of doors. Aim to have the work completed by the end of the month. Tulips, however, can safely wait until November.

Tubs, window-boxes, large pots and other containers can be planted up out of doors with narcissi, tulips, eranthis, muscari and erocuses for a spring display. It is a good idea to incorporate a little bonemeal in the compost. This acts slowly and will provide food material when the flower buds are forcing through the necks of the bulbs.

The bulbous irises and species crocuses do well in troughs, sink gardens and raised beds and can be put in now if they have not been planted earlier.

Plant up more pots and bowls this month. If a plunge bed cannot be provided out of doors, keep the bowls indoors in the coolest place possible. Put each bowl in a black polythene parcel and cover it with a sheet of stout brown paper, or several sheets of newspaper to exclude the light. Examine the bowls from time to time and continue to keep the fibre moist—never let it dry out. Plants plunged out of doors, should not need to be examined too often.

The method of wrapping the bowl in black polythene is the best way of keeping *Narcissus* 'Paper White' in the dark when the bulbs are planted among pebbles covered with water in a shallow bowl. The level of the water needs to be maintained while the bulbs are in the dark. Similarly, hyacinths grown in a hyacinth glass can be kept in the dark by covering with black polythene in a cool cupboard until they are ready to be brought into the light later in the year.

Finish planting spring-flowering bulbs in the garden and those best put in this month are alliums, ornathogalums and puschkinias.

In the greenhouse, keep the young growth of *Cyclamen persicum* sprayed over with soft water and encourage steady leaf formation now. *Nerine bowdenii* may still be in flower in pots, but reduce the water gradually as the growth dies down to rest the plants until next spring. Repot when necessary—about once in four years—during October.

New nerine bulbs will be delivered from the merchants now. Pot them up singly into a 4-inch pot or putting two or three into a 6-inch pot in a rich coarse compost. Where nerines are planted out of doors, probably at the base of a sunny wall, put some litter or other protective material over the crowns to prevent frost damage. Those in tubs and other containers can be brought into the greenhouse to be rested during the winter.

Once Gladiolus corms have dried off a little cut away the old roots, and cut away the top growth by making a clean cut in the stem close to the head of the corm with sharp secateurs. Remove the old withered corms from the base of the young corms.

Lift the half-hardy summer flowering bulbs like ixiolirion, sparaxis, acidanthera and ixia and dry them off immediately. Do not leave any soil or old roots adhering and rub away the outer papery scales before storing them in a dry cool, but frost-proof, place. Keep one kind separate from another and label them. It is best to store them in single layers in shallow boxes.

Once the foliage of gladioli begins to turn yellow, start to lift these corms and cut away the stems and old roots with sharp secateurs. Rub the corms free of soil and debris and leave them to dry off for a couple of weeks before storing them in a cool place, in labelled batches. The storage conditions of all bulbs and corms through the winter is of the utmost importance. It must be dry and frost free. If the temperature is too high, the corms will shrivel and where there is dampness in the atmosphere the corms will rot.

Make a habit of looking over bulbs and corms in store throughout the coming months and remove any that are decaying, to prevent the spread of disease. Precautions should be taken to prevent mice from finding stored bulbs and corms.

Flowers for Cutting

Berries of all shapes, colours and sizes abound, crying out to be used with the vividly coloured flowers of the month—perennial asters, border chrysanthemums, dahlias and, of course, the autumn leaves.

Many people would like to keep the berried shrubs indoors for several months. Most of them will last on the tree, if the birds do not eat them, but so far no one has found a satisfactory way of preserving them so that they remain plump and well-coloured. Branches can be saved for special occasions, even until Christmas, by pulling a polythene bag over the branch and fastening it tightly at the stem end.

It is possible to keep hips and coton-

If berries are needed for indoor decoration, they can be protected from the attacks of birds and wasps by covering individual sprays with a plastic bag.

easter and pyracantha berries plump a little longer after they have been cut by giving them glycerine solution. They should stand in the solution for two or three days. Some people dip the berries in shellac or colourless varnish, both of which will help to delay shrivelling. One answer to the problem is to cut extra branches and stand them in water out of doors, covered by wire netting against the birds. Berries keep plump longer this way than in dry houses and the stems can be brought indoors as they are needed.

If they are to be dried the gay physalis, or Chinese lanterns, should be gathered now and not left to spoil in the autumn rains and frosts. Cut the stems as soon as the first or lowest lanterns have turned colour—the remainder will turn while the stems are drying. The leaves should be removed from the tip and stems with scissors. Cut the tip away so that the stem seems to terminate naturally with the top lantern.

The stems can be arranged immediately, for they will continue to dry after arrangement. Alternatively, they can be made into small bunches, three or four stems to each, and tied together not only at the stem ends but also two or three times up the stem between the lanterns. If this is not done the stems will curve during drying and may be very difficult to arrange later. Hang them upside down in the manner recommended for drying other plant materials.

Gourds should be gathered as soon as they are ripe and before the frosts. The riper they are, the harder the external skin and the better they will keep. They should be handled with great care, for a knock now will bruise the fruits and cause them to rot.

Gather them with as much stem as possible. Often after drying some gourds shed this stem but it is retained by others and it makes mounting for arrangement much simpler. The skin is very tough and it is not easy to puncture it. Sometimes it is better to make the puncture in the side of the gourd which can then be displayed at an angle which shows its full shape.

However, gourds do not necessarily have to be mounted to be decorative. A bowl of them heaped on attractive leaves or made into a byzantine cone by building them up from circles of the largest specimens to the smallest, with a round paper mat between each layer, looks as attractive as anything elese.

Now is the time to skeletonise leaves. Select only tough-textured kinds such as magnolia, lime, some maples, pear and holly. Make sure that all are perfect specimens. A blotch on a leaf will not disappear. Place them in buckets or tubs of rain water.

The leaves should be kept in the water until it is impure. The bacteria in the water will break down the tissues of the outer skins of the leaves. Top up with rain water when necessary. After a few weeks see if the skin slips from its skeleton when handled. If it does, the leaf is ready. Remove the leaf, place it in a bowl, pour boiling water over it. When the water has cooled separate the skin very gently. Lay the revealed skeleton on newspaper to drain and dry. These skeletonised leaves can be bleached by soaking them in a solution of ordinary domestic bleach and water.

Fruit

This is the month when most of the late-keeping apples and pears are ready to pick (a very few may not be ready until November). Although these fruits may not be at their best for eating until mid-winter or even early spring, the same test for ripeness for picking applies as for the early and mid-season fruits: do not pick until the fruit parts company from the spur quite readily when you lift it without squeezing in the palm of your hand to a horizontal position.

The fruit store should be made ready to receive the new season's crop by scrubbing down racks and shelves with copper sulphate solution (1 ounce per gallon of water) or a hot strong solution of washing soda (1 lb per gallon of water).

The fruit store should be dark and an earthen floor helps to maintain equable conditions of humidity. Apples, however, require a somewhat moister atmosphere and a lower temperature than pears (ideally, between 37–40°F or 3–4°C). The temperature for pears should be 40°F (4°C) and, although conditions should be slightly drier than for apples, they should not be completely dry.

If possible, pick the late keepers in dry weather when the fruit itself is dry. Where this is impossible, lay the fruit out to dry before storing. In any case it is advisable to lay apples on a floor for a couple of days to sweat before they are put in the fruit store.

If you like well-coloured apples, an extra blush can be given to their cheeks by 'sun-dewing'. Pick at the usual time and then spread outdoors in a single layer on sacks or plastic. See that they are exposed to sun, but not wind, and arrange some kind of netting defence against birds.

Three weeks of exposure to dew by

1 When the fruit is ready to be picked hold it firmly, but do not squeeze. Bruised fruit will soon begin to rot. A test of ripeness: the stem should come away with the Pear—not remain on the tree.
2 Hold Apples in the palm of the hand and gently lift and twist to take them from the tree.

night and sun by day will increase the skin colour pigment. When the apples are dry bring them in and store in the usual way.

If you can, wrap apples individually in oiled-paper wraps before storing. Newspaper wraps are better than nothing, for wrapped apples keep better and if any do rot the infection cannot spread to adjacent fruits. An adaptation of the same idea is to put the apples in a polythene sleeve, separating each fruit with a rubber band.

An idea which has been tried with some success is to put apples (all of the same variety) in a polythene bag (not too thick: 150 gauge is ideal) and then to tie the mouth of the bag round a pencil, finally withdrawing the pencil so that a small opening is left. This imitates, in a rough and ready way, the commercial grower's gas store: as the apples ripen they give off carbon dioxide and as the concentration rises in the bag so the ripening process is slowed down. Some oxygen, however, is essential—hence the pencil hole.

Wrapping is unsuitable for pears because they ripen somewhat erratically and must be inspected more frequently. Lay them on shelves or racks, singly so that they do not touch their neighbours. Test pears for readiness by pressing the neck, very gently so that no bruising results. To bring out the flavour pears should be taken into a warm room, temperature about 65°F (18°C), for a couple of days before they are required.

Plant perpetual fruiting strawberries provided the soil is dry enough to work well. On heavy clay soils and in very cold districts (where early frosts may lift newly planted strawberries) it is preferable to ask for spring delivery. Set the plants 18 inches apart and position the rows 30 inches apart.

Plant grape vines late this month or early in November. If you receive the vine in a pot, break the latter to avoid damaging the roots.

Make preparations for the fruit planting season but do not make planting holes in advance. Buy and prepare stakes and order fastening materials. Patent plastic ties are excellent because they are adjustable and slightly elastic. Fix horizontal wires in readiness for fan-trained trees.

After the fruit has been picked, prune blackberries. Cut the fruited canes down to soil level and replace with the new growths, spreading them out over the available space.

Where the tips of shoots on blackberries or hybrid berries have been buried in the soil to root and form new plants, sever these now from the parent plants, but do not transfer to their fruiting quarters until next month.

To propagate black currants, insert 12-inch cuttings of well-ripened current season's growth. Plant the cuttings 4 inches deep in threes at 3-foot intervals in rows 6 feet apart, in the place where they are to fruit.

To propagate red currants and gooseberries plant cuttings about mid-month. These should be well-ripened shoots, 9 inches long after removal of unripened tips. Remove all but top four buds and plant 4 inches deep and 6 inches apart in a slit trench bottomed with sand.

Greenhouse

It is no longer safe to leave tender pot plants in frames, even with extra protection, so get them in as soon as possible. But first clean the pots and give the plants a thorough spraying against insect pests.

To keep these and other plants safe, heating will have to be used from now on. A temperature of 45°F (7°C) is adequate for such subjects as cinerarias, *Primula malacoides,* freesias and the greenhouse calceolarias. For cyclamen and *Primula obconica* a temperature of 55°F (13°C) is more suitable, although the plants will come along more slowly in cooler conditions.

Given the temperature mentioned (and maximum light for the cyclamen) these last two plants may be watered liberally but in a lower temperature the compost should be allowed to become almost dry before soaking it thoroughly, preferably from underneath. Cinerarias, *Primula malacoides* and calceolarias should also be watered in this way. Although dryness is unlikely to harm them, unless carried to extremes, one over-watering may kill them.

Cacti and most succulents need even less water—one soaking a month is more than adequate. Only enough heat to keep frost out is needed for them but the Christmas cactus *(Zygocactus truncatus)* does better in a temperature of about 60°F (16°C) with enough water to keep it evenly moist.

Where dormant plants of the tender *Azalea indica* have been ordered they should be delivered at any time now. If they are not already in pots make sure that the soil-ball on the roots is quite moist, then set each plant in a pot just large enough to take it, with a lime-free mixture such as 2 parts peat and 1 of sand being worked in firmly round the roots. Give a thorough watering with lime-free water (rainwater if necessary) then keep the plants in a temperature of about 50°F (10°C) and allow them to dry a little before giving more water.

Continue to pot up hyacinths, tulips and narcissi (including daffodils) and the smaller bulbs. Make sure that those in bowls under cover are kept adequately moist in a dark, airy place.

Some of the other bulbous subjects will be going to rest now. Gloxinias and tuberous begonias, for instance, should be allowed to die down gradually after flowering until the old stems and foliage can be easily removed. Begonia tubers should then be stored quite dry in a cool but frostproof place, while the gloxinias should be stored in a temperature of at least 50°F (10°C). Store the small tubers of achimenes in the same way as gloxinias. Hippeastrums should be left in their pots and kept perfectly dry in cool, airy conditions.

Some of the perennial bedding plants such as geraniums, fuchsias, heliotropes and gazanias will also need storing now. If they are left outside much longer they may be damaged by frost. The geraniums (zonal pelargoniums) may be placed close together in boxes of light soil. They should be kept almost dry in a frostproof place through the winter. Fuchsias may be similarly dealt with or potted up singly, with just enough winter watering to keep them alive. Heliotropes are best potted and stored in a temperature of at least 50°F (10°C). Gazanias, too, are best potted singly, but if kept almost dry

1

2

1 Most Cacti can manage with very little water now, but Zygocactus truncatus needs moderate water and a constant temperature of 60°F (16°C).
2 Zonal Pelargoniums need to be lifted and brought into the greenhouse for the winter. These are the leaves of Pelargonium 'Mrs H. Cox'.

1 Berberis x stenophylla provides a really decorative and impenetrable hedge. The glorious yellow flowers which colour the hedge in early summer are followed by berries.
2 x Cupressocyparis leylandii is a plant which can be relied upon to make a hedge quickly.

these only need enough heat to keep frost away.

Cuttings of all these plants will probably be well rooted by now and ready for boxing or potting for storage in the same way as the old plants.

Complete the housing of pot-grown chrysanthemums as soon as possible and make sure they have plenty of fresh air circulating around them, with just enough heat to keep frost away. Water thoroughly when the soil dries on the surface. Disbudding will still have to be carried out on the later varieties if large blooms are required, while feeding should be carried out until the blooms are almost ready for cutting.

Hybrid tea roses for pot culture are best potted this month. Set each one in a 7-inch pot with good drainage beneath a compost of good soil with a little old manure and enough coarse sand to keep the mixture open. A little bonemeal added to this mixture will also help. After potting, water the plants in, then stand them in the open until early next year, when they may be brought in for gentle forcing.

Cuttings of violas, pansies, bedding calceolarias, antirrhinums and penstemons may still be taken, while those that have already rooted should be grown on in conditions as cool and airy as the weather will permit.

From now on plants need all the light they can get so remove any shading and clean the glass. Keep the air in the greenhouse as dry as possible and do all watering in the morning so that the plants are fairly dry at night.

Hedges

As well as being one of the best months of the year for planting evergreen or conifer hedges, October is the time when deciduous hedging plants should be given their final trim of the season. New spring-planted hedges of vigorous growth such as beech, hornbeam and quickthorn—and, of course, the much-maligned privet—should be cut back to about 18 inches from ground level. Other less rampant subjects should have only a light pruning.

The drastic cutting back of the former shrubs will produce a hedge that is well-clothed at its base. More mature hedges should be clipped so that they taper slightly from bottom to top. A broad-based hedge with sloping sides is much less likely to suffer damage after heavy falls of snow.

When planting a new hedge, it cannot be too often stressed that the planting site should be well and deeply dug and provided with as much humus-rich material as can be spared.

It should also be wide enough to accommodate the ultimate spread of the hedge. If the latter is adjacent to a lawn, extra width must be provided so that the mower can cut right to the edge of the grass without falling foul of the hedge itself and damaging it.

Suitable hedging evergreens include the round-leaved and Portugal laurels, *Lonicera nitida*, the shrubby honeysuckle—*L. fertilis* is a newer and better variety than the type—box and holly. Autumn, however, is not the best time for planting a holly hedge—it does better if it goes in during April or May.

Berberis stenophylla and *B. darwinii*, as well as being evergreen, both make excellent flowering hedges. Evergreen berrying hedges are attractive as well and *Cotoneaster lactea* and most of the pyracanthas, or firethorns are useful subjects for this purpose.

For a hedge that flowers in winter as well as being evergreen there could hardly be a better choice than *Viburnum tinus*, better-known perhaps as laurustinus. The bud clusters, pink before the flowers open, begin to colour in January. They remain attractive until they open fully into beautiful white flowers in March and April.

One of the fastest growing conifers for hedge planting is x *Cupressocyparis leylandii*, a cross between *C. macrocarpa* and *C. nootkatensis*. Slower-growing, but more attractive, perhaps is the variety of *Chamaecyparis lawsoniana* known as 'Green Hedger' whose foliage, of a rich bright green, makes a particularly interesting hedge.

Herbaceous Plants

Every four or five years, herbaceous

Hebeloma crustuliniforme. Fairy cakes, often found growing in grassy clearings in the woods or on heathland. The caps are somewhat slimy to the touch and smell like radish but should not be eaten.

Amanita phalliodes. The death cap, so named because it is deadly poisonous, though no ill effect is experienced for some twelve hours after eating it – by which time it is too late. It is found mainly in beech woods.

Boletus erythropus. Usually found in coniferous woods and recognised by the reddish-brown spotted appearance of the stem. When broken the yellow flesh turns blue, purple, or even red quite quickly. It is not poisonous, but may have unpleasant consequences if eaten.

RECOGNITION CHART

Fungi

The mushroom is not the only edible fungus. The ones below can all be eaten. The ones above are strictly for looking at

Morchella esculenta. Morel, unlike the other fungi illustrated, is one which appears in spring, especially where a wood fire has been burned. The cap is club-shaped and criss- crossed with pale brown ridges.

Craterellus cornucopioides. Horn of plenty is found mostly in association with beech trees. It is of an agreeable flavour and can be dried and keeps well when stored.

Cantharellus cibarius. The funnel-shaped cap of the chanterelle is egg yellow in colour and smells of apricots. It is a delicacy and cooks well.

Lactarius torminosus. Woolly milk cap is found on heathland where birch trees flourish. This fungus has a hollow centred cap and is shaggy along the margin. A white peppery milk exudes when the fungus is broken.

Russula emetica. Sickener, so named because the acid taste of this fungus is persistent to the point of sickness. The bright red skin can be peeled from the cap easily. It is associated mainly with coniferous woods.

Amanita muscaria. Fly agaric found on poor soils and in birch woods and pine woods. It is poisonous but unlikely to prove fatal. Frequently the little brown patches appear to get rubbed off or washed away by rain. One of the oldest known fungi.

Boletus edulis. Among the best edible fungi it has a nutty flavour. The chief characteristic is the small rounded cap and wide stem in the young stage. The colour of the cap varies from pale amber to brown, according to the weather and situation.

Lactarius deliciosus. Saffron milk cap has brittle flesh which, when broken, exudes a saffron coloured milk which quickly turns to orange and emits an acid odour. The fungus is edible but not as delicious as its name might imply.

Fistulina hepatica. Langue de boeuf, or beefsteak fungus, is a bracket-like fungus, usually found on oak trees. It has a fruity aroma but acid flavour. The rich brown rot it causes to the wood of its host renders the tree valuable to the cabinet maker as 'brown oak'.

1

2

1 Now is the time to take root cuttings of Oriental Poppies. 'Plant' each piece in sandy compost in a seed pan. Cuttings should be about 1½ inches in length.
2 A one-colour border of herbaceous perennials can look very attractive indeed. But this is the kind of border that needs careful planning.

borders need overhauling. Lift and divide most plants in late autumn and deep dig and manure the ground. Paeonies are an exception to the rule. They resent disturbance so, unless they appear to be sickly, these lovely plants should not be moved.

Where farmyard manure is not available, ordinary garden soil can be enriched with hop manure, rotted vegetable compost, seaweed, or wool shoddy, digging it into the lower spit and adding bonemeal to the top spit. Some soils—clay, for instance—require slightly different treatment; compost, strawy manure or horticultural peat, together with sharp sand, should be worked into the top spit as well as the lower spit to help drainage and improve the soil texture.

Large borders should be tackled in sections, completing one part at a time so that the plants are not left out of the ground too long.

If it's your first experience of renovating a border, it pays to label the plants with their height and colour before lifting. Perennials are most effective when planted in groups of three or more of a kind or variety—not in straight lines but with the taller plants mainly at the back of a one-sided border (centre of an island border) with a few drifting towards the front to break up the contours. Plan for colour blending or contrast, arranging the plants according to season of blooming so that one group takes over from another.

One-coloured borders can be attractive, all white or all blue flowers being the popular choice, as a rule. White perennials for a feature of this kind could include: *Phlox* 'White Admiral' (2½ feet); Madonna lilies *(Lilium candidum,* 4 feet); *Chrysanthemum maximum* 'Wirral Supreme' (3 feet); *Achillea* 'The Pearl' (3 feet); *Gypsophila* 'Bristol Fairy' (3 feet); *Delphinium* 'Swanlake' (5–6 feet); *Paeonia* 'Duchesse de Nemours' (3 feet); *Pyrethrum parthenium* 'White Bonnet' (3 feet); *Pyrethrum* 'Avalanche' (2 feet); *Tradescantia* 'Osprey' (18 inches); *Geranium pratense alba plena* (2 feet); Christmas rose *(Helleborus niger,* 12 inches); *Campanula glomerata nana alba* (15 inches); *Astilbe praecox alba* (18 inches); *Aster* 'Snowsprite' (Michaelmas daisy) (12 inches) and *Dianthus* 'White Ladies Improved' (12 inches).

True blues are not so easy to find, but the following should provide a good framework for a blue border; *Delphinium* 'Capri' (sky-blue, 3 feet); *Delphinium* 'Naples' (3 feet); *Centaurea montana* (1½–2 feet); *Campanula persicifolia* 'Carillon' (3 feet); *Aster* 'Jean' (2–3 feet) and *Aster* 'Marie Ballard' (Michaelmas daisies) (3–4 feet); *Anchusa azurea* 'Little John' (2 feet); *Brunnera macrophylla* (18 inches); *Agapanthus* 'Dorothy Palmer' (2–2½ feet); *Eryngium tripartium* (3 feet): *Geranium pratense* 'Johnson's Blue' (18 inches); *Gentiana septemfida gigantea* (9 inches); *Iris* 'Black Magic' (3 feet); *Linum narbonnense* (1½ feet); *Tradescantia* 'Kreisler' (2 feet); *Veronica spicata* 'Blue Peter' (1½–2 feet) and *Viola* 'Lassie' (9 inches). In time, the enthusiast will collect many other beauties, among them the glorious blue poppy from Tibet *(Meconopsis betonicifolia,* 3–4 feet high) which should be grown in half shade, in moist loamy soil enriched with rotted manure and leafmould.

Spacing depends on the ultimate height and vigour of a plant. As a rough guide, leave 9–12 inches between low-growing plants, 12–18 inches between medium height plants, 2 feet between tall plants.

The majority of hardy perennials in a herbaceous border can be cut down close to the ground when the tops begin to wither. Remove any weeds and lightly fork over the soil. Deep digging is not advisable as it disturbs the plant roots but, after loosening the soil, it is a good idea to apply a 3 inch mulch of rotted manure to the surface.

Cuttings of penstemon should be struck at once if they are to grow into strong flowering plants by next year. Choose young side shoots, 3–4 inches long, inserting them in boxes or pans of sandy soil in a cold frame. Root-cuttings of oriental poppies *(Papaver orientale)* and anchusa can still be taken, too. The long thong-like roots should be divided into sections 2–3 inches in length, making a slanting cut at the base of each piece to ensure that the cuttings are planted the right way up. Plant with the tops just covered, in boxes of sandy compost, placed in a greenhouse or frame.

Most of the summer and autumn flowering bedding plants—petunias, antirrhinums, asters, dahlias and stocks—should be cleared by the end of the month to make way for spring flowering biennials such as wallflowers, forget-me-nots, polyanthus etc. Where wire-worms have given trouble, dress the ground with Gamma-BHC dust, working it into the top 4 inches of soil before planting.

Gladioli should be lifted from the middle to the end of October, shaking the corms free of soil and cutting back the stems to within a few inches of the crowns, before spreading them to dry in a cool, airy place. Leave for four to six weeks then remove the outer husks and store the crowns in bags or boxes in a frost-proof room.

Dahlias should also be lifted as soon as the tops are cut down by frost, cleaning off the surplus soil before storing in boxes of peat or sand, in a cool frost-proof place.

Any tuberous-rooted begonias grown outdoors can be lifted and stored in precisely the same way as the dahlias.

House Plants

House plants by their very nature should be able to live quite happily through the winter and to fulfill their decorative function during the whole of this time. But they give very little attractive or striking colour, so it is well at this time of year to leave them to their placid and undramatic role and to bring into the home the few plants which will bring added colour and drama.

An unusual and vividly flowered house plant which, with care, will produce its long lasting flowers not only in autumn and winter but almost the whole year through is the *Anthurium scherzerianum,* known variously and popularly as the palette plant, piggy tail plant and flamingo flower because of the unusual shape and colour of its flowers, seldom more than two or three of which appear on the plant at the same time. The flower is actually the 'piggy tail', the pale yellow or white spadix that arises from the vivid scarlet, pink or cream spathe. The secret with this plant is to give it plenty of moisture at all times and a special degree of humidity.

The leaves of Aphelandra squarrosa are dramatically striped and the flowers appear in the cockscomb of bracts. This attractive house plant is the ideal choice for a modern room setting.

The special added humidity demanded by the anthurium can be quite simply provided by using what has become known as the deep dish method. Take a bowl with a circumference roughly the same as the leaves of the plant and in its base place a saucer upside down. Stand the plant pot on the saucer and pour into the bowl sufficient water to reach just to

Plants which demand humidity, such as Anthurium, can be given moist conditions by standing the pot on a saucer in a dish of water. The evaporating water creates a humid atmosphere.

the top of the saucer, immediately below the base of the flower pot. The evaporating water from the bowl will surround the foliage of the plant with a microclimate of healthy humidity. In addition it is helpful to give the plant a light spray of clean water two or three times a week.

There are several varieties of winter flowering begonias which are also worth growing. These produce red, white or pink flowers in great profusion and with care the flowers will continue right through the winter. The plant is so easy to grow and to propagate that several can be kept growing at different stages of development to give a constant succession of bloom. Feed well and do not over-water.

The dramatic stripe-leaved aphelandra with its reddish-gold cockscomb is another good winter flowering house plant which, with normal care, will last a long time. The most easily obtained variety is *Aphelandra squarrosa leopoldii.*

The plant's leaves are lance-shaped, with the midribs cream coloured against the dark green background. The plant must be really pot-bound before it will produce the colourful golden bracts at its top. Aphelandra should also be kept moist at the roots and given generous humidity. The pot should either be plunged in moist peat or the deep-dish method of providing humidity can be employed.

The tender, beautiful and exasperating saintpaulia or African violet is another plant which will provide flowers during the winter. Some plants will flower almost the whole year through, giving continuously and lavishly of the dainty purple, blue, pink or white flowers double or single. Other plants, which have been given exactly the same treatment and indeed stood beside the first plant, will fail to flower or may even die. This is one reason why the plant is exasperating, for theories abound and methods of treatment vary widely, some methods being successful with some plants and failing with others. All that is generally agreed is that the saintpaulia demands clean air and that any degree of gas in the atmosphere will kill it.

The plant likes moist but not wet soil, an occasional feed, a moderately humid atmosphere, good but not strong light and moderate warmth. Few house plants can be lovelier when in good condition. They are inexpensive and saintpaulia devotees who fail to grow them successfully can easily and cheaply buy constant replacements.

Lawns

Unless the weather is exceptionally mild, the growth of lawn grasses will virtually cease during this month. In all probability, only three to four mowings will be necessary, and the last of these should be nothing more than a light 'tipping' of the grass blades.

This infrequent mowing with the cutter blades set high applies equally to both established lawns and those raised from seed sown in August or September.

Lawn edges, too, will require a final trim of the over-hanging grass. Short or long handled edging shears can be used or, where there is a long length of lawn edge to be cut, one of the wheeled or power-driven edgers will make quick work of the job. Any major improvement of lawn edges can be left for dealing with later in the year, say December, when there is little outside garden work demanding attention.

If earthworms are still being a problem, following treatment last month, a second application of a proprietary wormkiller can be made now when the weather is mild and moist. Even if treatment against worms was not carried out in September, a first application can still be given now.

During October, diseased brown patches and areas of moss may put in an appearance. Both should be dealt with promptly, by applying a proprietary mercury compound at the rate recommended by the manufacturer. Approximately 14 days following chemical treatment, the affected areas should be raked vigorously with a spring-tined lawn rake to remove the dead growth; this should then be lifted and burnt. To encourage the grass to become green again, spiking these areas and raking in an autumn turf dressing will improve the condition of the soil.

During this month, it is still not too late, either, to re-seed any patches that are very bare of grass. Sowing should be at a rate of about 1 ounce per square yard.

The seed should be lightly raked in, the soil firmed, and the area protected from children and birds by twigs.

If a really perfect lawn is to be created from a not-too-perfect one at present, it pays to dig out any tufts of coarse grasses during October. The bare patches left by the removal of these are raked, given an autumn top dressing and then reseeded with a grass mixture similar to that of the rest of the lawn.

Any bumps or hollows in the lawn surface should also be sorted out now. Bumps tend to become bare through regular 'scalping' when lawn mowing, and hollows usually are poorly drained and the grass is never cut short enough. The result is a patchy green lawn. Heavy rolling is not the answer, unfortunately; all it tends to do is to compact the soil and make matters worse.

Very shallow depressions can be levelled out gradually by applying $\frac{1}{4}$–$\frac{1}{2}$ inch layers of equal quantities of sifted top soil, peat and sand at intervals. Usually October and April are the best months for this, though in a mild June an application can also be given.

The most effective method of levelling bumps and hollows is to cut back the turf and either remove or add soil below as necessary.

The areas of the lawn to be treated in this manner should be cut with a sharp spade or turfing iron to a depth of 2–3 inches and then, using the same implement, should be sliced underneath and the turf rolled back. Where several square yards are involved, cross cuts may be made so that the turf can be rolled back in several directions. The fewer the cuts and tears though, the better for the grass.

In the bumpy areas, remove sufficient soil from the ground so that when the turves are replaced they are level. Conversely, in areas where there are hollows, add sufficient good top soil, mixed with peat and sand, and tread it down firmly, so that the turves will be level on replacement.

After returning the turves in position,

The most effective method of levelling bumps and hollows in the lawn is to cut away the turf, correct the level of the soil, then replace the turf.
1 To remove the turf so that this work can be carried out, cut the turf in long strips and then roll them back, just as one would roll up a carpet. Lift the turf evenly with a turfing iron.
2 Add or remove compost, according to the type of lawn renovation being carried out. Rake it level.
3 Test the level to make sure it is even.
4 Gently unroll the turf, to bring it back to its original position, but now it should all be at the correct level.

1

2

3

4

tread or lightly roll them, and fill the cracks with sifted top soil or peat.

The end of October and beginning of November are the best periods for making a new lawn from turf. Preparation of the soil—its weeding, feeding, levelling and tilth—should all be completed by now and the area allowed to remain idle for a fortnight or so for the soil to settle naturally.

The turves should be laid when the soil is reasonably dry. If there is a very wet spell, or the turves are delivered before you are ready for them, do not forget that you must unroll them and spread them out to prevent the grass turning yellow.

The best method of laying the turves is to 'bond' them like bricks. Then brush in a 50/50 dressing of peat and sand along the joints and roll them lightly to ensure full contact of the roots with the soil below.

Unlike spring turfing aftercare, there is little likelihood of the grass requiring artificial watering. Nevertheless, it pays to see that the new lawn does not suffer from dryness at any time during the winter months and to water it artificially if necessary.

Paths, Fences and Walls

October is the ideal month for the construction of a terrace or patio. The winter rains and frosts have not yet begun and the creation of a terrace linking house and garden can do much to cheer the prospect during the darker days.

The main essential of a terrace is that it should be carefully and adequately paved. The choice of materials for the paving can make all the difference between merely making a paved area outside the walls of the house or creating a terrace which is an integral part of both house and garden, neither fully one nor the other but a bridge between the two. The paving material should be selected with the house in mind. If the house is constructed of brick and the paving is therefore made of the same material, the terrace will appear to be too much a part of the house. But if the major part of the terrace paving is of stone with occasional inlet panels of brick, then the terrace is a perfect compliment to the garden and the house.

Whatever the type of paving, it must be well laid, bedded in at least 2 inches of concrete, with a very slight slope away from the house towards a drain, a soakaway or a flower bed capable of accepting and dispersing the considerable quantities of rain water that will on occasion be collected by the impervious paved area. Grout out the cracks between the paving stones so that the cracks themselves are up to a quarter inch below the level of the stones. This, in effect, makes a miniature drainage

October is the month for building paths and terraces. It is essential to choose the proper paving for appearance and safety in icy conditions.

Top **An Essex garden with attractive formal rectangular paving.** *Below* **A town garden with informal paths of cemented random crazy paving stones.**

Plants in containers on the patio and terrace need some attention before the winter weather sets in. Rain will have washed away soil. Top dress with peat to raise it to the correct level. Inspect the base of the pots and clear drainage holes by pushing through with a stick from the base.

system. For some reason this also appears to mellow the appearance of the paving, making it more pleasant to the eye.

The major part of the paving should be of one material, but this can be broken up with panels of a contrasting material. Where paving plants, such as thyme, are inserted or small beds left for later planting, keep these away from the main living or walking areas. It is an essential part of a terrace that there should be space to move without encumberances, so that one may use the site as a living-room.

Any low wall around the terrace should be broken at intervals, depending of course on its length, by openings into the garden proper. There may be steps, or the garden may be on the same level, but whatever the case always extend the paved area to extend for a foot or two into the garden as this acts both as an invitation and increases the feeling that the terrace is a link between the house and the garden.

The walls should always have some growing vegetation on them, such as a climbing vine, or in them, such as sempervivums and sedums. This again helps to link the area with the garden. Containers holding evergreens carry out the same task and have the added advantage that they can provide some sort of winter colour and decoration. Containers can be moved according to season and the amount of use the terrace receives.

Patios, Balconies, Roof Gardens and Window Boxes

Frosts can be expected in October and it is important to minimise their effects and to maintain on the patio, roof garden and balcony and in our window boxes as warm and healthy a situation as is possible. There are steps we can take, apart from installing a special electrical soil heating device, to ensure that both our plants and the areas they occupy will come through the winter well.

Winter snow, frosts and rain provide an excess of moisture, not only to the roots of plants but also to their foliage through high humidity. We must make quite certain that this excess moisture drains away quickly. This is not a simple matter, for several factors are involved. In the first place, beginning literally at the roots, any plants growing in a container in heavy soil are likely to find that these roots are surrounded by moisture, this is in the form of ice and so denied to the roots. A plant can die of thirst under these circumstances. It is therefore necessary to keep soil mixtures light, open and as warm as possible. To scrape away the top inch or two of soil in a container and substitute peat helps to warm the remainder of the soil and thus the roots. This slightly warmer soil reduces the likelihood of the root ball becoming frozen.

Summer rain may have washed soil down in the containers, blocking the drainage holes. It is generally possible to open the blockage by poking a strong stick through the drainage holes in the base of the container. This will permit a flow-through of moisture which is particularly important where special decorative containers are used, for frosty conditions in the containers can frequently mean that the container cracks beyond repair.

Finally, make sure that once the water has left the pot or container it drains away quickly. At this time of year heavy falls of leaves from the trees and shrubs can be blown into corners and down drain pipes, blocking them sufficiently to delay the drainage. Water can collect and lie about long enough to do serious damage to both plants and the containers, which should be standing off the terrace floor.

Any effort expended in clearing drains and removing fallen leaves and other rubbish is doubly rewarded, for millions of dormant insects, disease spores and fungus threads can shelter in these little collections to give trouble later in the year.

Where rubbish collected from these drains is soaking and half rotted it is wise to dispose of it by burning, as this gets rid of pests and diseases. Where collections of leaves and other rubbish are comparatively dry and clean they can either be placed on the compost heap to give good humus next year, or placed around the bases of over-wintering trees and shrubs to give some protection against frosts where it will rot down and provide healthy decomposed nourishment.

Nothing can take the place of inspecting the drains and clearing the blocked drainage holes. But electricity can certainly be employed to maintain floor temperatures above freezing point. Remember, however, that soil warming cannot make spring out of winter. All it can do is hasten the season by a week or two.

The object of soil warming during winter, particularly on a patio or roof garden, should be to maintain surface temperature at slightly above freezing, so that moisture can drain away quickly and roots breathe freely. Any attempt to use soil warming to bring on early foliage, flower or blossom must be allied to an increase in day length—a difficult, expensive and delicate operation much better carried out by the professionals in their automated or computerised greenhouses.

If by some chance the winter should be dry some plants are likely to require moisture at their roots. Never give warm water to thaw the possibly frozen soil and root ball, for this can result in damage or at the best can start the plant into unseasonal growth and so render it liable to damage by the next heavy frost. Use water at just above freezing temperature so that the difference between it and normal ambient temperature is slight and unlikely to cause damage.

Where damage by winter winds is to be expected move plants to a more protected place or give them some succour by a screen. Some of the slightly more tender plants may be given additional aid from forecast frosts by a layer of peat around their roots, by plunging their containers inside a bale of straw or by using a wire netting wall around them containing bracken or straw.

It is a good idea to plant up a trough garden with several low-growing evergreen shrubs. These will provide colour and interest throughout the winter.

Rock Gardens

Over the last two decades the demand for houses has resulted in more per acre thus limiting the space for gardens. Modern architecture, too, is more formal, having a tendency to be square in outline. This can be carried forward a step by introducing rock beds, troughs and sinks in which one can grow a reasonable collection of the better rock plants which, if balanced with the popular dwarf conifers, can give at least eight months of floral display. With troughs and sinks, it is now almost impossible to obtain the real thing except at a prohibitive price, but the construction of these is well within the scope of the ordinary handyman in these do-it-yourself days and they can be tailor-made to suit any available space. Troughs, and this applies to rock beds as well, can be constructed at any time of the year except during excessively frosty weather and this month is an ideal time to carry out the operation.

The shell is made with broken paving slabs. These are purchased quite cheaply from a local builder's yard or, if desired, small pieces of walling stone can be used. The advantage of paving slab is that it is uniform in thickness and easy to lay. First, about 2 inches of cement is laid over the area of the trough. This is made with a wooden firmer laid on a piece of brown paper on a level site then filled with a mixture two parts sand to one of cement.

A drainage hole should be allowed for in one corner while the cement mix is still damp and at the same time the first layer of slabs is pressed into the cement and levelled. The succeeding layers can then be based on a small amount of cement until the necessary height is reached making sure that the top row of slabs are level. Cover the completed trough with damp sacks for three days then rough up the cement joints with a large nail. Re-cover with damp sacks for a further week, by which time the cement will have set completely.

The rock beds are nothing more than long troughs—the size depends on the space available. If they are used as an edging to a lawn or garden bed no base is required, the natural soil being used for this purpose. If sited on a patio or other similar place the existing level will become the base, but a drainage hole or holes must be left in the first row of paving slabs or whatever type and size of stone is being used to build the rock bed.

One to two inches of drainage material is required and should be well sprinkled with an insecticide powder to keep the pests to a minimum over a long period. The drainage is covered by a layer of rough peat and then the trough or bed is filled to within one inch with a compost of equal parts loam, leafmould, peat and coarse sand well mixed together.

If possible at least one month should be allowed to elapse for settlement before topping up to the original level. For shade lovers or members of the heath family, *Ericaceae*, one extra part of peat should be added. When planting, small pieces of rock stone can be added. These will add height, provide shade for roots of the plants as well as creating an artistic setting.

Plants must be small in stature and non-spreading. Fortunately there are a good number suitable for the purpose and these, used with dwarf shrubs and conifers to give height, will give colour over nine months of the year. Nurserymen's catalogues dealing with rock plants will give plenty of information on the kinds of plants suitable for these rock beds.

The Asiatic gentians are at their best just now and should be given a light watering with liquid manure. If the natural water is from a lime source the fertiliser is best mixed with rain water as the majority of Asiatic genetians resent lime.

The peat garden and walls should be cleared of all dead foliage. Dead or diseased wood should be removed, then a top dressing of well rotted leafmould or peat worked down amongst the branches. This acts as a winter mulch and protection. In all but the smallest of rock gardens, where there is more than one outcrop of rock, an alpine meadow may be made. It can be the path which is laid between the outcrops, this being removed and the existing soil forked over, enriched with peat or leafmould and then a three inch layer of chippings or gravel placed over all. Paving stones are laid at intervals to provide access but here informality should be the keynote.

Plant in the bed of gravel lots of dwarf bulbous species, such as crocus, daffodils, snowdrops, tulips, irises and other dwarf bulbs. These are then overplanted with prostrate cushion and trailing plants, thus providing a colourful picture over many months. Some of the plants that will thrive are *Arenaria balearica, A. caespitosa aurea, Artemisia splendens, Campanula pusilla* 'Hallii', *C.* 'Miss Willmott', *Dryas suendermannii, Erinus alpinus, Frankenia thymaefolia, Gypsophila repens, Hypsella reniformis, Linaria pallida, Mentha requienii, Oxalis magellanica*, varieties of *Phlox douglassi* and *P. subulata*, *Raoulia* species, *Salix herbacea* and a large number of the carpeting thymes.

Any Rose buds that are showing colour between the sepals should be cut and put in water to open indoors. If they are left on the bush they will very probably be ruined by early frosts.

Roses

If no severe frosts occur, roses will continue to flower well into this month, and there is often a surprisingly good display. Nevertheless, it is advisable to bear in mind that sharp frosts may occur at any time, and there is no point in leaving flower buds to be ruined. Any which are showing colour, with the sepals separated from the bud, may be cut at this stage for opening indoors.

October is a time when autumn gales may be expected, and it is sound practice to shorten any extra-long growths and to tie-in to their supports the long new canes on climbing and rambling types. If this is not done the winds will not only damage the long canes, but will injure nearby shoots, too. The stakes and ties of all standard and half-standard roses, as well as those of weeping standards, should also be tested and renewed as required, without waiting for the plant to be blown over.

Spraying against black spot and powdery mildew will still be necessary, to avoid a build-up of these diseases which might well carry them over into the following season. As long as the plants carry plenty of foliage they will need protection against black spot at any rate, and with rain likely to be heavier or more frequent now, it is important to ensure that the spray is renewed whenever it is washed off.

Preparation of the ground for autumn planting should begin soon. The planting itself may be undertaken later in the month, if the plants can be obtained so early from the rose nursery. Most rose specialists like to defer lifting until some natural defoliation has taken place.

Nowadays, however, new chemical defoliants are sometimes used, and the plants are 'topped' at the nursery to remove the soft autumn growth. From the customer's point of view it is better to have a hard-wooded, well-ripened plant of moderate size than a larger one comprising mainly sappy, immature wood which may not survive the winter frosts.

In preparing the site for rose planting, one should be chosen which has not grown roses at all in recent years—otherwise, the soil is likely to be 'rose-sick' and new plants will not thrive. The best plan is to double-dig the bed, making sure that the fertile top-spit remains at the top and the less fertile second-spit remains underneath.

It is quite easy to ensure this if the bed

is divided into strips, about 1–8 inches wide, and the top soil from the first strip is carried to the opposite end of the bed to be used for filling up the final strip. The sub-soil of the first strip is loosened then manure (well-rotted), compost and old chopped turf should be added.

The top soil from the second strip is then used to fill up the first strip. The sub-soil of the second strip is loosened and manure and compost are added and the top soil from the third strip used to fill up, and so on for the whole of the bed.

Additional humus-forming material, such as moist granulated peat, old hay and clean straw and such vegetable waste may be thoroughly forked in as the preparation of the bed proceeds—it should not be left as a sandwich between the top-spit and the sub-soil.

On shallow chalk soils it will be necessary to remove some of the chalk, so that there is at least 18 inches of reasonably good soil above the solid chalk. Skimping this job now will probably result in a great deal of trouble later on from lime-induced chlorosis, a disease caused by iron deficiency due to the locking up of the iron which forms an insoluble compound with the chalk and causes yellowing of the leaves and poor growth. On hungry, sandy soils every effort should be made to improve their moisture-retaining properties. This can be achieved by burying old turf (grass side downwards), leafmould, old sacks, carpets and rugs cut up into strips, old clothes, newspapers and anything else that will absorb and retain moisture.

Care should always be taken to make sure that these materials are thoroughly moist before the top soil is replaced.

On heavy clay the problem will be to open up the soil so that it does not become a sticky, impervious mass in wet weather and baked to a brick-like hardness, with wide cracks, during dry spells.

There are a number of easy methods of breaking down heavy clay. Ridging to expose the maximum surface area to the action of severe frosts is the oldest method, and this can be supplemented by forking in generous quantities of compost, granulated peat and strawy stable manure, if the latter is available. It should be emphasised that this is a gradual process, extending over many seasons. For quicker results either hydrated lime or gypsum (sulphate of lime) may be used. A heavy dressing, normally applied to the sub-soil during the process of double-digging (up to 2 lb per square yard on a very heavy clay) will materially assist in breaking up the clay and making it more porous.

After the new site has been thoroughly prepared, several weeks should be allowed for the soil to settle and consolidate before attempting to plant. In areas of high rainfall it is a good plan to cover the bed with a large tarpaulin sheet. This will ensure that the soil is not too wet when the plants are delivered at the end of the month or in early November.

Where maiden plants budded earlier are available, it is often convenient to transplant these from the nursery rows to their permanent beds during October, before the November rains have made the soil too soggy for planting. If these maiden plants should still be in full leaf, due to a mild autumn, it is wise to cut off all the leaves and flower buds before transplanting, to prevent possible shrivelling of the wood from excessive transpiration

Trees, Shrubs and Climbers

An established shrub border that ha been kept free from weeds by mulching, light hoeing and the use of cover plants will need little attention from now until spring. This is an ideal time, however, to prepare the site for a new border by double-digging or bastard trenching, working in as much humus-rich material as can be spared in the process.

If the planting of evergreens cannot be completed by the end of the month, it is better to postpone the operation until March or April of the following year. Deciduous shrubs can be planted throughout the winter, given suitable weather conditions, as they arrive from the nursery or garden centre, most of which carry stocks of the more popular shrubs suitable for the basic planting of a new border.

The newcomer to gardening may find it easier to rely on the nurseryman's choice by investing in one of the special collections that are offered. These consist of tried and true favourites that are likely to flourish in a wide variety of soil conditions and situations.

Alternatively, the initial choice could be made from those shrubs that have received the Royal Horticultural Society's Award of Merit. Such plants, which can be identified in many nursery catalogues by the letters AM after their names, followed by the year in which the award was made, are of proven worth in almost any garden conditions.

But for those whose gardens are established, there can be few greater pleasures than those provided by the many trees and shrubs whose leaves colour brilliantly with the coming of

This is a ground plan of work for double-digging or trenching an area. Begin the operation by removing the soil from the top left-hand trench and put the soil outside the measured area.

Then work round the trenches, always throwing the top soil forward to the next trench, as indicated by the arrow. The soil set aside at the beginning is used to fill in the last trench.

An Acer dissectum, the Japanese Maple, which colours so beautifully at this time of the year, constrasts very well with the lovely Ginkgo biloba.

autumn—and October is the month when we see these at their best.

The maples include species and varieties that provide striking examples of this characteristic, and the smaller species make excellent specimen trees for the lawn or border. *Acer palmatum osakazuki* is a small and shapely Japanese maple whose green leaves turn into the fieriest of scarlets at this time of year.

The Canadian maple, *Acer rubrum*, is equally noteworthy for its vivid autumn colouring, but a tree that reaches 60–70 feet at maturity is somewhat large for the garden of average size. More suitable colouring species include *Acer capillipes*, *Acer cappadocium aureum* (golden-yellow autumn colour) *Acer ginnala* and *Acer grosseri*.

Other trees of medium size, whose autumn colouring is an asset to the garden, are found among the Japanese cherries. *Prunus sargentii*, one of the loveliest of these, is one of the first to flower in spring. It produces its delightful single pink flowers in March. Its leaves, too, are among the earliest of those of any tree or shrub to turn in autumn and *P. sargentii* sometimes displays its brilliant scarlet hues early in September—perhaps *too* soon for us to be reminded that the winter months are on their way.

Another cherry that colours attractively is that most widely planted of all the Japanese cherries, *P. sekiyama*, better known under its popular names of Kanzan or Hisakura.

There are several fine colouring species of sorbus, close relations of our native rowan, or mountain ash. *Sorbus discolor* is the best-known of these, with rich red autumn colouring, that is surpassed only by the vivid crimson hues of *S. sargentiana*, whose outsize pinnate leaves compete for attention with the large clusters of orange-red berries.

Among the many shrubs that colour brilliantly in autumn, the Ghent and Exbury strains of deciduous azaleas rank very high. Both assume vivid orange and flame colours that make the leaf display almost the equal of the colourful spring picture presented by the flowers.

A contrasting coral-pink colouring is provided by the foliage of *Euonymus alata* and *Cornus florida rubra* while that of *Berberis thunbergii* could scarcely be surpassed for its eye-dazzling scarlet.

Few evergreens and conifers provide autumn leaf colour, but there are some exceptions. The holly-like leaves of *Mahonia aquifolium*, the Oregon grape, for example, will, given favourable conditions, sometimes stage a brilliant display of scarlet that lasts throughout the winter.

Ginkgo biloba, the maiden-hair tree, changes the normal glaucous green colour of its unusual two-lobed leaves to bright golden yellow before they fall. The feathery foliage of that delightful conifer, *Cryptomeria japonica*, turns to rosy-scarlet.

Other conifers that colour attractively are *Taxodium distichum*, the swamp cypress (green to bronzy-yellow) and *Metasequoia glypto stroboides*, the so-called fossil tree that behaves in a similar manner to the swamp cypress.

Everyone is familiar with the autumn beauty of the Virginian creepers that so greatly enhance the beauty of many walls in autumn. If the better-known kinds are too rampant for the walls of a small house or bungalow, *Vitis henryana* will provide a similar effect more in keeping with restricted areas.

Utilityandautumnbeautyarecombined in some of the ornamental grapes. *Vitis vinifera* 'Brandt' has small clusters of edible black grapes that complement the beauty of the multi-coloured autumn foliage.

V. vinifera purpurea, the Teinturier grape, has autumn leaves of an appropriate wine-red colour. Both of these make good climbers for a south or west wall.

Vegetables

The main work of this month is preparation of the soil for next year's crops. Where gardens are large enough for space to be allocated to rotational crops, large areas can be dug and left fallow for the winter. Rotational cropping is an agricultural practice applied to gardening. It is not practicable in any but large gardens. It certainly is not practicable to follow completely the agricultural method which aims at cleaning new ground with root crops so that it may then be planted with cereals and after this be allowed to lie fallow for a whole twelve months.

In a garden, rotation consists more of dividing the plot and crops into three sections so that one may be planted with potatoes, a second with other root vegetables and the third with peas, beans and leaf vegetables. The next year the legumes and leaf vegetables follow the potatoes, the potatoes follow the roots and the roots follow the leaf vegetables. The third year the changes are rung once more and in the fourth year the cycle begins all over again. Onions do best on the same land continuously.

The plots need to be roughly the same area. As one can see, such a method cannot be applied to all gardens. Owners of small gardens prefer to crop intensively and to fill as much of the garden as possible with winter greens and salads produced under cloches. Even so, wherever possible ground should be dug deeply now and left rough so that it may be both pulverised and cleansed by winter weather.

It is advisable to test the soil from time to time. Where vegetable crops are produced intensively soil is often lacking in lime, an ingredient essential to the successful cultivation of so many vegetables, brassicas in particular. The continual application of home-made compost and mulches of lawn mowings also tends to make the soil acid. Manure and lime should not be applied at the same time, since one counteracts the influence of the other. Where ground cannot be dug because it is occupied by crops, well-rotted manure can be used as a mulch between the rows, where it can rot and be taken into the soil ready to be dug over in the spring. It is essential that where intensive cropping takes place the soil should be well fed.

Finish lifting and storing all roots now. Take a look at the salad crops and where possible cover them with cloches. Lamb's lettuce and land cress are both hardy, but if they are covered with cloches they will be both cleaner and more succulent. The same applies to seakale and spinach beet, both of which will continue to give a good crop if protected.

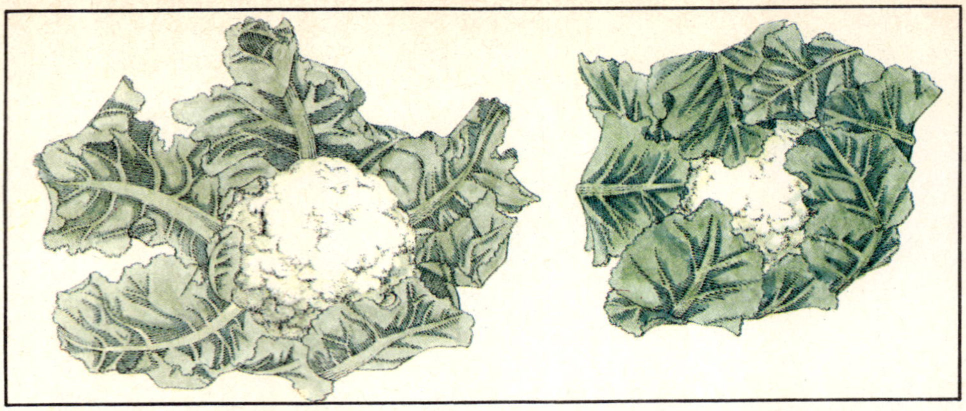

If the Cauliflower leaves are folded over the curd autumn frost damage will be prevented and this will then ensure that when the 'flower' is formed it will be white and appetising.

Cauliflowers which are beginning to form heads or curds sometimes become discoloured by the sharp frosts of early autumn. These can be protected quite easily by snapping, but not severing, a leaf or two nearest the curds so that they hang over them.

Fresh herbs can be enjoyed during winter if some roots of mint, tarragon and chives are lifted and either potted or boxed at the end of the month and brought into a cold greenhouse, or they can go on a window-sill in a frost-free garage or shed. Cloches placed over parsley and chervil will also ensure fresh leaves for use during the winter.

Although considered hardy, some endive should be moved to a frame to ensure supplies in severe weather. Cloches can be placed over those in open ground for the same purpose. Some may be ready for blanching. In winter the plants which have reached the required size may be blanched by covering each one with an inverted flower pot with its drainage hole plugged to exclude all light.

It may be necessary to hold up the leaves while the plant is being covered. Alternatively, the plants can be uprooted, planted close together in boxes and taken into a dark shed. Or they may be planted close together in a frame and covered with dry leaves. It is unwise to take up great quantities, since blanched endive does not keep well. Try to lift a few plants at intervals to give a succession.

Lettuce, winter and forcing varieties, can be sown in a frame now and transplanted to another frame or to a greenhouse later. When transplanting take care that the seed leaves are not buried. Plant quite shallowly. The seedling may appear to keel over a little, but it will soon right itself. Buried leaves, even seed leaves, are apt to cause damping off.

Spring cabbage may still be planted.

A THREE-YEAR ROTATION PLAN

FIRST YEAR	Beetroots Carrots Parsnips Potatoes Swedes Turnips	Broccoli Brussels sprouts Cabbages Cauliflowers Kale	Beans Celery Leeks Lettuces Peas Spinach Tomatoes
FERTILISERS TO USE	Fertiliser lime	Compost lime	Compost fertiliser
SECOND YEAR	Beans Celery Leeks Lettuces Peas Spinach Tomatoes	Beetroots Carrots Parsnips Potatoes Swedes Turnips	Broccoli Brussels sprouts Cabbages Cauliflowers Kale
FERTILISERS TO USE	Compost fertiliser	Fertiliser lime	Compost lime
THIRD YEAR	Broccoli Brussels sprouts Cabbages Cauliflowers Kale	Beans Celery Leeks Lettuces Peas Spinach Tomatoes	Beetroots Carrots Parsnips Potatoes Swedes Turnips
FERTILISERS TO USE	Compost lime	Compost fertiliser	Fertiliser lime

Water Gardens

The main work for October is to remove fallen leaves and plant remains, and to feed fish generously as long as the water stays warm enough to maintain their appetites. In addition, it is now time for some tidying in the borders around the pool where perennial waterside plants will be dying back. These should be cut down to 2–3 inches from the soil.

The crowns of gunnera must be protected from future frost with a covering of their own old leaves, or with bracken. Any zantedeschia (arum lilies) grown in the pool in containers should be moved into positions where they will have 12 inches (or more) of water over them until April. The tender water hyacinth, *Eichhornia crassipes,* must be wintered in a greenhouse. It need only be potted in soil which is kept moist until it is returned to the pool as a free-floating plant in early June.

Throughout October, and well into November while there is still some lingering warmth in the soil, is an excellent time for planting waterside perennials and ferns, rockery plants, dwarf shrubs and conifers. Fallen leaves which accumulate on the netting spread over the pool and rockery in September should be removed periodically to avoid the exclusion of light.

The extension of the water garden, whether by the installation of a bigger and better pool, or the construction of a series of waterfalls and cascades, is a job that tends to be put off until it is made urgent by the approach of the spring planting season. All too often it becomes a rush job at a time when the weather can be thoroughly uncooperative. There is a good deal to be said for getting this sort of work out of the way during this month and next, when the weather is seldom severe enough to interfere. This is particularly important if concrete is to be used.

Concrete is not now a fashionable material for pool construction. Most amateur gardeners prefer the labour saving advantages of the various kinds of plastics now available. Nevertheless some gardeners feel that concrete provides a better finish and a more natural appearance than can be achieved with plastics and persevere with this traditional pool-making material in spite of its undoubted drawbacks.

As a means of providing a waterproof lining to a hole in the ground, concrete is certainly far from ideal. It involves much labour and this alone will not guarantee lasting success. Really firm support is vital, since the most perfectly made concrete shell can easily break its back under the stresses imposed by soil movement beneath it. So a first essential is a thoroughly rammed hardcore foundation.

The excavation must always be considerably larger than the size of the finished pool to allow for the foundation and for a minimum thickness of 6 inches of concrete and rendering all round. Amateurs tend to make the floor thick and to taper off the thickness of the walls as they get to the top, with unhappy results. Material strength—and the firm support of the soil behind it—is even more important at the rim, which bears the brunt of ice pressure, than at the base.

The ingredients (3 parts coarse aggregate, 2 parts sand and 1 part cement) must be measured accurately and mixed thoroughly to a firm, even consistency. Reinforcement with wire mesh is advisable, and shuttering must be used to hold the walls in position until the mix is set. A rendering coat of 3 parts sharp sand to 1 of cement is applied 1 inch thick.

It is not safe to introduce plants or fish unless they are protected from the effect of the free lime in the concrete. This may be achieved by filling the pool, leaving for a week and emptying, and then repeating the process no fewer than three times. A simpler method is to paint the concrete with a colourless neutralising agent such as Silglaze.

Streams and waterfalls formed by slapping concrete down in scrapes between rockery stones are a common cause of frustration. Since the soil is seldom properly consolidated, settlement soon leads to fractures; and since it is not possible to make a watertight join between concrete and rockery stone, seepage occurs wherever a stone sticks up through the concrete. The result is a steady drop in the water level in the pool, and constant topping up because

1

2

3

1 A garden pool can be constructed relatively quickly and easily by lining the excavated area with 500 gauge black polythene, as has been done here.
2 A concrete pool will, of course, be a more permanent feature than a plastic or fibreglass-lined pool. Now is the time to begin such a construction.
3 The crowns of the Gunnera manicata should be protected from the winter weather. This can be done now by covering them with a tent of old leaves.

1

2

the real nature and position of the leak is not realised.

It is easy enough to avoid this unhappy state of affairs if sufficient soil and stone is first removed, and a continuous concrete shell is made to form the waterproof foundation of the watercourse, solidly bedded in thoroughly firm soil.

Rockery stones must then be placed on this shell and more concrete worked between them to create the finished pools and channels of the waterfall system. Any water that seeps down the superficial rockwork can get no farther than the underlying concrete shell and must ultimately find its way back to the pool.

Wildlife

Many animals which use the garden go into hibernation from about October until April. Bats, snakes, frogs and hedgehogs all go into a deep sleep away from the biting chills of winter. The hedgehogs, if a warm spell arouses them from their winter's sleep, may well come out for a night's foraging only to return to the warmth of their dens when the weather turns cooler again.

Any hedgehog found wandering abroad in October can be taken back to the garden, fattened up for the winter on mealworms and milk, and encouraged to stay by the provision of a special nesting box or a pile of leaves, grass and straw in a quiet corner. They are such useful and helpful animals in the garden and can make pleasant pets in spite of their nocturnal and somewhat verminous habits.

The squirrel is a 'cat-nap' hibernator. It will sleep for long periods but wakes up as soon as it feels refreshed enough and scurries about searching for its stores of nuts which it cached away earlier in the year.

3

1 and 2 At the end of October the last of our summer visitors leave, but the Goldcrests and the Song Thrushes arrive to take their place.
3 The Lesser Black-backed Gull is seen quite a long way inland in the autumn, following the plough. Although it is not a garden visitor, its presence in rural areas is a clear indication of the turn of the seasons.

The rabbit, fox and mole do not hibernate. They continue to scrape a bare existence from what is available, in spite of the frosty ground.

In October it is a common sight to see the plough followed by wheeling flocks of gulls and rooks. There are three main types of gull that come inland: the common gull, herring gull and the lesser black-backed gull. The common gull, despite its name, is in fact not very common and the herring and lesser black-backed gulls are generally more frequently to be seen. The rook is a very common relative of its larger, less known cousin the raven. Both belong to the crow family. While the raven shuns the company of other birds and is seldom seen in more than pairs, the rook is highly gregarious and nests in huge rook 'apartments'. More than 40 nests were once found in one Cornish tree.

In the newly-bared trees of winter those nests built in spring and summer stand out clearly against the frosted sky. The large dome of twigs that was the magpie's spring nest and the smaller sphere in which the wren brought up its brood are both now visible. The mud and daub nests of the swallows are deserted. Their former inhabitants are now happily swooping low over the Nile in search of insects.

By making a tour of the garden's trees, shrubs, hedges and walls the careful observer can tell which birds have rested in the garden during the past year.

In an old apple tree he may see the carefully bored hole of the woodpecker with a small heap of wood chips at the base of the nest on which the eggs are laid. Or he may find in a tangle of ivy the woven platform of twigs that is the wood pigeon's home.

There are two ways in which one can tell whether the nests were used in the previous spring. An old nest will be in poor repair with few fresh droppings beneath it, while a recent nest will still look comparatively fresh and will have beneath it a large area white with droppings. The old nest will have no infertile or addled eggs left in it whereas a more recent one may well have.

October ends, taking with it its last few late summer visitors and bringing in fieldfares, goldcrests, song thrushes and starlings.

The Month of November

Despite the dying down of the late summer blooms, there is plenty for the November garden to boast about. Trees and shrubs in fruit, such as Euonymus europaeus and Callicarpa giraldiana, the chrysanthemum and the perpetual carnation all combine to enliven the autumn scene

The dried seed heads of Dipsacus sylvestris, a plant of both garden and wayside, are invaluable for winter flower arrangement

1

2

3

4

5

6

1 Once the leaves fall from the deciduous trees the framework of branches can be seen. Most trees are identifiable from their branch structure.
2 The coral red autumn colour of Hamamelis x intermedia 'Ruby Glow' is at its best in early November. The winter flower buds are already forming.
3 Cotinus coggygria, the Smoke Tree or Wig Tree, has foliage of a deep plum-purple all summer. The colour heightens in the autumn before the leaves fall.
4 Picea glauca, a blue-grey fastigiate tree of good form, like all coniferous plants comes into its own in late autumn and winter, as it is evergreen.
5 The Holly berries are already gay and bright. Ilex aquifolium 'Golden King' is a form with creamy white margins to the dark green leaves.
6 Ilex x altaclerensis, the Broad-leaved Holly, is an imposing evergreen tree. The leaves are without spines, and wider than the true Holly.

3

2

1 Schizostylis coccinea 'Viscountess Byng', the Kaffir Lily or Crimson Flag, is a south African bulbous plant flowering late in the year and seemingly quite at home in sheltered spots.
2 Viburnum tinus, the Laurustinus, is often grown in towns where it tolerates the atmospheric conditions. It is an evergreen with white flowers which start to bloom in November and can be expected to continue until February.
3 The Ivy, Hedera helix, is a much taken-for-granted plant. Its creamy-green flowers appear in November despite short sunshine hours and damp weather.

1

3

2

4

1 Pernettya mucronata, the Prickly Heath, is an evergreen shrub with pinkish purple berries which persist until the early spring.
2 November is a month when most berrying plants are at their best. Callicarpa giraldiana is one of the most noteworthy, and has good autumn foliage.
3 Hippophae rhamnoides, the Sea Buckthorn, has bright orange berries along the length of its branches. Its grey leaves are evergreen.
4 Euonymus europaeus the Spindle Tree, is a British plant with orange and red seed heads in autumn and winter.

1 A greenhouse plant that continues to provide a good display during November is the Perpetual-flowering Carnation. Here is Carnation 'Dusty Sim'.
2 A large flowered incurved Chrysanthemum 'Golden Maylen'. In the greenhouse Chrysanthemums of all types are flowering.

2

1

1

1 Nerines, greenhouse bulbous plants from South Africa, start flowering in late summer and go on into late autumn. Nerine 'Plymouth' has red flowers.
2 The Cyclamen of greenhouse and living room is Cyclamen persicum. A range of colour is found in both flower and leaf. This is a silver-leaved form.

2

Sculpting the garden

Your garden reaches to the sky as well as to its boundary fences. Colour need not be its only quality. Tall plants, sunken areas, slim trees beside long hedges all contribute to its beauty

1

2

1 Fastigiate trees are used here with advantage to both emphasise and enhance a path.
2 In the border, considered selection and juxtaposition of plants makes for success.

The chief impression which any garden makes is one of colour—a background of green embroidered with vivid reds, blues, yellows and whites. But a more careful consideration of the colour will reveal that it is at different levels, advancing or recessed, with parts in bold circular splashes, parts in towering spires and parts carpeting the area.

This demonstrates that the colours themselves are only part of the impression and that the manner, shape and pattern in which they are displayed completes the effect.

Shape in the garden—a somewhat subtle element in design—is only occasionally obvious, and then in particularly dramatic form such as a meticulously clipped hedge, a towering line of poplars or a pleached lime walk. Yet the natural or artificial shapes of plants, the spacing between these shapes and the relationship one to another are essential to all good gardening.

People talk of a garden 'looking a real picture' and this attitude too frequently colours the approach. A picture is two dimensional and a garden is three dimensional—a sculpture rather than a painting.

The land itself, whether on the level or sloping, is also three dimensional. It is not a finite area with length and width, but an infinite space reaching up to the sky and out to the horizons over and above hedges, fences, walls and even buildings.

Space on the outside of the garden is in some ways as important as space inside it, and by varying shapes and levels within the plot it is always possible to create an impression of greater space than actually exists. Even the ground can be sculpted to create sunken and raised features.

All plants are to a greater or lesser extent in three dimensions and it is the exaggeration of one of these dimensions that gives certain specimens special interest and importance. A tall poplar or a delphinium towers above its neighbours with height as one of its most important characteristics, whereas a clump of heather spreads horizontally over the ground, never more than a few inches tall. In considering the major dimensional characteristic of any plant, however, you should not forget the other two. A row of poplars is more effective than a clump, because it exploits the individual heights of each of the trees. The effect of a clump instead of a straight line is to lose height and gain width and thickness, becoming a tall rectangle instead of a slim pencil.

When exploiting the special characteristics of plants you must take account of light and shade and their importance in highlighting those characteristics. A tall poplar throws a long, slim shadow. If another tapering or conical tree is planted so that at a certain time of day the shadow of one lingers on the other, that one will be almost hidden and will lose its effectiveness. You cannot, of course, always plant in an east-west relationship and you would lose many subtle pleasures by so doing. But where shadows are going to be significant and important it is as well to consider if the placing of a major tree or shrub will be more effective if the shadow it casts, or the shade it receives, can be made to fall in order that one plant will not affect another.

One of the reasons why garden design has moved away from the tyranny of straight lines and formal rectangular borders in favour of the curved or serpentine edge is simply so that light and shade can vary instead of being the same for each plant.

Just as some colours are advancing or aggressive and others are retreating and shy, so some shapes attract or reject attention. Because so many garden plants are amorphous, having no definite or characteristic shape but relying on colour for their interest, it is up to the gardener to use more definite shapes among them to give interest and pattern to the whole.

Basically, few shapes are available, but there are many variations. Using the analogy of colour again, there are actually very few basic colours in the spectrum, but the variations on these colours enormously extend the range. Red, for example, can vary from a blushed white through to blue—or purple-reds which are almost black. There can be, in fact, up to 50 or more quite different colours which are all basically red. So a columnar tree can be tall and nearly pencil-shaped with almost straight sides, or these sides can curve to create a shape like an exclamation point, or even more to be almost egg-shaped. Round or spherical trees or shrubs can also vary widely in

The ultimate in border design is a 'one colour' border. The silver border at Pyrford Court, Surrey, depends for effect upon textures and shapes of the plants.

shape and 'rectangles' can be almost any outline at all!

Beyond the question of basic shape or outline lies also the question of habit of growth. A fastigiate (tapering) tree must necessarily have an upright habit. Specimens having a round or rectangular outline can have upright, sideways or even drooping or weeping branches which together give the effect of a sphere or rectangle.

Because trees have the most obviously formal and recognisable shapes one is apt to consider their outlines but ignore the shapes of some of the smaller shrubs and almost all herbaceous plants. Mature trees show against the sky-line and become a theatrical backcloth for the garden scene in front. They are the largest of all our garden materials and are therefore the most important. They cannot easily be moved once they are established simply because of their size. It follows that their choice, their placing, their relationship one with another, their effect on the plants at the bases of their trunks, their purpose and their significance in the landscape outside the immediate garden are all of great importance.

It is possible today to obtain semi-mature trees of some 20 feet in height, but these tend to be both expensive and difficult to plant, particularly in a smallish garden. Where access is limited, cranes and tractors cannot get in or manoeuvre.

Most people instead prefer to rely on small, young specimens and wait, sometimes for years, before they achieve significance and importance. This drawback does have its blessings. It means that, in their early years, trees can be moved from one site to another if this seems necessary or desirable. Even the smartest gardeners make mistakes and it is reassuring to know things can be put right if you go wrong at your first attempt.

Remember, every garden is dynamic, never static. Every garden is changing with the growth of certain plants and the death of others. Gardeners must be equally dynamic in outlook and be prepared to make changes, even major ones, to improve their plots and keep pace with the changes created by nature. This may even include the moving (perhaps the complete removal) of such big features of the garden as trees. In their eagerness to clothe a new and empty garden everybody tends to plant too closely and, in time, thinning out and re-spacing become necessary.

So often people do not take full advantage of the facilities offered by nature and by nurserymen. One of the most popular flowering trees is the gorgeous cherry, grown for its blossom. Yet how many know that Japanese cherries can be planted in the shape of a pencil, a sphere, a fan or a tall or horizontal rectangle? How many take advantage of the fact that there are several varieties of weeping cherries available, and many, many other trees are also available in different shapes? In so many small gardens, where space precludes the planting of many trees, the careful selection of certain shapes, particularly the space-saving fastigiate shapes, allows a much greater density of planting than would be possible by haphazard choice.

Although trees offer the best example of architectural or sculptural shapes, all shrubs and all herbaceous plants follow the same basic shapes, and the same basic rules of planting apply. In a border against a fence, wall or hedge, for example, you would naturally plant the taller subjects at the back and the smaller ones in front. But this would make for dullness and uniformity if you carried it to excess. So try putting taller plants occasionally among the shorter ones to give a more irregular and interesting outline. It would be foolish and wasteful to hide mignonette or lily-of-the-valley among the taller plants at the back of the border. But an occasional group of kniphofias, say, could well come to the front beside a clump of foot-high gypsophila where each would gain from the other.

Gardeners usually have a much closer and more intimate contact with herbaceous plants than they do with trees and some shrubs. There are so many leaves on a mature tree, for example, that only occasionally is leaf shape as important as the outline of the entire tree.

The shape, colour, texture and habit of growth of small herbaceous plants, bearing perhaps as few as half a dozen leaves, achieve real importance in addition to the flowers produced. Leaves can be grass-like, hairy, ferny, fingered, feathery, prickly. They can be round, oval, irregular, spiky, spear- or strap-like, leathery or furry.

Herbaceous plants as a general rule must be left largely to their own devices as they grow. They are grown from seed or from young plants and, apart from occasional staking or supporting, there is little that can be done to help them grow in the shape and size required. A certain amount of pruning, cutting for flower decoration, and the dividing of perennials every few years will train the plants to a compact, floriferous and generally useful shape. The insertion of twigs in the soil around a paeony, for example, will keep the plant growing more or less bushy and above the soil rather than sprawling with the sheer weight of the bigger branches, but no amount of pruning or training will ever make a shrubby paeony into a tree paeony. They are different plants.

The neglected garden

When you resurrect a garden that has run to seed, look for traces of the old design for this was the result of somebody living with the garden. There will be good local reasons for its facets

Bringing a garden back to life after it has been neglected, even for only a few months, is a difficult matter. Beneath the dank, matted carpet of weeds, brambles and overgrown thickets there lies some sort of order and you must discover what and where this is before you can alter it to suit your own taste and convenience.

In summer it is difficult enough to identify half-hidden and overgrown plants. In winter it is almost impossible. Yet somehow you must decide which to keep and which to destroy.

It is tempting to raze the entire area and begin again, keeping only the mature trees and larger shrubs. But this may be unwise. The garden that existed before, now hidden by undergrowth, was the result of somebody *living* with the plot for some time. It was a reasoned and purposeful use of the land.

If you ignore what went before you may throw away the lessons learnt by the previous gardener, ignore his findings, neglect his experience. A tree may have been planted as a vital windbreak, a shrub may grow in a pocket of acid soil, plants may grow so lush because of the boggy nature of the ground where they are. If your predecessor found the solutions to problems by hard-won experience it would be foolish to ignore his findings and then undergo the same experiences possibly determining the same results.

It is wise, therefore, to try to discover

An old Yew hedge *left* cut back for renovation and young plants put in to fill the gaps. Drastic cutting back is needed. Golden Yew *right* which has been cut right back to encourage new growth to 'break' for the hedge.

what kind of garden existed originally before weeds and undergrowth took over and smudged its features.

First clear the ground so that you can find the overall plan. Cover every inch of the land carefully and slowly looking for rocks, logs, hidden plants, perhaps even a caved-in pool or a forgotten rake. The ground must be cleared around any tree, shrub or plant that might be important enough to save, clipping the overgrown grass with shears to expose the plant and save it from careless destruction.

Having cleared the ground and exposed every significant plant, cut down the weeds and undergrowth. Use a rotary mower for this, choosing one that is powerful enough to cope with tall growth.

Set the blades high enough to avoid hitting any obstruction missed in your earlier walks around the plot. This machine will chew the grass into short lengths and deposit it on the surface. Leave it to dry before raking it up into a heap and burning it.

The newly exposed, stubbly plot will now reveal some sort of pattern. You will see roughly what existed before and decide which elements of the original garden to retain and which to change. It is always tempting at this stage to embark on major long-term projects such as the digging of a garden pool, the creation of a rock garden or the laying of paving for a terrace or patio. But don't.

There are two main reasons why rehabilitation is wiser than construction at this time. In the first place you have not yet had time to live with the garden, to create your own patterns of use and activity.

The immediate, hasty building of a garden pool will prove a complete waste of time and effort if in the course of the next few months it is found to be in the wrong position because of aspect, drainage problems, overhanging trees or the necessity for some other garden feature in that spot. Only when you have lived with the plot for a full four seasons is it possible to recognise either the problems facing you or the natural advantages which you may make use of.

In the second place, while you are engaged in major constructional tasks you are bound to neglect the general maintenance of the garden and it cannot take its place as general living space.

Far better to spend the first year in your reclaimed garden accepting that it is not as you would like it, but cleaning, neatening and revitalising the area so that it is agreeable underfoot and comparatively pleasant to look at from the house. Your time will not be wasted, for while you are engaged in rehabilitation, the shape and pattern of the changes you wish to make will begin to form in your mind and will be actively linked with your own findings about the soil. During your weeding, pruning, mowing and spraying you will find that your feet lead you naturally along certain paths to the different sections of the garden. The paths you take will probably be different from the paths previously laid down and will determine to some extent the overall plan of the garden you gradually intend to create.

The grass which was left as a brown and uneven stubble after the first cut will begin to grow green and pleasant with several mowings and as the finer, shorter grasses take over again. There may be irregularities, bumps and hollows, but these can be smoothed out. Regular attention should be paid to trimming and neatening the edges to give a groomed appearance. If there are weeds in the lawns these can gradually be cleared by means of one of the selective weedkillers.

If the grass is not as fine nor the lawn as level as you would like, it can be re-seeded or re-turfed at a later date, but meanwhile repeated mowings and applications of food and weedkillers will change it from an eyesore to a more reasonable background for the remainder of the garden.

Although selective weedkillers, either in granular or liquid form, can safely be used on still days, they must be used with discretion and strictly according to the manufacturer's instructions on the bag or bottle. But the wholesale use of weedkillers, selective or total, is always dangerous in a strange garden as you cannot know all the contents and the unexpected, unknown or unrecognised plants can so easily be killed.

Once you have finally cleared the site, you can use paraquat weedkillers to clear sections of the garden for replanting and will quickly dispose of weed growth in paving, forecourts and driveways. It is usually possible to identify the various plants after a full year by referring to the encyclopedia, a friend, a nurseryman, the Royal Horticultural Society or your local Horticultural Education Officer.

The trees and shrubs which you decide to keep can gradually be pruned into shape and into increased fruitfulness. Do not attempt to cut away too much at a time as this may kill the plant. Prune gradually, looking at the shape both from the garden and from the windows of the house.

Where it is essential that a tree must come out entirely try to remove the major roots also. This can be a big operation and in some cases it is best to cut the tree down to ground level and kill the stump chemically.

To cut down a large tree in a comparatively small garden without damaging other plants or structures can be difficult. First prune the top and branches gradually down towards the main trunk, then cut the boughs, if necessary in stages. When little is left but the main trunk you can decide whether to clear this together with the roots or to cut it down leaving nothing but the roots.

In the first case leave as much of the trunk as can safely fall in the garden and attach to the top some stout rope. Then begin to dig around the roots, clearing away the soil and severing the roots as they are exposed. After a time it will be found possible to rock the trunk to and fro by pulling on the rope. This will loosen the soil and expose further roots. Eventually the leverage of the trunk by means of the rope will be sufficient to pull the tree down into the place required and it can then be sawn up and carted away. The remaining hole can be filled in and re-turfed.

If digging out the roots is too heavy a task, prepare the tree in the same way

1 

2 

1 At Moseley Old Hall, Staffordshire, the National Trust has carried out much renovation to the garden.
2 The reconstructed parterre, in keeping with the house of Elizabethan origin.

1

2

as before and then finally saw through it as near to ground level as possible. You will then be left with a considerable area of flat trunk and a major root system.

It is necessary to kill the root system and to decompose the trunk. Bore a number of large holes in the trunk at least an inch in diameter and 6 inches or so deep. Fill these with a solution of half brushwood killer and half paraffin and plug the top of the holes. Top up the holes with the same solution as it is absorbed by the wood.

After a few months the roots will have died and you can then either leave the stump and roots to rot away, which may take several years, or light a good bonfire on top of it. Because of the paraffin the stump and roots will gradually smoulder away, even below ground level, and when the process has been completed the area can be filled in and re-turfed.

1 The borders on each side of the path at Moseley Old Hall, Staffordshire, were badly neglected before renovation.
2 The character is maintained by improving the lawn and planting conifers.

Once the major clearing and grooming processes have been completed and the garden is no longer an eyesore, you can think about more creative work for the future. In the clearing process you will have got an impression of the various features you would like and will have discovered whether the soil is stony, chalky, clayey, sandy, peaty or composed of a good medium loam. It is now helpful to know whether this soil is acid, alkaline or neutral and a small soil testing kit from your garden store will soon settle this question for you. This is important to know for it will determine what kind of plants you can grow best.

You will also have noticed whether or not the soil is sufficiently well drained. If the land is obviously badly waterlogged a good working drainage system should be installed. Depending on the lie and slope of the land this can lead to a main drain or, where this is impossible, to a deep soakaway pit. In either case the preliminaries are the same. The length of the area should be dug to a depth of about 18 inches and land drains laid on a bed of rubble.

If the problem is a serious one the drains should be laid herring-bone fashion—side spurs every 20 feet or so leading into the main drain. More rubble should be laid over the drain pipes, then soil to fill and the turf replaced. The drain should empty out into the main drain at a slope of approximately 1 inch in 40. Where this is not possible the drain should fall into a soakaway.

This can be made by digging, in the lowest part of the garden, a pit about 4 feet square and 4 feet deep, depending on the length of the garden and the depth of the drainage pipe. This should be filled to within about a foot of the soil level with broken bricks and other rubble and then topped with good soil and turf. Excess water from the surrounding soil will drain into the pipes, thence to the soakaway, which will fill only in the wettest weather.

Most soils in most gardens do not need such drastic action and where drainage is faulty it can be remedied by deep digging and the incorporation of ashes or sharp sand into the top few inches. Peat and other humus-making materials are helpful in all gardens, whether wet or dry.

In periods of wet weather they absorb the moisture from the surrounding soil and in dry weather, or in dry and sandy soils, they hold moisture in suspension and release it slowly to the surrounding earth.

In all digging and all soil treatment remember that the top 9 inches or so is the important part. This is the top-soil that feeds the plants. Try to keep this topsoil rich and open and never bury it below ground by double digging. Plant fertilisers should be dug into these top few inches and not buried. Manures and home-made compost should be used on top of the soil and not buried.

Jobs of the month

November seems to be a dead month in the garden, but there are still many jobs that need to be done before beginning a spell of 'armchair' gardening. Construction jobs should be tackled. There is even some sowing that can be done now—and this is the perfect tulip planting time. All the jobs, from Bulbs to Wildlife, are summarised here and explained in full on the following pages

Bulbs

This is the tulip planting month. Always remember that shallow planting is the main cause of failure with these plants

Flowers for Cutting

House plants and flowers can be brought together in arrangements in a style known as pot-et-fleur

Fruit

The sooner fruit trees are planted, the better, although the planting season extends to March. But never plant in wet, sticky soil

Greenhouse

Greenhouse plants should be protected against fog and damp. Keep all ventilators closed while fog persists

Hedges

Begin planting deciduous hedging subjects this month. Planting sites should be deeply dug and well supplied with rotted animal manure or good garden compost

Herbaceous Plants

As late perennials finish flowering, cut down top growth. Weed and fork between the plants

House Plants

A thorough weekly examination of plants is essential — on the same day and at the same time of day. Plants may be dormant, but pests certainly are not

Lawns

Remove fallen leaves from the lawn regularly, using a proprietary leaf sweeper or a besom (twig broom)

Paths, Fences and Walls

Getting a car in and out of a garage can be very difficult during bad weather. Now is the time to give thought to improving access to the garage or car-port

Patios, Balconies, Roof Gardens and Window Boxes

Mulch all plants growing in containers with peat or dead leaves. When doing new planting, consider sun, shade, dryness and dampness of soil

Rock Gardens

Top dressings on the rock garden should be lightly stirred to allow air to reach the soil. A routine spray against pests during dry spells will help to clean plants and protect them through winter months

Roses

As soon as roses arrive from the nurseryman, remove them from their packing and sprinkle them liberally with water. Broken stems and roots should be cut away cleanly

Trees, Shrubs and Climbers

When planting trees take care not to cram the roots into too small a hole. Leave about one foot all round. Tender wall plants can be protected by canvas or polythene sheets

Vegetables

The Broad Beans 'Aquadulce Claudia' and 'Seville' should be sown now. Lift Chicory for forcing

Water Gardens

If you are thinking of installing a fountain or waterfall, now is the time to begin work. Give some thought, too, to the type of pump needed

Wildlife

Feed birds regularly, increasing the amounts of fatty foods. It is important to ensure that birds have a constant supply of water

November is the great Tulip planting month, when all the species and forms can be planted for the spring display. Here, Tulipa greigii 'Cape Cod', a good yellow cultivar, is used for bedding.

Bulbs

Bulbs planted in pots and bowls earlier in the autumn and now in the plunge bed will begin to show signs of growth, especially the early flowering ones. Such hyacinth varieties as 'Rosalie' and 'Vanguard'—the latter a miniature blue-flowered one—will be ready to bring indoors. Keep the bowls away from direct light for a few days until the pale green growth has deepened to a dark green and then the bowls can be put nearer to the light but kept out of sunshine. A cool room, hall or bedroom is the ideal place to keep them until there is some sign of growth. Then they can be brought into a warm room. Always keep the fibre moist.

The lachenalias planted in pots in August can be taken from the plunge bed now and put into the cool greenhouse where they will continue to grow without too much forcing. Bulbs of *Nerine bowdenii,* the Guernsey lily, are usually delivered in November and for greenhouse or house cultivation should be planted immediately on arrival in pots that allow only about an inch of compost around the bulb. Make up a rich compost of leafmould, loam, well-rotted manure and do not water until a flower spike begins to show next spring. This dry period is important for the production of good flowers the following autumn.

Nerines can be grown in a cool greenhouse or as room plants, or out of doors in mild districts, where they like to be at the base of a sunny wall. The flower spikes of those already established in pots will die down this month. Leave them without water, through the winter, until new flower spikes form. If the plants are pot bound, leave them alone rather than repot.

November is the tulip planting month and they prefer well-drained soil with some compost worked in, or bonemeal hoed in before planting. Plant the bulbs 4–5 inches deep and 4–6 inches apart. A trowel is the best tool to use for tulip bulbs and be sure to get them deep enough because shallow planting is the main cause of failure with tulips.

In pots or bowls for indoor culture, the routine is the same as for hyacinths and daffodils planted earlier in the autumn, except that tulips are often more successful in compost and pots than fibre and bowls. A deep pot can take two layers, one above the other, of the early single or double tulips. The bulbs' positions should be staggered so that none is immediately above another. All the shoots will appear about the same time and the bowl will be ablaze with colour at flowering time.

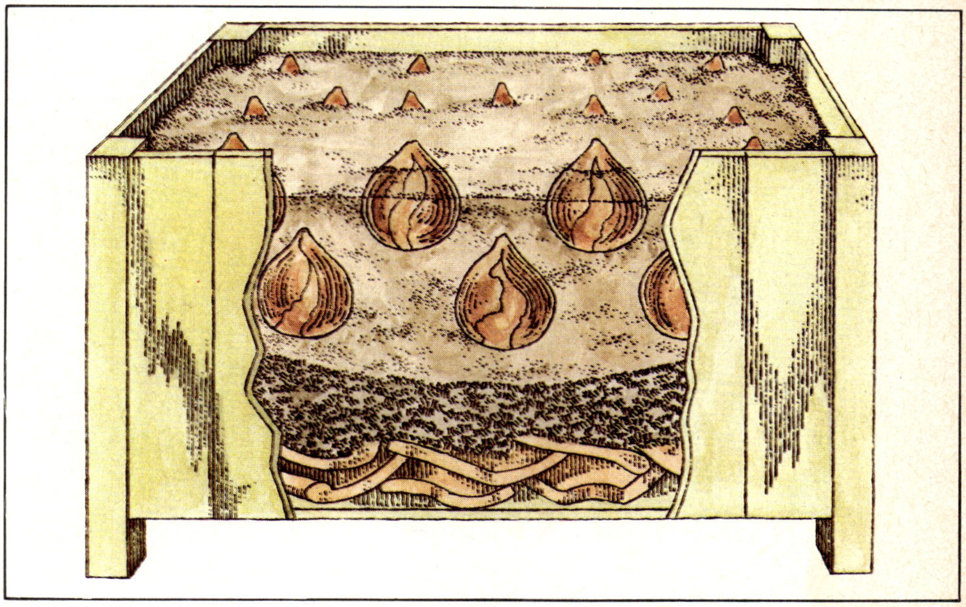

Tulips planted in tubs or troughs now can be put in effectively in a double layer and staggered in depth. All the bulbs will flower at the same time: this method allows for a good root run.

Flowers for Cutting

At this time of the year indoor plants tend to receive more attention than those in the garden. Consider bringing house plants and flowers together in arrangements in a style known as pot-et-fleur. These arrangements can be very lovely indeed, and are most practical.

All kinds of plants can be used and, generally speaking, the same loose flower arrangement rules apply: contrasting shapes with textures, arranging tall with short, broad leaved with spiky. Mainly foliage plants are used. Even if you do not have a great variety of plants to provide contrasts there are always the cut blooms and accessories. Branches of buds which you can watch open, lichen covered stems and driftwood, all can be used to achieve an effect. Many plants really benefit in these arrangements because they receive around them more humidity than they get in isolation.

It is best to select a container which will take two or three pot plants. Pedestal flower vases look elegant and

RECOGNITION CHART

Birds in the Garden

Diners at the bird table become dependent on this supply, so feed regularly if at all during winter. Try to provide natural foods

CHAFFINCH
More frequently seen in country districts than towns, usually in flocks, augmented in winter by visitors from the north. A well-wooded garden usually has a resident or two

GREENFINCH
Friendliest, most gregarious and garden-loving of birds having two, sometimes three broods a year and consequently frequently in need of food. Seed eaters

GOLDCREST
Tiniest British bird but an aggressive fighter for its territorial rights and its place at the bird table. Usually nests in conifers. Very Susceptible to hard winters so allow to feed well

STARLING
Noisy, untidy bird, usually travelling in flocks. Voracious and greedy eater of almost any food. Handsome plumage is speckled white or buff in winter

GREEN WOODPECK
Largest woodpecker. Feeds on ants and insect larvae with lo sticky tongue, so to attract it provide mealworms, or fat, seeds, oatmeal in winter

GREAT SPOTTED WOODPECKER
Shy and timid, so do not disturb. A gay and vivid acrobat and a regular visitor if given peace, seeds, nuts, fat in winter

COAL TIT
Our smallest. shyest and most timid tit, visiting the bird table rarely and alone, unless a close dweller. Feed with seeds, nuts, fat, milk

REDWING
Our smallest thrush and a winter visitor from the north. Hungry during frosts which if prolonged will kill large numbers. Feed with berries, fruit, most kitchen scraps

BLUE TIT
Brave, bold, gregarious and a regular and constant visitor when food of almost any kind is about. Acrobatic, charming and quite unafraid of humans

GREAT TIT
House loving resident, delightful to watch, clever, agile and eating anything. A great friend to gardeners in spite of attacks on fruit blossom

ROBIN
Britain's national bird, a lover of man and hater of other birds, jealously guarding his own territory. Eats anything, best of all a worm from under the spade

BLACKBIRD
Beautiful songster, first in the dawn chorus in town and country. Regular visitor if provided with fruit, raisins, fat, cheese and most kitchen scraps

NUTHATCH
Only British bird to go headfirst down tree trunks. Wedges nuts in bark crevices to smash them open with beak. Prefers seeds and nuts but will eat almost anything

1

2

1 Winter flower arrangements need to have the same flowing lines as the summer arrangements. Dried material, fruit and evergreens are used together in this predominently orange group.
2 Dried Clematis and Fern together with Physalis, evergreens and Holly berries are brought to life with fresh red Anemones.

display the plants well. They should be deep enough for the pot rims to be hidden below the container's edge. The chosen container should be part filled with peat, crumbled and secondhand Florapak or Oasis, shingle, or whatever one has which will remain moist but not sodden, and the pots should rest on this. They should be packed, tilted and wedged in place by more of the same material or, alternatively, by moss. Stones, shells, coral or small pieces of driftwood can also be used and can form part of the ensemble just as they do in ordinary flower arrangements.

The flowers are arranged in a separate container which is thrust down among the pots. Metal cones, sold by the florist sundriesman, cream cartons, large tablet tubes and sometimes even small polythene bags are examples of what can be used. These must be hidden of course and the flowers should rise prettily from among the plants.

The plants help to determine the colour scheme for the finished arrangement and the flowers should match them. Most green plants have other colours in their stems or leaf undersides which can be matched by other plants and blooms. Only a few flowers will ever be needed, sometimes only one should this be, for example, a spray of cymbidium orchids. As one might expect, arums and zantedeschia look well with house plants and so do any smooth stemmed flowers grown from bulbs. Leafy flowers, such as chrysanthemums, should be restrained; two or three blooms or sprays are usually sufficient. Posies of tiny flowers, such as hardy cyclamen and gentians, look charming arranged at rim level as though they were growing.

Fruit

Have saws and secateurs reset and sharpened in readiness for the winter pruning season.

Greenhouse fruits want plenty of air now, and ventilators need be shut only when hard frost is expected.

Nurserymen start lifting fruit trees as soon as they are dormant. Although the planting season extends from November until March the sooner trees go in, the better—provided that the soil condition is satisfactory. Never plant in wet, sticky soil: it should be dry enough to crumble readily and trickle in around the smallest roots. Planting in frosty weather is permissible if the surface of the planting site has been protected in advance or if the frozen top soil can be removed and a sufficient supply of unfrozen top soil is available for filling in over the roots. Never let frozen soil go into the planting hole.

Give priority in planting to the trees which are earliest to flower—apricots, peaches and nectarines.

To avoid root damage insert stakes before putting trees into their planting holes. Tie or fasten immediately after firming but inspect fastenings several times in the next few weeks in case the soil settles. Fan-trained trees should have their branches tied with soft string or plastic tape to canes which, in turn, are tied to the horizontal wires.

Prune greenhouse grape vines as soon as possible once they have shed their leaves. Sweep up the leaves and burn these with all prunings except for any shoots required for use as cuttings. Foot-long shoots may be inserted to half their length in good soil now. Alternatively, suitable lengths of grape vine prunings may be heeled in now for planting as cuttings next spring or for providing propagating eyes for rooting in pots in proper warmth next February.

1

2

1 When a fruit tree is to be root pruned a circle is marked out around the tree and the turf removed from one half of the circle ***top left.*** **Sever most of the roots that are exposed as the work proceeds** ***top right*** **and then work fine soil around the remaining roots and level off the soil surface** ***below left.*** **Replace the turves to their original position. Work in the same manner around the other half of the tree the following winter.**
2 When tying in a fan trained fruit tree first tie the shoots to bamboo canes and then fasten the canes themselves to the horizontal wires.

Prune down to soil level the weakest shoots on black currants planted last autumn or winter. Prune the established black currants if this has not already been attended to.

Root-prune over-vigorous trees which will not settle down to fruit production. Plum trees often come into this category and too vigorous stone fruits cannot be restricted by the easier method of bark ringing because of the risk of silver leaf infection.

Operate on fifty per cent of the roots one year and on the other half the next year, digging a trench halfway round the trunk about 3 feet from the trunk and sawing through any thick thong-like roots or downward tap roots you may encounter. Try to preserve all the fibrous roots. See that the tree is well-staked afterwards. With wall-trained trees make a trench 3 feet long and 30 inches away from the stem at right angles to the wall. Then make another trench parallel with the wall so that approximately half the root system can be dealt with.

Transfer to their fruiting quarters the rooted red or white currant and gooseberry cuttings which were taken in October two years ago.

When other priority work has been done, make a start on winter pruning established trees.

Greenhouse

Fog and damp are the main enemies of greenhouse plants this month and against the former all you can do is to keep the ventilators closed while the fog persists. When it goes, ventilate freely and give a little more heat to freshen and dry the air. Avoid splashing when watering and make sure that there is ample room for air to circulate freely around the plants. If botryits (a grey woolly fungus) appears remove affected leaves or plants immediately and give more air, even if it means lowering the temperature a little.

Pot-grown hydrangeas should now be brought in if their leaves have fallen. Place them in a cool, airy part of the

1 

2 

3 

1 Botrytis or Grey Mould can cause much damage in the greenhouse, especially if the atmosphere is not kept buoyant. This shows Botrytis on Tomato.
2 Tomato crops should be cleared and not allowed to stand suffering from Grey Mould, otherwise the fungus spores flourish in the greenhouse conditions.
3 Bulbs newly taken from the plunge bed and brought into the light. Crocuses are not removed until the buds are fat, and Hyacinth buds are in the neck.

greenhouse and water them only when they have become almost dry.

Dahlia roots from outside should also be brought in—after the foliage has been blackened by frost. After lifting and roughly drying the tubers, store them loose in a box where they will be safe from frost. Each one must be labelled.

Cyclamen from an August sowing will be ready for pricking out as soon as they have made two or three tiny leaves. Use the John Innes potting compost No 1 made firm and level in a seed-box and set the tiny corms about 1½ inches apart, with the top of the corm just level with the surface. Subsequent waterings will then bring it to the correct level, with the upper half of the corm showing. After pricking out keep the seedlings on the dry side in full light, preferably in a temperature of 60°F (16°C) to encourage quick rooting.

Some of the hardy bulbs planted in pots or bowls in September will be ready for bringing inside if they have made an inch or two of growth together with plenty of roots either coming through the drainage holes in pots or pushing up round the sides of bowls. If they have reached this stage bring them into gentle heat and give them gradually more light. Small bulbs such as crocuses, scillas and snowdrops should not be brought in until the flower spikes are visible.

For a spring display in a cold greenhouse, polyanthuses, wallflowers, astilbes, Solomon's seal (*Polygonatum multiflorum*), *Dicentra spectabilis* and *D. formosa* 'Bountiful' should all be lifted and potted in good, well-drained soil. After potting bury them to the pot-rim in the ground outside to become established in the pots, then bring them in early next year.

Where the climbing passion flower (*Passiflora caerulea*) is grown under glass its rampant growth may shade other plants too much. In this case it may be safely cut back to about 18 inches and kept fairly dry through the winter.

Schizanthus plants sown in September should now be strong young plants in 3-inch pots. Keep them as cool and airy as possible, preferably on a shelf close to the glass, and water sparingly.

Pot lilies, as they become available, in well-drained pots half-filled with an open, porous soil with plenty of leaf-mould added, and lime where necessary. Then stand the pots in a cold frame until growth starts.

Hedges

The planting of deciduous hedge plants can begin this month and continue, during periods of favourable weather, until the end of March. The planting sites should receive generous treatment, be dug deeply and well supplied with rotted animal manure or good garden compost, supplemented by a dressing of coarse bonemeal at the rate of 2–3 ounces to the square yard.

Many popular deciduous shrubs make excellent boundary or interior hedges, but where long stretches are being planted the cost can be a drawback. However, many nurseries sell large quantities at favourable rates.

Crataegus monogyna, the common quick-thorn or May of the hedgerows, is probably the cheapest hedging plant. But it would hardly be a suitable choice for a small town or suburban garden as it affords little privacy during the winter.

Beech and hornbeam, at approximately double the cost of quickthorn, are both good choices. Although deciduous by nature, both retain their dead foliage in winter when grown as a hedge and regularly clipped.

A more offbeat, yet extremely colourful hedge can be obtained by planting a mixture of myrobalan plum 'Green Glow' and *Prunus atropurpurea* 'Purple Flash' in the proportions of one plant of the former to two of the latter. This is sometimes known as a 'tapestry' hedge and the medley of two such rich leaf colours certainly does form a dramatic backcloth in gardens where this planting has been used.

Such a 'combination' hedge will reach a height of up to 10 feet. Growth is rapid, but the annual increase in height should be restricted to between 18 inches and 2 feet. The plants should go in at 2-foot intervals.

For low informal dividing hedges the dwarf barberry, *Berberis thunbergii atropurpurea nana,* with striking crimson-purple foliage, is very effective. Like its taller relation, *B. t. atropurpurea,* it is noteworthy for the brilliant colouring of its summer and autumn foliage.

One of the more compact philadelphuses, or mock oranges, will provide a slightly taller interior hedge, with intensely fragrant creamy-white double blossoms in early summer. The dwarf barberries should be lightly trimmed in winter, but the philadelphus should be trimmed immediately after the plants have flowered.

Viburnum opulus compactum is a more compact form of the guelder rose that grows only 2–3 feet tall. This is a shrub of threefold virtues—it has the beauty of summer flowers, richly-coloured autumn leaves and scarlet winter berries. It is an ideal hedging plant for chalk soils.

By the middle of the month, the leaves will be starting to fall. Tidy gardeners will waste no time in raking them up and, it is to be hoped, not burning them but rotting them down for compost.

Whether it is better to do this or to leave them to be slowly absorbed into the soil is something that two opposing schools of gardening thought are not likely to agree on. In most instances, it seems, the desire for a neat-looking garden takes precedence.

Herbaceous Plants

Tulips and narcissus (this includes daffodils) should be planted now. Some tulips are more suitable for planting in a herbaceous border than others. Especially recommended are the elegant lily-flowered tulips with their pointed reflexed petals: the varieties 'Jacqueline', a lovely rose pink and cerise softening to silvery pink at the tips, and *T. elegans alba,* a pure white with cerise pink edging, the huge double, sweetly scented Paeony-flowered type and the well-known stately Darwins.

Planted 4–5 inches deep, 6–7 inches apart, in groups of six or more, tulips thrive in medium to light soil enriched with compost or sphagnum peat—the Paeony-flowered, in particular, lasting a long time in bloom given a sunny, sheltered position. It pays to dust the bulbs with Botrilex as a precaution against tulip fire, if the ground has been used for tulips before.

Most narcissus, planted 5–6 inches deep, 6–9 inches apart, will grow in almost any soil, in sun or shade, though they prefer rather stiffish loam to which bonemeal has been added. They can be left undisturbed for three years or more, but in a herbaceous border it is usually better to lift and dry off the bulbs after flowering.

As late perennials finish flowering, continue cutting down the top growth, weeding and forking over the soil between the plants. Polyanthus (primula), sweet William (dianthus), wallflowers (cheiranthus), foxgloves (digitalis), sweet rocket *(Hesperis matronalis),* forget-me-not (myosotis) and Canterbury bells (campanula) should be planted without delay.

Foxgloves and Canterbury bells thrive in sun or shade. Plant Canterbury bells in largish groups towards the front or middle of a border and plant foxgloves —the 'Excelsior' strain which bears florets horizontally all round the stem instead of drooping to one side—massed at the back of a border.

Hedging provides a useful and attractive background to a border, acting as a windbreak as well as a foil to flower colourings. Not all shrubs are suitable for this purpose. Privet (ligustrum)

A hedge provides a useful and attractive background to the herbaceous border. Even a deciduous one makes a useful windbreak for plants in the winter months, often minimising frost.

tends to rob the soil of nourishment. Among the best of the deciduous shrubs for planting now are beech *(Fagus sylvatica)* and hornbeam *(Carpinus betulus)*. Hornbeam is very well suited for planting in heavy, sticky ground.

Climbing roses trained up 8-foot larch poles spaced 6–8 feet apart, also form an effective backing to a wide border, especially if some of the shortened side-shoots are left on the pole so that the roses can be trained sideways as well as upwards.

Christmas roses *(Helleborus niger)* can be planted in rich light to medium loam, in a shady part of the border. Established plants should be mulched with peat or leafmould, scattering slug pellets between the foliage.

House Plants

By now practically all house plants should have settled down into their winter torpor, alive and attractive but dormant, growing so slowly that change is almost impossible to see from week to week. But their inactivity does not mean that they require no attention. This is, in fact, the most critical time in their lives. A mistake in the handling of them or a little neglect now can be most damaging to the plants.

In the winter daily attention is hardly necessary, but a thorough weekly examination of each plant is essential, so get into a routine of going around each plant at the same time on the same day each week.

First look for any dead leaves or shoots or any that are behaving oddly—perhaps twisted, mis-shapen or curiously coloured. Any of these could suggest insect attack, possibly by red spider mite. These pests flourish in a dry atmosphere, and are almost impossible to see, but can be detected by dropping a pinch of powder or some cigarette ash on the affected part. If this is caught up in fine webby hairs, then red spider can be blamed.

Dead or dying leaves and shoots should be pruned away at once and any fallen leaves removed from the surface of the pot.

Wash the entire plant thoroughly, preferably using white oils. Then spray the plant with a solution of white oils. As a preventive measure increase humidity or give the affected plant a weekly spray with an atomiser.

Examine foliage, stems and joints for insects. Aphids will be causing no trouble at this time of year, but you may find a woolly white tuft which on examination is found to contain an insect.

This is mealy bug. The creature can be picked off with a matchstick and the plant cleaned with white oil. Or you may find a small, grey, scaly blotch adhering

1

2

1 A woolly white tuft upon examination may be found to contain an insect, which is a Mealy Bug. Pick it off with a matchstick, clean the plant with white oil immediately to prevent infestation.

2 A Scale insect on a Balsam or Busy Lizzie. This is rather difficult to take off, but hand picking is the best way to eradicate the scales, then wash with oil right away.

to the underside of a leaf. This will be a scale insect, more difficult to pick off, but also necessitating a thorough cleaning of the plant with white oil.

Leaves wilting or turning yellow usually indicates a condition of dryness at the roots or of over-watering.

Finally look at the general shape and appearance of the plant. Is it still attractive enough to keep? Does it look healthy? Is the shape pleasing? Does this shoot need tying in or pruning?

All house plants in time will outlive their attraction and should be discarded, for after several repottings even house plants become old, tired and unpleasing in appearance. The first function of a house plant is to be decorative in the home and when it fails this purpose it is time to replace it with a young, fresh, clean and virile specimen.

Do not wait until spring to buy new plants. Any reputable supplier will have plants in good condition in the winter, in warm premises protected against frosts. But make sure that when you carry your purchases home they are suitably wrapped and protected against winds and frosts.

Lawns

If the weather is very mild during November, it may be necessary to mow the lawn once during the month. This should only be a light tipping of the grass to prevent it growing too long and looking unsightly during the next few months. But the grass should not be cut when the weather is frosty or the ground very wet.

Fallen leaves often become a lawn problem this month and, however infuriating it may be, it is advisable to remove these regularly. If leaves are allowed to lie, they encourage earthworm activity and, in their rotting state, are detrimental to the health of the grasses.

On small lawn areas, a besom (a birch twig broom—like a witch's broom) or a rake can be used to gather the leaves into piles. These should then be picked up immediately and added to the compost heap. If heaps of leaves are left standing on the lawn, either the wind will blow them about again or the grass will turn yellow below the heaps.

For larger lawns, it is much easier to use some form of mechanical sweep to collect the fallen leaves. There are several proprietary leaf sweepers available. Basically these consist of two wheels, a revolving brush and a collecting bag. Alternatively, some of the motorised rotary grass cutting machines with collecting bags can be used for this purpose, with the cutter blades set high enough not to cut the grass at the same time.

If earthworm activity is still noticeable on the lawn area during warm periods a further application of a proprietary mowrah meal, derris, chlordane or lead arsenate wormkiller should be applied. The manufacturer's instructions and precautions for the use of these must be followed carefully.

A new lawn area from turves that was not completed last month can be finished during the early part of this month, provided the soil is not too wet and the ground has been well prepared in advance. If it appears that the soil is not going to dry out sufficiently for the job to be done, a useful tip is to rake an inch layer of a good coarse grade of *dry* peat into the top 2 inches of soil. Then roll the surface or tread it lightly, so that the peat and soil particles are in close contact and the peat can absorb the excess moisture. Turves should then be laid immediately, before the rain again delays this job.

1

2

1 Where Earthworm activity is still to be seen in the form of worm casts on the lawn, give a dressing of a proprietary wormkiller in a mild spell of weather.
2 If land that has been levelled and prepared for turves is not dry enough and shows no sign of drying out now, rake it over again and add a thin layer of dry peat, then rake again before turfing.

Paths, Fences and Walls

As the darker days of winter descend and transport becomes increasingly important, few things can be more exasperating, sometimes even alarming, than to have difficulty in getting the car into or out of the garage because of bad weather conditions. It is essential to have a properly paved access which can cause no trouble for the car, regardless of weather conditions.

The simplest means of providing good access for the car is merely to have two parallel concrete tracks from gate to garage, car-port or standing area. This is not particularly attractive to look at and is difficult to keep neat and pleasant. It is generally very little more trouble or expense to pave the entire area rather than the two tracks.

A wide and level entrance to a garage is the most convenient if space permits. A tarmac drive provides for access to the garage and both the back and front entrances to the house.

If possible try to slope the driveway slightly away from the garage to avoid water entering. If this is not possible, as for example when the garage is at a lower level than the road, provide means for heavy rain to be diverted to the sides, to a drain or soakaway or to a gulley beside the garage. If concrete is used for the drive, make sure that the surface is roughened or slightly corrugated so that in conditions of snow and ice tyres can still get a good grip.

Where there is space and conditions permit, it is always helpful to be generous with car space in front of or beside the house. Allow space for visitors' cars to park. Ease the problem of turning and reversing.

Gates should be made wide enough and turning points large enough for easy movement without the risk of scratching. Keep trees, shrubs and climbers sufficiently clear to allow not only good vision of the road and pavement, but easy access, too.

If sufficient space exists for two gateways and a throughway drive between them, indicate in the designing or even by signs where you would prefer cars to park or tradesmen's vehicles to stop for their deliveries. Bad driveway design can lead to confused parking and the irritation of being blocked or having to move a car to allow access for another. Purpose-made parking bays can be indicated by whitewashed stones or similar methods.

Patios, Balconies, Roof Gardens and Window Boxes

Winter conditions can begin in earnest this month, so this is the time for

looking ahead. It is the ideal month to lay paving or build walls provided heavy frosts are not expected, which can ruin concrete unless it is protected.

Clean up all containers holding flowers or shrubs, including wall troughs and raised beds. Where these contain clumps of perennials, lift, divide and replant where this appears necessary. A few plants prefer to be moved when conditions are warmer. Leave these until spring. They include delphiniums, some Michaelmas daisies, kniphofias, scabious and pyrethrums.

Some gardeners leave dead and frosted stems on plants in the borders because of the extra protection they give to the plant below. This protection is so slight in containers and so disfigures the architectural form and appearance of the terrace or roof, that it is wise to pay meticulous attention to grooming.

When the clearing up has been completed mulch all plants in containers with peat or some of the leaves that have been falling from the trees in the past few months. Where this mulch is apt to be dislodged by winds, anchor it down with a few pebbles.

Where new planting is considered necessary choose plants for the patio, roof garden or balcony with special care, for in these places shape, form and size are vital for a good effect. Also take into

A small town roof garden in which space is well used. In order to have a colourful display year after year it is necessary to renew the soil, and the late autumn is the best time for doing this. Import new soil or feed old soil.

consideration factors such as sun and shade, the dryness or dampness of the soil, the ultimate height and spread of the plant and its tolerance for city living if the site is urban.

Town soils are frequently over-worked, under-fed, thin and lacking in humus and sick with the inevitable chemical deposits from polluted air. For containers it is always wiser to use a good standard soil, such as the John Innes mixtures, rather than to rely on normal garden soil. Where plantings are made directly into a border it is helpful to dig out a foot or so of the existing soil and replace with John Innes. If the labour or expense of this is considered too great, then sprinkle the soil area with ½ lb of lime per square yard to sweeten it and dig in a good bucketful of peat into which has been mixed a large handful of bonemeal.

If this seasonable renovation is not in progress, the patio can be put to its proper purpose and be used for the barbecue party on bonfire night. Foil wrapped jacket-potatoes can be baked and sausages grilled, to serve to the guests. Supplementary lighting can be supplied in one of several ways, but it needs to be properly protected in damp atmospheres.

Rock Gardens

From now until March all deciduous shrubs can be planted. The ground must, of course, be clear of frost when this operation is carried out. This is also the period when deciduous dwarf trees can be safely transplanted. The position in which they are to go should be prepared as for evergreens.

Tulip species and varieties as dry bulbs are best planted now. Unless the rock garden is large, only the species should be used. The large varieties and forms are out of place in a small rock garden. The species are planted 3 inches deep and about 6 inches apart in a light, rich well-drained soil in a sunny position. They are best left undisturbed for four years, then lifted and divided. A top dressing of bonemeal, 4 ounces to the square yard, is beneficial when applied at planting time and each succeeding autumn.

A watch should be kept for falling leaves. These should be removed at once. If they are allowed to remain on the cushion or prostrate plants they will often kill the part on which they rest.

In the scree beds, troughs and other parts of the rock garden where the choicer plants are grown, the chippings or other top dressings should be lightly stirred to allow air to reach the soil and prevent packing. Renew all bait for slugs and snails, for if a mild spell occurs during this month these pests can create havoc.

There are still a number of plants that will provide interest during the month when the weather is fine: *Cyclamen neapolitanum* and *C. ibericum;* the many autumn flowering crocuses such as *C. longiflorus*, *C. medius*, the Saffron crocus *C. sativus*, *C. pulchellus* and *Polygonum vaccinifolium*, an evergreen shrub with small spires of pink flowers.

The conifers take on a new lease of life at this time, many turning to golden bronze, yellow or blue-grey. The berrying shrubs are at their best, too, and provide a bright picture on dull November days.

If there is a mild spell during the month a routine spray against pests will finally clear the plants and provide protection for the winter months ahead. Weed seedlings are best removed before they gain a foothold, but here care is necessary that these *are* weeds and not seedlings of rock plants. Pans or pots containing seed should be looked over and if there is any sign of liverwort or moss these should be gently removed with tweezers or a blunt stick. Both are

Where small cuttings of rock plants are housed in cold frames, some ventilation must be given during the day at this time of year. Condensation and a stagnant atmosphere encourage damping off.

injurious to the seedlings if allowed to remain—more so in pans of rock plant seeds which may have to be left for a period of up to two years.

If a cold frame is used to house either rock plant seedlings or rooted cuttings growing on for planting out next year, air should be given when weather permits, for a stagnant atmosphere will quickly make these liable to damping off diseases. The only time the frame should be closed is during heavy rain or prolonged frost.

Roses

This is the earliest month that the rose specialists can usually hope to dispatch the plants. In the average season the wood is not ripe enough for lifting with complete safety much before November.

Nearly all roses are now dispatched in multi-ply paper sacks, and while these are strong enough to protect the plants from damage in transit they are not really frost-resistant. So the roses should be unpacked as soon as possible. If there should be a frost when the package is received it should be placed in an unheated, but frost-proof shed, where the plants will come to no harm for a few days. As soon as this can be done they should be removed from the package and sprinkled liberally with water. If the roots are dry they should be stood in tepid water for several hours.

There is quite a wide variation between different nurseries in the amount of trimming undertaken before dispatch. The larger rose specialists remove the soft growth from the tops before lifting mechanically. Some, but not all, remove the leaves, but usually there are many of these still on the plants dispatched in November. All of these leaves and any flower buds or soft, sappy young shoots should be cut off as soon as possible. If the leaves are allowed to remain they may lead to shrivelling of the stems from loss of moisture due to transpiration. In addition, any broken stems or roots should be cut away cleanly just beyond the damage.

If it should happen that the consignment is delayed in transit it may be that the stems will be shrivelled when the package is opened. It is a waste of time

When planting a Rose standard ***below*** **stake it first and plant it to the correct depth, that is so that the swollen union is just covered with soil. You should always ensure that the roots are well spread out** ***right*****.**

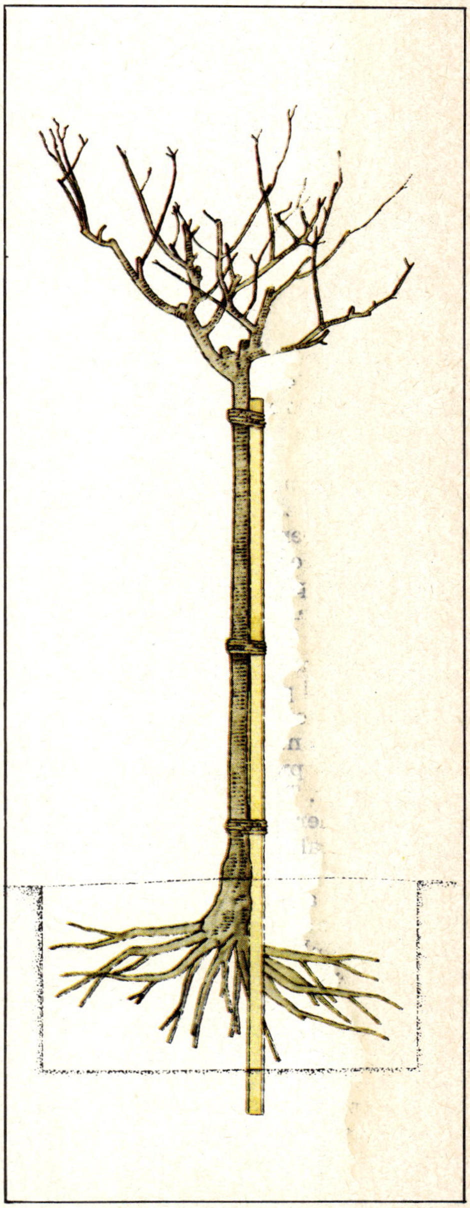

Rose plants packed and pruned ready for dispatch from the nursery to the buyer. The polythene wrapping keeps the ball of soil intact and moist until planting.

planting with the stems in this condition.

The most effective treatment is to dig a fairly deep trench, lay the plants horizontally at the bottom and then cover them completely, both roots and stems, with 6 inches of soil, firming this so that there is complete contact between soil and stems.

If the soil in the trench is at all dry the trench should be watered well after burying the plants. After a week or ten days the plants should be unearthed and by then the wood should have plumped up, allowing the roses to be planted normally.

The correct planting depth is when the budding point, i.e. the swollen part from which the top growth emerges, is just covered with not more than an inch of soil. Standard roses should always be planted as shallowly as possible, so that the top roots are only just covered. A stout stake should be driven home before the roots are covered to avoid possible injury. Dig a hole large enough to take the roots when spread out to their maximum—they should never be bent round to fit into too small a hole.

Finally, plenty of moist granulated peat, to which a little bonemeal has been added, should be mixed with the soil in direct contact with the root system and thoroughly firmed to ensure proper contact between roots and soil.

Trees, Shrubs and Climbers

During this month, the planting of deciduous trees and shrubs, apart from those of doubtful hardiness, can continue. November, in fact, is one of the best months for this operation. There should be no severe frosts to delay planting and, given comparatively mild weather conditions up to Christmas, the plants will make root growth that will stand them in good stead when leaf growth recommences in spring.

Planting positions for trees require the usual careful preliminary preparation, with plenty of space left for the roots. Ample space is doubly important where specimen trees are being planted in a lawn.

The holes for planting should be deep and wide enough to allow for the full spread of the roots, with an additional margin of about a foot for initial growth all around them.

Cramming the roots of a tree or shrub into a hole too small for them can often cause unsatisfactory development and even complete failure.

When a tree is planted, the base of the root system should rest on a shallow mound of soil in the planting hole. The nursery soil mark is a reliable guide to the correct planting depth, but the soil should reach an inch or two above this to allow for sinking. Before planting, any roots that are damaged should be cut back to sound material with a pair of sharp secateurs.

If the operation is to be a one-man job, it will help if the tree is tied to a batten of wood laid across the top of the planting hole. This not only helps in determining the proper planting depth but also keeps the tree firmly in position while the hole is being filled and the soil firmed in.

Standard trees will need staking with a stake that is sufficiently stout to do its job efficiently. Round chestnut stakes, if obtainable, are very satisfactory. Chestnut is a good rot-resistant wood and stakes of this kind will easily last for the two or three seasons that their support is required.

The best method is to drive the stake into position before the tree is planted. This avoids damaging the roots as they can be spread round the stake after it is in. The top of the stake should not come above the point where the head of the tree branches from the main stem. If it is too long, damage by rubbing may result. Ties should be wide and soft enough to prevent them from cutting into the bark. Patent plastic or rubber ties are ideal for this purpose.

Winter protection of tender shrubs should be one of your main concerns. Delicate climbers and wall shrubs, as well as tender shrubs in exposed situations, will need some form of winter protection, especially for the first season or two after they are planted. Many shrubs are not completely hardy when young but acquire greater resistance to cold conditions as they mature.

If a young tree or shrub is to be planted single handed, tie it to a stout piece of wood so that the plant can be held upright while the soil is packed around the roots. It is also possible to plant it in this way to the correct depth.

1

There are several ways of providing the necessary protection. In the shrub border, hessian screens can be erected round young plants to shelter them from freezing winds. Alternatively, a circle of wire netting, loosely packed with dry bracken, can be used. Shrubs susceptible to late spring frosts, such as hydrangeas, tree paeonies and others, can be protected in a similar manner when the need arises.

Anything used as a protective covering should always be removed as soon as the danger of severe frosts is past in spring.

Wall plants of doubtful hardiness can be protected with canvas or polythene sheets, while shrubs such as chaenomeles, lilac and forsythia, whose dormant flower buds are especially susceptible to damage by birds, can be protected by pieces of old fruit netting or by threading black cotton through the branches.

This is more effective than bird repellent sprays which, excellent though they are while they last, need renewal after periods of rain. These, however, can be useful where larger and more mature shrubs and climbers are in need of protection.

1 When tender shrubs are grown against a wall, protect them in winter with peat or bracken packed around them and held in position by polythene sheeting.
2 A rough canvas screen on the windward side of a newly planted shrub, like this Mahonia, will prevent rocking until the root system is established.

2

Vegetables

It may seem paradoxical to be talking of seed sowing at such an obviously dead time of year, but in the south and in other sheltered gardens where the soil is warm, or where cloches can be used, both broad beans and early peas may be sown in the open ground.

Some varieties of both these vegetables are more suitable than others for this purpose. Broad beans to sow now include the modern dwarf broad bean. Because this plant is so compact it can be wintered and cropped under cloches and so give really early pods. 'Aquadulce Claudia' is for autumn and winter sowing only and should never be sown after January. 'Seville' is another very hardy variety giving shorter pods which mature early.

Peas include the sugar pea which comes very early if helped by cloches. It is a round-seed pea and it is these varieties and not the wrinkled peas or marrowfats which should be sown now. 'Feltham First' and 'Meteor', which some consider to be the hardiest variety, are two others that can also be sown. It is important that this crop should only be sown when conditions are right; otherwise it is best to wait until the spring.

Chicory can be lifted for forcing now. Roots should be placed upright close together in deep boxes or pots in ordinary soil and covered with sand. They should then be brought into a dark place which has a temperature of about 60°F (16°C). The chicons should be ready in about two weeks. It is best to lift for succession.

Seakale roots can also be lifted now and stacked under a north wall covered with sand, ready for lifting as required. Pot the crowns in succession, three or four in a 7-inch pot, and bring into a warm greenhouse for forcing. Seakale, too, should be forced in complete darkness.

Jerusalem artichokes should be lifted now and stored in sacks in the same way as potatoes. Horseradish is also best lifted and can be kept fresh merely by laying the roots on the floor and covering them with dry sand or soil.

In case of hard weather, lift some parsnips and salsify. But continue to

1

3

1 Garden Peas of varieties such as 'Meteor' can be sown in suitable localities this month. It is one of the hardiest varieties, and withstands frost.
2 Roots of Chicory can be lifted and put in deep boxes of ordinary moist soil, under the staging of the greenhouse.
3 A dwarf Broad Bean, 'Aquadulce Claudia', is for autumn and winter sowing only and should not be sown after January.

2

take supplies as required from the garden while the soil is not frosted hard or snow covered. Store the lifted roots in sand. Dig whenever possible and wherever necessary.

It is important to complete digging as early as possible because nature prepares the soil right for spring much better than can Man. Frost, snow, and winds will pulverise the soil, breaking down clods into small particles which, by the time we are ready to sow seeds in the spring, will fall easily into a good fine tilth.

Dig while the weather is right. When any plant becomes unproductive, root it out and dig. Don't break down soil clods, let them weather.

Water Gardens

Really severe weather is rare before Christmas but it is as well to be prepared, and now is the time to instal the floating pool heater which is the most effective way of preventing the fish pond from freezing over.

If a fountain or waterfall pump is present it will probably be a good idea to disconnect it, and connect up the heater in its place. At the same time the pump can be cleaned and given whatever annual servicing is recommended in the manufacturer's instructions and—if it is a submersible pump—put it away until the spring.

If there is no fountain or waterfall, this may be an excellent time to think about the advantages of adding one. Installation can, of course, be carried out at any season.

1

2

3

1 A 100-watt Otter pump will prevent ice in the pool in winter and once the autumn clean up of growth has been completed the heater can be installed in readiness.
2 A floating submersible heater being lowered into the pool.
3 A water course can be made of a series of fibre glass bowls transversing a sloping piece of ground. Each bowl is level itself and water overflows from the pouring lip, along the course.

The virtues of moving water arrangements are part practical and part aesthetic. The murmur and splash of water is a delightful sound during the summer months and can do more than anything else to give the garden an out-of-the-ordinary character. A practical advantage is the benefit the fish derive from the oxygen carried into the pool with every bubble in the waterfall and every droplet in the fountain spray. At the same time it should be remembered that water-lilies dislike currents and cold water. For their sake, moving water effects should *never* be created by a continuous supply from the mains but only by circulation of the water from the pool itself. Currents are avoided by careful positioning of the pump as close as possible to the waterfall; in other words, taking the water out as close as possible to the place where it comes in will ensure that disturbance is confined to the smallest possible area.

There are many pumps suitable for powering fountain and/or waterfall arrangements and choice will depend on the number and scale of the effects desired. Pumps are divided into two categories—submersible pumps and surface pumps.

Submersible pumps simply sit in the pool and need no plumbing or fixing. A surface pump is mounted outside the pool, housed in a dry pump chamber. It draws water from the pool through a suction line and then pumps it along polythene delivery lines to the fountain and/or waterfall outlets. Surface pumps are generally more audible than submersibles.

For small- or medium-sized pools

which require no more than one fountain and/or one waterfall, submersible pumps offer decided advantages. For schemes involving combinations of several fountains and waterfalls the lower cost of surface pumps may well outweigh the disadvantage of having to construct a pump chamber. Specialist suppliers of water garden equipment will offer helpful advice, given details of the effects desired. In particular they will want to know, in the case of waterfalls, the horizontal distance the water will have to travel and the vertical lift—that is, the height of the top of the watercourse above the water level in the main pool.

A simple, though perhaps costly method of constructing a watercourse is offered by glassfibre watercourse units. These are made in the form of basins or troughs with pouring lips and the most sophisticated types have a rough, rocky finish that makes them very fair imitations of rock pools and stony streams. They can be set in a rockery in any combination and with any convenient vertical distance between them provided, of course, that they overlap just enough for the water pouring from one to fall into the next. Even one, set a foot or so above the pool, can be very effective.

Always bear in mind that the pleasant murmuring splash of water can be enjoyed with a very modest stream. Miniature Niagaras are not necessary or particularly desirable. The planting of ferns and waterside plants can continue in the open this month.

Wildlife

Now that the winter has really arrived the feeding of resident and migrant birds should become not a casual activity but a regular and important one. It is better never to feed birds at all than to put out food for a period and then to forget, for many birds become dependent on what is offered and will surely die of starvation if the food they have come to expect is denied them.

Increase the quantities of fatty food—this gives strength, stamina and warmth. Pieces of suet stuffed into a netting 'bird stocking' will be enjoyed by some birds, but it is better still to make up a special bird 'pudding'. Mix together seeds, nuts, pieces of cheese, soft biscuits, stale cake, boiled potato and other scraps and place in a large cup or similar receptacle. Pour hot fat over the mixture and allow to cool and set. Turn this out on to the bird table. Or put the pudding into a jam jar on its side. Water cannot get into the jar but small birds are able to do so.

Water is as important as food. This should be in a receptacle shallow enough to let birds both drink and bathe, probably not more than 4 inches deep and made of something with a rough surface. The birds will not be able to support themselves in a container made of a smooth substance, such as plastic. The water should be changed frequently and never allowed to freeze solid. This may mean changing the water several times a day in really freezing weather conditions.

If bird baths freeze quickly it is helpful to use a pond heater provided, of course, there is an electric point nearby. Never use anti-freeze, glycerine or any similar substance to keep water from freezing, for it will seriously damage the birds' plumage.

The importance of water in winter is that it helps the birds to maintain healthy, well-oiled and warm coats. A bathing bird never gets really wet. It cleans itself of surface dust, shakes its feathers free of moisture and then gets down to the serious business of preening. With its beak the bird smoothes its feathers into position and then dips its beak repeatedly into its oil gland and spreads the waterproof substance smoothly along its feathers. This complex preening process is vital to the warmth and protection of the bird.

Blue Tits enjoy a coconut suspended from the trellis. Encourage them to come to the garden in winter for their entertaining ways. They can be amusing acrobats while feeding on nuts and fat.

Birds become very engrossed when bathing and are apt to lose some of their natural wariness, so make sure that the bird bath is in a position near cover, to which the bird can dart if surprised by a cat, dog or squirrel.

If there is, in fact, a cat or dog in the family it is wise not to allow birds to become too tame. By all means feed them and encourage them into the garden, but respect their shyness and do not lure them too close to the house or encourage them to feed from the hand. Neither cats nor dogs can be, or even should be, trained not to attack or even stalk birds. Instead, make it your own responsibility to keep your animals in the house or shed for certain periods, such as twilight, so that the birds may be allowed to feed and bathe in safety.

The Month of December

The joys of the December garden are partly for sophisticated tastes with muted reds, browns, yellows and greens. But there is plenty of brightness too: brilliant poinsettias, the ripening berries of Crataegus prunifolia and the sharp white flowers of Convallaria majalis

Euphorbia pulcherrima 'Viking', the Poinsettia, is one of the most popular of flowering plants indoors at Christmas

1

3

2

4

1 Primula obconica with large somewhat floppy flowers is a favourite to have in the house at this time of year.
2 Capsicum fru[illegible]escens (syn. C. annuum) has several for[illegible]s that can be grown for indoor decorat[illegible]n. Other kinds which are larger, are the Peppers, grown for flavouring and culinary use.
3 Convallaria[illegible] the Lily-of-the-Valley, can be force[illegible] [illegible]nd encouraged to flower in the green[illegible]se. Bring the pots indoors to enj[illegible]he scent in the warmth.
4 Solanum [illegible]astrum, the Winter Cherry, is [illegible] for its brightly coloured f[illegible]

1

2

3

1 Snow can transform the garden into a picturesque scene with a new dimension, changing proportions and emphasising shapes. Where wind-blown snow rests, the enlarged proportions of an inconspicuous plant can make it important.
2 Frost traces the outlines of Ivy leaves against a wall, changing the texture and emphasising the shape of the leaves.
3 Hoar frost adds a furry edge to Rose leaves, enlarging them and altering the shape and outline.

1

2

3

4

6

5

7

There is a wide variety of form in the cones that are carried by some trees. Frequently they are a distinguishing feature of the tree and are specially in evidence during autumn.

1 Pinus griffithii, the Bhutan Pine, is almost exclusively an ornamental tree in Britain. The bark and cones when young are remarkably resinous. The long cones hang down.

2 Pinus coulteri, the Big-cone Pine, is from California and has strongly hooked spines on its big cones.

3 Abies procera, the Noble Silver Fir, bears large and decorative cones that are quite long and erect.

4 The 'cones' of Chamaecyparis lawsoniana, the Lawson Cypress, are the ripened female flowers.

5 The chocolate-coloured cones of the Monterey Cypress, Cupressus macrocarpa.

6 The smooth, resinous cones of Abies lasiocarpa, from the western shores of North America, are resinous at first.

7 The Monkey Puzzle, Araucaria imbricata, has conical spikey cones.

2

4

3

5

1 In mid-winter coniferous trees provide colour—greens, gold and blue-greys—against the bare background of the deciduous trees.
2 Crataegus prunifolia is notable for its large persistent fruits and foliage that take on a good autumn colour.
3 Mistletoe, Viscum album, is one of the plants traditionally used for Christmas decoration. It is a parasitic plant that grows on the branches of trees.
4 Ilex aquifolium bacciflavum is one of the yellow fruited Hollies.
5 Iris unguicularis will be in flower before Christmas in many sheltered corners, and will continue to bloom through most of the winter. Its delicate blooms are slightly fragrant.

Jobs of the month

This is the time to carry out those essential tidying up operations. Neglect these and the garden takes on a ragged and scruffy look in winter. December is a good month, too, to study garden catalogues and draw up plans for the work that must be done when the spring arrives. With careful planning now you can have colour in your garden for next December

Bulbs

Lily bulbs delivered this month should be plump and firm. If they are shrivelled pack them in damp peat for a week or two to restore their quality. Dust corms in store with an insecticide

Flowers for Cutting

Because of the lack of blooms in the garden, evergreens come into their own. They may be dusty, so clean the leaves before using them in an arrangement

Fruit

Prune secondary growth on cordon apples and pears. Do not prune stone fruits. Pull off and burn mummified fruit to prevent spread of brown rot. Pick off and burn second crop figs

Greenhouse

Take first cuttings of perpetual carnations now. As midseason chrysanthemums finish cut them down to about 8 inches, wash soil from roots and set close together in boxes of good compost

Hedges

Gardeners considering planting new hedges should look round now at the berry-bearing subjects. These should be at their best this month

Herbaceous Plants

This is the time to prepare new borders, do deep digging and manure the ground in readiness for spring planting. Protect delphiniums and lupins against slug damage

House Plants

Plant arrangements are good Christmas gifts. When planting these, choose subjects and containers with care. When receiving a planted bowl examine it at once to see if it needs water

Lawns

Remove dead leaves from the lawn. Now is the time to pay special attention to messy and uneven lawn edges. Where edges have been worn bald, it is a good idea to turn the worn piece of turf

Paths, Fences and Walls

If new paths are to be laid, it is well worth laying soil-heating cable under them to thaw ice and snow. In some districts it is worth storing some road salt

Patios, Balconies, Roof Gardens and Window Boxes

Consider the kind of plants suitable for these situations in large cities. Pyracantha, forsythias, Daphne mezereum and many berberis all do well in city air

Rock Gardens

Birds can damage cushion plants in winter, so it is a good idea to cover them with chicken wire. Labels should be checked. Those where plants have died or been ruined by pests should be removed

Roses

Rake off fallen rose leaves from beds and burn. A start can be made on pruning hardy shrub roses, the Kordesii group, the Wichuraiana ramblers and even some of the floribunda-shrub group

Trees, Shrubs and Climbers

There are many trees and shrubs that will give plenty of colour in December. Some will flower from November to March. But gardens with year-round colour must be planned with care

Vegetables

In the vegetable garden this is a month for tying up loose ends. The real task this month is forcing and planning salad crops and seakale to ensure a constant succession

Water Gardens

This is the perfect time to sit down with a paper and pencil to plan new pools, waterfalls and cascades, or improvements to existing water gardens

Wildlife

As farmers have to cut down more trees and hedges, it is up to gardeners to provide homes for birds and host plants for the insects which provide their food, for birds kill so many garden pests

Bulbs

The Christmas-flowering hyacinths and Roman hyacinths will be in flower now. Although their perfume is as intense as the mid season kinds, they do not normally last quite as long. Out of doors in sheltered spots the buds may be appearing on *Iris stylosa* (syn. *I. unguicularis*). Pick these and bring them on indoors to enjoy their winter blooms and delicate perfume, or the birds will nip them off and ruin them. More buds will be produced in years when there has been a dry spring to help to ripen the plants after flowering.

Hoe over bulb beds where narcissi and tulips have been planted. A residual herbicide applied on a calm dry day will save much time in spring when there will be so many other jobs to which attention must be given. A powder fungicide hoed in around the tulips can be especially effective against such diseases as basal rot, botrytis and fusarium.

Lily bulbs will be available in the shops before Christmas, and those ordered earlier will be delivered now. They ought to be plump and firm to the touch but if they have shrivelled, pack them in damp peat and/or leafmould for a week or two to restore their quality before planting.

Late autumn has long been recognised as the best planting time for lilies but bulbs potted up now or planted out of doors at the turn of the year, or even during February if the weather is open, will do well. The soil they need out of doors—or the compost if they are potted—must have plenty of humus and drainage material. Slug pellets should be pushed into the ground near lily bulbs out of doors—both the newly planted ones and the established ones—because slugs love the fleshy leaves of the lily bulb at this time of the year and the bulb has no outer coat for protection as have most other bulbs.

The early flowering gladioli can still be planted if the weather is open and the ground covered with bracken, peat or other protective material after planting. Incorporate some bonemeal in the ground when planting. Such forms as *Gladiolus nanus* 'Cinderella' (coral), 'Peach Bloom' (soft pink), and 'The Bride' (white and red) are attractive and will provide early flowers for cutting next summer.

Gladiolus corms lifted during October can be cleaned off this month if this has not been done already; the old shrivelled corms broken away and discarded and the corms rubbed free of outer skins. Dust them, and any corms already in store, with an insecticide such as BHC or malathion against thrips, especially if the pest was troublesome during the summer. Carefully examine corms in store and *burn* any that appear to be ribbed or corrugated or seem spongy.

Sturdily grown Hyacinths in bowls and pots are coming into flower to decorate the greenhouse. Alternatively this is the stage at which they can be brought into the house to be enjoyed.

Flowers for Cutting

Although every bloom is double precious now, this is the season when evergreens come into their own. But because they are so tough outdoors, evergreens of most kinds need a little sympathetic treatment when they are brought indoors, where they are in an alien environment.

Many will be very dirty and dusty. They will last better if they can breathe properly through their leaves, so they are worth cleaning. It is essential that they take up water quickly and it is surprising just how much will be consumed, so prepare all branches by plunging the stems in hot water until they become turgid. Once arranged, keep the water level topped up daily. Keep a little house plant food solution ready mixed and top up with this from time to time.

When gathering conifers for Christmas decorations, bear in mind that the tighter the needles grow the longer they will be retained on the branches. Blue spruce, for example, in perpetuelle arrangements, will never shed its needles, while Douglas fir will not hold its leaves for more than a week or two. *Thuja*, chamaecyparis and cupressus are all very long lasting when cut.

There are foliage fixatives specially formulated to reduce respiration rates and thus increase the life of leaves or needles on tree branches. Other methods which have been tried and found useful include painting the branches with cellulose wallpaper fixatives and spraying branches with colourless varnish or hairspray.

It is surprising how much colour one can create from a collection of evergreen snippets—colour which can be emphasised by the inclusion of a few fresh flowers or berry clusters. Yellows, orange, russet and blues appear as if by magic.

If chrysanthemums are arranged with plenty of foliage they will remain looking attractive long after their own leaves have faded. Arrange the flowers in such a way that a branch of evergreen stands before each bloom's stem. Remove the chrysanthemum leaves as necessary, but keep the pattern of the arrangement intact.

Narcissus 'Paper White' is a good early flower for forcing, and can be relied upon to bloom for Christmas in both the greenhouse and living room.
It is one of the bulbs that can be grown in water.

One can begin cutting branches of early blossom to force indoors in the warmth as soon as the shortest day is past. Even catkins cut then will open soon.

Choose a mild, moist day for your cutting. To hurry on the branches first immerse them in tepid water for an hour or two and then stand them in a warm greenhouse and spray them daily.

Fruit

Where secondary growth on cordon apples and pears has not yet been pruned attend to this now, cutting these new shoots back to one bud beyond their point of origin.

The leaders of cordons need not be cut, either in summer or winter, unless the trees have reached the limit of space available to them, or unless they are not making sufficient new sideshoot growth. In the latter case, the leader may now be shortened by up to a third of the growth it has made during the previous season. With young trees this may delay cropping, but it will stimulate the production of more laterals. If, on older cordons, the fruiting spurs have become crowded, this is the time to shorten them.

Cut back to one bud beyond their point of origin any secondary growths which have appeared on pyramid apples and pears since their summer pruning. Cut the central vertical leader back to about 9 inches of new growth, making the cut just above a bud pointing in the opposite direction to the bud to which the previous winter's cut was made.

Prune established standard, half-standard or bush apples and pears and newly planted fruits.

Do not prune stone fruits, but burn mummified fruit to prevent the spread of brown rot disease. Do not prune trees which have recently been root-pruned.

Vine rods are painted with Gishurst Compound against mealy bug in winter when growth is dormant. Rub the rods free of loose bark before painting so that the liquid will reach the insects hiding deep in the bark fissures.

Pick off and burn second crop figs on outdoor trees. These will never ripen and may well prove a disease risk by contracting mildew.

Give newly planted fruit trees, bushes, canes and strawberries a 2-inch mulch of well-rotted manure or garden compost to help conserve soil moisture in the event of a spring drought. If you have a fruit cage, remove the netting roof before snow comes to weigh it down and bend or break the supports.

Birds can do considerable damage to fruit trees and bushes during the winter months, pecking out the buds. Gooseberries are particularly subject to this trouble and for that reason their pruning is often left until March. Netting on trees provides the best defence against birds, or you can drape trees and bushes with rayon web or black cotton.

After pruning greenhouse vines, brush or peel off all loose bark from the main rods and paint with Gishurst Compound or 5 per cent tar-oil. Finally, unfasten the main rods and lower them on strings until horizontal.

Peaches and nectarines under glass also need tar-oil treatment to kill scale insects and aphid eggs. Spraying with tar-oil inside a greenhouse can be very messy, and it is better to apply the oily liquid liberally with a paint-brush.

Cut back, to one bud beyond their point of origin, any secondary growth that has been formed since the summer pruning of Apples and Pears. This can involve removing quite long whippy growth. The leader can be shortened on young trees or if the tree is not fruiting.

Inspect pears and unwrapped apples in store and remove any which show the slightest sign of rot.

Greenhouse

If all has gone well there should now be a good show of cyclamen, *Primula, obconica, Solanum capsicastrum* (the Christmas Cherry), *Azalea indica* and the first of the potted bulbs, such as *Narcissus* 'Paper White' and 'Soleil d'Or' and the earliest 'prepared' hyacinths. All of these may be in bloom by Christmas (or in berry in the case of the solanum) but the plants should not be over-crowded as this will only encourage pests and diseases. If possible, stand them on tiered shelving on the staging so that each one has ample room.

The beautiful foliage plant *Begonia rex* is another one that can add to the display, but this needs a temperature of at least 50°F (10°C) if it is to keep its leaves. At this time of year give *B. rex* the benefit of full light and keep the compost just moist.

As the mid-season chrysanthemums finish cut them down to about 8 inches high, wash the soil off the roots and set the roots (stools) close together in boxes of a good compost such as the John Innes potting compost No 1. Then keep them cool and fairly dry until they are started into growth early next year. The December-flowering varieties can then be spaced out farther apart to ensure a good circulation of air around them.

Zonal pelargoniums (geraniums) and fuchsias now in store will need an occasional look-over to make sure that they are not too dry. They need very little water but should not be allowed to dry out completely. A thorough soaking about once a month should keep them safe.

Where perpetual carnations are being grown the first cuttings may be taken now. Established plants should be kept in an even temperature, with a minimum of 45°F (7°C) at night, by careful regulation of the heating and ventilators. The plants need little water now but make sure that, when watering is necessary, the compost is wet right through.

Climbing plants of all kinds should be trained in as necessary and kept on the dry side. This is a good time, too, to erect any necessary supports for them, using wires, trellis or one of the various metal meshes that are available.

H.T. roses that were flowered in pots under glass last year may be brought in now for harder forcing. Renew the top inch or two of compost in the pots, prune the roses in the usual way and bring them into an initial temperature of 45°F (7°C). Water moderately and increase the temperature as the plants grow. Plants potted last autumn should not be started off until early next year, with only very mild forcing for the first season.

It is of course too soon to make any sowings for next year yet but the necessary materials for sowing, pricking-out and potting should be got in hand before the weather clamps down on operations of this sort. A good supply of loam should,

Simple Christmas decorations can be made by spraying branches of evergreens and cones with silver paint and using them in conjunction with fresh Anemone-flowered Chrysanthemums.

The beauty of Begonia rex leaves can be easily lost at this time of year. They drop quickly if the plants are not given enough light. Maintain a temperature in the greenhouse of 50°F (10°C).

for instance, be placed under cover so that it is dry enough for sieving and possibly sterilising when it is needed and a supply of peat should be sieved ready for use.

Sand, too, is another item needing to be kept dry, otherwise it may be frozen solid when you need it. Pots, boxes and so on should be thoroughly cleaned and dried ready for use.

Hard frost may also loosen the cuttings that have been inserted in frames for the winter, so if necessary firm them back into the soil, at the same time removing any dead leaves, weeds and other debris. It will also help if the soil between the cuttings is lightly pricked over by running the point of a dibber between the plants.

Finally, if the greenhouse plants do happen to get frozen spray them with cold water as early as possible next morning. This may just save them by preventing the too rapid thaw that does most of the damage.

Hedges

Deciduous hedging plants can still be planted this month whenever the weather is favourable. Normally there are no really long spells of severe frost in December to hold up planting. The problem is more likely to be excessive wetness, particularly for people who garden on heavy clay soils. It would be risky, to say the least, to try to plant hedges in soil that is wet and soggy after continuous heavy rain.

With the soil saturated, the roots cannot be firmed in properly, so there is a danger of leaving air pockets round them after the soil has dried out.

The best procedure, if weather conditions make planting impracticable, is to take out a shallow trench at one end of the planting site.

The shrubs, after careful removal from their packing materials, are placed in the trench, their roots being covered with some reasonably dry soil.

They can stay this way for some weeks without coming to any harm. As an additional frost precaution, sacking can be laid on the soil above the roots, held securely in position with bricks or large stones.

Berried hedges should be at their best in December and it is a good idea to look round other people's gardens with a view to noting suitable subjects for planting. The berries on a barberry hedge are very attractive in their translucent crimson beauty, but they are equally attractive to birds, who find them early in the season and bring the display to an untimely end.

Some of the cotoneasters make much better berried hedges. The scarlet berries of *Cotoneaster simonsii,* for example, remain on the bare brown stems until spring, as also do those of the evergreen *C. lacteus*. Its long-lasting scarlet fruits show up well against the olive-green foliage.

Some of the Cotoneasters make thick, sturdy hedges. Cotoneaster simonsii is one that holds on to its berries throughout the winter. Thus the hedge is green during the summer, but red in winter.

Pyracantha hedges, too, produce a mass of berries that persist until well after Christmas to provide a late winter feast for thrushes and blackbirds. *Pyra-*

cantha atalantioides, with red berries, is generally considered to make the best hedging species.

Hippophae rhamnoides, the sea buckthorn, makes one of the finest berried hedges for seaside districts. Both the twigs and narrow, willow-like leaves are silvered and the latter make a striking contrast to the clusters of orange-red berries.

As a change from red, the white mothball-like berries of the snowberries, symphoricarpus, can be attractive, especially as the birds seem to leave them alone to remain on the bushes throughout the winter. 'White Hedge' is a good hedging variety, with masses of white berries. It is a compact variety growing only about 4–5 feet tall.

Another interesting subject for a dwarf berrying hedge is *Viburnum opulus compactum*, a low-growing form of the native guelder rose that does not exceed 3 feet in height. The flat white heads of summer flowers are followed by red berries.

Herbaceous Plants

To lengthen the stems of Christmas roses, mulch the plants with clean straw or peat moss. *Iris unguicularis* (syn. *I. stylosa*) should be protected with cloche or handlight if the plants are to produce unspotted blooms for Christmas decoration. Scatter slug pellets among the Iris foliage to prevent damage to blooms. Such lovely flowers as these should be gathered before they are fully expanded if required for decorative indoor arrangements.

Most herbaceous plants should be cut back to within 6 inches of the ground now. Rake all rubbish and leaves from borders and burn or stack them in heaps to rot down into valuable compost.

The soil between perennials can still be forked over provided the ground is free from frost. Hardy plants such as Michaelmas daisies (aster), the shasta daisy *(Chrysanthemum maximum)*, helenium and golden rod (solidago) can be lifted and transplanted where necessary but do not divide roots until the spring. This is a good month for preparing new borders, deep digging and manuring the ground in readiness for the coming spring planting.

Delphiniums and lupins are extremely prone to slug damage, especially when they are grown in heavy clay soil. To deter this pest, scrape the soil from the tops of the crowns and cover with a conical-shaped heap of sharp cinders or sharp river sand. In early spring, the soil can be replaced, then treat the ground and any new shoots with a liquid slug killer.

Protect hardy fuchsias in winter with a few inches of soil and leafmould or peat, on clay soil covering the roots with 6 inches of fine weathered ashes. The tops of the plants, which give extra protection, should not be cut back until March.

Given reasonably mild weather, corms of the lovely poppy anemones *(A. coronaria)*—the semi-double 'St Brigid' and the single de Caen—can be planted for early bloom or cutting. These beauties thrive in sun or part-shade, planted on edge, 2–3 inches deep, 6 inches apart, in

1

1 Cut back the stems of Rue, Ruta graveolens, in late winter to encourage compact and bushy growth next year.
2 The corms of Anemone coronaria, the Poppy Anemone, can be put in when the weather is mild and the ground frost free. The St Brigid strain is semi-double and possibly sturdier than the de Caen type with single flowers.

2

RECOGNITION CHART

House Plants

Any part of the house can be decorated by house plants if consideration is given to the amount of light each plant requires

RHOICISSUS RHOMBOIDEA
A wall upon which light is reflected from a window is the best place to let Rhoicissus rhomboidea, the Natal Vine hang or climb. Ficus elastica likes a similar situation

NEPHROLEPIS EXALTATA
A north-facing windowsill is the ideal spot for Nephrolepis the Laddern Fern, Aspleniums, Platyceriums and other ferns

CHLOROPHYTUM COMOSUM VARIEGATUM
Where a windowsill is screened from bright sunshine by a thin curtain Chlorophytum comosum variegatum, the Waterfall or Spider Plant does well. (Azaleas and Saintpaulias given humidity can be grown in the same place)

OPUNTIA
Give cacti like Opuntias the sunniest place in the house

X FATSHEDERA LIZEI
Where semi-shade can be provided X Fatshedera lizei and its forms, Fittonias and Fatsia japonica will be happiest

SPATHIPHYLLUM WALLISII
Where there is gloom or shade, Spathiphillum wallisii will be happy, together with Hedera helix and Philodendron scandens

AZALEA
For a central position in any room Azaleas, Marantas, Cordyline and Crotons are the most reliable

BEGONIA
Where the morning sunshine strikes an east facing window the Begonias will be happiest, together with Plectranthus

ASPIDISTRA
Adaptable plants that do not mind being moved about are Aspidistra elatior, the Parlour Palm, Sansevieria trifasciata laurentii and Aechr[illegible]s

CYCLAMEN
Where there is constant good light but not direct sunlight the Cyclamen persicum will do best. Choose also Euphorbia pulcherrima, the Poinsettia, Dieffenbachias, Scindapsus aureus and its forms for similar positions

MAMMILLARIA
Mammillarias, and other cacti, need as much sun as they can get

dampish well-drained soil liberally enriched with rotted cow manure and leafmould. In cold districts plants should be protected with a cloche.

Autumn-planted bedding plants—wallflowers, forget-me-not (myosotis), polyanthus—need firming in after frost. The same applies to newly planted carnations and pinks. Both the latter will repay a dressing of ground lime during the early spring.

Although perennial, the chrysanthemum produces earlier and better blooms if new plants are raised annually by means of cuttings. Stools should be lifted and planted in a cold frame now with the idea of encouraging basal growth. Straight, sturdy shoots 2–2½ inches long, removed immediately below a joint (node), are suitable material, the lower leaves being stripped off so that no foliage comes into contact with the soil when the cuttings are planted.

Plant firmly, 1 inch deep, in a propagating bed, round the edge of a pot or in boxes, filled with equal parts sharp sand and damp peat or in John Innes potting compost No 1, aiming at a temperature around 50°F (10°C). Hormone root promoting substances, in dust or liquid form, can be used before insertion, but chrysanthemums are not difficult to root without these aids.

House Plants

Plant arrangements make excellent presents. There are, however, some important points to watch.

Select your plants and their containers with care. The containers must be large enough to hold the requisite number of plants without crowding, yet on the other hand there should be a minimum of ugly bare soil showing between them. The bowl or other container should be deep enough to hold the root ball of each plant and still allow enough space for watering, yet not so deep that some of the attractive foliage is hidden in its depths.

The container need not have drainage holes if planting is carefully carried out. Its colour should not clash with the plants it is to contain and any pattern on it should be unobtrusive.

Plants should be chosen to give contrast of shape, form, colour and texture, yet all must have the same cultural requirements. Never put cacti and succulents, for example, in the same bowl as an aphelandra and a cyperus, for their water requirements are completely different.

When selecting, choose some plants that grow tall and upright, some that are rounded and bushy and some that will hang or trail attractively over the rim of the container.

Make sure the bowl is clean and then place a layer of coarse drainage material

1

2

1 House plants provide colour and interest during the winter months and should be given regular attention. Take off dead leaves, water and keep a stern eye for pests.

2 Groups of house plants raised in your own greenhouse make acceptable Christmas gifts. Assemble them in collections of varying leaf colour and form and put them together in one container.

in its base. On this pour a layer of finer material such as pea gravel and then finally the soil mixture. Use a good sterilised soil mixture such as John Innes.

While the plants are still in their pots practise arranging them on top of the soil in the bowl to see exactly where they should go to give the best effect. When you have found the most pleasing effect you can begin planting.

Knock the plants from their pots one at a time and tease away a little of the soil around their roots. With your fingers clear a little hole in the soil of the bowl and place the roots in position, firming soil around and over them so that the plant is held securely. Do the same with each plant in turn. When the bowl is completely planted spray the plants gently with clean water, using sufficient to trickle into the bowl. Do not water in addition for the first couple of days, but spray the plants again, this time watering the bowl generously. Then set it to one side to dry out almost completely. When this is done it will be ready to receive its normal routine waterings.

Clean the bowl thoroughly of any soil particles adhering to it before you give it away. If it is to travel try to find a strong and secure box for it rather than risk damage to the plants.

If the recipient of the plant is unversed in the care of house plants it is a kind and helpful thing to give brief written instructions or a copy of a little book or leaflet. Most flower stores have free leaflets or inexpensive books which you can obtain for just this kind of purpose.

When receiving a planted bowl the first thing to do is to examine it carefully to decide if it needs water. Once this has been dealt with, place the bowl in a cool and airy room rather than in the main living-room, which is too likely to be warm and stuffy—the wrong environment for a newly planted bowl. Only after it has had several days to acclimatise itself to its new surroundings should the bowl be brought into the living-room and its more or less permanent home decided.

For the first few waterings examine each plant the pot contains to make sure that all are in good health and uncontaminated by pests or diseases. Only when you are reassured on this point can you begin to treat the plant as a part of your furnishings, which after all is its function.

Lawns

December is very much the tail end of the year as far as lawns are concerned. There is virtually nothing that *has* to be done, but there are still the odd jobs which can be carried out now to the advantage of the general appearance of the lawn next season.

Any dead leaves lying about should be removed and if the weather is very mild and open, lightly tip the grass, which is still growing slightly, with the mower blades set high.

Another job which can well be done this month, or at any time during the autumn or spring, is the tackling of uneven or unsightly lawn edges. Very often these get into a mess each year, purely as a result of normal family wear and tear.

Where it is just a question of straightening the edges, a sharp spade or turfing iron can be used to chop away unwanted soil or grass. If the lawn should have straight line edges, and you are not too certain how good your eye is, it pays to peg a length of twine or string along the edge, and work to that as your guide line. Where the lawn has a curved or shaped edge, a length of garden hosepipe, positioned as required, can serve the same purpose as a guide line to obtain even edging.

If after edging the lawn you still feel there is a 'wear and tear' appearance around its perimeter, a useful way to overcome this for the following season is to lift and turn the worn pieces of turf.

With a sharp spade or turfing iron, first cut a piece of turf into a square then slice underneath it and lift it clear of the ground. Turn the turf so that the old, worn edge is facing the centre of the lawn, replace it, firm it lightly by treading and fill the cracks with topsoil. Maybe this need only be carried out in one or two places, or perhaps the entire perimeter of the lawn will benefit from a turn around in due course.

Whatever work is carried out on the lawn during December, at no time should it take place when the ground is very wet, frozen or snow-covered.

Paths, Fences and Walls

December's frosts and snows quickly indicate whether garden paths, front entrances and garage drives have been efficiently and intelligently planned and made.

A sudden thick snowfall can cover and hide a path completely and where residents may know the way from front door to gate, a visitor or tradesman can

Renovate lawns and grassy paths when the weather is open and frost free. Cut a turf of reasonable size so that it can be handled without breaking, with a turf-cutting iron. Lift it carefully and evenly and relay it the other way round. The thinly worn grass will then be able to recover and the thicker grass take the wear of the constant traffic. The adjoining worn turf (not shown) needs also to be turned in a similar way.

A level and well-laid path is easy to clear of snow in winter. Thought should be given to the snow hazard when planning and laying paths and driveways. A solid surface is always more practical.

easily blunder over flower beds, suffer inconvenience and embarrassment or even do significant damage.

Important paths, such as those to the front door or garage, should always have visual evidence of direction and width. They should be sufficiently well drained to carry away excess water quickly.

If new paths are to be laid, in some areas and under some circumstances it is well worth considering the advisability of laying a length of soil heating cable under them so that snow and ice can be dispersed quickly. This applies in particular where the slope to or from the house is steep and possibly dangerous under snowy or icy conditions. Soil warming cable is relatively inexpensive, easy to lay, foolproof, inexpensive to run for the brief periods necessary and of tremendous value where conditions are difficult or dangerous.

Alternatively, it is worth while in some districts to lay in a bag or two of road salt on the approach of winter. This can be ordered from most builders' merchants.

A reasonable scattering of the salt in the morning can clear drives and pathways of snow or ice in a few hours. It is inexpensive and can be stored easily in plastic bags in the garage.

Winter rains and snows also indicate the value of a definite though slight camber to any path. So long as the main path is clear it does not matter that the drains or gullies at the sides contain water which is steadily disappearing. Where the site is flat and the path has been efficiently edged it may take some time for this excess water to disappear, so when laying pathway edging always allow small drainage openings.

Patios, Balconies, Roof Gardens and Window Boxes

When considering what to plant in large cities, poor soil is not the only problem to be overcome. Polluted air and lack of good light are two more problems often met that also affect some plants. Even the rain that falls is frequently contaminated by chemicals in the air through which it travels on its way from cloud to ground.

There are plants which are able to withstand these difficulties. They include a surprising variation in type, running from the tough and obvious lavender, Michaelmas daisies, chrysanthemums and monarda to the lighter and more delicate violas and pansies, Solomon's seal and lily-of-the-valley—the last so tolerant and prolific that it can almost become a weed in some areas.

Among the smaller shrubs suitable for container planting and which tolerate city conditions is the invaluable pyracantha with its dark green glossy leaves and its multitude of autumn berries. Buddleias also do well, as do forsythias and practically all of the many berberis. *Daphne mezereum* stands up well to city air.

The best roses for cities include the old but still unbeatable thornless 'Zephirine Drouhin', 'General MacArthur', 'Frau Karl Druschki', 'Else Poulsen', 'Hugh Dickson' and 'Betty Uprichard'.

Ivies and Virginian creepers make good self-clinging climbers and wall plants for cities. They tend to get dirty and dusty and are improved in appearance by an occasional spray of clean water.

Much more exotic and interesting are such seemingly delicate climbers as *Hydrangea petiolaris*, wisteria and several of the honeysuckles.

Do not forget that wall plants, and particularly climbers, frequently suffer from drought because the wall both protects the plants from rain and tends to absorb it from the soil, so make sure that these plants are watered.

Shrubs that will tolerate fairly dry soils include lavender, brooms, heathers,

A firm and well constructed entrance to a town house. This area can be used in summer for sitting out, or changed in appearance by the introduction of container-grown plants in season.

Foliage plants in a London garden where they have to tolerate the unpromising conditions of the town atmosphere. With careful selection plants can be grown under such seemingly adverse conditions.

escallonia and laburnums. Helianthemums are, of course, particularly tolerant of dry conditions.

Window-boxes and container plants can get dry very quickly in hot and sunny conditions. Where conditions do not allow liberal watering, in some cases as frequently as twice a day, it is wise to choose plants which will not mind occasional dryness at the roots. These include thymes, several of the cheerful pinks, alyssum, the hardy geraniums, arabis and all of the wide range of sempervivums and stonecrops.

Rock Gardens

This is possibly the one month of the year when plants in the rock garden are more or less at a standstill.

Perhaps the only colour one can expect in December is displayed by the dwarf varieties of heath. These are varieties of *Erica carnea* and will succeed in an open sunny position, in any loamy soil well enriched with peat, irrespective of whether the soil contains lime or not. Their height ranges from 4–12 inches and each plant covers approximately an area of 18 square inches. These plants are foolproof but they need both an annual top dressing of peat in spring and cutting back with shears after flowering. This treatment keeps them compact and tidy. Their flowering season is from December to March and cold holds no terror for them. There are many varieties among which 'James Backhouse' (pink), 'King George' (deep red), 'Queen of Spain' (light pink), 'Winter Beauty' (deep pink), 'Springwood White' (white with outstanding brown anthers) and 'Vivellii' (crimson) are representative.

Where a number of cushion plants are grown in the rock garden, scree beds or troughs, birds can be a nuisance especially during cold periods, when they take a delight in pulling the plants to pieces. The troughs present little difficulty: a framework in the shape of a box large enough to fit round the edge made up of 1 inch by ½ inch wood battens to which a covering of chicken wire netting is nailed will provide complete protection.

In the rock garden or scree beds it is not so easy. Here it is best to make small cones of chicken wire either to cover one or more plants. Primulas too often suffer from bird damage. It is the flower buds that are the attraction and the birds unfortunately seem to prefer the rare Asiatic species.

The birds, deprived of fresh food during the winter often attack and pull out growth from cushion-forming plants in the trough garden. Protect such plants from birds by making a temporary frame of wood covered with chicken netting.

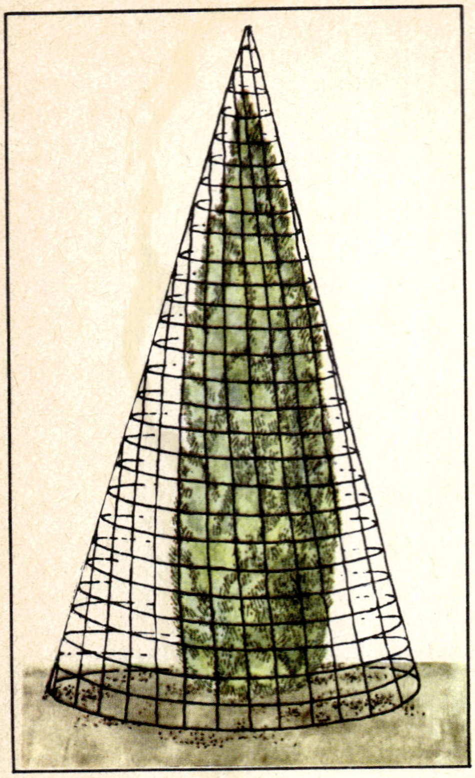

It is more difficult to protect plants in the rock garden itself because of the uneven ground. Make cones or wigwams of chicken netting.

Labels should be checked this month, and removed from sites where casualties have occurred. If a system of labelling is in use that entails keeping a record book, the entries against the numbers on the labels in the record book must be deleted. These numbers and labels can then be used again.

During December alterations in the rock garden can be carried out, such as the renewal of parts that have become overgrown through faulty planting. It is better to start with fresh stock than to retain old worn out plants that have outgrown their use. The whole of the site should be lightly forked over. To help drainage, dig in some of the surface chippings. Then add a liberal dressing of peat or well rotted leafmould and, after resetting the rocks, leave the site to settle until the following March, when it can be replanted.

Roses

Rose planting should be continued if the weather and soil conditions are suitable. If plants are received when the soil is too wet for planting, they should be 'heeled in' until the soil is friable enough for permanent planting. A trench should be dug in a sheltered part of the garden and the plants laid in singly, at an angle of 45 degrees.

The roots of the plant and the lower part of the stems should be covered with soil, or a mixture of soil and peat if the soil is very heavy, and firmed moderately. Care should be taken to see that the labels are well above soil level, and the plants should be spaced out so that one may be removed without disturbing its neighbours.

When properly 'heeled in' rose plants will come to no harm, even if planting in their permanent quarters has to be deferred until March.

All fallen rose leaves should be raked up from the surface of the beds and burnt. This is particularly important when severe attacks of rust or black spot have occurred during the previous season.

To take a further precaution against the carry-over of disease to the following season it is a wise plan to spray the plants during this month with Bordeaux mixture or, alternatively, with copper sulphate, at a strength of 1 ounce per gallon of water. One gallon of the dilution is sufficient to spray the plants in an area of about 8 square yards. Copper sulphate in solution should only

1

2

1 Some of the Rose pruning can begin before the end of the year and dead wood, as seen above, needs to be cut away first and burnt. Shrub Roses and Wichuraianas can be pruned now.

2 Rake up all fallen Rose leaves and burn them to prevent the spread of such fungus diseases as Black Spot. The spores survive the winter on decaying material. Keep garden rubbish composted.

be mixed in a plastic container, it can corrode metals.

There is no reason why a start should not be made on the pruning of some groups, such as the hardy shrub roses, the Kordesii group, the Wichuraiana ramblers if these have not been dealt with earlier, or even some of the floribunda-shrub group. Dead wood may be cut out of roses belonging to any group as soon as it is noticed, as this wood can only harbour disease spores and cannot possibly benefit the plant. Many of the shrub roses will benefit by thinning out some of the twiggy wood and by cutting out completely any canes which have obviously become exhausted. These often show a yellowish tinge and do not carry any strong side-shoots.

In addition, it is useful at this time to look at the shape of shrub and hedging roses and to practise some judicious trimming to ensure a more symmetrical outline. This applies more particularly to large specimen bushes. Any dead or diseased wood and trimmings should be burnt as soon as possible.

When the ground is frozen is a good opportunity for barrowing soil, manure and compost, as it would be difficult to do this to any extent in mild weather without damaging the turf. Usually it is possible to push ahead with any reconstruction work at this time, such as the clearing out of old shrubberies, the preparation of new borders, the erection of pillars and rustic screens.

Pot roses which have been sunk up to their rims outside since June should be brought under glass during December and kept in cool conditions for a few weeks. They may be pruned hard back towards the end of the month for flowering at the end of April.

Trees, Shrubs and Climbers

No single month in the garden need be entirely lacking in colour as far as trees and shrubs are concerned, and December is no exception. *Prunus subhirtella autumnalis*, for example, one of the loveliest of winter-flowering subjects, produces its semi-double, white cherry blossom at intervals from November to March. There is also a variety *rosea*, with flowers of a delicate pink. Both are compact enough to make fine specimen trees for the smaller garden.

In the shrub border, too, *Viburnum fragrans* will be bringing both colour and fragrance to the garden in December. This shrub, which should find a place in every garden, produces its clusters of pink-tinged white flowers from November to the end of February. Their intense perfume fills the air for a considerable distance on mild, still winter days.

Chimonanthus praecox, aptly named wintersweet, is another shrub in which fragrance is allied to winter blossom. It will be in flower by Christmas in a favourable season, particularly if it is grown against a south or west wall. The waxy, pale yellow, purple blotched flowers cluster thickly on the bare stems and branches.

There are a number of varieties with larger or more intensely coloured flowers than the type, but in these a certain amount of the characteristic perfume is lost.

The wintersweet may take some years to reach the flowering stage, but it is a shrub that is well worth waiting for.

1

2

1 Jasminum nudiflorum, the Winter-flowering Jasmine, blooms through the shortest and coldest of winter days. The blossom is a clear yellow and fragrant.
2 Viburnum fragrans, one of the winter flowering Viburnums, lives up to its name and is strongly perfumed during the shortest days of the year.

There will be no such waiting period with *Hamamelis mollis*, the witch hazel. In fact, a specimen in bud, planted early this month, will give quite a good display of blossom by Christmas. The flowers are unusual, like yellow spiders with curiously twisted, narrow petals. Witch hazel flowers have a delicate primrose scent.

On the house walls, winter colour is provided by the tiny yellow trumpet flowers of the winter jasmine, *Jasminum nudiflorum*. This is another shrub that flowers profusely from November to February and although batches of bloom may suffer damage in very severe spells, there are always others waiting to take their place as soon as milder conditions return.

As a substitute for flowers, the gold and silver-splashed leaves of variegated evergreens can be extremely useful in providing continuity of colour and interest in winter, and gardeners are especially thankful for these in December, both for outdoor and indoor decoration.

It is nice to see that old favourite, *Aucuba japonica maculata,* the so-called Japanese laurel, returning to favour. Its green-and-gold leaves are a cheerful sight in the shrub border in winter. As well as the common variety, affectionately known to our Victorian forebears as 'spotted Dick', there are others with more pronounced variegation, such as *A. j. picturata,* with elongated golden markings and a newer introduction from Cornwall, 'Goldenheart', in which the entire centre of the leaf is an attractive bright gold with a speckled margin of green and gold.

Variegated hollies are equally colourful and make fine specimen shrubs for the lawn or border. Among the best of these are 'Golden King', the gold leaves of which have a narrow edging of green, 'Golden Milkmaid', 'Silver Queen', and 'Mme Briot'. In the last-named, the variegation of 'Golden King' is reversed, the dark green leaves being edged with gold.

Variegated ivies can fulfil a similar function in brightening up a north wall in winter. Many varieties of *Hedera helix,* the common ivy, share this useful characteristic and there are gold and silver variegated forms of striking appearance.

Vegetables

December is a month mainly for tying up loose ends. Finish all digging now—there may be no other opportunity for some time. Remember that the work the weather does in pulverising the soil relieves the gardener of many hours of hard work in spring, when breaking down soil clods can be difficult and raking wearisome. Soil, well-weathered, needs only the slightest touch with the rake to be reduced to fine crumbs.

The only real task which continues on through this month is forcing and planning the salad crops and seakale so that there is a constant succession. If salads should be scarce remember that large brussels sprouts finely sliced are nutty and sweet. They do not have the strong flavour of raw cabbage and savoy, which some people find offensive. Red cabbage is also good for salads and is delicately flavoured.

Write for seed catalogues: you will then receive yours as soon as firms begin mailing their new issues. This really is important. Some seeds may be in short supply and only early applicants will be successful. Again, if one can get ahead in the new year with certain vegetables sown under glass, crops are earlier and consequently more appreciated.

December is a good month for pottering about in the shed. See that there are enough trays and that these are clean. Then seed potatoes, as soon as they arrive, can be stood, eyes upward, to get the light and so begin shooting. Earlier crops are produced this way.

Look over marrows, squash and so on to make sure that all is well. Turn over shallots and onions to look for any which may be affected by rot or fly. These should be burnt to destroy the pest.

If the shed seems not quite warm enough remember that insulation can be simply and easily installed by pinning sheet polythene over ceiling and sides.

Put down bait or traps if there are any signs of mice and rats.

Bring a pot or two of chives and mint into the warm kitchen and place on the window-sill. The plants will quickly

1
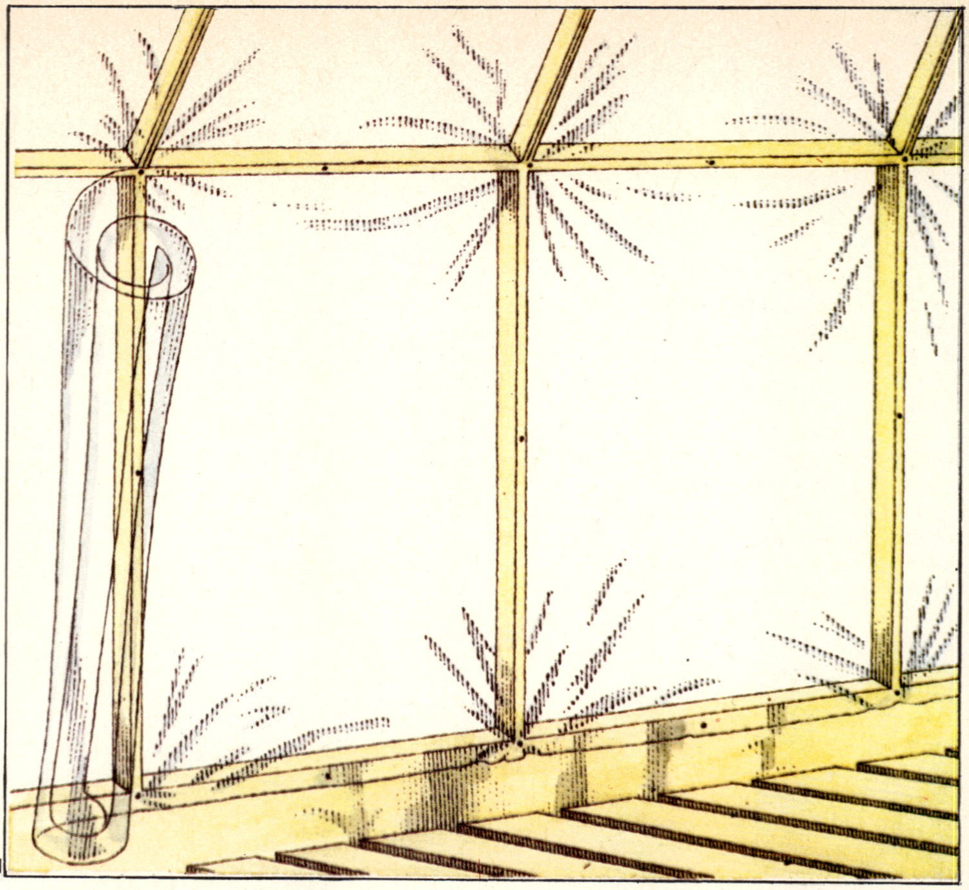

2

3

1 If the potting shed seems uninviting and chilly in December, line the windows with thick polythene sheeting. It will give some insulation and prevent draughts from the window frames.
2 Sprouts are in season now and cleanly grown ones may be used uncooked in winter salad. Shred or slice the sprouts finely before serving.
3 During December make sure trays are ready and dry to receive the seed Potatoes as soon as they arrive.

grow and although they may become drawn there will be sufficient growth to flavour a few dishes. Keep a succession of herbs in pots which can be brought into the house.

Water Gardens

The only work to be done in the water garden this month is to depress the switch that operates the pool heater if the weather is so cold as to threaten ice formation substantial enough to persist through the day.

This leaves plenty of time for recollecting the successes of the past summer, and considering the improvements and extensions that will make the next even more pleasurable. Plans might now be made for a completely new pool, particularly by those who started cautiously on a very small scale and, having tasted the pleasures of the water garden, have the urge to create something bigger and better.

With pools, bigger is always automatically better. The larger the volume of water, the less drastically it will be affected by extremes of heat or cold, making it much easier to establish and maintain a balanced and flourishing pool community.

Design considerations are not complicated by increased pool size. The shelf or shelves provided for water iris, arrowheads, bulrushes and other marginal plants in containers will still be 9 or 10 inches below water level. The main depth of the pool might be increased from the usual 18 inches to 24 inches or, in very large pools, to as much as 30 inches, but need never be greater. No other complications of depth are necessary since, with container planting, minor adjustments to suit the needs of particular plants can so easily be made by supporting the container on bricks or oddments of paving stone.

A marsh garden may be included in the overall design by incorporating within the pool boundary a substantial area with the 9 inch depth level and filling this with 12–15 inches of soil (i.e. to a height of 3–6 inches *above* water level). This soil will be divided from the pool proper by a brick partition with apertures to ensure that it is always soaked.

Whatever one's views are on the virtues of concrete, there is no doubt that its disadvantages increase with pool size, and serious consideration must be given to the several alternatives now available.

These alternatives are all loosely referred to as plastics, but they vary considerably in character and it is desirable for an intending purchaser to be aware of the the differences. Plastic pools which are supplied in preformed shapes, more or less rigid, are either fibre-glass or moulded polypropylene. Fibre-glass is the more rigid, substantial and lasting; it is an excellent material and an expensive one. Moulded polypropylene pools are cheap and, in comparison, less rigid and more flimsy in appearance. They are good enough value as a temporary or small 'spare' pool. Both fibre-glass and polypropylene pools are available in a range of predetermined shapes, none of any considerable size.

The other plastics are in the form of straightforward sheets which are used to line an excavation of virtually any shape. Disregarding the various proprietary names, these sheet plastics are basically butyl rubber, PVC, PVC reinforced with terylene net, and polythene.

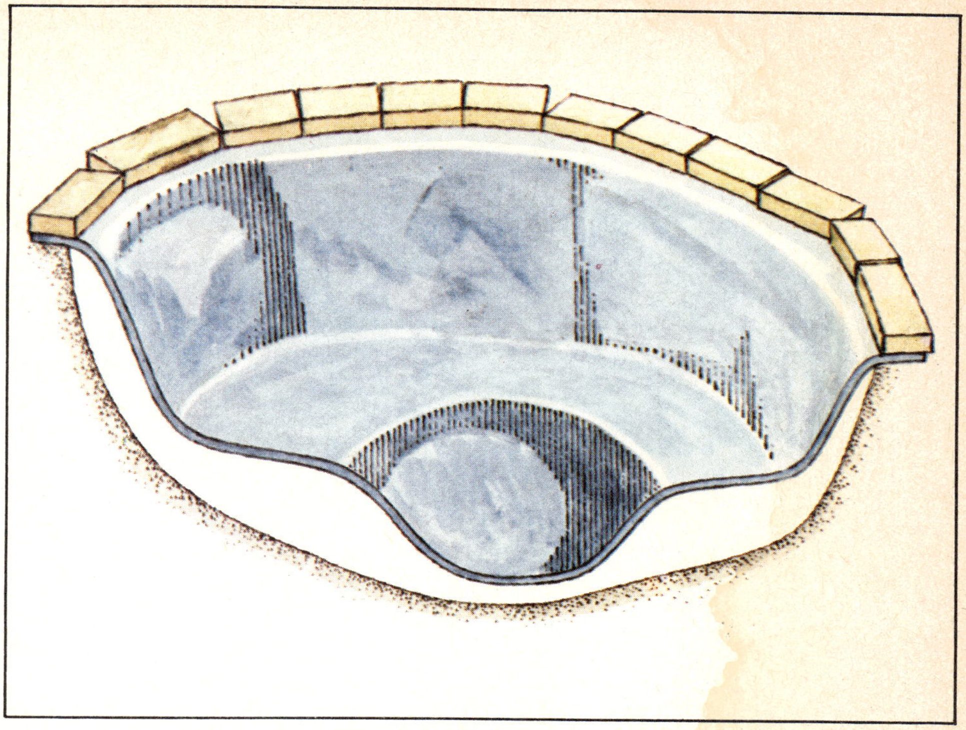

1 If a fibreglass mould is used to make a pool in the garden, ensure that the hole is dug deeply enough. There is no need to fill in the space between soil and fibreglass. Stones set around the edge both hide and secure the rim.

2 When the pool is constructed by using polythene sheeting the hole needs to be irregular in shape to form an interesting pool. Fill in the contours with fine soil or gravel so that the sheeting can be moulded into shape.

Polythene is cheap, easily damaged and not easily repairable and, except for a temporary or reserve pool, not a serious possibility in this context.

Straightforward PVC, which looks very much like polythene but is chemically very different, is much less likely ever to need repair but is, in the event, easily repairable. It is admirable for pools up to about 100 square feet in surface area, but for anything larger greater strength is perhaps desirable.

For the larger pool, where one is contemplated, it will be seen that fibreglass, polypropylene and polythene are non-starters, straight PVC is doubtful, and the choice is narrowed to butyl rubber or reinforced PVC. Both are excellent for the purpose, being available in any required size and having the elasticity to adapt themselves without strain to any shape the gardener fancies. They are not troubled by ice, and subsequent soil movement beneath the liner creates no problems for such flexible materials. They need to be settled on a layer of building sand or sifted soil as a matter of prudence, and to have part at least of their perimeter paved to stand up to the heavy foot traffic inevitable around such a frequently visited garden feature.

Now it only remains to write to your favourite supplier of water garden equipment to earmark a copy of his new season's catalogue, and settle down by the fire to sketch out the details of next year's projects.

Wildlife

Faced with the necessity to raise the level of productivity on their land, farmers tend to cut down trees and remove hedges. This makes life difficult for many species of wildlife—birds in particular. Not only are they denied their normal nesting sites, but wild grasses are lost to them and many insects living in the weeds of verges lose their homes. Spraying for efficient farming also kills many more insects and beneficial weeds: caterpillars lose their host plants.

It is therefore, up to the gardener to provide both homes and food for the birds. Nesting boxes and bird tables are helpful, but they are not the whole answer. It is far better to provide trees and shrubs for the birds and to grow plants which will either feed them or act as hosts to the insects on which birds feed.

In giving thought to the birds which help to decorate the garden, be realistic rather than romantic. Birds in the garden can cause damage. You must equate the damage they do with the pleasure they bring. Certain plants, particularly fruit and vegetables, should be protected from attack by a well made permanent fruit cage. The fruit blossom of cherries, apples, pears and so forth can be protected by spraying with a non-toxic chemical or by the safe webs of plastic deterrents. Never use netting in which birds can become trapped. They become so caught up in it in their attempts to escape that they cannot be cut loose.

Allow birds to use certain old and unproductive fruit trees, both at bud and blossom time and while the fruit is on the tree or fallen to the ground. Plant plenty of berrying plants, those with red fruits for the birds and those with yellow for yourselves, because for some reason yellow berries appear to hold far less attraction for birds. Allow seed heads of sunflowers, Michaelmas daisies, teasels, thistles to remain on the plants. Birds love them.

In some hidden spot allow a few nettles, ragwort and other weeds to grow. These are hosts to many insects and caterpillars. Plant a cabbage or two in this hidden patch and allow the cabbage white butterfly to plant its eggs. Allow just one rose bush to become infested with aphids. With systemic insecticides it is easy enough to prevent the pests from doing any damage to the other plants.

By doing these things, as well as providing food on the bird table, you will attract more birds into the garden and so obtain natural and inexpensive predators against so many of the insect pests which normally cost you time and money to clear.

Use pesticides with care and responsibility. Sensibly used and sensibly chosen they can enormously increase productivity in the garden and do the minimum of harm. Use only approved chemicals bearing the large 'A' on the label. Both manufacturers and Ministry officials are bound by law to test materials and it is up to the gardener to read labels and follow directions carefully to avoid unnecessary damage.

1

2

Make provision for the birds to have food and fresh water on the bird table. Remember that if birds are encouraged they will also visit the garden in summer. Order some proprietary protective material (1) for the fruit bushes, or erect the posts to hold netting or a fruit cage (2) when the fruit sets.

The year-round garden

You cannot have a permanent blaze of colour but, with intelligent planning, you can always have something at its best to help keep interest and beauty flourishing in your garden

Too many gardens can become dull and uninteresting during the winter months unless the gardener has done some careful planning. There can be a lull in the floral display at almost any time of the year, and it is at such times that if pays to have taken into account the inter-relation of foliage colour, height and form, which makes your garden attractive to look at even when there are no flowers.

A creative and imaginative gardener always manages to have something of interest showing throughout the year. It is, of course, impossible to have your garden a blaze of colour all the time, and perhaps it is not particularly desirable, since each season has its individual mood and character. Nevertheless, you can always arrange to have some plant approaching its best as its neighbour passes the peak of perfection.

From spring through to autumn it is possible for your garden to have a constant display of flowers. But if you rely for colour on flowers alone, late autumn through to early spring will be a drab time indeed.

Fortunately gardeners have a wide range of plants available to them and by thinking also in terms of berries, foliage, fruits, barks, seed vessels and other portions of plants than flowers alone you can widen and enrich the garden in a way which may not always be brilliant but at least will be interesting.

There are several components of the year-round garden, but before discussing individual plants here are some general principles. In the first place everyone knows that even in high summer there can be gaps in the garden, times when one series of plants appears to have passed its best and the next has not yet reached its peak. These gaps can be avoided easily, for there is much to choose from at this time of year.

Unless you want definite seasonal bedding schemes where one group of plants is removed completely to be replaced immediately with another, such as is done in parks and botanic gardens, it is advisable to plant for succession, each group of plants being placed next to others which will come into flower in succession as their neighbours fade. This should be done throughout the entire garden rather than in selected and isolated sites, except perhaps where you want to keep one area of the garden cool, green and restful during summer.

Remember too that even in summer all interest does not come solely from flowers. Keep contrasts of plant material, shapes and textures always in mind so that vivid poppies can show against the green of recently flowered rhododendrons or white lilies can stand, regal and dignified, against the dark green of conifers; so that the spicate leaves and flowers of lavender contrast with round roses, delphiniums and foxgloves rise from rounded shapes in the mixed border.

Hydrangeas are in full bloom during August and as the flowers fade so they take on changing colours, as a bonus.

Picea pungens glauca procumbens is one of the low-growing evergreens that add colour and forr at all times.

Although during winter the herbaceous borders are bare of flowers, they need not be completely lacking in colour or interest. Some perennials take on a wonderful tan, copper or brown as they are struck by the frosts. Although they are sometimes cut down for neatness, you can get an added bonus of colour, plus some measure of protection of the bases and roots, if you let them remain standing until spring is near.

It is the evergreens, however, that really come into their own in winter. Their summer dullness is transformed as they reveal themselves to be green and awake in a world so largely surrendered to the brown sleep of winter. All evergreens, though, are not green and many hues of gold, silver, blue and copper, many variegations, bi- and tri-colours can be used to stand out against the winter landscape. The range of evergreens available is large indeed and although many will have been chosen originally because of their flowering qualities, their value in winter should be taken into account when you are selecting yours. Spots nearest to the windows of the house or those most frequently seen from them should always be planted with a special thought for winter appearance because in winter the garden is more often seen only from indoors. Something, therefore, is required that will give the eff ct of life and colour.

A range of tal r growing conifers and other evergreens will give a winter promise of life against the skyline. Against the soil, long-lasting results can be obtained from he thers or ericas. In the past few years more and more foliage ericas have been available, usually golden or orange and whether or not these are in flower their colour still shines through the winter murk. *Erica carnea* will actually grow and flower underneath the snow and *E. darleyensis*, considerably taller, will flower from about November onwards. Both of these require a neutral if not a positively acid soil, but this can easily be achieved by liberal applications of acid peat, a contribution which is well worth while. The tree heath, *E. arborea*, which grows to 10 feet or so, gives greater height and is followed by *E. mediterranea*, perhaps a little shorter. These are splendid winter plants, suitable not only for the garden but for tubs and window-boxes as well. A selection should always be planted so that they can be seen from indoors. They are tiny plants at first but grow into dense clumps with little attention and they live for years, smothering the ground, and any weeds beneath, and giving the benefit both of their flowers and their colourful foliage.

Another vastly underrated plant is the camellia. It is hardy, evergreen and colourful, even when not in flower

Heathers make good ground cover plants and at the same time provide year-round interest and variation in colour.

because of the lovely shape and glossy surface to the leaves. Some camellias, particularly the williamsii strain, flower from about January onwards, regardless of the weather. The pretty flowers appear to be delicate and this has probably given rise to the false belief that they are fit only for the greenhouse. In fact they are tough, but it is wise to place them out of the early morning sun, otherwise their gorgeous blooms are apt to burst their tissues as it strikes and warms their frost-filled petals. Face them to north rather than east or protect them from the direct rays of the sun. This is another plant which prefers an acid soil. In fact nearly all the most effective and interesting winter plants like their roots in a slightly acid soil.

Winds will, however, affect the golden *Forsythia suspensa*, usually grown as a climber when it will reach to 10 feet. Stake or support it well against a wall and, if possible, even give it just a little mulch at the roots as protection against the fiercest bites of winter. *F. intermedia spectabilis* can be even earlier and stems can be cut for forcing into early bloom in the home. Neither is particular about its soil. Both are easy, tolerant and rewarding for winter delight, so although they are perhaps a little dull and uninteresting for the remainder of the year it is worth growing a plant or two especially for winter colour.

Rhododendrons, spectacular and even flamboyant in spring and early summer, can provide valuable colour in winter too. Not only do they give us a solid green background which is so valuable against winter greys, but a few flower so early that they precede the normal season by some months. Rhododendron 'Christmas Cheer' can really give flowers for Christmas. If you wish to use it for indoor decoration at this time cut stems when the buds are just showing colour and let them open and develop in the warmth and comfort of your rooms. The brilliant red *R. shilsonii* is also early and in the normally damp and dismal rock garden the almost prostrate *R. repens*, with its waxy red bells about the size of gentians, is also useful.

Ericas always live well with rhododendrons and they serve a useful purpose also by shading from the later summer sun the roots of these plants which, like clematis, enjoy having their heads in the sun and their feet in the shade.

Given the protection of a south-facing wall *Clematis calycina* will flower in January and February, invaluable garden decoration and a heart-warming hint of the spring that is not now far away. It carries creamy white flowers. White also, though with a hint of pink instead of yellow, are the flowers of *C. armandii* which follow it. Both, as suggested, like some protection from the colder days and both should be pruned immediately they have finished flowering to allow them time to ripen their wood for next year's blooms.

The clematis take up little space in the smaller garden, for both are climbers growing up a wall or fence. The willows *Salix britzensis*, with almost sealing wax scarlet shoots and *S. vitellina*, bright yellow, are equally space-saving. They give brilliant bark colour in the winter but to get this colour they should be cut down almost to the ground in about March each year. Both will make quite large trees if allowed to grow without pruning, but the older the wood the less colourful it is, so it is best either to cut them down annually or to allow them to make a single trunk before lopping or pollarding the top.

Other vivid bark colours can be obtained from the dogwoods, again red and yellow. Choose *Cornus sanguinea atrosanguinea* for the red and *C. flaviramea* for the yellow. All these vivid barked trees are hardy, provide useful decoration for the remainder of the year and require absolutely minimum attention during the year except for the annual trimming of whippy shoots.

Among the earliest of the blossom trees are the prunus family, the cherry, almond and plum. Perhaps the best for longevity, as opposed to massed flowers, is the well-known *Prunus subhirtella autumnalis*, which has small pink tinted flowers. It will, in some years, begin flowering in the late autumn or early winter and continue right through until spring or even early summer—a continuous season of six months or so, surely a record hard to beat! The tree is attractive at all times and because of this and its determination to make no demands on the gardener it should find a place in every plot.

A shrub that can be almost guaranteed to produce its arching pink flower sprays for Christmas is *Viburnum bodnantense* 'Dawn'. Other members of the family are *V. tinus*, also known as laurustinus but less fragrant than the slightly later *V. carlesii* and hardier than *V. macrocephalum*, which has green flowers changing to white.

Yet in this recital of the trees and shrubs that can give us winter interest, we must not forget the bulb flowers that grow at their feet.

The dainty snowdrop or galanthus will bloom happily beneath the snow and be unworried when it melts. Varieties can be obtained up to a foot or so in height. 'Peeping Tom' and 'February Gold' are two of the first narcissi to appear, golden and unconcerned, long before the main drifts have progressed much farther than sending their first exploratory spears above soil level.

Winter aconites, *Eranthis hyemalis*, only 3 or 4 inches tall, also begin to appear from January on. Drifts of all the earliest flowering bulbs should be planted near enough to the house to be seen from the windows.

Above, rather than through the snow grow the deliciously scented witch hazels, several varieties in several hues but all early. Cut a twig or two to bring indoors to scent the rooms with spring. Bring indoors also a few sprigs of the early flowering currant, *Ribes sanguineum*, to burst into flower in the warmth and guarantee the beginning of another gardening season.

Gardening catalogues

Plenty of useful armchair gardening can be done in the long winter evenings. It is important, however, to understand catalogue presentation to get the best value from your reading.

This is the season when seed catalogues begin to appear on the doormat. They are followed at intervals right through to early summer by further catalogues from general and specialist nurserymen, from rose growers, bulb merchants and all the hopeful suppliers of garden and gardeners' needs.

Generally a seed catalogue contains only details of flower and vegetable seeds, which can include bulbs, corms, tubers and so forth, although a few bulb merchants offer excellent specialised catalogues. Some, nevertheless, contain a special section on herbaceous plants, usually grown from the seed listed.

A nurseryman's catalogue on the other hand lists plants entirely, without mention of seeds. The plants can be divided into trees, shrubs, climbers, conifers, dwarf conifers, roses, fruit, herbaceous, alpines and maybe more sections.

Sadly for the novice gardener, plant names are both confused and confusing. Most nurserymen list plants according to established botanical names, sometimes with popular or familiar names cross-referenced. Many seedsmen, however, seem to prefer listing their seeds under their popular names and seldom make cross-references.

Many people, comparing the prices of seeds with those of established plants, wonder whether they cannot grow a pear tree, a rose or a maple from seed much more cheaply than buying an established plant. Perhaps they can. But in the first place it may take years of careful cultivation before trees or shrubs grown from seed can be of a size significant enough for the border. In the second place only species can be grown true from seed. In other words, although it is easy enough to grow a pear or a peach from a seed or stone, the resulting plant will not be the same as that from which the seed or stone came originally, for these have been hybrids. Roses are grown not from seed but from cuttings grown on alien roots to get a better performance. And remember, when comparing prices, that in growing the plants for some years the nurseryman has had to charge for labour, time, materials and even a part of the rent of his land.

Many gardeners wonder why F_1 hybrid seeds are more expensive than normal types. The answer is that the seed is produced from pure first generation strains, often by hand pollination and meticulous protection against the casual bee, insect or wind-blown pollination. Seeds from F_1 hybrids should not be kept because they will not come true to strain. You will have to go back to the parents.

You may have a regular nurseryman or seedsman from whom you have bought for years, because his products have proved themselves in your garden. All the same it is worth while obtaining a few other catalogues from his competitors to compare prices, varieties and the range of subjects listed. One may give a little extra information, a hint or recommendation for planting or care, a suggestion for unusual use or a description not contained in your usual guide.

When a nurseryman has a surplus of certain plants or finds them particularly easy to grow he may make a special offer of a collection which will give you a real bargain. He may find that his customers are interested in a package deal of a collection for a south-facing border, for a rock garden or a paved area. All *collections* are cheaper and well worth examining.

It is sometimes puzzling to find several varieties of a single species listed in a catalogue at widely varying prices. *Cornus canadensis,* for example, may be listed at 35 pence a plant, while *C. alba* Westonbirt is 75 pence and *C. Florida rubra* is one pound 58 pence. The reasons for this may be various. One variety for some reason may be heavily in demand, or take several more years to grow to marketable size. It could also be that this variety is so difficult to propagate that only one in ten baby plants survive to maturity.

Occasionally a particularly hard winter leaves nurserymen all over the country short of certain plants. If these have been killed in the nursery they are certain to have died in many gardens, so next year there will be a heavy demand for replacements with which the nurseryman cannot cope so prices will rise by the law of supply and demand.

Most catalogues carry somewhere a statement that where a certain ordered plant is out of stock the nurseryman reserves the right to substitute something similar, unless specific instructions to the contrary have been received. So if you order a particular plant and are

1

2

1 Modern garden centres provide an unprecedented choice of plants and equipment for the gardener.
2 Many nurserymen sell rooted cuttings in pots, and these can be transferred, at any time, to the garden provided that the instructions are followed.

unwilling to make do with a substitute you should always make this clear.

On the other hand, bear in mind the fact that the exclusion of a certain plant from his lists does not mean that the nurseryman does not stock it. He may have failed to list it because stock is limited in this particular year. But even if his stock is completely sold out it is quite possible that he will be able to obtain a single plant or two from some other source; so it is usually worth asking if he can do this.

Although the prices of good, viable seeds and plants seldom differ significantly between various reputable suppliers, there can be hidden differences. Some seedsmen may sell by the packet while others sell by the ounce or, with some vegetables, by the pint. An ounce may provide more plants than you need so a smaller packet could be more suitable.

One particular nurseryman may offer a 2½-foot tree for the same price at which his competitor offers a smaller or taller specimen. So long as the supplier is reputable and provides the usual guarantees of name, quality and replacement, then by choosing the less expensive plant you can either save money or increase your order.

A considerable proportion of seeds and plants are bought in bulk by seedsmen and nurserymen for wholesale sources in this country and abroad. Just as a confectioner does not make his own sweets, so nurserymen and seedsmen do not necessarily grow their own plants. Seeds of 'John Smith's selected mixed candytuft' can come out of the same original bag as 'Peter Brown's special brand of mixed candytuft' sold by the competitor down the street, and the original bag may well have come from abroad. As when buying groceries, you should go for the well-known name, the established reputation, the man who knows you and cannot afford to let you down.

All gardeners are safeguarded to some extent by the Seeds Act which controls purity and germination rates for many seeds. Lots of nurserymen specify in their catalogues that all the stock they offer conforms to the specifications published by the British Standards Institution. These appear as BS 3936 Nursery Stock, Part 1 Trees and Shrubs, Part 2 Roses, Part 3 Fruit and Part 4 Forest Trees. For a copy of these standards write to the British Standards Institution, 2 Park Street, London W.1.

Nursery stock, delivered by mail or rail, usually arrives during the dormant season, about October to March, and should be planted right away. Some plants, such as alpines and many of the climbers, which are pot-grown can be planted at other seasons. In addition, an increasing number of nurserymen and garden centres offer container-grown plants for a cash-and-carry trade.

Because container-grown plants are designed for this type of trade they are not always listed, and catalogues are not issued. However, if you have a catalogue from a local firm it is always worth asking whether any particular plant of your choice is available for collection, container-grown.

Every seedsman or nurseryman must pack a great deal of information into as little space as possible, so he must catalogue according to categories and he must also resort to a large number of abbreviations. It is a good idea to list these on a piece of paper to use as a book-mark and thus save yourself the chore of continually turning back to stop making a mistake. When looking for a subject you must be aware of its category, whether, for example, it is a hardy annual or suitable only for the greenhouse, whether it is a tree, shrub, climber, conifer or hardy herbaceous perennial.

Many catalogues, particularly those from seedsmen, list what are called novelties. These are new introductions—seeds of plants that are new for the season, perhaps with different colourings, heights, fragrance or some other quality that makes them different from plants previously available. Prices are likely to be significantly higher and the differences in the plants are sometimes minimal so, as a general rule, only if you specialise or seek particularly the new qualities advertised is it worth spending extra money for these. On the other hand, the new qualities gained by hybridising may be a significant breakthrough and exactly what is needed: a new non-bolting lettuce, a new golden foliaged matricaria or a culinary pea especially bred for the deep freeze. So look carefully.

Never allow yourself to be so overcome by the delights of colour, shape, size, flavour or performance, offered verbally, that you lose sight of more practical considerations. Check carefully the ultimate height and spread of your trees and shrubs or you may find that they grow too large for where you plant them. Check dates of flowering or fruiting so that you can get a continuation of colour or interest.

However expert a gardener you may be read carefully any cultural instructions printed in the catalogue. Perhaps, because of the particular soil in the nursery certain plants will require or benefit from a slightly different technique from that which you normally practise and the printed notes may make all the difference to your results. Almost every catalogue printed contains somewhere special notes or instructions.

Quite apart from the fact that very many of these are models of concise clarity and good gardening sense, they may contain that tiny tip or suggestion, missing from the more erudite and profuse gardening manuals, which fills some small gap in your gardening knowledge.

Remember that the catalogue, the plants, seeds or bulbs it lists and the prices charged for them are to a certain extent under your control. If you accept everything without making suggestions, complaints or congratulations, then the catalogue will remain much the same year after year.

Order early, carefully and correctly and leave the nurseryman or seedsman to carry out your order at the correct time. Do not hinder and confuse him by changes and enquiries when he is at his busiest.

Let him carry out his various collecting, packing and dispatching formalities with the least possible disturbance. Then he can keep down his overheads and the prices he charges you.

INDEX

STEWART COWLEY